# Envy Theory

# Envy Theory

*Perspectives on the Psychology of Envy*

Frank John Ninivaggi, M.D.

ROWMAN & LITTLEFIELD PUBLISHERS, INC.
Lanham • Boulder • New York • Toronto • Plymouth, UK

BP53

Published by Rowman & Littlefield Publishers, Inc.
A wholly owned subsidiary of The Rowman & Littlefield Publishing Group, Inc.
4501 Forbes Boulevard, Suite 200, Lanham, Maryland 20706
http://www.rowmanlittlefield.com

Estover Road, Plymouth PL6 7PY, United Kingdom

British Library Cataloguing in Publication Information Available

**Library of Congress Cataloging-in-Publication Data**
Ninivaggi, Frank John.
 Envy theory : perspectives on the psychology of envy / Frank John Ninivaggi.
  p. cm.
 Includes bibliographical references and index.
 ISBN 978-1-4422-0574-1 (cloth : alk. paper) — ISBN 978-1-4422-0576-5 (electronic)
 1. Envy. I. Title.
 BF575.E65N56 2010
 152.4'8—dc22                                                    2010010841

∞ ™ The paper used in this publication meets the minimum requirements of
American National Standard for Information Sciences—Permanence of Paper for
Printed Library Materials, ANSI/NISO Z39.48-1992.

Printed in the United States of America

1/19/12

# Contents

# Introduction

This book introduces *envy theory*. It is a conceptual exploration of hypotheses and conjectures about the mind's fundamental cognitive and emotional makeup—its infrastructure and developmental potentials. Introducing the *envy model* and attempting to unravel the meaning of envy illustrates this orientation. Aims are to contribute to the psychological literature, improve patient care, and stimulate new research.

*Envy theory* addresses basic propositions about human psychology, consciousness, and the meaning of personhood. Challenging clinical work with children and adults in psychiatric contexts over three decades has provided the data for *envy theory*. It suggests a number of explanatory factors to make it socially interesting and of practical use, for example, as a research paradigm. Many aspects of *envy theory* await testability.

The significance of envy descriptively, developmentally, and as a typical state of mind, universal but dimensional in degree, in all psychological functioning is presented. Rather than being simple and discrete, envy is a diverse set of urges, emotions, and cognitions with a tonic presence that waxes and wanes over time and experience.

*Envy theory* is a complex and comprehensive analysis of the conscious and unconscious factors that result in the self-destructive manifestations of envy. Unmet needs and desires pressing on consciousness and fostering feelings of envy and the actions that result can seriously undermine psychic health. Endowments of envy, however, are not as bleak and unsparing as they at first may appear. An understanding of *envy theory* would be incomplete if its clinical significance were not recognized or underestimated. That significance pivots on the fact that, properly identified and managed, *a healthy maturation of envy* may occur from which successful advances both personally and socially may arise.

*Envy theory* draws from psychology, psychoanalysis, phenomenology, and aspects of the humanities in constructing models of envy in the human condition. The task of understanding and attempting to explain human nature and mind is far too broad to use only a single perspective, especially since there is no bedrock to understanding. Each branch of knowledge studies a subset of reality that depends on a variety of factors studied in other branches. Scientific realism suggests that conjectures arrived at in one area often help in understanding other areas. *Envy theory* presumes an intrinsic orderliness in human psychology, the details of which are mostly undiscovered. Inductions from one class of facts—for example, psychoanalytic psychology—may be shown to coincide with inductions obtained from the study of properties emergent in other classes—for example, neuroscience. This suggested complementariness and agreement, in fact, represents a consilience across disciplines, creating a common, realistic, and orderly groundwork for explaining the yet uncharted depths of how envy exists in the mind. The author has found such a bold methodology essential to explain envy.

*Unconscious envy is the primitive sensation and conflated feeling of privation, powerlessness, inferiority, and hostile distress coupled with the urge to rob and spoil in the face of advantages and their enjoyment existing elsewhere.*

Envy is biting the breast that feeds. This is part of envy's paradoxical nature. Ironically, envy cannot be taken personally. It is akin to a reflexive response to another based on the *envier's idiosyncratic phantasy construals*. In this sense, it is insular and "impersonal."

Phantasied omnipotence (strivings toward exerting power) and a need to control are the pillars upon which unconscious envy stands. Power in all its connotations suggests holding great resources along with the authoritative force, strength, and ability to act. Envy and an underlying sense of powerlessness go hand-in-hand. Conscious recognition of envy, for example, resides in many folklore ideas such as "evil eye" and "jinx." Both connote identifying something exceedingly good with the implication that this powerful talisman will contribute in some way to its spoiling and destruction.

The varied phenomena subsumed in the construct of "power" as played out in all human relations, from the intrapsychic to the interpersonal to the extended group, can be seen and described from different perspectives. Conceptually, power denotes sufficient force required to do work and the capacity to produce change and achieve outcomes. Power can also be defined as the ability to control, influence, or coerce others and environments by manipulating resources. Throughout *envy theory*, "power" is given its psychodynamic appellation—namely, the construct of *omnipotence*, the unconscious platform organizing all human power strivings.

In *envy theory, unconscious phantasy* (Isaacs 1948)—how the mind experiences/pictures itself—represents information and its lived processing. It is largely though not entirely self-generated. *In this book, this spelling of the term "phantasy" is used to differentiate it from conscious "fantasy" denoting, for example, imagination and daydreams.* The idiosyncratic meaning attributed to experiences and, for example, the subjective feelings implied by the concept "qualia" used in formal psychology arise from the personally constructed matrix of unconscious phantasy.

The consciously experienced features of envy are often reflected in those who feel themselves or are seen by others to be insecure. People who feel insecure and inadequate always look outside themselves and compare what they have or feel they are with what they perceive others to be or to possess—usually something ideal. Envy arouses questions about fairness and equal distribution of resources. Scavenging for hidden treasures and exploiting the acquisition of what is perceived to be free also imply underlying envy. Envy, in isolation, can be destructive to psychological processes; envy, recognized and intelligently managed, transforms and may spur admiration, emulation, aspiration, empathy, and developmental advantages—*the healthy maturation of envy*. This is one of *envy theory*'s principal themes.

*Envy theory*'s focus is *unconscious* envy, the central theme of this book. Envious attitudes that are conscious may be benign (nonhostile) or contain willful maliciousness. Unconscious envy, difficult to capture empirically, however, ordinarily has malignant potential since its signature urges are primitive, robbing, and corrosively spoiling. On a conscious level, these correlate with invasion, ruthless exploitation, and scavenging the spoiled resources. Pain is felt when envy on any level is activated. The envier feels pain, but the person toward whom envy is directed feels perplexed. Surface actions mask the envier's unconscious aims.

Pleiotrophy, one innately endowed predisposition influencing a variety of different expressions as development proceeds over time, characterizes *nuclear envy*. It is a presemantic set of sensations and responsivity, independent of conscious thinking, out of which automatic attraction and responses to fear, reward, and novelty emerge. Cognitive processing, for example, partakes of envy's cascade of iterative changes in receiving and transforming information.

What are the practical consequences of excessive envy? The details of envy's mental mechanisms will unfold throughout this book. The following, in principle, outlines consequences of envy—its experience-near negative effects. Envy's infrastructure is made up of mental splitting and projection. Envy has intrinsic disintegrative properties that foster and enhance such splitting. This denotes the phenomenological experience of mental disorganization, attention that incessantly drifts and falters, and the inability to gather mental focus. This obstructs cognitive, emotional, and physical integration and engenders disorganized self-experience and "single-mindedness." Projection denotes the ongoing attribution to all aspects of perception the intrinsic contents of the subjective mind, typically phantasy and imaginary ideals and wishes. Along with this, one's already tenuous attention becomes identified—trapped—in this outer-directed array. Attention so trapped becomes controlled in willy-nilly and vapid ways; thinking and willful action, in turn, are disabled. Clear-mindedness, volition, and performance suffer.

When envy, however, is identified and modulated in a mindful way, its hold over attention is significantly mitigated. This enables one to think more clearly, plan more effectively, and carry out goals, aspirations, and ambitions in a more deliberate and successful manner. In other words, *the healthy maturation of envy* is an internal accomplishment that enhances odds of success for external accomplishments in real-life situations.

In *envy theory*, each human being is considered a *biomental entity*. When the physical body of the whole person is referenced, terms such as "human organism" or physical body are used. When the psychological level of the whole person is addressed, the term "self" is used.

The philosophical problem of "the one and the many" is also embedded in *envy theory*. In the developmental process, one's sense of self slowly arises, in part, from an indistinct experience of the changing groups of mind-body functions (multiple "I's") toward a more cohesive sense of their "togetherness." These multiple aspects always remain mentally active—often experienced as competing dimensions of the self. Dissociative states, indecisive and erratic thinking, and fickle-mindedness, for example, reflect an insufficiently integrated self.

As emotional and cognitive maturation and development proceed, however, conscious awareness locates itself in only one or a select few sectors of biomental experience. Gradually, a psychological character forms and an individual comes to perceive and believe that he or she is that crystallized "one self"—in isolation or dissociated from the other self aspects present. The remainder of one's biomental functions, even though still operating, become nonconscious, not remembered. These varying aspects of the self are often contradictory and arouse conflict. The nonconscious search for unity not only stimulates but, in part, arises from such dynamic dualisms that largely drive envy.

*Envy theory* expounds the meaning, functions, and significance of *nuclear envy* in self-experience and the self's experience of others, especially when its spoiling impulses arise in conscious thinking, motivation, and action. Although aspects of self (experiencer) and others (experienced) may be described in terms of "parts," there are no parts in mental apprehensions. *Only "shifts of focus" are being described.*

*Envy theory* may be regarded more an individual and interpersonal rather than social psychological perspective since its focus is studying and understanding the person as a biopsychological individual whose major axes of orientation are self-relevance (perceiving others to share characteristics similar to oneself) and maintaining a sense of self-meaning in relation to others. Yet envy is not entirely an interpersonal phenomenon; social consequences are significant and have real-life impact. Cognitive and affective pathways tempered by envy may be adaptive and health promoting or destructive when envy is excessive and unopposed by the forces represented by love (for example, affiliative attraction, empathy, mutual cooperation) in all its integrative dimensions. The quality and quantity of one's constitutional endowment of envy may be viewed as a heritable risk factor activated by environmental stress. The stress-heritability-coping model of vulnerability-resilience (mix of risk and protective factors) in adaptation correlates heavily with this.

*Envy theory* comprises one principal foundation on which a more general psychology can be constructed. The broadest frame of reference is psychoanalytic psychology, particularly object relations theory. This view sees all individual psychology as simultaneously engaged in and informed by intersubjective and social interactions.

The manner in which an individual idiosyncratically perceives his or her emotional and cognitive relation to others in the interpersonal world denotes that subject's "object relations." In other words, that to which the subject becomes related is the relation to the object. The term "object" used here roughly denotes the subject's emotionally charged attention, particularly the encoded mental identification, recognition, and interpretation of another person—technically termed "the object." Most important, "object" denotes the subject's object of desire. The "object" typically takes the form of a largely unconscious action image between two persons or parts of persons.

"Object" and "object of desire" emphasize the idiosyncratic nature of how other persons are construed.

This genetically endowed object relations pathway expresses itself at birth in the intimate interpersonal and extended social field of the mother-infant dyad. This reciprocity is the crucible in which the infrastructure of mind assimilates impressions and experiences that enhance growth, maturation, and development.

This infantile urgent focus is the first and becomes the primary object-specific relation. It remains the nonconscious prototype for all subsequent conscious object strivings—in other words, interests and emotionally charged preferences toward persons deemed interesting and significant.

How human minds begin to understand the world arises from how the biomental infant can act and react in relation to its mother. Somatic action patterns, cognitive pathways, and affective moods develop and coalesce early on and dynamically reconfigure throughout growth, maturation, and development. Motivation, volition, and emotion, therefore, are always about aspects of this primary relation that remains the nonconscious trigger stimulating further exploration along the developmental course of one's life. Although an exclusive relation to the mother can vary in many ways, such as actual physical presence, duration of attentiveness, and emotional intensity, some form of it exists in everyone.

*Envy theory* asserts a fundamental axiom: two overarching inferred primary instincts, *life instinct and death instinct*, act as the archetypal compass directing and orienting mind and behavior. *Envy theory* denotes this use of *the construct "instinct" to mean an innate biomental preparedness having an extremely sensitive, flexible responsivity, rather than absolutely automatic reflex action, that waxes and wanes as it takes concrete shape in the experiential social environment.* Both classes of instinct *in unison* aim toward adaptive survival imbued with meaning. The strength of these biomental forces is endowed constitutionally; the developing ego and environmental facilitators and constraints, however, contribute to their activation and expression. In other words, genes do not predetermine performance; experience decides and shapes behavior.

This conjectural framework denotes that the inner "life instinct"—whatever complex biomental and neural network processes compose and correlate with it—drives the biomental self to actively seek greater and greater *degrees of affiliation, creativeness, and vivifyingness.* The power to expand and create accompanies these indefatigable life impulses. Love as experienced and enacted in all human relations may be the broadest instantiation of this life instinct. The idea of a life instinct is an archetypal construct inferred chiefly by its effects.

These impulses, however, must exist in dynamic conjunction with the in-ferred "death instinct" that counters this life drive by forceful impulses toward constraint, aggressive control, disintegration, and destructiveness. Varying degrees of reconciling consequences dynamically emerge and continuously reorganize these ongoing dually operating creative and destructive life scenar-ios. Anxiety, hateful and spoiling attitudes, and manifestations of destructive actions may be the broadest expressions of death instinct processes.

Both innate predilections and human cultural reinforcements make hu-man subjects uniquely sensitive to experiencing intense pleasure, satisfac-tion, and comfort in relation to one another—the raison d'etre behind object relations. *Envy theory* describes the milieu of "birth, breath, and breast" as the incomparable mating of subject with subject that launches for baby in states of nurturance with mother the founding moment of biomental activity and the canalization of mental space.

The first awakening of mind is a mixture of the cognitive and emotional apprehension of the animate world of relationships having idiosyncratic per-sonal significance. Such social cognition is the infrastructure of the human infant's intelligent and meaningful adaptation.

The use of the term "object" denotes a reference, in technical terms, to the subject's *idiosyncratic construction of a personalized figure other than the self/experiencer*. This apprehension and encoding may be partial/featural or holistic/configural in its processing and structuralization. Detail and pat-tern processing, respectively, have different developmental trajectories and influence cognition and emotion differently. These crucial bias signals are established in earliest infancy and guide the flow of emotional and cognitive neural circuitry by the prototypical patterns they establish. Object relations are the foundation of all social attachments, the universal building blocks of the meaningfulness underlying culture and civilization. Object relations underlie all forms of social cognition and communication.

At the start of life, information-processing capacities have both hard-wired and software elements that develop and expand by growth, matura-tion, and experience with the environment, especially significant people. These capacities, which are essentially plastic and mutable, are more active than merely passive and reactive. *Envy theory* sees these as transcending mere computational mechanics. Therefore, the tenets of cognitivism in psychology and functionalism in philosophy, however useful, are only par-tial descriptions of how the mind, especially consciousness, works. In other words, explanations of the neural instantiation of the subjective nature of mental and bodily states are partial approaches to understanding the whole person.

For example, the elements in the bottom-up computational substrata of cognition in isolation are more passive; the entire cognitional system takes active direction from top-down sweeps of the consciousness that guide them whether consciously/explicitly or nonconsciously/implicitly. Information processing at different strata and at different times may function in a number of ways—for example, sequential or parallel, either of which may be centralized or decentralized and distributed. They become connectionist when the strength of neuron-based connectivity increases.

Sensory abilities and perception in healthy individuals is reality-oriented, able to perceive and construct realistic aspects of the real environment. Simultaneously, innate unconscious phantasies, vivid nonconscious images largely determined by the form of the human body and its action impulses (emotional and somatic feelings), arise. These phylogenetically conserved orientations are typically characterized by omnipotent strivings and expectations, and flood information processing. From birth onward, innate phantasy and realistic perceptions of external reality—the simultaneous and bidirectional operation of projection and introjection—modulate and shape one another to produce a rich tapestry of emotionally and conceptually active information-processing systems.

*Envy theory* also has strong features of a cognitive psychology. Cognition here connotes the encoding, processing, storage, and use of raw sensory data, perceptual information, and emotional experience. To introduce *envy theory* as a novel class among associationist, stage theories, and information-processing approaches (chapter 2), current empirical insights from cognitive developmental psychology, cognitive developmental neurosciences, and philosophy are briefly reviewed. Conscious and nonconscious cognitive processes, along with motivations arising from *unconscious phantasy*, structure the construals or epistemological constructs that an individual uses to make sense out of self and the world. Unconscious and conscious values, choice, and volitions emerge from this.

Unconscious phantasy is continually processed in dynamic fashion within two basic developmental units/positions or ontogenetic states of mind that persist throughout life. Their rudiments occur in early infancy and are elaborated thereafter. This nonconscious, regularly occurring mental activity results from the oscillation between the *paranoid-schizoid position* and *depressive position*.

These "positions" are psychoanalytic constructs that describe normative, typical, *healthy*, and expectable psychological development from birth on (Klein 1935, 1940, 1946). They are certainly grounded in neural net profiles that develop by hierarchical integration, ongoing differentiation, and reorganization. This cognitive and epistemological theory of development suggests continuous yet distinct interactions of featural and holistic object recognition, respectively. Iterations of the affective and cognitive elements of these positions over the course of life add complexity to mental functioning. Healthy developmental successes signal that the ability to experience "absence" in novel and creative ways has been achieved.

*Envy theory* connotes an epistemological architecture with an initial and persisting developmental genesis. The embodied infant is situated in an embedded relationship with its primary caregiver, typically the mother. In analytic terminology, the mother is the "primary object" and all connectivity to her constitutes the basis for "object relations" during the entire course of psychological ontogenesis. Experiential envy arises from this self-generated matrix. The infant brain-mind is born in expectation of its central evolved psychological mechanism for survival—mother. In other words, *envy theory* uses this model as its framework for a developmental cognitive psychology. *Envy theory* orients itself by its emphasis on intrapsychic attachments. This complements other valuable attachment theories that are more empirical and describe measurable behaviors. The recent discovery in neuroscience of "mirror neurons" lends neuroanatomical and neurophysiological credibility to the actual measurability of real biomental connections of identification and attachment in infantile experience—cognition, learning, affective states, and behaviors (chapters 2 and 7).

*Envy theory* proposes an exceedingly novel construct termed "the infant's dilemma." This denotes that, along with primary love, the infant experiences primary envy toward the mother. Primary love is normal attachment characterized by a raw love or elemental idealization. Primary envy, by contrast, suggests threatened attachment characterized by excessive idealization and the impulse to spoil what is sensed as ideal.

*Envy theory tries relentlessly to emphasize that the inner forces of primary love and love in all its expressions are the foundations of the infant's attachment to mother.* The vicissitudes of the infant's love establish basic trust, hope, and belief in goodness. This goodness is not merely a theoretical abstraction. Goodness for the infant is *concretely experienced nurturance*—being fed, loved, and understood. This promotes survival and enhances interest in experiencing the real world in real time.

Along with love, envy is also felt. This envy is not a craving for the advantages possessed by mother, but an intolerable anxiety that prompts the infant, in phantasy, to wish to strip and spoil those sensations, perceptions, and emotional states that connote the very existence of such value, salience, enjoyment, and goodness not felt as self-possession.

*The core dilemma is maintaining primitive love as normal idealization, not excessive idealization, which is intolerable and ultimately destructive.* In earliest infancy, what later develops as more conscious and empathetic love first arises as a naked and raw impulse of affiliation in the form of normal idealization. *Excessive idealization provokes envious anxiety and leads to envious spoiling of what had been felt as extremely but unbearably good, not bad.* Envy theory correlates raw love with normal idealization and raw hate with excessive idealization leading to envious destructiveness. Cognitive processes thereby become distorted leading to adaptations that are less realistic both mentally and behaviorally.

To reiterate: The principal developmental task and achievement in earliest infancy, the paranoid-schizoid position, is that *internal loving feelings and attitudes of the infant* sufficiently supersede internal envious destructive impulses. This facilitates basic ego integration and the genesis of attitudes of admiration. The infantile ego, therefore, is enabled to receive and assimilate the nurturance—food, love, and understanding—given and shared by mother. This process makes possible the introjection of the "first good object" into the ego that, in turn, may act as the nucleus around which continued integration, less splitting, empathy, gratitude, and further healthy self-expansions may proceed. It is the basis for all further good identifications. This process, however, varies in degree and is never complete. *Envy theory* regards this *nuclear love* as a focal point of the expression of primary love.

The developmental process defines, organizes, and is the matrix out of which love and hate play out in the psyche and behavior. In other words, love and hate are dynamic processes that have organic growth by a series of progressive changes toward an end that, in itself, may change during the process. Envy, by contrast, is characterized less as a process and more as an eruption in toto, almost a *fait accompli.*

Love in all its developmental permutations as a process both opposes and modulates this core conflict—attraction and envious spoiling. Emphasis here is on the inner endowment of loving attitudes that the infant has and can mobilize. This inner complement of love has a strength and intensity that significantly influences perception, assessment, evaluation, and interpretation of everything in the environment. This makes the experience of actual "goodness" or "badness," to some extent, subjectively determined.

Love in *envy theory* is a complex interpersonal attitude characterized by attraction, benevolent affiliation, and nonviolent mutuality. As development proceeds, love takes on increasingly intelligent features fostering healthy adaptation and survival. This applies to the infant's loving attitudes and those of the mother and caregiving environment. Ideas that associate love with *indiscriminate sentimentality, cheap pathos, mawkish deference, and blind acceptance* are not included here.

*The healthy maturation of envy*, a novel proposition introduced by *envy theory*, enhances the capacity to tolerate envy's core unpleasantness without repugnance, ill will, and falling apart. The cognitive yield of this core dynamic is the unquenchable epistemic search for meaning to repetitively solve uncertainty and reduce confusion.

The orientation at birth toward the mother—the primary developmental object stimulus—is innate. Mother and aspects or perceptual parts of her are the most relevant and salient stimuli for infants. The brain's expectation pathways include an unconscious awareness of the breast (part-object) and the mother (whole object). The immediate and formative relationship established is termed "primary identification." It denotes an instantaneous recognition of mother as the necessary "other" needed to sustain life and reduce distress. The mother is the infant's first mirror and acts to dynamically reflect back—in a modified way—a variety of cognitive and affective building blocks that the infant may use to establish an experiential self *in statu nascendi*. A great deal of research using neuroscientific methods and neuroimaging techniques such as functional magnetic resonance imaging (fMRI), especially on the role of mirror neurons and interpersonal attraction, sexual desire, love, and self-expansion, has steadily been advancing (Ortigue, Bianchi-Demicheli, Hamilton, and Grafton 2007; Ortigue and Bianchi-Demicheli 2008a, 2008b).

The infant uses the geography of the mother's body to explore the world and, in turn, correlate and assimilate these experiences with its own mental and corporeal self. By witnessing objects in the external environment, principal of whom is mother, the infant vicariously experiences anatomical parts and functions of its own body—gesture, eating, moving, spitting, urinating, and so forth. As the infant explores (detection and recognition) what it sees, hears, smells, feels, and tastes, it relates these to its own body. The mother is the primary object used by the infant to release its own innate predispositions. This occurs within the intersubjective dynamics of the mother-infant dyad. The important role of father comes to the fore slightly later in infancy. Father offers the developmentally more mature infant the first chance to explore new objects.

Identifying parts of the self with parts of the other in this early concrete fashion is the basis for the later development of abstract symbol formation, one significant achievement of the developmental depressive position around the middle of the first year. Shortly thereafter, the use of pragmatic language reflects how words are used to refer to inner feeling states and attitudes.

In *envy theory*, *projective internalization* is the cardinal mode of cognition used both in infancy and later. At its core is the exploratory, communicational, and defensive mechanism of *projective identification* in which the developing mind looks outward in its attempts to recognize, identify, aggressively control, and so reconfigure itself. Projective identification operates nonconsciously whereas projective internalization also has conscious components. The microcosmic mind orients itself in the macrocosmic extended environment and forges links of identity.

Greater mental integration occurs, and the breadth of mental operations expands. Randomness transforms toward coherence in more unified thinking and affective attitudes. Through this *projective internalization* of perceived relationships, the infant gradually begins to imagine/feel/conceive how its own body is assembled. Mind develops. The chief vehicle used for this cognitive buildup is the mother's body and her caregiving. This shapes the infantile template of cognitive organization—attention, perceptual coordination, concept formation, memory, problem solving, and preferences—as development proceeds.

*Envy theory* presumes a preeminently biomental orientation. From historical precedent and inextricably embedded in language, a heuristic division has been made between the material body and the psychological mind. These dimensions of the whole person, in fact, operate in unison. Any discussion of mental processes always assumes simultaneous changes in their biological base. The body, then, is an essential part of the circuitry of thought, feeling, behaviors, and adaptations in a social context. For example, when ego integration is posited as an aim and parameter of *mental* health, psychopathology can be conceptualized as an expression of suboptimal integration, weak coordination, and dysfunction among *neural networks*.

The psychogenetic past not only influences later development but also remains a living, albeit nonconscious, part of all current mental activity. Understanding challenging real-life situations presumes understanding as far as possible their nonconscious roots. The dynamics of envy stimulate ongoing cognitive and affective exploration and motivation, while both instigating conflict—experientially irreconcilable opposites—and presenting novel opportunities for conflict resolution, self-integration, and social cooperation. *Envy theory adheres to this positive rather than bleak orientation regarding the potential value of envy.*

❖

The scope of applicability of *envy theory* is enormous. *Envy theory* provides new avenues for future research in neuroscience and sociopolitical theory, as well as integration in clinical practice. Besides its basic contribution to a general psychology of mind, it outlines a theory of cognitive development in infancy and cognitive processing throughout the lifespan. Thinking, affect, and motivation-volition arise from the way genes, brain regions, neurotransmitter pathways, and experiences are psychologically felt and interpreted. Envy is a basic element in the intersection of objective neuroscience and the subjective sense of self and self with others. Research models and basic science measurements may develop from *envy theory's* delineated novel perspectives, especially since envy typically evades awareness, and because self-reports may be intentionally or inadvertently inaccurate. *Envy theory* attempts to probe envy dynamics beyond face, appearance, and commonsense explanations.

*Envy theory* can inform research in social and political sciences by new ways of exploring irrationally destructive trends—greed, aggressive control, and war—that appear related to upward social comparisons unduly resistant to change. Using *envy theory's* insights in how envy and greed operate in indolent and ultimately spoiling ways gives insight into the dilemma modern financial institutions have created. In addition, organizational consultation may benefit from insights into how enhancing helping-based, less envious interpersonal behaviors are essential to team building and can significantly improve teamwork and business efficiency. *Envy theory* presents philosophical psychopathology with a broad discussion of value attribution in its elaboration of idealization as central to cognitive processing and motivation. Viewing *nuclear envy* as a universal core in human nature expressing itself idiosyncratically in cultures by *adaptive diversification* may enrich the hypotheses of sociocultural anthropology.

Additionally, *envy theory* has pragmatic therapeutic uses when used thoughtfully, prudently, and judiciously. A leading example is its integration in clinical psychotherapy. Personal change is challenging. A fundamental prerequisite is insightful recognition of a need to change coupled with an enduring perseverance. The overwhelming difficulty of this decision and its enactment is often underestimated. Motivation and volition leading to change is complex. The interpersonal and social dimensions of psychotherapies that create conditions in which envy is identified and properly addressed are significant means facilitating envy's healthy maturation. What *envy theory* terms excessive "outsight" or focus on outer accomplishments to the neglect of inner self-development is remedied by *the healthy maturation of envy*.

The cutting edge of modern neuroscience, barely a decade old, is beginning to provide hard evidence that the brain's neuroplasticity—ability to substantively change and reorganize—is very real (*Neuropsychopharmacology* 2008, vol. 33, no. 2, whole issue). This includes responsive expansion and adaptive growth on various levels: neurogenesis, gliogenesis, synaptogenesis, axonal sprouting, dendritic arborization, receptor trafficking, and long-term potentiation (LTP). Not only can these expansions of learning and memory be stimulated by pharmacological and electrical (electroconvulsive therapies) interventions, but also by carefully targeted sensory and motor stimuli, including psychotherapies. Moreover, the latter may be regarded not only as treatment but also as a form of neuroprotection.

The pragmatic yield of *the healthy maturation of envy* enables the "power to change" as a valuable outcome. Volition on all levels is enhanced so that motivated courses of action, to whatever extent individual choice and social considerations influence these, may come to fruition. *Envy theory* boldly asserts that such a process is a "disease modifying treatment," and not merely palliative.

The effects of psychotherapy on positively changing brain function have been demonstrated by precise volumetric measurements derived from magnetic resonance imaging (MRI) data and regional brain activity changes observed by fMRI (Carter and Krug 2009). In other words, the cortex (thought processes) may be enabled to teach the amygdala (raw emotion); mind can change brain (LeDoux 1998; McNab et al. 2009). For example, the fourth leading cause of disability worldwide with a lifetime prevalence of ~15 percent to 20 percent is depression (Rubinow 2006). *Envy theory* advances the idea that treatment-resistant depressions have a core in pathological envy that, when identified, may be influenced by psychotherapeutic interventions. This yet unexplored area opens exciting possibilities not only for further research but also for meaningful personal change.

*Envy theory* is advanced not as a series of answers but a range of propositions, conjectures, and questions to stimulate interest and further exploration of what it has offered as the *nuclear envy* that is dynamic in human psychology.

# PART I

# ENVY THEORY

# CHAPTER ONE

# Love and the Complex Problem of Destructiveness

### *Envy Theory*

This book attempts to describe how the mind works—its mental functioning. It is a study of mental faculties, particularly colored by envy, and how these experiential states are managed and controlled. Health promotion and wellness are leading values. An analysis of love in attitude and action (helping behaviors) and *the healthy maturation of envy* are central to understanding envy. *Envy theory*'s central proposition rests on the relevance and meaning that *nuclear envy* has for all mental functioning. The psychology of envy provides hypotheses for future research as well as guidelines for clinical applications.

*Envy theory*, introduced here for the first time, is a working analysis of emotional and cognitive information processing. Information processing denotes a complex array of neurologically based epistemological systems—pathways that both actively seek and generate knowledge. Specifically dedicated biomental circuits detect specific types of sensory data and perceptual information. The interplay among neural pathways, cognitive faculties, and emotionally colored lenses stimulates recognition of both ecologically expectable and novel stimuli. Both brain and the developing psychological self attempt to coordinate these diverse findings by using conscious and nonconscious strategies. Signal information gradually refines its clarity amid filtered out background noise. This occurs maturationally, developmentally, and through conscious, intentional information seeking.

*Envy theory* is a broad framework suggesting testable hypotheses. To this end, some fundamental operating principles behind human experience are proposed. Phenomenological and psychoanalytic perspectives outline a wide-ranging description of inferred mental processes. Psychoanalytic psychology and intensive clinical work with children, adolescents, and adults have been instrumental in unearthing the dynamics driving envy. Findings gleaned from cognitive science add to this framework. *Envy theory* attempts a bold integration of such differing approaches.

Psychodynamic operations, the dialectical interplay of unconscious forces and unconscious mental contents, all of which unfold in social contexts, are meaning-laden processes. This conception of dynamisms connotes impermanent arrangements in constant flux. The term "psychodynamic" encompasses both mental conflict and cooperation. In psychoanalytic psychology, the collision of opposing experiential forces elicits the dissonance felt as anxiety. This, in turn, stimulates the mind to defend itself against and adaptively cope with these. Hence, the mind's defense mechanisms develop and are experienced, in phenomenological terms, by "unconscious phantasy"—subliminal mental images, for example, and also those images witnessed in the dream state. Defense mechanisms ward off abrupt mental short-circuiting and psychological decompensation.

Mind is seen as an interior universe populated with meaning. It experiences itself as a vivid inner world in dynamic motion. The meaning-laden links organizing mind serve to orient and motivate thinking and behavior. Love and hate work to ensure survival. Love and envy provide the scaffolding on which meaning arises. Both these pairs in tight unison operate as a person's overarching orientation. They shape and guide personal experience and interpersonal engagements in the social environment. The thematic orientation of this book is that meaningful survival is the ultimate end product achieved by the complex interactions of love, hate, and envy. Love and hate are obvious. Envy is the mind's hidden module.

Understanding individual psychology, moreover, provides the basis for insight into groups and complex social systems. This includes the psychology of mental processes, attitudes, and performance seen in small and large groups—namely, social and cultural psychology. *Envy theory* emerges from an "object relations" psychology. This denotes that within the individual mind there exist innate expectations, templates, and a readiness for experiences in real social contexts. Out of these social contexts emerge dominance hierarchies and social status stratifications whose impact both on individual and group functioning unquestionably affects the strivings and quality of life for all.

The meaning of social context encompasses not only the real but also imagined, innately expectant, and construed presence of other people. In psychoanalytic psychology, the construed other is termed "object." Such a context is a complex organization. It reflects dynamic interactions, features of the settings in which behaviors occur, and expectations and norms that typically govern both individual behaviors and interpersonal interactions in particular settings. In the real world, the power of actual social situations to influence and control attitudes and behaviors is evident.

*Envy theory* highlights the manner in which groups provide opportunities for the intrinsic dispositions of individuals, especially unconscious and primitive impulses, to manifest themselves in concrete ways. It may identify productive and counterproductive trends previously hidden. Unconscious envy isolates itself from conscious awareness; hence it is secretive. When envious attitudes approach conscious awareness, often, they are intentionally masked in an attempt to blunt social criticism. These are defensive "impression management" strategies.

## Love-Hate and Love-Envy Paradigms

The binary opposite of love has traditionally been regarded as its natural counterpart—hate. This seemingly intuitive coupling—love and hate—has been part of the history of the struggle to make sense of human motivation, feeling, thinking, and behavior. This hedonic, appraisal-laden pairing has emerged in various ways in the propositions underlying the wrestling of ideas and values in religion, philosophy, psychology, and sociology. Biology, less personalized, has as a basic postulate the complementary forces of attraction and repulsion driving an organism's interaction with the environment in its organic struggle for survival.

*Envy theory* is born out of a context of discovery, a new way of thinking about universally experienced psychological phenomena. It reconceptualizes the long-established love-hate proposition and introduces a new "love-envy" paradigm. Its serious intent speaks to the complexity of human psychological development. Its particular focus on envy is clearly just one part of the entire story behind mind, motivation, and culture. To magnify the subtle yet indispensable significance of envy, envy is purposely taken out of its virtually amalgamated real-life context.

To be sure, a true understanding of the meaning of human experience is much richer than any one system of concepts can explain. Each attempt at such a study can be informative by itself, but no one study's findings can be designated as definitive. In clinical applications, for example, a study or set of studies may explain outcomes for the group a patient belongs to, but not the probability of that patient's individual outcome, especially since most studies are explanatory rather than pragmatic.

Hence, a reasonable perspective is seeing how each body of propositions, such as those comprising *envy theory*, best fits the overall tapestry of fact, conjecture, and contextually pragmatic life experience.

*Envy theory* should be viewed as a novel construct theory. It is a grouping of hypothetical processes that structure and make personality function. These emerge from a biomental base in infancy and undergo a lifetime of biopsychosocial development. It endeavors to provide a single explanation of the intangible abstractions—love, hate, and envy—as they are experienced mentally and in observable behaviors. The confirmed accuracy of *envy theory* as true or false does not lend itself to being proved directly since it is a construct theory by nature. Its value, therefore, lies in its utility: its usefulness in describing, predicting, and managing the subject matter it purports to expound. Hence, the principal criterion for evaluating the worth of such a contribution is its usefulness, for instance, in research studies and psychotherapeutic applications.

Love, hate, and envy in all their permutations are basic driving forces in mental life. As orienting principles on the broadest level, they make up the root causes of behavior reflected in both mental experience and expressed physical action. The complexities of these motivations comprise implicit amalgams essentially unconscious. They are the dynamically unconscious subtexts, especially in their primitive forms, that act to elicit causal action experienced in preconscious and conscious dimensions of ego awareness-perception, conception, and behavior. These nonconscious drives and emotions combine in each individual's primary-object/person-seeking need and wish for human attachment. Coming together, they prompt the developing ego to integrate to become a more stable and cohesive self/experiencer. No period in human development is motivationally neutral.

## Ego, Object, and Self

*Envy theory* uses the psychoanalytic construct of ego and defines it in psychodynamic, phenomenological, and information-processing terms. Using the term "ego" throughout *envy theory* is intentional. Ego is that aspect of the person that makes contact with the world. Experiential contact is essential to survival. Ego is the self's group of tools coordinated to pick up data and apply information processing to make sense out of being alive. This cognitive and phenomenological reality is *envy theory*'s ultimate point of reference.

*Ego denotes perceiver, witnesser, and processor of experiential information commensurate with current abilities and developmental capacities. As a biomental entity, ego denotes the manner in which perceptions are experienced.* Its hardware is both the brain and its innate psychological dispositions. Its software emerges from its hardware as it encounters experiential information both subjectively and in social contexts. The ego is the incubator in which the organic growth of emotions by a series of progressive changes leads to complex attitudes of love and hate. Plasticity and change, moreover, are essential features of brain, ego, and behavior.

In *envy theory, what is perceived, witnessed, and processed in respect to something other than the experiencer is termed object(s).* Object typically denotes the ego's construal of another person. *Since the terms "ego" and "object" assume crucial importance in explaining envy theory, understanding their denotations and implications is essential.*

Ego as processor of experiential information has many complex functions. Some of these include the following: sensation of raw data; perception of information; the unconscious experience of emotional physiological arousal; the formation of affects, the unconscious aspects of a consciously felt "feeling"; thinking; memory; executive regulation; control of impulses; a synthetic and integrative capacity to generate meaning; the ability to feel anxiety and sense danger in order to construct psychological defense mechanisms; the need to seek other persons ("objects") with whom to attach in emotionally meaningful ways; the ability to apprehend reality in a rational, deliberative manner in order to make intentional choices ("secondary process thinking"); and neuromuscular motor control for behavioral action.

Using the aforementioned, the ego functions to achieve ongoing adaptation to its nonconscious and conscious biomental self in the context of the external environment to realize meaningful survival. Such states of mind denote cognitive processes and emotional salience, both of which count heavily in forming attitudes. The ego orchestrates consciousness, and, in part, is the reservoir of conscious awareness. Consciousness denotes acuity of sensitivity to and validity of assessment of self and environment; consciousness, in principle, is the process of biomental experiencing. Self is the phenomenological experiencer of consciousness.

The construct of a *self as a biomental unit* denotes that neural processes experience the entire physical organism and register this experience in what we call "mind." The experience of mind arises from the entire organism as a whole, not merely the central nervous system in isolation. An individual, therefore, from birth is a biomental self—an experiencing entity on a dynamic trajectory of growth, maturation, development, and ongoing integration.

Accordingly, the self (a structural construct) and its consciousness (a functional process) denote the distributed, dynamic interrelations occurring in mind-body rather than merely being localized in or restricted to, for instance, only a specialized part of the central nervous system. The gradually integrating forces in consciousness play a large part in directing the self—its orientation, attitudes, inclinations, and actions. Nondualist perspectives on mental functioning have gained neuroscientific credibility in the last twenty years (Varela, Thompson, and Rosch 1991/1993). Thinking of mind separate from body is imprecise.

The somatic or bodily aspect of the self sensed and made meaningful by the brain denotes mind, mental functioning, and an individual's psychological reality. Although the meanings of ego and time are on different levels of abstraction and discourse, it would not be incorrect to assign an intrinsic identity to them since both connote measurement, progression, and cumulative change. Time and how the mind emerges, therefore, are inextricably correlated. Conscious awareness and thinking are experienced as linear progressions. In psychoanalytic psychology, this is called *secondary process thinking*. Nonconscious processes that underlie this alert state of awareness operate more in "nonlogical" simultaneity and so make irrational thinking and dreams a fact. This is termed *primary process thinking*.

In *envy theory*, the ego is defined as an organizing agency that serves as a means or instrument for perception, cognition, emotion, memory, and their neuropsychological integration. In other words, the ego mediates cognitive-sentient levels of awareness of the inner and outer environments and between them. It is both aspirational performance—thinking, feeling, and phantasying—and operational performance, in that its motoric capacities are able to pragmatically implement its intentions.

The ego, as a whole, integrated agency, consolidates in principle during the early developmental era (Klein 1935, 1946) of the "depressive position"—middle to end of infancy. Only when the depressive position is established can the crucial sense of "depression"—intentionality, harm, loss, sorrowful suffering, and an urge to repair damages—be experienced to varying degrees. A major characteristic of all depressions is the sense of being stuck, imprisoned in a static, colorless state where time freezes in abeyance. In essence, this is the experiential belief that no change is, can, or will occur. This "sense of no change" or the faltering of time implies the qualities intimately correlated to depression—hopelessness, helplessness, loss of pleasure and interest in the future, and anhedonia. This contributes heavily to the unyieldingness of clinical depression to current therapeutic interventions.

## Envy as a Paradigm of Stressful Life Events

Envy theory may be regarded as a bridge between neuroscience and mental health. Stressors are life experiences that involve change from one mode of activity to another. Such changes include both attitudinal shifts as well as physical adaptations. Stress itself is typical and an inevitable part of everyday experience. Inordinate and unpredictable stress, however, may become chronic and lead to a variety of biomental changes that are traumatic and deleterious—anxiety, depression, mood dysregulation, and metabolic syndromes. Stress increases circulating glutamate and cortisol, and reduces proper neurotransmitter functioning (for example, serotonin, norepinephrine). Its effects reach down to gene expression by altering transcriptional factors (Sanacora 2008). It is now well established that stress is a neurotoxic event and may lead to multiple neurological changes such as reduction in neuronal dendritic spines, reduction in the length and complexity of neurons, and in impaired neurogenesis—the birth of new, healthy neurons (Pittenger and Duman 2008). Major depressive disorders correlate with these changes.

Envy theory suggests that the subliminal experience of envy is always a fundamental dimension of stress, anxiety, and depression. The ongoing, healthy neuroplasticity of the brain, therefore, is impinged upon by unrecognized envy. For example, the hippocampus, long thought to be a center of learning and memory, becomes diminished in size and functionality by chronic stress as well as by depression. Only recently has it been demonstrated that a range of interventions that includes antidepressant medications, electrical stimulation, and psychotherapies can reverse such neurotoxicity and confer degrees of neuroprotection (Sanacora 2008). Awareness of envy's role in anxiety, stress, and depression opens new vistas in designing effective treatments.

## Envy Theory's Core Thesis

Envy theory's core thesis is that unconscious envy is the central mode and expression of primitive, innate destructiveness encompassing a corrosive spoiling to both the subject as well as the object. Envious destructiveness aimed toward the object is usually direct, whereas envy's destructiveness to the subject who envies is indirect yet more insidious. This differentiates envy from hate since hate aims at object destruction while carefully sparing the subject. Envy is psychological violence by the self to the self.

Envy theory considers envy as the nuclear, elemental core of destructiveness in the entire personality on the deepest level. As described in the constructs presented, envy embodies two mental forces: love as excessive idealization, and destructiveness as complex spoiling.

Unconscious envy is the primitive sensation and conflated feeling of privation, powerlessness, and distress in the face of advantages and their enjoyment existing elsewhere. The term "primitive" in *envy theory* encompasses several meanings: primary process nonconscious, active information processing; primitive unconscious defense mechanisms such as omnipotence, denial, splitting, projective identification, and idealization; and the psychodynamic processes inherent to fundamental chronological and long-lasting developmental configurations: the paranoid-schizoid and depressive positions. These configurations are not psychopathological. On the contrary, they reflect trends that normative as well as atypical emotional and cognitive development and information processing typically use to function. They constitute the primary nonconscious dimension of mind.

For example, the psychodynamic construct "splitting" denotes fundamental psychological operations on multiple levels. Although often considered a defense mechanism, splitting has adaptive value and promotes development. Two leading areas are cognition and emotion. Cognitively, splitting refers to the hardwired capacity to differentiate and recognize differences in any experience. In earliest development, information processing exists as a blur of undifferentiated experience that only gradually begins to organize over time, mature, unfold, and develop. Experiential data, at first apprehended in large conflated chunks, is slowly disentangled as perceptual systems come on line. Distinctions, differences, delimitations, and boundaries between and among experiential entities sharpen. When this occurs very early in infancy, the splits between perceived objects appear wide, in other words, largely unintegrated. Different objects are perceived as juxtaposed in linear-like fashion.

Only later in development, when the capacity for abstraction and symbol formation emerges, does this change. The essential change involves apprehending perceptual entities, not statically, but as involved in a myriad of interactive relationships—for example, self with other, other with other, self with others (relationship to father and mother), and also self with self (developing self-observation, self-awareness, and awareness of conscious conflict). From an epistemological perspective, at all developmental levels, one is more aware of differences/distinctions rather than commonalities/similarities. Sameness seems to be concealed beneath apparent differences. Perception of differences typically connotes emotional aversion rather than attraction.

The emotional dimension of cognition attaches polarized feelings of love/goodness versus hate/badness to cognitive distinctions. The mechanics of information processing are prompted to organize their data input by such fundamental discriminations. Through repeated reconfigurations of the effects of splitting, impressions, evaluations, and preferences form themselves.

Melanie Klein (1957) thought that splitting processes in early infancy acted to preserve the emerging ego by an adaptive dispersal of destructive impulses and internal persecutory anxieties. She said that a certain amount of splitting is essential for integration and the later synthetic functions of the ego. If splitting, however, becomes excessively driven by constitutionally primed destructive forces, it results in fragmentation. When splitting acted to preserve what is good from what is bad, then it acted as defense.

## Melanie Klein's "Primary Envy" and *Envy Theory*'s "Nuclear Envy"

Melanie Klein (1882–1960), a British psychoanalyst, first formally introduced the proposition of unconscious, primary, innate envy (Klein 1957). She oriented this construct in her theory of developmental positions (paranoid-schizoid and depressive). *Envy theory* is a further expansion of her seminal discovery. In *envy theory*, inherent, primary envy is called *nuclear envy*.

This expansion of "primary envy" includes a unified foundation with a trinity of three roots: the *primordial* envy of ego to its id; the *primal* envy of ego to the part-object, breast; and the *primary* envy of ego to the whole object, mother.

In addition, *envy theory* adds a unique dimension. Envy may undergo a healthy, reality-oriented, and adaptive refinement—*the healthy maturation of envy*. This arises when the "internal good object" is sufficiently established in earliest infancy or, to some extent, retroactively later on. This process varies in degree and is never complete. This internal good object correlates positively with what *envy theory* calls *nuclear love*. This focal point in the ego transduces the vital energies of the life instinct making them available to further integration, lessen splitting, and enhance feelings of admiration and gratitude. In this way, the goodness of nurturance is recognized both as an inner experience and through perceptions of the environment. This optimizes receptivity and permits the ego to assimilate experience in health-promoting ways.

Growth, maturation, and development create nuanced characterological styles, all of which may be explored thus enabling change and modification. The essence of this psychological refinement denotes the gradual integration of all dimensions of consciousness: conscious awareness, preconscious subliminality, and unconscious mental life.

To explain this trend toward coherence, a novel proposition, the *episte-mophilia* within the self, is advanced. It denotes the inherent, self-directing, biomental drive toward *meaningful survival*, anticipating future experiences and promoting successful adaptation. This biomental impulse to seek and understand meaningful experience emerges through contact with significant persons and is mediated by the infinitely variable interactions of the life-and-death instincts throughout development. Moreover, unconscious envy is named as the missing theoretical and clinical link in unsuccessful adaptation, impaired biopsychosocial functioning, and treatment-resistant psychiatric cases.

## Love and Envy: Primary Phenomena in an Indissoluble Union

Envy is one of the foundational, dynamic mental operations that provides a significant underpinning for all human experience. The term "dynamic" refers to both the conflictual and creative dialectical interplay between opposing psychological forces. Envy not only acts to motivate and drive impulses but also to maintain and push all mental processes toward a state of dynamic unconsciousness. This is the state of repression—an obdurate nonconscious stratum of information storage.

Phenomenologically, love begins with wide-eyed attraction, a subtle smile, and an internal sense of "yes." Envy begins with wide-eyed arousal, incipient rage, and an internal sense of "no." All these states occur on various levels of consciousness, simultaneously.

Consciousness in *envy theory* denotes experiential states of information processing that include a wide spectrum encompassing both nonconscious and conscious. Both are predominantly active rather than only reactive. This broad conception is not restricted to conscious awareness of and responsivity to the external environment.

Consciousness denoted here goes beyond fluctuating levels of alertness or vigilant states of the sensorium. On both conscious and preconscious levels, consciousness may loosely connote degrees of awareness of mental content and bodily states. Mental occurrences take shape at a variety of levels of sensitivity that includes awareness and nonawareness. Human consciousness is flooded with emotion and motivation, which, as a whole, direct thinking and behavior.

This mental sentience ranges from an inception that is undifferentiated toward becoming more defined neuropsychologically. For example, the unconscious physiological arousal of "emotion" gradually becomes the unconscious aspect of a more consciously felt "feeling." On any level, it triggers reverberating responsivity, which thereby produces varying degrees of changing self-regulation. In this sense, the *experience* of consciousness is a dynamic, impermanent, ever-changing state of flux conditioned by both internal and external qualities. These attributes are inextricable mixtures of bodily emotional states, mental feeling sets, and environmental stimuli.

The analysis of envy centers on its root form in unconscious dimensions of the mind. These domains constitute "split-off" sectors of unconscious envy. In this sense, it is inconspicuous, and very unlike love and hate. All permutations of envy derive from this unobtrusive base.

*In speaking about envy, split-off and unintegrated unconscious envy are postulated.* In understanding *envy theory*, it is essential to remember that it is unconscious—not conscious—envy that is being addressed.

Envy as a conscious attitude, by contrast, is an uncomfortable experience marked by comparisons occurring when a person positions himself in relation to a supposed superior other ("upward social comparisons") who is perceived to be enjoying unobtainable advantages. It is a feeling on the surface of awareness and more integrated into conscious experience. Such feelings of desire are more easily recognized, much less obstinate and destructive, and generally more manageable. The spoiling aim at the base of unconscious envy is absent. Whatever the extent of conscious envy's hostile destructiveness, it is less corrosive and insidious. Although unsettling, conscious envy may stir reasonable ambition and competition. Most conventional discussions of envy revolve around conscious envy—the envied person having superior and self-relevant, shared characteristics that are desired. *Envy theory*'s inclusion of the essential factors of spoiling and destructiveness are not included in conscious envy.

## The Conceptualization of "Primary" in *Envy Theory*

Envy and its complement, love, work both interactionally and in dynamic tension to regulate the mind and progressively establish character and personality. Together (along with hate), they act to orient and calibrate all psychological processes—intrapsychically, interpersonally, and behaviorally. Whereas love and envy manifest as complex phenomena, each may also be understood as unitary—that is, partially modular. In other words, each is an elemental or primary operating force although consisting of subgroupings and subconstituents. Each essential unit (love, envy, and hate) has virtually irreducible and nuclear status. In this special sense, "primary" means not derived; it has no cause other than itself. The personality needs love, hate, and envy to survive, amass experience, and develop. All mental processes originate from this matrix of emotional and cognitive information processing.

"Irreducible" in this sense means they act as fundamentally organized units, a minimum distinctive unit that cannot be divided further without losing its meaning. For example, an artist's pragmatically used primary colors (for example, red, yellow, and blue), however they are open to variations, and the inferred primary emotions (fear, sadness, surprise, happiness/elation, disgust, anger, and contempt) (Darwin [Ekman] 1998) in this sense may be viewed as "primary" and "irreducible."

The terms "primary" and "irreducible" used to describe envy are akin to the meaning of the term "atom." Atom denotes a basic unit of matter. These units are used in coordinated groupings to form more complex aggregates or derivatives having different individual identities. Primary envy and *nuclear envy* fit this definition. They are the basic units of psychological matter. *Envy theory* sees excessive idealization, robbing, and spoiling as envy's subatomic components.

It is suggested that such reductionistic groupings with heuristic value derive from hardwired, innate, and phylogenetically older structures in the brain's limbic system. In other words, they do not primarily emerge from complex frontal lobe associations, those derived from learning, acquired experience, civilization, and reason.

As root emotions, love, hate, and envy are primary in that they are un-learned, innate processes serving as invariant templates with no fixed action patterns. They, however, are not the equivalent of the innate instincts attributed to animals by ethnologists. These unitary human processes—love, hate, and envy—once activated, subsequently launch massive secondary, complex developments (for example, defense mechanisms) that then become the principal focus of attention with which their primaries become identified. It is critical to add that experience, culture, and learning very early on in infancy give idiosyncratic shape and content to these primaries, notably enhancements and constraints. Learning causes enormous behavioral variations and reinforcements.

The term "primary," then, is used here to spotlight some axiomatically central emotional and cognitive root orientations. All so-called primaries probably are useful in that they are *pragmatic fictions*. They function as imaginary variables or imperfect yet economical compromise constructs adopted heuristically for specific purposes in context-specific models such as in *envy theory*.

## Self and Other in *Envy Theory*

The concept "self" refers to the whole personality, including the psychic organizations denoted in classical psychoanalysis by the constructs *id*, *ego*, and *superego*. The actual physical body is also included; hence, *envy theory* regards self as a *biomental* entity.

*Envy theory* goes to great lengths to emphasize that, when different structural and functional aspects are described, only shifts of focus pertaining to how the mind is experiencing aspects of itself are meant. This underscores the dynamic quality of all biomental reality underlying their conjectured makeup. Terms used here are best regarded as simplified approximations of highly complex processes.

The self is (consciously and nonconsciously) aware of the here-and-now and incorporates conscious and nonconscious elements of past, present, and future as memory develops. The concept "ego" is a subset of self. Ego as a structuring dimension of self acts as the self's functional experiencer—witness to what is happening. In this sense, ego, as mediator, is the point of contact—experience—between self and stimuli.

The concept "self," by contrast, is not a mediator; it is a construct about an individual. Self is characterized by dynamically flexible, coordinated sweeps of the entire biomental entity that, as a whole, correlate with a person's self-identity. At their core, both self and mind are not separate from how they function; they are, in essence, the experiential process, itself. The axis of the self, then, is an ever-shifting dynamism of nonintegrated and integrating biomental associations. Major components comprising self are self-awareness, self-continuity, self-agency, degrees of self-coherence, self-aspirations, and self-boundaries. The individual, for example, in differing orienting contexts may be termed the physical self, the social self, and the spiritual self.

From a neuroscience perspective, neuronal circuitry, neurotransmitters, the strength between neurons and coordinated neural pathways, and other neurotrophic substances like oxytocin and vasopressin reflect in measurable ways (for example, by fMRI studies of activation and deactivation) thoughts, feelings, attitudes, and behavioral repertoires that we attribute to ego and self.

The phrase "objects of experience outside the experiential self" refers, in different contexts, to any of the following: id, intrapsychic objects, superego, and the factual presence of an interpersonal other in the external environment. When the ego, as seat of the self's unconscious and conscious experiential scanning, senses "not ego," for that moment, this focus becomes an entity experienced as "not me" located seemingly outside the self. Such experiential distinctions begin in infancy and etch themselves in the *biomental self*. These imprints are "re-membered" thereafter both corporeally and by retrospective narration. Mental distinctions and differentiations are formed in this way.

Envy, for example, although prompted by an awareness of something *apparently* outside the self in the form of a construed envied object, is essentially a self-centered and self-directed solitary process. Envy fosters isolation and, in general, the breakdown of growth and creative development. The majority of envy's dynamics have an intrapsychic orientation. Their nonconscious mechanisms suppress reason and make them phantasy configurations rather than realistic assessments on almost every cognitive level.

Throughout this text, the idiosyncratic, paroxysmal, and spontaneous aspect of the nature, arousal, and ultimate actions of envy is emphasized by using the prefix "auto." This highlights various aspects of envy's egocentric insularity. Only when envy undergoes a healthy maturation does it transform into attitudes and behaviors more observable and outwardly reasonable.

For example, equitable and benevolent states of mind—one's moral compass—expressed in ethical conduct marked by empathy, sharing, helping, a sense of justice, and fairness are all indications of envy's normalized maturation. These attitudes are markedly affected by individual construals of deservingness of both merit and misfortune. While the ethical standards established in social systems tend to be objective and unvarying by consensus, an individual's moral judgment about what is good and bad on a personal level is more subjective and changing. *The healthy maturation of envy* shifts mental operations from a base in phantasy toward reason and consensual validation, lessening major splits between personal and social standards although discrepancies in emphasis may remain.

## Psychoanalytic Frameworks and Envy

Introducing psychoanalytic concepts is necessary because *envy theory* originated in this discipline and requires these ideas since they form an important part of its framework. Theoretical and clinical familiarity is not necessarily assumed. Hence, terms and their connotations for *envy theory* will be elucidated throughout this book.

The phenomenon and experience of primary envy is *first and foremost unconscious*. It is neither solely an impulse nor an affect or defense of the ego, the perceiving and information-processing aspect of the self.

From a metapsychological (abstract psychoanalytic theory) point of view, envy is the action of the id. *The id is the nonconscious, unknowable mental reservoir of instinctual love and destructiveness as it refracts itself through the prism of the experiencing ego. The id is the mental aspect of the physical body, specifically, though not exclusively, the central nervous system. In other words, the id is the body in the brain.* The id's formal inception coincides with the primordial inception of the relation between id and ego at birth when experience outside the womb occurs.

The ego's experience of its id is a total response of the self to itself when the self senses the *experiential presence of "another."* This primitive and inchoate experiential differentiation in some way starts at birth, and results in mind having a nonconscious side (id) together with an increasingly more conscious side (ego) that becomes able to sense—in only shadowy fashion—its nonconscious base, the id.

The id functions as a subliminal background state of mind; and it is always active in some way. Mental processes remain largely outside of conscious awareness. The nonconscious id with its surface of burgeoning consciousness—its ego—continues to structure and influence every aspect of mental life and behavior.

*Envy theory* uses the Kleinian constructs (1935, 1946) of two fundamental developmental positions originating in infancy. In attempting to approximate these nonverbal chronological eras, adultomorphic language is used. What the infant actually experiences remains unknown, although how they are characterized in recognizable adult language gives a conjectured "sense" of how they operate. These positions recur as oscillating states of mind throughout life.

The *paranoid-schizoid position* present at birth is characterized by fragile ego relating to a part-object. The infantile unintegrated ego is aware of partial aspects of its objects of attention and desire. They are typically felt as extreme states of mind. In the paranoid-schizoid position, conscious memory and memories of recent experiences are essentially absent; unpredictability, therefore, is the norm. This gives the paranoid-schizoid configuration an undertone of anxiety and fear that has a persecutory coloring. Unconscious phantasy predominates.

In the paranoid-schizoid position, where envy first organizes itself and remains based, there is never a clear division between the self as ego and the construed object. *What dominates mental processes is the experience of ego-object confusion and extremes of good and bad. Vacillating experience is felt as either ideal or imperfect.*

The *depressive position* beginning in the middle of the first year is characterized by greater differentiation between a more integrated ego ("self") and its more distinct awareness of and relation to a separate and whole object (another person). Here conscious awareness begins to expand and cognitive processes of reason begin to overshadow but not eliminate subjective phantasy.

## Comparisons between Love and Envy

Impulses toward approach, seeking, affiliation, benevolence, and creative bonding reflect the concept of "love" used here. Love denotes a highly complex, multifaceted configuration. How the subject experiences love for its objects is versatile and nuanced. It includes more than what is termed romantic love, sentimentality, or even everyday kindness.

Love's multifaceted dimensions include active and focused searching, discriminative differentiation, affiliation, linking, *shared* attachment, bonding, creativeness, fecundity, potency, normal idealization, admiration, esteem, empathy, gratitude, nurturance, kindness, enjoyment, and happiness. This "vivification" results from the unique integration and reorganization that emerge out of differentiating ego-object (observer-observed) self-experience beginning in the first year of life, the paranoid-schizoid and depressive positions, which usher in progressive expansions of meaning, self-identity, and subjective well-being. In other words, how the developing infant perceives and loves its mother becomes richer and more complex over time.

*This attachment organizes, achieves stability, and becomes secure to the extent the infant without excessive envy and greed lovingly accepts and assimilates mother's nurturance—being loved and understood.*

The abstract concept of love is infinitely varied in its concrete expressions both personally and interpersonally. Its manifestations in feelings and behaviors toward the self and others may be quantitatively more apparent than the expressions taken by *nuclear envy*. Whereas love seeks to be born, held in awareness and nurtured, envy is secretive and wants to remain hidden and invisible. Love seeks contact; envy seeks to delete contact.

Although the essential significance of love in human development and relations cannot be emphasized enough, this book highlights the details of unconscious envy rather than focusing on a more detailed elaboration of love and its experiential derivatives. It would be a mistake for the reader to think that in *envy theory* love is not as important as envy. In fact, *the healthy maturation of envy* is predicated on love taking center stage when change is sought and mental health succeeds.

Envy, unlike love, is a strong mixture of both primitive love (inherent libidinal instincts or life instincts) and destructive forces (innate destructiveness or death instinct). More precisely, *the love component within envy takes the form of excessive idealization and the destructive component takes the form of spoiling.* Envy as such is not primarily ambivalent, which would strongly suggest an indecisive cycling of feelings of love and hate. Envy's mood, by contrast, is primarily flooded with feelings of ruination and deletion.

In envy, there is a profound emphasis on the impulse of destructive spoiling, which negatively affects the envier. Hence, there are always psychotic and self-destructive elements, however subtle, in operation. Envy is the ego's diathesis toward perpetual suffering. This proposition is essential for understanding the meaning and implications of the *nuclear envy* concept.

Pure cultures of unconscious envy do not exist. Isolates of envy are theoretical abstractions used to intellectually analyze how the structure and functioning of envy may operate in concrete contexts. Conscious forms of ambivalence, greed, and jealousy typically overlay envy after early infancy as both cognitive and emotional development advance. This is crucial to remember when trying to fathom the nature of unconscious envy within *envy theory*, especially since envy is presented at times *as if* it could occur in isolation from all else and present itself directly. Envy always fuses with and masks itself amid other more obvious, less dire phenomena.

Envy, like its companion, love, is a complex life regulator with cognitive, affective, motivational, and volitional dimensions that are indispensable for meaningful survival. As such, both love and envy are primary mental orientations. This primacy lies at the base of their complicated clinical expressions, which always include amalgamations of other mental phenomena developed from acquired life experience. In other words, what one can see as the final product is the outcome of love and envy with numerous additions.

In the history of psychoanalytic theory building, for example, the classical juxtaposition of love and hate has been used to describe two primary classes of mental forces. This has been and continues to be heuristically useful, especially because this coupling has a more obvious rationale for counterpart status. This premise issues from Freud's proposition of the life instinct associated with love and the death instinct associated with hate and observable aggression, violence, and assaultiveness. Although complementary, these two classes of human mental "instincts" are neither symmetrical nor isomorphic. They are not parallel in structure, form, or function, although they always exist and must operate together.

*Envy theory*'s discussion of envy is framed on a variant perspective. Its approach is phenomenologically sensitive and clinical. It juxtaposes and contrasts experientially felt love with experientially felt suffering, the principal cause of which is *nuclear envy*. Hence, *envy theory*'s model rests on a love-envy paradigm.

## Aspects of Intrapsychic Phenomenology:
## Experience and the Problem of Consciousness

The term "conscious" is broad. It typically denotes wakeful alertness with some degree of experiential noticing, phenomenal awareness, recognizability, and discrimination. These sentinel functions comprise the state of the active sensorium—the five senses of hearing, seeing, tasting, touching, and smelling, and their coordinated and integrated receptivity. The abilities to attend, concentrate, remember, communicate verbally and nonverbally, and direct voluntary motor activity characterize this state of conscious alertness.

The conscious aspect of the mind is the most conspicuous and transparent aspect of personal and interpersonal experience. Yet it represents only a small, if not the smallest, part of the broad range of human experience. Even in the awake state, an individual may be described as adequately "conscious" in a technical sense, but may not be fully cognizant of most of the nonconsciously sensed elements in the internal and external environments. The quality of unwittingness, both unawareness of the full range of facts of a situation and of unintentionality, characterizes the average state of conscious wakefulness.

The term "nonconscious" is used in psychophysiological studies and cognitive science to denote experiential states marked by inferred reactivity (cognitive activation and cognitive processing) to unrecognized (not consciously perceived or noticed) and unprimed stimuli (Stapel and Blanton 2004, 2007; Badgaiyan 2006).

Experiential consciousness reflects configurations that include both awareness of and responses to experiential events on nonconscious and conscious levels. Nonconscious mental processing, preconscious memory, and consciously unattended information, for example, are accepted theoretical propositions used in contemporary cognitive science research (Kihlstrom 1987; Velmans 1991). For example, studies have shown that complex information processing—without attention and awareness—operates on sensory inputs before conscious recognition of them occurs (Bechara et al. 1997; Kubovy et al. 1999).

In *envy theory*, reasons for such extensive considerations of consciousness rest on two basic premises: (1) states of conscious choice and conscious motivation are starting points for the examination of experience and for sustained self-inquiry, and (2) by using *envy theory*, the goal of such self-inquiry—the integrative refinement or cultivation of consciousness—is given a pragmatic framework for successful attainment through *the healthy maturation of envy*. Achieving insight reflects such cognitive and emotional integration.

# Envy Theory: The Evolution
# of Personality and First Principles

Character and personality emerge from a complex pool of sources over time. Included are an individual's genetic endowment, processes of growth and maturation, and the interaction of these with experiential factors. Actual environments—impoverished or enriched—clearly have a real impact on the developing person. Yet how subjectivity—the inner world—is experienced arises largely from idiosyncratically construed transactions with the environment. Upbringing, the quality of nurturant, empathetic care, experiences of frustration, and early and later traumas are just a few such influential transactions that are phenomenologically relevant.

*Envy theory* correlates the experience of envy with self-suffering. The experience of suffering in this view, for example, is seen as an important expression of the subject's willingness to continue to carry forward, in the here and now, those anxiety- and pain-bearing beliefs that occurred around past traumas and conflicts. *Envy theory*'s emphasis on the causation of current mental pain, therefore, is not exclusively tagged to past events. It is the result of current construals.

Suffering is a direct correlate of how all past and present life experience—both good and bad—is interpreted, appraised, and reconciled experientially in the present moment. Such considerations avoid the "genetic fallacy" of reducing all psychopathology exclusively to its antecedents in the past. In addition, the fallacy of a "genetic omission" is also avoided by not dismissing the real impact of infantile and childhood traumas on current maladaptive functioning. In this way, perspective and attributional balance temper an understanding of the psychogenetic continuity of all development.

The suffering experienced in envy is influenced by how love of self and love of objects is felt. Considering the ego as the experiential center of the self, self-love includes both *normal narcissism* (healthy self-love) and *pathological narcissism* (excessive and omnipotent self-love). The ego also has the capacity for *object-love* (love for others). All three love domains are major *energetic (instinctual)* aspects of *experiential (phenomenological)* love.

Neither self-love nor object-love arises exclusively from a series of developmentally progressive stages. Both forms of love, in principle, are primary, exist simultaneously, and begin at the start of life. They are interactive and dialetical, not linear. They develop in complexity over time, like the ego, the physical body, and the entire personality, but their substantive inception is at birth. This conception does not see self-love and object-love as mutually exclusive. Rather, they possess a dynamic tension with almost inverse proportions. Both undergo transformations as development proceeds over time.

## Envy Directed at the Object Deflects on the Self: Autodestruction

Masochism is the energetic or instinctual state of self-induced suffering and self-induced pain. It is primarily destructive—that is, an expression of the human biomental death instinct as it operates within. It exists, however, in the first place, because it has an important libidinal (life instinct) component that gives it a quota of pleasure that makes it a reinforcing event. This sense of excitement is the first glimmer that attracts the envier to the envied object. When envy runs its course, only the pain of suffering remains.

Autosuffering is the end product of envy's complicated trajectory that begins with envious attacks prompted initially by desirable attributes misperceived to exist outside the self. Intolerance to what one does not have makes the envier attempt to spoil the object eliciting envy. Spoiling is the envier's feeble effort to stop self-suffering in the envy process. These spoiling attacks rapidly reverse and become self-directed. They ultimately boomerang and finally result in a state of emotional autodestruction.

In other words, *envious processes initially appear instigated and aimed at something outside the self*. This something is attractive and exciting at first. As it becomes intolerable, spoiling is almost reflexively aroused. The spoiling aim in envy seems to be an attack focused in this outward direction. The repercussion of this is the ultimate retroflection or turning backward upon the self of this spoiling destructiveness. Envy, in the end, results in aspects of the self (usually via the sadistic superego in which envy ultimately pools) destructively attacking and spoiling perceived aspects of goodness in the very self that generated the destructive spoiling in the first place. Envy is a reflexive verb that acts upon the actor. Its end product is the experience of masochism or self-suffering.

Envy uses the mental mechanisms of projection, introjection, and identification. These act in unison in the form of *projective identification*. This mechanism like so many other mental processes is always self-reflexive. It is a two-phase psychodynamic operation. The first phase is an active process of featural detection and local, component recognition—an interesting object is scanned and identified. The second phase is passive; the targeted object is brought inside the self and merges to become part of the self. The subject/actor, almost simultaneously, first acts on what is felt to be outside (projection) the self, then secondly is *acted upon (introjection) by his own first action*. The final phase of projective identification is the return to the ego (identification) of what was initially projected.

Envy first aims at destructive spoiling of the object's goodness to quell the anxiety of the envier's own sense of deficit. Massive attempts at spoiling consume the envier. The spoiling eventually becomes self-directed, and a paradoxical action results. The subject's own capacity to experience goodness becomes spoiled.

Envy-driven destructiveness operates and remains virtually inside the subject. This results in autoerosion. This crash becomes a cognitive dissonance felt as an experiential descent into bitterness, emotional miserliness, fear, isolation, and self-loathing. It plays itself out in full splendor principally as a grim intrapsychic drama.

*Although its seeming first aim is to damage the object, envy paradoxically causes enormous damage—primarily and ultimately—to the self.* The envier, in effect, turns his envy on himself. This may not be an intentional turning against the self; it is, in fact, the only way that envy can operate. Both in masochism and envy, destructive and spoiling aims result in suffering within the ego, not in the object. According to *envy theory*, the illogic of this reflects the illogic of how nonconscious processes work because the death instinct, in one sense default chaos, rules their operations.

Envy ultimately spoils those aspects (envied objects) in/of its own ego that participate in the envy dynamic. In the inner world, if objects (for example, featural cognitive presentations, mental representations, affective structures), in some way, are the ego's mirror, then when the ego directs its spoiling envy toward its envied idealized objects, the envy deflects back upon the core ego, itself. The details of this process of autodestruction are discussed in later chapters.

## Normal Self-love Regulates Envious Self-suffering

*Envy theory* places envy in bold relief as a premier cause of self-suffering. To the extent that envy plays a part in mental disorders and stressful life events, the envy dynamic exacerbates the distress and malaise felt.

Love directed to the self in the form of self-love is envy's balancing counterpart. In earliest development, elements of self-love emerge coterminously with elements of object-love. These include the intrapsychic and interpersonal experiences of normal idealization, admiration, empathy, gratitude, and *sharing*. The "object" is the intrapsychic proxy, the ego's creative image of its interpretation of external figures in the environment. Ego is observer; object is what is observed. In other words, the object is the ego's construal of a significant person. The ego fills its inner world with objects of significance. The ego, as it were, is a universe of self-created objects.

Envy and love as discrete, functional entities comprise coherent and distinct psychodynamic forces. They are part of the basic underpinning of mental life. Each is motivational, goal-directed, and suffused with meaning. In this sense, each of them has fundamental and primary status. Although not isomorphic, in some ways they behave as polar opposites. More precisely, they are complementary and exist in varying degrees of interaction, counterbalance, and fusion. This is the ultimate basis for self-regulation. When love and envy are excessively imbalanced, mental impairments emerge.

## Ego and Id: Setting up the Blueprint for all Experience

The blueprint for how the ego experiences itself and others is set up in earliest infancy by the way the id and ego interact. In *envy theory*, the fundamental hypothesis is that the original sense of "the other" is the primordial awareness that the ego has of its biomental source—the id. *The term "id" denotes the mentalized, nonconscious experience of the physical body—its genetics, physiology, and anatomy, and all somatic experiences from birth onward.*

Although the id is primarily a mental structure, it is intimately allied with the corporeal self. In other words, the mental id has a prominent somatic hallmark. Having this corporeal soul, the id remains mostly nonconscious in the ego's awareness. The id's concreteness, as such, is the polar contrast to the ego's capacity to be awake and conscious, and use memory and language, which only retrospectively can sufficiently describe the experiential id—feelings, attitudes, and dreams that were once unconscious.

*Id relations describe the ways the id relates to its ego.* The impact of this on the ego correlates with how the ego experiences itself in relation to others. Two important mechanisms by which the ego handles nonconscious experience are splitting and idealization. Nonconscious splitting and idealization unrealistically exaggerate features of both ego as subject (with characteristics of absence, impotence, lack, imperfection, inferiority, and impoverishment) and id as object (with characteristics of omnipotence, fullness, might, richness, superiority, and perfection). The genesis of this is in earliest infancy. This primordial polarity between self and other persists as a subliminal blueprint for all information processing throughout life.

This primitive magnification of such primordially sensed differences is extreme. The *wide split* underlying this "primordial comparison" in mental ontogenesis influences the developing sense of self. For these reasons, all experience and cognition are subsequently guided by this polarized template in the background of all experience. This harsh dissonance ultimately evokes distress, resentment, anxiety, unbearable intolerance, feeling persecuted, and hostility. These signals anticipate excessive envy's ulterior destructive and spoiling intentions—the attempt to halt these unbearably painful tensions.

As the experience of love unfolds and influences how the infant feels about itself and its environment (objects), love acts to modulate envy by normalizing excessive idealization. It diminishes exaggerations and reduces polarizations in information processing. It aims at creating union, fostering creativeness, advancing mental integration, maintaining integrity, enhancing conscious processes, and fostering pleasure. Its clinical expressions appear noble and generous in intent, aim, and behavior. Its self-soothing and self-regulating derivatives are closer to conscious awareness.

Love is a positive experiential presence; envy is a negative, masked, and more silent presence. Love and its expressions are luminous. They stand out in more obvious ways in mental life and behavior.

Envy causes a general blindness in understanding, notably clear recognition of its unmasked self. Envy's hidden agenda exists as an underground empire that, along with love, implicitly governs mental life. Envy is the premier secret maker that globally weakens vitality. Conceptual and experiential correlates closely related to envy are absence, gap, deficit, lack, emptiness, void, and bitter unpleasure.

## Summary

The natural companion and contrast to hate has traditionally been described by the term "love." This book reconceptualizes the "love-hate" model and introduces a novel and developmentally earlier "love-envy" paradigm. Love and envy, a primary couple, along with love and hate, another primary couple, are the superordinate dialectical forces underlying and shaping all mental functioning. In fact, *envy theory* proposes that both love and hate are the two major components making up envy.

The existence of hate and destructiveness in human experience is conspicuous and unquestionable. Both have observable and direct experiential equivalents in conscious awareness. The propositions advanced here offer a wider frame of reference for mental functioning. While acknowledging that hate and envy coexist and are intertwined, *envy theory* singles out the proposition that unconscious envy is the primitive, nuclear core possibly at the base of all modes of destructiveness. Admittedly, this is controversial, if not provocative and disturbing. Equally arguable may be the assertion that envy's ultimate object is the envier himself rather than the envied object, which merely acts in prop-like fashion to organize envy's emergence.

Love's aims reflect an affectionate approach. Love seeks a positive embrace to improve both subject and object. The aims of hate are aggressive, often destructive, control and containment of a perceived enemy. Envy, a mixture of primitive love as excessive idealization and destructiveness as spoiling, initially perceives the object as excessively ideal but quickly acts to dissolve this since this first impression of goodness is felt as intolerably painful. Emotions are felt as unbearable at envy's onset—excessive idealization—and at its offset—spoiling.

The nuclear status of love and all its mental and behavioral manifestations is also presumed in *envy theory*. Libidinal/loving strivings are discussed but not elucidated in detail since this book's principal focus is a comprehensive exposition of envy. The dual forces of love and destructiveness denote the dialectical interactions of love and envy as they unfold in the mind and display themselves in behavior. Simply put, love is creative affiliation and envy is destructive dismantling.

Klein (1957) was the first psychoanalyst to introduce the proposition of unconscious, primary envy. Besides accepting the validity of this view, I refer to the entire constellation of primary envy as *nuclear envy* and go further by suggesting that *it may undergo a healthy maturation*. This emphasis makes the envy concept presented here more a health paradigm rather than erroneously suggesting a deterministic fatalism. In contrast, it underscores a rational, perhaps guarded, therapeutic optimism.

Envy, I propose, is the missing theoretical and clinical link in many treatment-resistant psychiatric cases. If managed properly, it may be the springboard for insight and greater psychological well-being.

Using a psychoanalytic and phenomenological vocabulary, human consciousness is seen as arising on two ontological levels: (1) participation in an unconditioned base of primordial somatic aliveness, and (2) the psychological dimension of a conditioned phenomenological consciousness ranging from nonconscious experience through conscious attention. Experience denotes both nonconscious and conscious information processing.

Conditioned consciousness includes three substates: (1) alert conscious awareness, (2) preconscious, subliminal unattended information, and (3) a more rigidly inaccessible unconscious biomental base of information storage. The ego is made up of these three topographical levels. A central goal of *envy theory* is the integrative refinement of consciousness. This denotes the progressive achievement of a more fluid and adaptive integration across all substates of consciousness, forged by and ultimately reflected in cognitive and emotional experiential insight.

*Envy theory* proposes that the phenomenon of "self" consists of a *biomental unity* that includes an ego-id organization as the mental dimension of a corporeal self. Id relations denotes how the nonconscious, somatic self is experienced by its ego—the self as perception. Object relations denote the self's inherent *epistemophilia*—how the ego searches for knowledge of others, its objects.

*Envy theory* discusses how love and envy have counterpart status. Love subsumes narcissism (self-love) and object-love, both having normal/balanced as well as abnormal/unbalanced (pathological) dimensions. The proposition that envy represents the premier experience of elemental self-suffering (primary masochism) is advanced. Masochism is the end product of envy's complicated and seemingly, outwardly object-directed trajectory.

Envy unmodulated by love becomes a rogue wild card in mental life. It ultimately results in an abrogation of pleasure propelling the self on a course of paradoxical autodestruction, a self-induced mental annihilation arising from within.

The *epistemophilic impulse* is *envy theory*'s term for adaptive forces impelling toward the search for and exploration of novelty and new information. The aim is to discover and structure relational meaning. This is the raison d'etre for growth, maturation, and self-development. It derives from the innate impulse to observe, search for truth, understand, resolve confusion and ambiguity, and experience meaning.

Motivated goals toward change are forged through interpersonal relatedness. This is the quintessential search for the "good object." Its reward—meaningfulness—exists in part from birth and continues as an aspiration throughout life. The overall aim of self-development is to enhance *meaningful survival*.

Personal change and *the healthy maturation of envy* focus on internal accomplishment. Typically, the odds for success in life—external accomplishments—are improved when envy is recognized and modulated. Individual, interpersonal, social, and cultural factors interdependently coalesce to produce a developmentally emerging sense of self. This construal of self reflects both an experientially vivid inner world and its expression as concrete transactions with other persons in real life.

# CHAPTER TWO

# Inborn Envy

That the capacity for primary unconscious envy, innate and rooted in genetic antiquity, is part of the phylogenetic history of the human species is a presupposition of this book. *Envy theory* denotes the biomental self's inherent trends toward self-orientation and self-organization as being innate, hardwired, and "phylogenetically conserved." These endowments operate in the context of environments that afford great mutability and change in such biomental structure and functioning.

*Envy theory* refers to these endowed proclivities as *nuclear envy*. Sigmund Freud's own proposition of "wishful impulses which have never passed beyond the id" (1933a [1932], 74) suggests the existence of a unique dimension of repression whose primitive contents have never been conscious and remain dynamically unconscious from the start of life and thereafter.

Freud (1916–1917) describes a complemental series of etiological factors (innate constitution, childhood experience, and later trauma) acting in concert to produce the expressions of mental illness. In other contexts (1922), he clearly recognizes the contribution of organic factors in producing mental phenomena. This consideration, he stresses, should not relieve us of the obligation of examining the psychological processes connected with their biological underpinnings.

*Envy theory* positions *nuclear envy* within the arena Freud describes. Although the validity of this notion is arguable and far from being proven, it may be reasonable to suggest that envy, to some extent, has both hereditary and constitutional elements. It would be fair to say that the idea of envy as

43

an innate endowment is either dismissed or apparently not relevant to most psychoanalysts with very few contemporary exceptions (Fonagy 2008).

In any event, although scientifically inconclusive, the heuristic appeal of this view is useful in *envy theory*. In the broadest sense, provisional truth must always exceed reasonable proof; scientific inquiry embraces this. Therefore, *envy theory* proceeds in a context of discovery before elements of it can be justified through research.

## Cognitive Developmental Psychology and Neuroscience: An Overview of Current Empirical Insights

Cognitive science encompasses numerous disciplines—for example, psychology, neuroscience, linguistics, computer science, and philosophy. Cognitive psychology, in turn, addresses matters of attention, perception, learning, memory, thinking, problem solving, language, motivation, and human intelligence. Cognitive developmental theories describe how knowledge is acquired, its mechanisms, and how a child's understanding of self and world changes as a function of age and experience.

Cognitive neuroscience studies of the infant-mother dyad, sometimes referred to as "attachment theory," have begun to address the neurobiology underlying human attachment. Given the explosion of research findings, only some representative classes of findings will be outlined as an orienting backdrop to *envy theory* and its propositions. The upshot is that current empirical findings increasingly substantiate early infancy as an active period in which cognition is significantly more competent than had been believed. Whereas empirical studies tend to emphasize the role of learning, *envy theory* acknowledges the importance of learning but also stresses the evolved innateness of cognitive structures including the selective experience of preferred content. The environment provides opportunities for releasing, constraining, and transforming innate proclivities.

Cognitive developmental theory asks how knowledge is acquired and used. A developmental framework sees this expansion as a process beginning in infancy and becoming more complex as growth, maturation, and development by experience occur. Three broad approaches are delineated, each having a different theoretical base and perspective. These are associationist theories, stage theories, and information processing approaches.

The *associationist* view regards the infant, in a general sense, as a "blank slate" that meets an environment with mixed sensations. According to the laws of association, the frequency of and proximity between sensations and responses establish epistemological connections. These connections traverse a bottom-up journey from the sensory-motor to the perceptual and then, by cross-modal associative learning, to the abstract and conceptual. Jean Piaget, Jerome Bruner, and Lev Vygotsky represent stage theorists. The latter two theorists put emphasis on the way caregivers in the environment are needed to help a child develop knowledge. Social, cultural, and historical contributions are emphasized.

Piaget (1952; Piaget and Inhelder 1969) has outlined a theory of concept formation and the development of the ability for abstract thought. He suggested that children's intelligence universally proceeds, mostly in serial fashion, through a series of four stages of organization and development. Both quality and quantity of information varies in this cumulative process. The classical Piagetian four stages emphasize the contribution of the subject's ability to assimilate and accommodate information, but also admit that exposure to and interactions with appropriate environmental stimuli are needed. These stages are the sensorimotor, preoperational, concrete operational, and formal operational.

During the sensorimotor stage, from birth to two years of age, bottom-up sensory and motor coordinations arise without developed language, symbol, and concept formation. At about six to nine months, the cognitive achievement termed "object permanence" occurs. This suggests the emergence of a substantive capacity to be aware of objects and people even when they are out of sight. It implies some degree of memory and developing mental representation. In the preoperational stage, between age two and seven, language and symbolic thinking emerge. In the succeeding concrete operational stage, from seven to twelve years, the principle of conservation, the knowledge that quantity may be unrelated to the arrangement and physical appearance of objects, is established. The concept of reversibility becomes measurable. The fourth and last stage, from age twelve to adulthood, is termed formal operations, when abstract thinking, logic, and problem solving develop.

Although Piaget has contributed one of the best-known classic models of cognitive development, his theories have been criticized on several fronts. Children, for example, do not seem to adhere to the rigorous linear timeline proposed. Some developmental theorists suggest that cognition proceeds in a more continuous fashion, one more quantitatively cumulative. In addition, Piaget clearly underestimated the abilities and capabilities of early infants. Recent evidence suggests that infants as young as five months, some even younger, have rudimentary mathematical skills and numerical discriminatory abilities (Wynn 1992; Carey 2001).

The *information-processing approach* emphasizes cognitive processes such as attention, processing speed, memory, decision-making, problem solving, and metacognition. The problem of whether what is known facilitates or hampers the learning of new knowledge is also addressed. As has been said about associationist and stage theories, information-processing theory puts important emphasis on first-order sense data as the concrete foundation on which more abstract concept formation and complex knowledge systems develop during infancy.

Rochel Gelman (1993, 2001), in contrast to bottom-up cognitive theorists, has suggested a rational-constructivist and symbolic connectionist approach to infantile cognitive development. She suggests that infants are endowed with some innate ideas, modules, or domain-specific structures of mind. These "skeletal-like" structures are ready to assimilate and accommodate domain-relevant inputs in an interactional and plastic manner. Skeletal mental structures are attuned to information in the environment at the level of universals, not merely surface details. She proposes that "[y]oung learners can have abstract concepts."

Last, the work of Myron Hofer and Regina Sullivan (2001) on the neurobiology of attachment suggests that the classical "attachment theory" of John Bowlby (1969), trained in part by Melanie Klein in London, can be supported by research evidence. Although these researchers heavily rely on the impact of early learning, even in the prenatal period, they endorse the fact of the infant's unflagging need for proximity to its own mother, its early, almost instantaneous recognition of her, and the psychophysiological distress caused by separation from her. They speculate on prospective clinical studies from infancy to childhood that could shed light on the mechanisms underlying the hypothesized residues of early attachment on later behaviors, both personal and played out eventually in the parental behaviors of adults.

## Envy Theory and Innate Aspects of Envy

*Envy theory* uses the idea of primary envy, whose taproot is inborn, as a reasonable working hypothesis having utility as both a construct and an orientation in therapeutic strategies. The dispositional inclination toward envy, at least, may be genetically coded and part of the evolutionary program that supports the immense diversity in the organic world. Envy is part of the genetic package that individuals inherit as members of the highly social human species. It is important to emphasize here, as will be addressed frequently throughout this book, that envy is not absolutely fixed and unalterable. Developing *insight*, learning *envy management skills*, and *the healthy maturation of envy* can change subjective attitudes and behaviors influenced by envy.

*Envy theory* suggests that understanding primary envy as a preconceptual, subliminally affective, and innate predisposition, inclination, readiness, and anticipation, in fact, does it justice. This faculty acts as a template to structure and organize awareness and impute value, salience, and meaning to all experience *in selectively preferred ways*. The mind, whether awake or asleep, remains in a perpetual state of tonic readiness to activate and hedonically appraise experience when aroused by phasically introduced novelty. This novelty may be generated endopsychically (for example, emotion and unconscious phantasy) or by sensations and perceptions triggered by environmental stimuli.

The way inherited susceptibility translates itself into an experienced mental state and behavior is complex. The sequence of events leading to the expression of biogenetic (biologically based) and psychogenetic (psychologically based) predispositions is heavily influenced by an individual's microenvironment (intrapsychic environment) and macroenvironment (external milieu).

The plasticity and mutability of both these environments is dynamic. Continuous reconfigurations are typical and normative. Moreover, *envy theory redefines the construct of "hardwiring" of brain and behavior to denote innate templates that are not only directed toward specific emotional and cognitive aims but also toward multiple, nonfixed circuitries, a major function of which is adaptive compensation. Neuroplasticity and change, therefore, are norms across life's chronological thresholds.*

In neuroscience terms, those who have a greater genetic predisposition to develop biopsychosocial complications of envy may be more susceptible as far as gene expression to envy-provoking environmental stimuli. Genes do not determine; experience ultimately determines final outcomes.

Consistent exposure of the ventral tegmentum and nucleus accumbens to such stimuli, for example, may form permanent changes in the second messenger, intermediary systems inside neurons of the central nervous system. Second messengers regulate the function of neuronal membrane ion channels, neurotransmitter synthesis and release, and protein kinase activity. Gene transcription and translation factors are involved in such processes. This may influence the turning-on of genes, which then may not only activate but also reinforce one's psychology—instinctual and motivational drives that perpetuate envious scenarios.

The selective processing of aspects of these sensations is a filtering that leads to highlighted perceptions. The German term *einstellung* connotes such a state of cognitive readiness—namely, a mental set structured to grasp and interpret information in a selective manner. In the awake state at any developmental level, preattentive processing using parallel, not linear, information registry (multimodal, integrative perceptual systems) can detect, to some degree, global, holistic, and gestalt aspects of whatever is experienced. This, in part, underlies the neurocognition of envy's activation.

On an observable, interpersonal level, the choice of envied object is based on "lock and key" and "glove and hand" mechanisms. The envier scans the environment for some hint of common ground between himself and another. The link is an inverse connection based on perceived absence in the envier and presence in the envied one. When the envier sees a figure in the environment that appears to possess what the envier lacks, that figure is used as a potential key to enable the envier to unlock his own wished-for potential. The hand of the envied one signals that a fit into the empty glove of the envier would bring about satisfaction and completion. This negative correlation always remains a phantasied experience of anticipation and subsequent disillusionment.

Recent work in cognitive science (Bargh and Ferguson 2000) strongly suggests that higher mental processes (the "secondary processes" of psychodynamic psychology), once viewed as the domain of deliberate choice, free will, internal goal structures and pursuit, judgment, and interpersonal and social behavior, occur without conscious choice and attentional guidance. Unconscious determinism here counts heavily.

*Envy theory* considers inborn envy a functional capacity possessed by an ego/experiencer that is operational neonatally. Envy is a faculty of presemantic sensations that elicits basic emotions like fear and anger independent of conscious recognition or thinking. Both ego and its capacity for envy begin in a state of *ateliosis*—that is, incomplete development.

Inborn envy, like temperament, may be a primary given, a minimum distinctive disposition, that is secondarily elaborated together with progressive ego maturation and development. One of envy's principal features is that of pleiotrophy. *Nuclear envy* is a genetically endowed disposition responsible for and influencing a multitude of different phenotypic expressions. This one innate base affects many cognitive and emotional pathways across chronological development. It is also shaped by environmental, situational, and interpersonal experiences. Envy, like temperament, must be contextualized to activate, organize, and be expressed. Modern neuroscience continues to produce research that yields evidence substantiating the transactional nature of infant and child development (Hane and Fox 2007; Perez-Edgar and Fox 2005; Schmidt and Fox 2002).

*Envy's inferred constitutionally based capacity is not to be equated with its fully developed or stable expression. The expressions of envy in everyday life are not ready-made products that merely appear.* Moreover, envy does not have a so-called preadaptive status, which again might imply the somewhat mechanistic, predetermined unfolding of a rigidly unalterable adaptive ability. Maturation and learning from experience, with its numerous environmental modifiers, heavily influence individual development. The results make the mental and behavioral expressions of envy intensely personal and idiosyncratic. The nuances of changing needs at different chronological ages significantly contribute to the way envy is expressed.

Whereas descriptions of the phenomenology of envy may be plausible, assertions and conjectures about its constitutional basis, notably its being a primary motivating mental force, are admittedly speculative. Research tools, for example, using conventional and standardized psychological testing parameters, including a validated Dispositional Envy Scale (DES), have been developed to further examine the role of envy (Smith, Parrott, Diener, Hoyle, and Kim 1999).

Some, although not all, physical traits such as gender, height, body conformation, and so forth have been shown to be under at least partial genetic control. Heritability studies have demonstrated that many important personality traits are influenced by genetic factors (Loehlin et al. 1998). Meta-analyses in statistical reviews of aggression have shown clear-cut genetic overlap between twins and between adopted-away children and biological parents (Miles and Carey 1997). The genome project and the emerging field of behavioral genetics developed over the last ten years have given greater scientific credence to the effects of heredity on behavior (DeFries, McGuffin, McClearn, and Plomin 2000; Plomin 2004). *Envy theory* proposes that primary, innate envy, perhaps like temperament, has similar genetic status. It is a biopsychosocial measure especially sensitive to environmental influences.

Envy, therefore, *cannot* be understood as an assertion connoting unmodifiable biopsychosocial determinism. Envy can be understood as a stochastic phenomenon—namely, having a probability distribution or pattern that may be characterized but not predicted precisely. The expressions of envy emphasized in this book are not entirely constitutionally driven. Envy may be a constellation of traits with a threshold for expression, both experientially and behaviorally, that takes on varied expressions within and from one interpersonal, social, and cultural context to another. State fluctuations occur in most people. From birth onward, this legacy is further shaped through acquired learning, conscious and unconscious thinking and feeling, active adaptation, and developmental maturation. One's constitutional temperament—for example, *nuclear envy* and *nuclear love*—transacts experientially with the environmental influences of family, society, and culture. It gradually develops over time to create a unique self-signature that reflects individual character and personality.

What is inborn, therefore, acts as a matrix of elemental building blocks for mental structure and functioning to organize in preferential ways. This matrix is always contained somehow in all that follows from it. Similarly, the early experiences of infancy and childhood have continuity over time. They, however, like the latent dream thoughts (nonconscious raw stimuli prompting active information processing) at the base of a dream, undergo secondary revisions and re-present themselves in masked ways, as does the manifest, often remembered, content of a dream. Human psychological development over time is comparable in many ways to the structure and development of a dream.

Primary envy, understood here as a *temperamental set point*, therefore, is qualitatively and quantitatively constitutional, to some extent. An individual's envy load reflects the degree of envy experienced. It determines, to some extent, the way information processing is made up—its preferences for detection, recognition, and attribution. Its expression is subject to important modification because of the context in which it emerges. It is an innate mental program, which activates largely, though not exclusively, in spontaneous and autonomous fashion. It is not exclusively reactive or secondary to frustration, although such situations augment, reinforce, amplify, and typically accompany its operation, as will be discussed in later chapters. While elucidating at length the idea of *nuclear envy*, much of it can be applied *mutatis mutandis* to the idea of *nuclear love*, in many ways "the first equal among equals."

The proposal that envy is constitutional with an inferred predetermined strength may make it appear inherently intractable and, at times, refractory to important modification. Although the existence of innate factors can put a limit on how far mental integration and well-being may be achieved, how one handles and manages what is already constitutionally given is potentially amenable to change.

Envy is always overlaid, fleshed-out, and stratified with experientially acquired conflict, unconscious phantasy, and behaviors along developmental pathways. These elements, in themselves, are potentially accessible and subject to change. *The accretions around envy can be understood and analyzed—that is, sufficiently explained by clinical observations. The irrational core of envy, however, remains a black hole inexplicable by clinical explanation. This reflects its genetic bedrock.*

## Intrapsychic Predispositions Are Activated
## By Environmental Exposure: Subject and Object

*Envy theory* elaborates the phenomenology of psychic reality—namely, the conscious and unconscious experiential processes that make up mind. Including the concept of intersubjectivity encompasses a conceptual view of psychic reality (mind) that emphasizes the intimate and almost inextricable identity of intrapsychic and interpersonal experience. It frames the base from which self and the larger environment interact.

The term "intersubjectivity" aims to describe the dynamic structural and functional mental configuration between two individuals. The interiorized relation itself reflects an overarching experiential whole. The subject's lived inner world, as such, has a share in another subject's lived interior world. The last decade has produced numerous studies with a plethora of conjectures in this regard, especially in relation to the infant-mother dyad (Trevarthen and Aitken 2001; Gallese 2005a, 2005b; Lohmar 2006).

Intersubjectivity in *envy theory* is distinguishable since it does not equate this construct directly with that of "empathy." The two concepts reside on different levels of abstraction. *Empathy* connotes more a dynamic affective process in contrast to intersubjectivity, which connotes the structure of a state of relatedness. Empathy contributes to an individual's active, intuitively poised grasp of another. Empathy, for example, underlies the active process of intuitive listening by a therapist, or the affectionate, dynamic attunement of a mother for her infant. All varieties and nuances of projective identification lie beneath the unconscious communicational dynamics of both these personal and interpersonal states of mind.

Empathy is instrumental activity. In therapy, it can be used as a tool. It has highly charged affective and transient participatory characteristics. Intuition may follow empathy and is supported by a subliminal cognition. More consciously developed insight and understandability subsequently emerge from these.

Intersubjectivity, by contrast, is the state of mind that reflects object-related mental contents. Intersubjectivity reflects the mental interplay between two subjects as both a process and structural state. The first and primary example of such a relationship is that of infant and mother. Intersubjectivity is the matrix for cognitive and affective development. As a functional container, this conduit contributes to the abiding template, structured as nonconscious cognition, for information processing and communicational transfers throughout life.

Intersubjectivity, established in infancy, is the field from which the developing self experiences the entirety of its environmental milieu even beyond the powerful ministrations of the mothering figure. The essential role the environment plays in the growth, maturation, and development of mind and personality is complicated. The significance of environmental and situational factors, such as interpersonal contact and caring, interspersed with actual and perceived emotional and physical insufficiency and trauma cannot be overemphasized.

In addition to the person of the mothering figure, the material conditions to which the infant and child are exposed—food, clothing, shelter, harmonious sounds (music), pleasant colors, grass, trees, birds, running water, and so forth—are important. Enriched or impoverished environments make a difference. Upbringing, culture, and environmental opportunities play critical roles in ego formation, object relations, learning, and expressed behavior.

The interactions and transactions between self and environment are so tight that separating them is challenging, if not daunting and almost impossible. In other contexts, I have termed this aspect of the individual's environmental embeddedness *eco-corporeality* (Ninivaggi 2008). All these considerations are of enormous importance. Environmental interactions and the embeddedness of the self in the real world are critical throughout life.

Hence, the developmental formatting of an inner world in *envy theory* is always interactional. Personality and mind cannot arise from a solipsistic, biopsychological unfolding. The "myth of the isolated mind" is just that—a mythological fiction. On the contrary, individual character and personality emerge in a complex field of recursive interplays between the developing biomental individual and other developing individuals. All mental functioning is participatory and interdependent with other minds and people. It is not only simple but also misleading to view psychic processes within and between individuals in a polarized fashion. Psychological theories based on "one-body" or "two-body" phenomena or "one-person" contrasted with "two-person" interactional models are imprecise.

The term "intersubjectivity" used here suggests this dynamic viewpoint. Individual minds develop along pathways that are similar yet idiosyncratic and unique. The term "intrapsychic," for example, has been used historically in psychoanalysis, as well as in this book, to emphasize this individual, personalized locus of mental activity—that is, the inner, experiential world. It is the subjective landscape, the microenvironment of the self. This view avoids the misleading epistemological polarizations that characterize the psyche from either the perspective of naive subjectivism or that of naive objectivism. Integrative links between classical psychoanalysis and modern cognitive science are made throughout this text to further illustrate this basic assumption—an intrapsychic perspective in an intersubjective field.

The abstract concept "object," as defined here, refers to the subject/self/ego's experience of meaningful affective and cognitive affiliative awareness of its observations. Loosely defined, object denotes the subject's salient experience of another person. The psychoanalytic construct "object relations" is the subtext, often unconscious, for observable social relationships.

The psychoanalytic term "id" is used purposefully to suggest the complex array of fundamental mental operations, including the neurocircuitry linked to emotion, concept formation, interpretive construals, drive, and motivation. In psychodynamic theory, the id is the source of *libido (motivational and affective drive), existing as the life instinct in the ego. This life instinct—spurred on by its protoplasmic impulse to survive—seeks to express itself creatively by expanding itself on all levels, especially by cognitive and emotional proliferation.* The construct of a life instinct is a heuristic hypothesis in *envy theory.*

In a concrete way, the infantile experience of the nurturant breast as the primary object of desire may reside in a powerful, unconscious belief that the breast is the representative of the life instinct. In the beginning of life, this nonconscious authoritative force is felt as the first manifestation of potent creativeness. This biomental experience, a sense of vivification, takes shape as a mental object in association with the mothering figure in the infantile environment. In the most general sense, "object" is ultimately the object of consciousness, specifically a conditioned consciousness. Conditioned assumes that consciousness must somehow respond. Responses, in turn, precipitate out as experiential "objects." Thus, the mind populates itself with objects, and, in fact, all these must be structured as relationships to objects. This "object relations" framework is *envy theory's* basic frame of reference.

An individual's unique projective tendencies impact how he or she experiences a given assemblage of perceptions. A heightened experience colors the resulting mental registrations of the experience. These registrations coalesce as objects. Experiencing objects, in this sense, is what I term *projective internalization.*

## Projective Internalization

*Projective internalization,* a concept unique to *envy theory,* is the mechanism underlying all epistemic operations in infancy and thereafter. The mind or ego automatically "autoimprints" aspects of itself in its experience of sensing and becoming aware of what it considers nonself or other. Recognition consists of bidirectional, causal loops: combinations of the subject's innate contributions to and the impact of incoming stimuli in the environment. Information exchange emerges from this interaction. In addition to sensation (visual, auditory, touch, taste, and smell) and information derived from interactive perceptual systems, corporeal action patterns also become registered and internalized. Both nonconscious and conscious components make up *projective internalization*.

*Projective internalization* is an autorecognition that spurs the developing ego's undeveloped potentials. This then launches the development of new and fresh experiential material not previously developed in the ego's repertoire. In *envy theory*, *projective internalization* is far more complex than processes suggesting mere confirmatory bias. It facilitates information exchange, cognitive-affective processing, and new adaptive learning from experience.

*Envy theory* adheres to the construct "eco-corporeality," which sees the individual as an integral aspect of the extended environment. The human organism is regarded as a biomental entity embedded in an environmental matrix of which it is more similar rather than alien in makeup. *Projective internalization* processes reflect this continuity. Such a perspective, though not denoted as such, is not foreign to modern cognitive psychology (Wertz 1987).

*Projective internalization* uses what cognitive science terms "priming." Priming denotes the nonconscious, subliminal recognition and identification of words, objects, and relationships that become stored and part of memory systems. Priming processes influence further incoming and already stored information, especially affecting information retrieval. Vast amounts of nonconscious information both enter and exit the mind on a regular basis. Priming is an innate form of presemantic, cognitive learning that takes advantage of visual information—pictures, shapes, faces, perceptual interactions—having ecologically adaptive aims (Tulving and Schacter 1990).

Neuropsychological studies (Aurell 1989; Panksepp 1998; Newton 2001) strongly suggest that cognitive processes innate to brain-mind have strong and predominant self-generated activity. Findings seem to suggest that anticipation and expectation of events evoke attention and a scanning-like interest that perceptually locks onto environmental objects that are synchronous with these already existing potentials.

Research on the neural bases of corporeal awareness continues to demonstrate how brain mechanisms underlie the mental representation of the body. An implicit knowledge of body structure by neonates antedates the adult body schema (Berlucchi and Aglioti 1997).

The discovery of "mirror neurons" (Gallese, Fadiga, Fogassi, and Rizzolatti 1996; Rizzolatti, Fadiga, Gallese, and Fogassi 1996) in 1995 in the ventral premotor (area F5) cortex of the macaque monkey, and later in the inferior frontal gyrus and inferior parietal cortex of humans (Rizzolatti and Craighero 2004), has lent neuroanatomical and neurophysiologic support to *envy theory's* construct of *projective internalization.*

Researchers hypothesize that "mirror neurons do not discharge in response to object presentation; to be triggered they require a specific observed action" (Rizzolatti and Arbib 1998, 188). Thus, neural responsivity is not general. Specific—matching—stimuli trigger their intrapsychic neural correlates. Mental experience, therefore, matches in some relatively objective way what it observes.

Mirror neurons—for example, in the central nervous system—fire when the subject performs an action, and also when that subject merely observes the same action performed by another of the same species. Researchers believe mirror neurons match observed events to similar, internally generated actions, thus establishing or revealing an intimate mind-body link between observer and observed (Braten 2004; Falck-Ytter, Gredeback, and von Hofsten 2006; Iacoboni and Mazziotta 2007; Rizzolatti and Gallese 2005; Uddin, Iacoboni, Lange, and Keenan 2007; Gallese 2005b; Brass and Heyes 2005; Stanley, Phelps, and Banaji 2008; Adolphs 2009).

The crucial point emphasized in *envy theory* is that the subject's mirror neurons are only triggered when the subject attentively targets material in the environment—recognizable since significant elements of it are already somehow present in the innate makeup of the neuron itself. These neurons in the matrix of the mind projectively lock on and react to environmental objects that match the subject's innate capacity to recognize them. Mirror neurons encode abstract concepts of actions, including some understanding of goals and intentions. These processes also include language development and theory of mind (for example, empathy) skills.

For example, it has been found that, at about two to three months after birth, the typical infant exhibits a measurable developmental milestone—"social smile"—in response to observing and imitating significant others. *Envy theory* would posit that this response reflects the fundamental operation of "projective identification," a part of *projective internalization* (see chapter 7), especially its role in prompting, exploring, and communicating. These findings, which are consistent with emerging neuroscience studies, suggest that the cognitive inferences presumed in the projective identification construct have a measurable basis in the central nervous system, as, for example, in mirror neuron findings.

*An upshot of these considerations is that regardless of the goodness or badness— positive facilitators or traumatic stressors—in the environment, innate dispositions, to some extent, profoundly color perceptions and how the environment is experienced.*

## Perception, Cognition, and "Ego" as Active Information-Processing Beacon

At all chronological ages, environmental stimuli have varying degrees of ambiguity and uncertainty. This typically produces an affective and cognitive experiential dissonance that, in turn, prompts a need for perceptual and cognitive resolution and, therefore, experiential tension reduction. Management strategies to reduce anxiety and confusion become activated, at least, on a tenuous basis.

Recognition of environmental stimuli, accordingly, depends on unique systems of configurable processing: analysis of small differences in details and spatial relations of features in the context of a prototypical organization that is internally biased. Recognition remains in a state of anticipatory readiness. The ego's nonconscious and conscious sentinel abilities attach to correlated and corresponding trigger features in the environment, launching incremental degrees of recognition, experiential significance, and meaning.

For example, findings from modern cognitive science (Haggard and Libet 2001) have described measurable readiness potentials (initially outside of the conscious awareness of the subject) that occur well before subsequent decisions and behaviors. From a biogenetic and evolutionary point of view, some researchers hold that nonconscious bottom-up cognitive process detectors attune to recognize salient (adaptive) features in the environment and orient attention (Yantis and Jonides 1996). The important role of limbic system circuitry, especially the hippocampus, contributes emotional specificity to these cognitive processes. Whether attention is first oriented by bottom-up or top-down activity may be too polarized a way of explaining attentional processes. Both play into orientation, attention, and focus although *envy theory* assigns a more active, leading role to top-down sweeps of consciousness (explicit or implicit) as being executive in directive power.

Recent research, for example, on interpersonal attraction, sexual desire, and the experience of love has used sophisticated neuroimaging and fMRI data to corroborate the essential role of higher cerebral centers in determining such emotional selectivity (Ortigue, Bianchi-Demicheli, Hamilton, and Grafton 2007; Ortigue and Bianchi-Demicheli 2008a, 2008b). Higher regions may be priming the visual cortex to be more sensitive to certain kinds of information, instructing visual pathways toward what kind of person is perceived sexually desirable. The cortical brain regions that handle self-awareness and understanding others may also be telling the emotional centers (for example, limbic circuitry) what to feel.

In the last ten years, the fundamental neural substrates of attention and memory have been examined in detail (Baddeley 2003; Miller and Cohen

2001). Attention is regarded as a multitiered process resulting from reverberating interactions of working memory, competitive selection, top-down sensitivity control, and bottom-up automatic filtering for salient stimuli (Knudsen 2007). These work in consonance. The prefrontal cortex plays a leading role in exerting executive control. Working memory identifies the selected objects of attention in a tonic field of ongoing competition among information-processing hierarchies actively vying for access to working memory. Top-down bias signals, based on decisions made in working memory, deploy the entire process. Innate elements of already established orienting neural circuitry bolster signal strength and selectively enhance stimuli. Central nervous system information about the world, stored memories, and internal states regulates new information acquisition. While these formidable hypotheses in cognitive neuroscience do not prove *envy theory*'s postulate of *projective internalization*, they contribute further insights that add to its plausibility.

*Envy theory* describes cognition and information processing as major ego functions. The self-system of id, ego, and superego along with the physical body comprises the entire person—mind and body or mind/body seen as unitary. The self is the noumenal reality; the ego is the inextricable shadow of the entire self. The topographical dimensions of the ego as self-orchestrator include conscious awareness, preconscious awareness, and unconscious mental activity. While unconscious aspects of mind constitute the overwhelming majority of the self, the preconscious (nonconscious aspects of ego, in part) in tonic readiness continuously scans for salient information so that conscious awareness may temporarily activate and use *projective internalization* to increase new knowledge and understanding.

To illustrate this perspective metaphorically: id is the blind, black ocean on which preconscious awareness of ego—a lighthouse—may intermittently illuminate an object so that the conscious awareness function of the ego as sentinel may stop, focus, and further illuminate the object of attention.

In *envy theory*, this miniscule cognitive spotlight—the preconscious ego—acts as the dimly lit beacon that only periodically illuminates itself sufficiently to become more fully conscious—a state of focused attention. Underlying this tonic arousal, unconscious splitting (disintegrative) processes in primary process cognition typically cause information processing to revert back to its default state of polarized differentiation in binary-like fashion. This "base two" reference platform becomes the experiential template for all preattentive and wakeful states of perception, emotion, and cognition.

The way conscious experience—the triggering of value appraisals—correlates with and can set off envy arises from the mind's binary predisposition. The universal proclivity of the mind is to resolve—"repair"—these unstable discrepancies—"conflicts"—toward equilibriums—"integrations" and "plastically responsive reorganizations"—that appear fair and equitable.

*The ego, moreover, operates as the perceptual beacon of the entire self. It holds the privileged status of being the unique spotlight in consciousness (both nonconscious and conscious dimensions of self) that has the potential ability to effect change in the entire psychological system of the self. Such changes are intermittent achievements that come about, for example, when insights into motivations and self-understanding arise, especially in psychotherapeutic situations. In its conative or volitional functions, the ego is a bridge between desire and action.*

*Envy theory* posits, for example, that innate instinctual predispositions fuel and direct attention. These instincts are pathognomonic, defining qualities unique to human psychology. They are qualitatively distinguishable from the reflexive behavioral repertoires of animals.

*Human instincts (Triebe)* are flexible biomental pulsatile impulses with no fixed action pattern. Their mode is either nonconsciously driven attraction or destructive repulsion, and they subserve motivation. Instincts drive the ego's sentinel function of attention. Attention sets in motion both noticing specific stimuli and experiencing their appearance in idiosyncratic ways. An individual's attention increases the effective salience of stimuli and contributes to shaping overall phenomenological experience. Hence, both innate proclivities and acquired reinforcing information expand cognitive bandwidth. The power of information processing increases as development proceeds. The transient attentional abilities of the early infant may be especially instrumental in boosting the perceived contrast of stimuli, their discrimination, and their mental registration. In this process, the ego, the self, personality, and character develop.

An important illustration of this process of experiential exaggeration in the formation of self-experience is the psychodynamic construct of *idealization*. When anxieties begin to soar, idealization functions *both normatively as an adaptive strategy and also defensively to contain anxiety*. As development progresses, attentional exaggeration is an important dimension of the ego's beacon of conscious awareness. Its role in the envy dynamic is crucial. Its impact on mechanisms of insight is discussed in chapter 9.

Although some aspects of psychological development can be correlated with cognitive and neuroscience substrates, the clinical object relations propositions outlined in this book do not stand or fall on their biological foundations. They assume a tightly unified biomental reality whose psychological dimension rests primarily on personalized meaningfulness organized in the form of experiential unconscious phantasy. Meaningfulness—the *epistemophilia* in the self—has its intrapsychic reference point in the relation sparked between ego and object. Its interpersonal/intersubjective/attachment-based reference point is the relationship between two intimately committed people. Hence, personal meaning, itself, has privileged status. It is counted heavily in unique ways. Both phantasy and the extended, tangible environment of people shape construals of personal meaning.

To reiterate, the approach taken here is centered on psychological experience. Formidable aspects of constitutional endowment are postulated. In addition, the activating effects of environmental exposure on the direction that developing mental processes and personality take along all developmental lines are also emphasized. Environmental tutoring acts to enhance or inhibit/constrain levels of innate potential, disposition, and temperament. From birth on, the individual's developing information-processing abilities and capacities largely determine how environmental factors and situations are perceived-conceived—that is, how animate and inanimate events manifest themselves to the observer. Although innate forces drive, experience chooses.

It is worth noting that Melanie Klein (1952b) addresses the interpersonal realities that influence aspects of mental development in infancy in her paper "On Observing the Behaviour of Young Infants." Klein focuses on the importance of the inner world and the development of meaningfulness derived from and shaped by the specific fashion in which the mother handles (emotionally and materially) her infant. She also describes concrete examples of actual maternal care in relation to specific infant behaviors. The following citations reflect her emphasis on the importance of the relationship.

If we are to understand the young infant, though, we need not only greater knowledge but also a full sympathy with him, based on our unconscious being in close touch with his unconscious. (94)

From the beginning of postnatal life and at every stage of development, external factors affect the outcome. Even with adults, as we know, attitudes and character may be favourably or unfavourably influenced by environment and circumstances. And this applies to a far greater extent to children. (94–95)

The conclusion is that with all children the mother's patient and understanding handling from the earliest days onward is of the greatest moment. (98)

In the present paper I have repeatedly pointed out that an understanding mother may by her attitude diminish her baby's conflicts and thus in some measure help him to cope more effectively with his anxieties. (116–117)

## Perception and Environment: A Bidirectional Loop

From the neonatal period onward, innate predispositions mix with acquired mental and physical skills and are stored as neuro-muscular-mental (*biomental*) dispositions. This is a fundamental reserve contributing to and residing in developing memory stores. Hence, a natural, automatic perceptual orientation to grasping stimulus information is set in motion. All perception actively establishes developmentally optimal adjustments of sensation and cognition for the pickup of information in the respective field of exploration targeted.

This innate capacity to apprehend, in realistic ways, self, others, and the world underlies the ability to recognize aspects of the environment in particular ways. Additional experience further enriches and reinforces this preferential perception of the world. Experience and memory structure learning as it incrementally develops from birth onward.

*Envy theory* proposes that an individual is always in relationship with others and environment, in states of knowing that may be termed "entrainment" and "equilibratory resonance." These tight cognitional links may even have qualities that transcend conventional cognitive concepts embodied in constructs such as mental representation and memory. From a neurocognitive perspective, these registrations are patterns of activation of neural circuits that produce neural net profiles containing information. What one has already stored in experience immediately appears in the way the world presents itself. The invitational quality of perception (for example, the "suckability" of the nipple of the breast, or the "shakeability" of one hand with another) determines, in part, how one experiences these solicitations from the environment (Gibson 1991; Ellis 2006). The psychoanalytic construct "unconscious phantasy" denotes the cognitional base of these mental metaphors drawn from the mental experience of a bodily self.

The prototype of this resonating entrainment is the infant-mother dyad, a mutually shared experience of lived intersubjectivity. Affective, ideational, and corporeal action patterns are experienced and registered in this urgent focus. The mind structures itself as a receptive and idiosyncratically understanding container of information.

In infancy, the first personal object is the total mother. Intimate contact with aspects of the mother, and with the mother as a whole, facilitates the transformation of the corporeal into the mental—the canalization of infant mind. *This is the mentalizing process.*

*Mentalizing* in *envy theory* denotes the gradual transformation of mental structures and elements (id and ego) from, or their precipitating out of, their corporeal matrix. Cognition and emotion make up mind from elements of somatic experience. This denotation is qualitatively distinguishable from other psychological theories that roughly equate the term with conceptions of self-reflection, identifying with others, and empathy.

For example, stimuli both from the outer and inner environments automatically elicit unconscious physiological arousal throughout the body, especially mediated by the autonomic nervous system. Arousal correlates with hedonic tone: attraction and pleasure contrasting with avoidance and unpleasure. Neurotransmitters such as dopamine and also the opioid system play major roles in such mediation. These value-valenced responses are experienced as "emotions." As this brain circuitry (cortical, subcortical, and limbic structures) activates, cognitive appraisals or construals quickly occur and somehow meaning develops. These accompanying construals emerge both simultaneously with and after emotional arousal.

From nonconscious emotions, "affects" crystallize as the unconscious aspects of more consciously felt "feelings." In turn, further concepts elaborate themselves and thinking organizes. Relatively distinct categories of emotions differentiate themselves in this process. Emotions, affects, and feelings may motivate behaviors, some of which are constrained and remain unexpressed; others become manifest as behaviors that demonstrate and reinforce the accompanying feelings.

Realistic perceptions influence and, in turn, are shaped by unconscious processes—unconscious phantasies and their affective interaction scenarios. The common expression, "perception: real or perceived," therefore, is ambiguous at best. All perception has elements of idiosyncratic phantasy and a realistic assessment of the actual environment.

Envy theory adheres to a psychodynamic developmental theory that emphasizes the simultaneous and bidirectional psychological processes of projection and introjection from birth. These are foundational epistemic elements, the substrata of both cognitive and affective pathways. These mental givens may be likened to exhalation and inhalation as physiological processes instinctive and necessary for life. Projection and perception ride on one another. Perception is illuminated with the spotlight driven by projection. Mental encodings take shape and become introjected. This to-and-fro dynamic activity starts the process of mental structure formation by gradually establishing differentiated boundaries—self and other as well as intrapsychic distinctions.

This entire bidirectional process functions, largely, to increase attention, organize motivation, and strongly influence behavior. A fractal dimension of this transformative process, moreover, is repeated, mutatis mutandis, in psychodynamic therapies and is the basis for their mutative therapeutic actions.

All these considerations address the way the subjective nature of the self is formed in concert with contributions from the experience of the objective world of other people, most important of whom is mother.

## Adaptation, Defense, Early Memory, and Character Formation

Infancy has long been viewed as a period of helplessness and dependence on a significant caregiver to ensure adequate physical and psychological survival. Although it cannot be denied that these altricial features make the attentive and interactive presence of the mothering figure essential, the real psychological competence of the infant must neither be overlooked nor underestimated.

Sensory capabilities begin in the neonatal period. At birth, they far exceed the development and expression of motor skills. Sensorial receptors absorb stimuli, perceptual information is detected and recognized, and mental architecture is laid down as its circuitry comes online robustly and in increasingly complex ways.

Theories of infantile amnesia are knotty and unsettled. Infantile amnesia denotes the relative inability to consciously recall data, information, and events that occur in the infantile period, the first twenty-four months of life. *Envy theory* and many other developmental theories regard this period as uniquely important, especially because the infant-maternal relationship is exquisitely sensitive in facilitating the infant's bodily survival, psychological adaptation, and homeostatic regulation (self-regulation and adaptive conformity to the environment). Important implications for the trajectory taken developmentally into adulthood underlie this consideration. In other words, leading questions include: How receptive are early information-processing mechanisms? In what forms are earliest experiences encoded? What is the state of their pragmatic accessibility (conscious and nonconscious) throughout development?

*Envy theory* tends to regard learning more as a process of reperformance of an earlier experience rather than an exclusive process that enables the conscious verbal accession of earlier mnemonic encoding. Explicit learning is based on the storage of information at the conceptual, typically linguistic level, while implicit, nonconscious learning tasks typically involve data-driven tasks that operate at preconceptual, nonlinguistically dependent levels. Implicit, in contrast to explicit, memory systems form multiple and dissociable subsystems that are cortically based, operate at a presemantic level on domain-specific perceptual information, and support nonconscious expressions of memory (Schacter 1994, 260; Stanley, Phelps, and Banaji 2008).

Two important parameters affecting learning are context dependency and state dependency. *Context-dependent learning* denotes that the actual environment in which experience occurs is intimately associated with the ability to recall and recollect it later. *State-dependent learning* denotes that learning and memory are intimately associated with the physiological and psychological state (original construal state) of the individual when experiences were encoded.

Because the infantile period is preverbal and chronologically removed from the more linguistically and cognitively developed capacities of later childhood and adult life, it has been argued (especially in the early history of psychology) that either little experience has been learned and laid down in memory tracts or that whatever experience has been encoded is virtually opaque and inaccessible. The latter is hypothesized because an individual cannot return to the original infantile context and unmatured infantile state in which original experiences occurred. Some comments on these unsettled matters about the penetrable and impenetrable aspects of early experience from psychodynamic and neuroscience perspectives follow.

Adaptation and defense as psychological constructs refer to processes in the developmental buildup of personality; both reside on a continuum. Ordinarily, *adaptation* denotes a relatively realistic apprehension of self (depending on developmental level) in the context of successfully cooperating with the environment, and the subjective and objective measures taken to approximate a healthy, advantageous interactive fit. Adaptation may be measured by the degree to which biopsychosocial needs and standards are successfully met to achieve a personally and socially reasonable quality of life. This may include effective coping with commonly recognized life demands such as the perception of discrepancies, uncertainties, and challenges.

Adaptation in adolescence and adulthood connotes meeting standards culturally believed fitting for negotiating dependence/independence appropriate to chronological age and social context. The ego is the principal domain in which the heterogeneous processes of adaptation are orchestrated. Nonconscious and conscious dimensions of the entire biomental self are thus continually recalibrated and reconfigured. This occurs regularly over time.

*Defense*, by contrast, ordinarily connotes psychological mechanisms also erected by the ego. These mental strategies, largely unconscious, are used to manage emotionally laden problems, the effect of which could be potentially overwhelming anxiety. The management of such problems requires containment to ward off trauma and prevent decompensation. Although originating mentally, they quickly spread into bodily functions and correlate with body movements and positioning.

Examples of defense mechanisms include denial of reality, suppression of distressing ideas and feelings, projection, introjection, identification, splitting, repression, rationalization, intellectualization, dissociation, regression, and somatization. Defense mechanisms are erected nonconsciously but are experienced as attitudes, characterological styles, and ways of behaving. Over the course of time, these defenses become so ingrained and automatic that they condition a person to act in habitual ways, by rote. They set thoughts, feelings, and behaviors as nonmindful automatic reactions arising spontaneously and by response to most environmental stimuli. Inflexible behavior patterns become established and cut off opportunities for fresh perceptions, fresh responses, and new learning.

Typically, anxiety implies conflict—opposing or competing forces, especially perceived as irreconcilable. When defense mechanisms are used flexibly in moderation to appropriately contain anxiety so that forward development may progress, they are healthy. When excessive, defense mechanisms act as impediments and slow or distort normal development. Personality disorders and psychiatric conditions may result. People's character conditioned and formed by defensiveness, then, takes on the role of a feigned "pose" that misrepresents and precludes recognition of more genuine aspects of the self.

Hence, adaptation and defense are closely related processes with important psychodynamic consequences. They function both as assessment instruments of experiential states and reactive modulators resulting in mental and behavioral responses. For example, one might appear to have no other choice than to use a psychotic means to adapt to the inner and outer worlds if environmental circumstances (for example, severe child abuse or war trauma) require such a tenuous, imaginary, and nonrealistic survival strategy.

Some have categorized defense mechanisms as immature or primitive in contrast to more mature and reality-oriented strategies. If managing one's survival is viewed in its most general sense, then one may use the broad concept of adaptation to include all degrees of survival-based mechanisms, conscious through unconscious, used to address experiential responsivity. Whereas adaptation ordinarily connotes cooperative action, defense suggests conflict modulation. Both are inextricably tied to survival at all developmental eras and contribute to personality and character formation. Hence, learning from experience and its memory reserves are frameworks subserving conflict resolution and adaptation in general.

From a neuroscience perspective, the somatic marking of *memory* has been suggested to reside in the functioning of the orbitofrontal cortex (Damasio 1994). As the soma (body) responds to experiential events by forming nonconsciously aware emotions, these responses become registered or marked, it is speculated, in a region of the parietal lobe in the nondominant hemisphere, usually the side without language specialization. These somatic or emotionally felt changes in the body are used to mark perceptions in brain regions devoted to "working memory." These anatomical sites include areas in the dorsolateral prefrontal cortex and hippocampus. Such brain-marked bodily arousals may take the form of nonconscious emotional appraisals that correlate heavily with the types of knowing called intuition and "gut feeling." These orientations are laid down in earliest infancy and contribute to self-regulation and social intelligence (Schore 2002).

The role of awareness and consciousness has been linked to the concept of working memory (WM). Working memory refers to the temporary maintenance and processing of information used to guide behavior, particularly when that information is no longer present in the environment or the object of direct attention. Storage, rehearsal, and executive control are required for WM to operate. Posterior brain regions are linked with storage processes. Prefrontal regions subserve rehearsal and executive processes (D'Espositio and Postle 2002).

Some research has suggested that the dorsolateral frontal cortex of the dominant or language-specific hemisphere may be essential for the complexity of consciousness unique to human beings (Charlton 2000). Thus, the gradual development of working memory links awareness of inner body states or feelings and awareness of the perception of experiential events, especially in the external environment. The developmental unfolding of conscious awareness parallels the gradual refinement of this capacity. The extent to which implicit, nonconscious learning and memory contribute to this remains an open question.

Recent studies have confirmed that both selective attention and explicit memory are active in prelinguistic children (Fulchiero Gordon 2005, 3025). This issue had been heavily argued in the negative (negligible attention and memory) for many years until recently. The registration of memory, therefore, is now recognized as possible in infancy. Even lacking self-conscious awareness in the first two years of life, solid information is continuously being laid down in the brain. The fact that stored memories can be retrieved and expressed without conscious awareness is technically called "implicit memory." Studies on the development of face processing in infancy have suggested that the speed of memory formation in the newborn and the robustness of the memories formed are clearly demonstrable (Pascalis and Slater 2001).

Cognitive science suggests that highly complex events are stored as nonconscious contents in the mind, and have the potential to reemerge in everyday living outside conscious awareness and intention. In fact, recent neuroscience studies (Gold 2002) have added support to the theory of multiple memory systems that both selectively and in coordinated fashion take in specific types of information both explicit and implicit. It has been suggested that the basal ganglia, for example, may be specifically involved in the acquisition of the ability to use nonverbal information to make automatic social inferences (Knowlton 2002; Adolphs 2009). Such information processing is implicit for the most part and occurs through nonconscious mechanisms. Automatic connections, procedural memory, and habit learning do not require language and occur nonconsciously.

These emerging findings in neuroscience shed light on the psychological perspectives in *envy theory*. The anlagen for the structuralization of *character*, a person's idiosyncratic style of thinking and behaving, which will endure throughout life, are rooted in constitutional endowments *and developmental vicissitudes*, especially early on. The affordances and opportunities that interpersonal experiences provide through learning from experience contribute to conflict resolution and greater refinement in adaptive skills. These processes give one's character its particular melody and nuanced shading over time.

Exposure to a variety of experiences facilitates the elicitation of mental capacities that might otherwise have remained latent. Psychotherapies, for example, from time to time can simulate infantile states of *context- and state-dependent experience* and, by design, work on restructuring them. Personal change is always enhanced in positive and negative ways by the mode of an individual's unique integration of perception, interpretation, evaluation, and emotional registration—one's subjectivity. Somatic and physiological needs that require food, shelter, medical care, and so forth must be supplied in adequate fashion for life to continue. Additionally, both the way these are given and the way their acquisition is interpreted through experience combine to determine their positive or negative net effect on the infant, child, and adult who receives and assimilates them.

To reiterate: The mind, in conjunction with the actual impact of the environment, draws on external occurrences in an internally guided fashion, in effect, using them as props. These props are points of attachment acting as conduits joining what is interior to what is exterior. These contrasting positions are mutually dependent reference points. These environmental props are cues *selectively attended to* and used to activate, instigate, and reinforce inner predispositions, preferences, and tendencies. Opinions, beliefs, and a wide variety of other appraisals both rational and irrational are formed and become the cumulative elements guiding further interpretive experience. These cognitive and emotional mental sets may and probably do have a strong basis in actual genetic endowments. Experience during one's lifetime fine-tunes and enriches what an individual brings into the world at birth.

Thus, both self-modification and one's sociocultural environment collaborate in the buildup of cognition, intelligence, and emotional states of mind—in a word, "character." Infancy is not a period of absolute helplessness; cognitive and emotional processing are more active than previously thought. "Sense of self" denotes their confluence as relatively stable, individual differences influencing attitudes and behaviors. The self acts as container filled with object relations organized in culturally adaptive ways. This overall interpretive mental construction of meaning as a whole—what I have termed the *epistemophilia* of the self—adds to the makeup of the inner world—psychic reality and its contents. This impulse to seek evokes anticipation and attention, and shapes perception and the construal of psychological material. These accruals contribute to the mind's wealth as well as to its impoverishments. Moreover, these "contents," when expressed in language and behavior, are the material of therapeutic observation and intervention and thus become the currency of psychic change.

## Why Does Envy Exist At All?

Given its overall destructive outcome, one might ask why envy exists at all. A complete answer cannot be given in a simple way. If envy is innate and characterized by spoiling and destructiveness—notably, an autodestructive program—how has it been able to survive during the extended course of human evolution?

Far from being a bleak and unsparing predisposition, the broad scope of attitudes and behaviors prompted by envy offer crucial opportunities for personal and social advancement. From an evolutionary perspective, envy may be an evolved solution to the natural competition for resources necessary for adaptive survival. Natural selection may act to reinforce what is an innate potential capability. In *envy theory*, social competition only secondarily, though in exceedingly important ways, reinforces what is already an inevitable intrapsychic configuration.

Whether originally innate or acquired or some mixture of the two, envy, although typically destructive, is *not "absolutely" destructive*. Part of the essential envy dynamic is recognition of a perceived advantage at that moment not possessed but sensed as "out there," that is, possessed by another. The resulting sense of disappointment, along with the desire for more perceived to be available, engenders emotional movement in the aspiring envier.

In fact, envy spurs incentives to explore and consider options. In *envy theory*, such an evolved innate module exists in tight and complementary fashion with the growth-promoting forces of love. In this dynamic balance, envy and love act to manage and modulate each other.

Envy (together with love and hate) is one of the innate capacities that equips individuals and groups to scan the environment to recognize potential survival advantages. Adaptive acquisitions, in fact, are often accompanied by destructive actions on some level. Simple examples include hunting for food, preparing and cooking food, physical exercise and the burning of calories, building a house and using wood from once-living trees, and so forth.

In its more primitive and unmatured states, envy appears dominated by destructive forces. However, in its simultaneously experienced affiliative recognition of attractive, albeit "idealized" aspects of the object, it denotes a wish for contact, recognition, and some rudimentary, primitive object-relatedness. A major root of the capacity for social cognition—identifying and understanding attitudes and intentions of others—arises from innate envy.

From a more theoretical perspective, *envy theory* posits a major instinctual force within envy—the life instinct. In its most primitive form, it is experienced as primitive love, its earliest developmental form—elemental idealization. The value of this libidinal aspect resides in its trend toward attempting to promote *significant adaptive and meaningful survival* by establishing a linkage with an object. In *envy theory*, idealization, when not extreme, inordinate, or excessive, is normative and not a defense mechanism. One of the essential parameters of the life instinct is the seeking of and attachment to objects (persons eliciting a uniquely strong attraction with novel significance). This is, perhaps, the most elemental form in which life expresses itself—a creative expansion. The envy principle motivates the ego to regard the object as meaningfully appealing—an irresistible promise of imparting vivifyingness.

The qualitative and quantitative features of object relations, however, always remain fluid. In other words, the ego construes an object in positive (for example, admiration, empathy, and self-development promoting) or negative (controlling and destructive) ways. The state of object relations always has transitional features. These changing states are common to both more extreme forms of narcissism (closely related to part-object relations characterized by feelings of fusion) and more mature object-love (characteristic of whole-object relations where separateness is felt).

*Envy thus affords one the opportunity of going beyond the exclusivity of the self.* This can act as a major developmental route rather than constraint, in fact, underlying the establishment of both early and later object relations. Culture and the establishment of societies are rooted in this.

Furthermore, in its healthier, more normalized condition, envy enables a variety of cognitive and affective processes to occur: an almost automatic awareness of comparisons, *differentiation and discrimination of good from bad*, superior from inferior, and attractive-desirable from repulsive-unwanted. Not only are these basic intellectual functions of the ego but they contribute to superego discrimination and evaluation. Interest, appreciation, and the expectation of novelty arise from this.

Perceptual discrimination, judgment, and valuation are intimately allied with the envy dynamic. When comparisons highlight bold discrepancies, envious distress is often stimulated. When comparisons indicate asymmetry, more benignly felt efforts to restore balance come into play. The clear survival value of these abilities—when not excessive or extreme—cannot be underrated.

The emotions, affects, and feelings associated with envy, especially disgust, are rooted in the mammalian limbic system and are essential to adaptation, survival, and evolution. In its adaptive function, envy contributes to, if not fuels, the drive to search for and find provisions for survival. It is neither the death instinct, as such, nor the force of the life instinct, in isolation, that engenders survival. Envy, a peculiar blend of both, is crucial to successful adaptation when envy takes on mature forms.

From a developmental point of view, mechanisms of idealization accompany envy and early states of persecutory anxiety. When envy and persecutory states are excessive, idealization acts in a defensive way to quell those anxieties. Defensive idealization counteracts and protects the ego from the hated object, first construed as a persecutor, by making it an unrealistically dazzling figure. By contrast, *when envy and persecutory states are not excessive, normal idealization has both organizational functions and psychic structure-building aims*. In all situations, however, idealization is temporary and shrinks quickly. After infancy, for example, if states of excessive idealization persist, conditions of hypomania, mania, and delusion are seen.

Envy's underpinnings, therefore, are intrinsic to processes of perception, intention, motility, thinking, and development in general. Speech, language, and facial expressions are important communicational aspects of envy. Facial expressions, in particular, which are an almost automatic display of basic emotional attitudes, reflect and display these nonconscious affective dynamics. These undoubtedly are manifestations of envy's underlying dynamics and communicate the powerful emotions correlated with projection, introjection, splitting/differentiation, denial and omnipotence, excessive idealization, identification, and degrees of internalization.

Recognition, evaluation, ambition, emulation, learning, and successful adaptation, therefore, are grounded, in part, in the dynamics of envy. They are also grounded, although more constructively, in the affiliative and integrating forces that the connectivity fostered by love provides.

In this positive sense, the existence of innate envy, an impulse that is *selectively preferential*, may be understood to be one of nature's gifts. Rather than acting solely as a constraint, it is the giving of an opportunity to spur development. It is, in part, a compelling force, a potentially survival-based incentive, that offers an almost limitless range of potential opportunities for spurring mental integration, complexity, development, and robust psychological enrichment.

In a broad cognitive sense, envy functions as an appeal, request, and search. This is its quintessential experiential motor. It acts on multiple emotional and intellectual levels in its attempt to obtain more information, seek further clarification, and search for confirmation of unconscious hypotheses. At root, this is the search for the good object, which is the reward resulting from meaningful information acquisition. These impulses aim toward increasing the *epistemophilia* and storehouse of meaning within the self. They build up the richness of the ego. This is part of the progressive threshold toward *the healthy maturation of envy*. The developmental pull forward is thus given exquisite momentum by envy at every chronological age.

From an interpersonal and group perspective, for example, social dilemmas may result from mixed motivations toward selfish versus cooperative gain, and thus engender conflict. In the theory of envy, a fundamental presumption rests on the inevitable comparisons that arise within all aspects of mental functioning as a natural part of everyday living. Given the premise that individuals orient their values by comparing themselves (what they have, earn, and are given) with what others are perceived to possess, *envy theory* can be used to illuminate some important mechanisms behind basic social processes.

From pragmatic social relevance perspectives, envy may create "zero-sum" situations in which gain by one necessitates a correlated loss for another. *Envy theory* formulated here, however, emphasizes the possibility of *the healthy maturation of envy*. This denotes cooperative gain and a "win-win" philosophy resulting from collectively oriented, beneficial behaviors. Inherent in such behaviors is the principle of reciprocation or mutually beneficial sharing.

*The healthy maturation of envy* increases the chances of having an attitude disposed toward sharing and helping. This sort of reciprocation in interpersonal and social behaviors derives from elements of empathy, compassion, and low envy in an individual's mindset. These elements also significantly drive social motivations. It is undeniable that such a social perspective has real value toward peaceful and mutually enriching outcomes on individual and social levels. Mutually beneficial outcomes make a difference and advance positive changes.

## Summary

Like Melanie Klein, modern *envy theory* hypothesizes the biomental core of primary envy to be innate, inborn, and constitutional. Such a bold assertion is admittedly unprovable at this time. As a clinically heuristic working hypothesis, however, it is a useful exploratory instrument.

The phrase *nuclear envy* covers an expanded constellation that was initially referred to by Melanie Klein as "primary envy." Envy is a preconceptual, subliminally affective, innate predisposition, inclination, readiness, and anticipation. This faculty acts as a template to structure awareness, preferentially filter and organize it, and impute hedonic value and meaning to all experience in selectively preferred ways as determined by an individual's unique constitution. The companion to *nuclear envy* is *nuclear love*. Both are focal points in the experience of self and others.

*Nuclear envy* is characterized by pleiotrophy—that is, one innately endowed predisposition influencing a variety of different expressions as development proceeds. It is a presemantic set of sensations and responsivity, independent of conscious thinking, out of which automatic responses to fear, reward, and novelty emerge. Envy, together with love and hate, forms a superordinate orientation for mental functioning.

The emotional and motivational value of perceived stimuli triggers all aspects of attention and cognition. Because experiential stimuli are typically ambiguous and uncertain, projective mechanisms within the dispositional bias of an individual activate to organize what is experienced initially as emotionally and cognitively correlated yet dissonant.

An individual's selective cognitive and affective encoding—*projective internalization*—makes *the apprehension of experience idiosyncratically meaningful*. Meaning denotes the identity that arises from the ego's salient recognition of aspects of itself in the environment. Meaning results from bidirectional processes, causal loops. This process of attribution is the basic manner in which the ego functions. This is part of the inherent *epistemophilia* of the self. Its meaning-laden linkages organize one's unique inner world of object relations, the ego's experiences of the other. Idiosyncratic emotional meaning is the glue that binds cognitive apprehension of real social stimuli. "The other" is forged from elements already available in the image of the self.

Meaning derives from the *relation* to the object, not the object. Primary envy may be compared to a temperamental set point with *ateliotic* features—namely, to a basic state of experiential readiness that is primarily undeveloped. It is only with environmental releasers that envy becomes secondarily elaborated and expressed in an individual's experience and interpersonal transactions.

Envy's innate proclivities are not immutable; they are not obdurate constraints. Environmental exposures influence these dispositions in profound ways, and can be perceived as significant opportunities toward more refined personal development. *The healthy maturation of envy* pivots around *nuclear love*, the establishment of the internal good object.

The acquired accretions (new experiential material perceived and processed by the ego) around envy can be understood and analyzed—that is, sufficiently explained—by clinical observations. The irrational core of envy, however, remains a black hole that is intrinsically "un-understandable."

# CHAPTER THREE

# An Introduction to the *Nuclear Envy* Concept

## *Nuclear Envy*: Rethinking the Details of Klein's Primary Envy Concept

*Nuclear envy* is the core conceptualization of modern *envy theory*. It is an expansion of Melanie Klein's concept of *primary* envy (1957, 183, 221). Her discovery was crucial not only to a new understanding of human nature but also launched a qualitative advance in the fundamental conceptualization of human psychology. She knew exactly what she was saying, even though some Kleinian and non-Kleinian commentators have disputed this. Her bold assertions in a changing psychoanalytic world in London and North America made acceptance even more of a challenge. It would not be incorrect to say that psychoanalysts, other than those of the British School of Melanie Klein, either have avoided recognizing or dismissed entirely the consideration of envy as a core module of mind.

For these reasons, the envy concept has been largely left out of serious consideration in the United States until recently. Although Klein's ideas about envy were intermittently developed in both British and South American psychoanalysis, more penetrating analyses are needed to address the unclear and vexing aspects that make up this complex idea. *Envy theory* and *nuclear envy* attempt to fill this gap. While acknowledging an inestimable debt to Melanie Klein, *envy theory* represents a further, independent contribution to the psychology of personality and character development. In other words, without the political and ideological constraints that affiliations with institutes and societies bring, *envy theory* has evolved. Moreover, envy is cast as an exciting opportunity toward insight, internal accomplishments, and self-development.

The literature on envy is relatively sparse. Important though limited psychoanalytic contributions began in the early 1920s with the work of Karl Abraham (1919, 1921), Michael Josef Eisler (1921), and Melanie Klein (1928, 1932). Joan Riviere (1932, 1952) in London discussed envy, jealousy, and the negative therapeutic reaction, the paradoxical impasse arising in some analytic situations. Susan Isaacs (1935, 1949) discussed issues of property, possessiveness, and their unconscious meanings in child behavior as they related to envy. Sigmund Freud's principal contribution was his idea of penis envy as part of female psychological development (1908, 1914a, 1925, 1933a, 1937).

Kleinian analysts (Bion 1962a; Rosenfeld 1952, 1971; Segal 1973, 1993; Racker 1968; Etchegoyen 1999) have made major contributions. Hanna Segal (2007), a distinguished proponent of Klein's concept of envy, comments that envy has remained underutilized in professional circles for two reasons. First, it may have been overinterpreted early on after its introduction by Klein in the 1950s and 1960s. Second, its full realization is the hardest one to bear for both patient and the analyst who interprets it.

Whereas psychoanalytic literature has been relatively sparse, the psychological literature over the last decade and a half has generated some important work on envy. American psychologists have recently consolidated the few studies made during the last two decades, and produced a remarkable collection reviewing findings from a broad range of disciplines. In these valuable studies, the more conscious aspects of envy, for the most part, are addressed. In addition, this literature remains descriptive and theoretical rather than primarily treatment-oriented. The contributions of Richard H. Smith are especially noteworthy (Smith and Kim 2007; Smith 2008).

A valuable collection of papers revisiting Klein's *Envy and Gratitude* has recently become available (Roth and Lemma 2008). Over a dozen contributors bring interesting and varied insights to current views of envy and its impact on development and mental health. No general psychology primarily oriented around envy, however, is advanced. This diverse collection is a welcome contribution to the psychoanalytic literature on envy. Peter Fonagy, distinguished psychoanalyst and developmental researcher, has contributed a particularly noteworthy chapter. He says, "I intended to celebrate Melanie Klein's contribution by showing its relevance to current thinking in developmental psychopathology. . . . While Kleinian theory was courageously adultomorphic . . . it peculiarly might just turn out that Mrs. Klein's fictitious developmental ideas were more relevant to the scientific basis of the discipline and closer to reality, as established in infant laboratories, than most of us were willing to acknowledge" (2008, 210).

*Envy theory*, however, owes its greatest debt to psychoanalysis, which forms the framework for this exposition. Klein's seminal paper on schizoid mechanisms in 1946 introduced the construct of projective identification, the principal mode of operation of envy. These were elaborated in *Envy and Gratitude* (1957) published before her death in 1960. Envy, for Klein, was the chief expression of a foundational mental force—the death instinct. She described envy as innate, largely constitutional, essentially unmotivated, primary, dyadic, and directed at the primary object, the mother, specifically "the feeding breast." Envy was a part-object phenomenon characteristic of the paranoid-schizoid position.

*Envy theory* attempts further theory building. Klein's lexicon like Freud's included the structural theory of psychic agencies: id, ego, and superego, the genetic point of view, the notion of primal phantasies, and emphasis on the impulses of the innate life instincts and the death instinct. The "economic point of view," a description of the way the energetic forces of these instincts infuse and drive the personality, was central. It provided an early action model of the circuitry of information processing, phenomenally suggesting how emotions and defense mechanisms structure cognition. Additionally, the role of the object (interpersonal proxy generated mentally in idiosyncratic ways) as an inherent aspect of the biomental life of instincts was stressed. The "object" incarnates in the mind in the presence and *absence* of an actual, external interpersonal environmental figure.

Klein framed her exposition of primary envy using the twofold set "envy and gratitude." *Envy theory* restructures this coupling in terms of "envy and love." Love in its primitive form is elemental idealization. Pleasure, satisfaction, and happiness stemming from idealization is raw, primitive, and tenuous. As normal idealization matures into love, it becomes more empathetic and only then does it give rise to gratitude.

In paranoid-schizoid configurations, the "internal good object" is established when internal loving experiences supersede destructive envious ones. This process varies in degree and is never complete. Melanie Klein introduced this idea in 1946 in her seminal paper, "Notes on Some Schizoid Mechanisms," and reiterated its crucial importance through her career (Klein 1948, 1952a, 1955, 1957, 1958, 1963a, 1963b).

Primary love structures the internal good object as the nidus of inviolate *nuclear love*. This becomes the ego's focal point for the recognition of inner and outer goodness and the assimilation of nurturance—food, love, and understanding. With ego integration and the capacity for admiration, enjoyment couples with gratitude and galvanizes the achievements brought about by what *envy theory* calls *the healthy maturation of envy*.

Loving gratitude is based on the enjoyment that adequate satisfaction, pleasure, and happiness bring. These are more complete, rather than partial and fleeting, experiences. When gratitude soars, happiness merges into delight and joy. Primitive love, however, begins as a preverbal idealization that gradually develops into a more reality-based capacity for self-love and love for others. Gratitude, in a manner of speaking, becomes the serene and trustful enjoyment felt in the company of self and others.

Envy is primary in many ways. First, its original object is the primary object, the mothering figure. Additionally, envy is inherent in human nature, constitutionally based, and virtually elemental. Envy is made up of the life and the death instincts. These nonfixed instinctual action patterns encompass broad trends with strong emblematic connotations. *In envy theory, these instincts are archetypal forces whose presence can only be inferred by their effects.* Envy's loving side reflects the primary mental expression of the fundamental biomental life instinct: attraction, expansion, and connectivity. Envy's destructive side is the force aimed at opposing and spoiling these.

The life instinct and death instinct have a necessary and delicate balance. They are not antagonistic but complementary and form a normative integrative dialectic. In fact, the death instinct, in a figurative sense, needs to ride on the waves of the life instinct to fulfill one of its principal aims—to taste the sensuous corporeal world. *For the two instincts, as such, to exist, they must exist together*; it is impossible for either to operate in isolation. The ego orchestrates their dynamic balance. Their proper integration in the ego reflects mental health.

Unconscious envy is designated *nuclear* and primary to stress its powerful, authoritative, unique, and core psychological rank. Envy is central, has primitive roots in infancy, and is part of *a nuclear mass around which normal as well as atypical and disordered development consolidate in dynamic fashion*.

How *nuclear envy* and its complement, love, are sensed, their "qualia," is presented in this book in language that attempts to be experientially near. This attempts to convey the way envy manifests itself in everyday life, especially in clinical situations.

Some of the epistemological issues relating to the early infantile experience of knowing, considerations of affective and cognitive development, and recent scientific findings are addressed. The numerous expressions of envy, for example, in anxiety, guilt, suffering, hate, disgust, desire, lust, loneliness, romantic love, and psychosis are enumerated.

Psychic structure, mental mechanisms, organization, and functioning are discussed using metapsychological propositions. This terminology nowadays is infrequently used, even disdained. This classical terminology, however, has provided a necessary instrument to expose envy and suggest hypotheses for further examination, perhaps by cognitive and neuroscience studies.

*Envy theory* necessitates introducing various new hypotheses: *biomental self, biomental corporeality, the infant's dilemma, projective internalization, id relations, ego relations, the epistemophilia within the self, primordial anaclitic dependency, the concept of the chaperone, envy's developmental triad, adaptive collapse, dynamic spot psyche, self-signature updating, lived goodness, and the healthy maturation of envy.*

*Envy theory's* proposal for a concept of *the healthy maturation of envy* is unique in that it reframes the envy concept to suggest that envy does have a beneficial potential rather than being a "dead end" to significant change. Envy is neither a condemning stricture nor predetermined fatalism. In fact, such a pessimistic view was never part of Klein's own theory of envy.

*Envy theory* adheres to the debatable, if not controversial, proposition of a death instinct. The conceptual explorations in this book have maintained an open-minded willingness to explore its possible meanings. Similar to the concept "id," the concept "death instinct" is deliberately used to suggest the vast array of destructive forces in mental operations that are undeniably present but whose detailed etiology (mechanisms and neural substrates) remains undiscovered and insufficiently explained. Freud understood it as silent in its interior operation. *Envy theory* regards the internal death instinct as a violent, biomental phenomenon whose outstanding expression in the ego is anxiety. All anxiety is palpably experiential. True to its nature, envy exists as a negative presence so rooted in nonconscious processes that its makeup attempts to perpetuate this invisibleness. Whether the death instinct is silent in its interior operation, its expression in envy is always muted, whereas its expression in aggression is loud and glaring.

Additionally, viewing the death instinct as a "death wish" is misleading and incorrect. For the same reason, diluting the concept and calling it an "aggressive drive" is equally a misinterpretation of Freud's discovery and Klein's use of the idea. Moreover, any attempt to describe the aim of the death instinct as one that serves defense and self-protection is not consistent with the pointedly destructive aim that both Freud and Klein maintained. Freud (1933b [1932]) described the death instinct as noticeable only when it is diverted outward as an instinct of destruction—aggression toward the interpersonal object.

*Envy theory* regards both the life instinct and the death instinct as foundational. They denote archetypal primordial forces inferred only by their experiential and at times empirical effects. These are the primary energetic forces of the whole personality—id, ego and its substructures, and superego. The body is its corporeal platform. All these component factors intimately suffuse one another. The personality, the self as a whole, therefore, has as its principal wish: "To live, not to die." The action of the death instinct on the self, however, necessarily activates autodestruction. This cannot operate in isolation from the action of the life instinct, usually in functional ascendancy.

The overall thrust of individual motivation and behavior is toward life and meaningful survival even in the face of envy's continuing attempts to instigate mental self-defeat, in effect, a self-endangerment. This shows itself in information-processing confusion. Self-defeating choices or instances of "acrasia" are reflected in envy's pulsions toward the self-denial of the experience of goodness, the intolerance of experiencing oneself or the object as good. Self-defeat denotes envy's undermining of love as a positive motivation toward enhanced self-development.

For human life to exist in all its complexity, *envy theory* posits the proposition, however provisional, of a death instinct. Its functional operation deliberately creates emotional and cognitive dissonance. Additionally, envy elicits the rumblings of anxiety and distress in order to shape and prune the life instinct whose aim is to spur ingenuity, exploration, creativity, and expansion. This dialectical action of the forces of life and death provide the ground for paradoxical self-destruction and clear-cut adaptation. This is the raison d'etre of envy.

## Vitiation, Reparation, and *Epistemophilia*: The Geometry of Ego-Object Relations

The nexus of human psychology in *envy theory* is centered in the ego's experience (witness) of the object (witnessed). The formal designation of this relational dynamic is termed *object relations*. This includes the ego's own experience of itself, *ego relations*. Both constitute the dialectical interplay between loving and destructiveness. *The ego is the self's seat of experiential responsiveness, both conscious and nonconscious.*

The concept of object relations denotes how the self experiences emotional "meaning," the ultimate end product of all information processing. Some meaningfulness, both nonconscious and conscious, is inherent in the way the ego functions from birth. This bears the hallmark of the ego's experiential grasp of the object.

The ego's object relations are driven by the *epistemophilia* inherent in the self. This is the epistemophilic wish to know and meaningfully understand. In *envy theory*, it proceeds from both the life and the death instincts. Anticipation, expectation, attention, and perceptual exploration arise from the innate matrix of this adaptive impulse to seek. The biomental life and death instincts (*whatever real forces these provisional abstractions may approximate*) are the fundamental matrix out of which primary love, hate, and envy emerge. These are the three axes of cognitive and emotional information processing around which mental forces dynamically battle and ultimately mate.

The *epistemophilia* within the self is driven by libidinal urges toward exploration and novelty seeking—notably, the search for good objects. *Envy theory* understands this as universal and intrinsic to the hardwiring of the brain. All aspects of these explorations are sharpened by the pruning and shaping that destructive trends introduce. Cognitive science attributes the heterogeneity of novelty seeking to yet undiscovered moderators and complex variables. The impulse to search yields both pleasure and a reduction of anxiety. The *epistemophilia* within the self nourishes the seeds of creativity and human thinking. It has both emotional and intellectual dimensions. Envy dampens the epistemophilic experience of reward. It acts to blind insight and blunt impulses toward creativeness.

The ego's overall aim is adaptive assessment of what is safe and unsafe for survival. *Meaning derives from the intuited and perceptive interpersonal links discovered during experience.* This contributes to the buildup of a sense of reality. The safety and survival forged, secured, and consolidated through these links with objects is sought instinctively. The first object of desire and knowledge is the mother's body.

The infant's body and mind use the mother as the premier object for survival on all levels. The phylogenetic and biological roots of this enduring corporeal given cannot be overemphasized. The mental dimension of these roots exists as a perpetually active process in *the unconscious as a system*—that is, in phantasy life in both infancy and thereafter. These "phantasies" are largely nonconscious information-processing transactions that are innately active. They are primitive mental operations.

On this basic biomental platform, gradually evolving psychological change, insight, and self-understanding become consolidated. Emotional conviction results. Infantile concrete experiences become "mentalizations"— transmutations of somatic cognitions into psychological entities. They are engendered by the flesh's transformative morphing of its own personal and interpersonal biomental interactions. Creativeness, destructiveness, and self-understanding in this process drive *meaningful survival* for both self and extended social group.

The phenomenon of hating may express itself in numerous ways ranging from self-hate to hate of the object. Hate's destructive action is described conceptually as aggression. Observable aggression connotes the outward deflection of destructiveness as forceful violence. Aggression also takes the form of intimidation and menacing. *Envy theory* elaborates the wider roles that hate plays in consciousness, in its specific manifestation as an essential component of unconscious envy. Primary envy is reflected in the emblematic unconscious phantasy of the ego's robbing the ideal object of all aspects of its creativeness, as well as putting badness into it through projective identification. The nuances in this construct are immense and include the exploitation of resources and scavenging the spoils.

The term *vitiation* describes *the spoiling qualities of envy* that are object-directed and inevitably become self-directed. Envy's vitiating action is, in effect, a de-vivification on experiential and material levels. Envy sucks the life out of the envier. Envy instigates impotency and barrenness in mental functioning. It nullifies emotional creativity and truncates the developing capacity for proper thinking. It not only spoils what is ideal; it acts to negate creativeness.

*Envy theory* describes the details of envy's vitiating and spoiling characteristics and introduces the possibility of envy's *healthy maturation*. The complex processes of reparation, integral to Melanie Klein's psychoanalysis, correlate strongly with this healthy maturation.

Vitiation and spoiling are the primitive forms of destructiveness characteristic of envy. Beginning in infancy and perpetually cycling throughout life, life-affirming (also called libidinal) strivings interact with and modulate hate and destructive envious processes through the *epistemophilia* in the self. These three factors—vitiation, reparation, and *epistemophilia*—are the axiomatic pillars that drive all mental development. They are the geometry of the mind. Unconsciousness is the universe, the atmosphere in which this geometry organizes. The epistemophilic impulse toward meaning consolidates by means of emotional intimacy, affective bonding, and investments of identification and internalization beginning in infancy and continuing thereafter. These iterations impart the complexity characteristic of cognitive and character development.

*The healthy maturation of envy* transforms envy's spoiling aims toward healthier states: awe, silent wonder, respect, hopeful anticipation, and reverence. *Nuclear love* at the core of the ego drives this. These states of burgeoning admiration and emulation set in motion further complex reparative impulses toward mending damages done to ego (the envier) and its objects (the envier's inner world).

*Reparation is much more than mere expiation, making amends, correcting a wrong, or compensating for damages done. It is the essence of integration, consilience, confluence, and justification of previous disparate parts. Ultimately, reparative trends fueled by the vital forces inherent in life and all positive libidinal strivings emerge as conscious feelings of empathy, compassion, sharing, gratitude, generosity, and helping behaviors. These crucial humanizing developments define envy's healthy maturation.*

## Nuclear Envy: An Outline of Essentials

*Envy theory* purposely reaches beyond what is empirically verifiable and scientifically measurable. The proposition that the root capacity for envy is an innate psychological dynamic has been controversial from its inception. Attributing such major significance to a "trait" with such seemingly negative connotations is difficult and disturbing. Yet envy's profound implications are bold statements regarding human nature, particularly its dark and threatening side.

Innate and acquired traits can never be differentiated precisely since the two are so inextricably bound. These categories can be cast as two directions existing on one continuum. They always transact to produce a final product. The innate direction (for example, envy, love, hunger, and breathing) suggests the universal possession of an ever-present trait or need existing on some level of expression. The acquired direction (for example, suntan, wearing clothing, and a name) suggests that a state or condition could be absent or present depending on an individual's responsiveness and conditioning in the environment. "Innate" only suggests that a change in overall status is relatively more difficult to effect. It does not assert a fixed, rigid condition in which change or modification is impossible. Furthermore, imperviousness to change does not necessarily denote the presence of an impenetrable or unknowable innate factor.

Hence, while the faculty for envy is normatively embedded in opaque ways in human psychological functioning, its expressions can become accessible, understood, and transformed to permit change. Envy's strictures are elastic.

The two concepts, primary envy and *nuclear envy*, are similar although each has a slightly different emphasis. Primary denotes an envy that is directly elemental, without antecedents, axiomatic, and organized in earliest infancy. This occurs through its relational structuring with the primary whole object, the mother, and specifically, the primal part-object, the breast. Nuclear denotes envy's innate, primordial, primal, primary, and central mental nexus, a pivotal relational core around which mental functioning organizes both in infancy and thereafter.

*Envy theory* uses primary envy/*nuclear envy* and primary love/*nuclear love* to connote a system of mutually and, at times, inversely related, prime orienting coordinates. *Nuclear envy* has relatively more passive and reflexive characteristics compared to *nuclear love*, which requires more ego activity to instantiate and establish it securely.

These multiordinate terms refer to numerous mental phenomena that can achieve satisfaction on multiple levels of need. Primary also implies without antecedents, endogenous, and virtually irreducible. It may also suggest a faculty not resulting from conflict, but an element that, itself, is necessary for the generation of conflict. The attribution of being primary is always relative, since antecedents can be discovered in most cases other than, for example, a hypothetical, spontaneous creation out of a void. The term "primordial" is closer to such a concept of de novo phenomena. In the analysis of envy's arousal stimuli, its causative roots, *envy theory* goes to great lengths to delineate three component parts that span an ontogenetic range from primordial, primal, and primary through reactive and brushed with conflict (see chapter 6).

With these qualifiers, *nuclear envy* is understood as virtually unmotivated, unconscious, and having an elementally privileged primitive status. The primordial and primal roots of primary envy fuse with experience over time and yield the clinical complexes that manifest and express themselves as mixtures of primary envy. Secondarily acquired envious accretions, which may take conscious expression, are additive. Primary elements as products of conflict or arising otherwise are prerequisite components generating amalgams of conflict. *Nuclear envy* denotes this entire constellation. Conflict, as used here, has both positive and negative dimensions; it not only generates anxiety, it may also promote development by stimulating adaptive resolutions to what had been perceived as irreconcilable.

In what ways can the experience of envy be described? Envy when excessive and unmodulated is always base, ignoble, invidious, undermining, and spiteful. The roots of unconscious envy exist as subliminal experiential states. They are far below the threshold of conscious awareness. Envy begins as a kind of praise, which then rapidly sours. This praise is an idealized overvaluation rather than a benign admiration. Souring is the vitiating process that characterizes envy's spoiling matrix.

The envier resentfully and agonizingly senses himself or aspects of himself to be bad, inferior, poor, flawed, powerless, or even absent. At the same time, the envier desires to possess what are perceived to be personally missing attractive, advantageous features felt to exist in another. Such a discrepant perception embodies the essence of unfairness and injustice. Envy is marked by the abiding perception that distributions of assets and resources are inequitable, unfair, perhaps undeserved despite logical considerations. Conceptual and emotional attitudes of justice, equity, fairness, and deservedness are complex mental states characteristic of developmentally advanced people. Their roots, however, are felt early in life in inchoate ways. A subjective sense of perceived injustice, stimulating dysphoria and hostility, typically accompanies envy.

The object of envy is imbued with perceived prosperity and better fortune. Ironically, this is a reaction based on internal phantasy, idiosyncratic to the envier. This stirs a sense of unhappiness and resentment in the envier. For example, on an empirical level, envy may be observed in the penetrating and silent stares that accompany feelings of bitter resentment, whether the envied person has merited this or not. The role of the eyes in envious states is often alluded to metaphorically in literature and folklore. Phrases such as "penetrating look," "intent gaze," "evil eye," and "if looks could kill" imply envy. The gaze of the eyes has a projective, penetrating quality that correlates with the unconscious mechanism of envy and the aims of projective identification underlying its operation (chapter 7).

What is idealized is, in fact, that which is *present yet underdeveloped* in the experience of the self. That which is envied is not actually absent in the envier, but only missing because its potential for fullness is not yet sufficiently developed. In other words, the idealized entity is not absolutely absent; its fullness is merely not yet sufficiently unconcealed.

An interesting correlation to Aristotelian philosophy can be made here. The experience of the ideal state being present in all its fullness (*physis*) is not a *fait accompli* because two dimensions needed to complete what is already there (*morphe*) are missing: *hyle*—unfolding of yet latent features—and *steresis*—a privation of the essence of what might be ideal felt to be irreversibly absent. This psychological proposition is not identical to the Aristotelian notion of "entelechy" or the inner blueprint that merely unfolds independent of environmental influence. The development of any mental process can never occur in the absence of actual environmental factors that release and constrain expression.

What is envied or wished for is the transformation of what is sensed as flawed *or perceived as vacant* in the self into what is desired to be present, richer, and perfected. Only that which, in fact, has some "substance" or presence in the self can emerge as an object of serious envy. Bion (1962a, 1962b) has alluded to the phenomenon of these innate, undeveloped substances, which include hardwired anticipations, aspirations, and hopes. He terms them "innate pre-conceptions." He viewed these prefigured *expectations* as making up a large part of the dynamics of unconscious phantasy. Unconscious phantasy, then, is the repository of subjective "if-then" innate nonconscious action sequences. Dynamic, intersubjectively shared environmental experiences release the ego's innate predispositions and interests. Together with concrete, instance-specific experiences, they manifest themselves as the object-related/ interpersonal dramas in which envy unfolds.

Envy is a titanic amalgam of clashing unconscious forces that expresses itself as a premier state of unpleasure, suffering, and unhappiness. This is accompanied by the envier's simultaneous belief that the envied one, by comparison, is ideal and superior and possesses what are perceived as exceedingly valuable, advantageous, and almost perfect, though unattainable, traits, powers, possessions, or resources. Envy's intrapsychic reference point is an ideal construction, whether structured in the unconscious or elicited preattentively in preconscious imagination. These belief states are subliminally ingrained in the ego's perception of both the inner and outer worlds. An adaptive dimension of envy, however, is its essentially orienting feature, which, in part, contributes to the ego's interminable striving to make sense out of its experience.

Envious idealization, when excessive, acts as a reference point with unrealistically exaggerated value. As this floods the superego's good-bad construal filter, the overall ego response is a perception of discrepancy. This is the felt experience of unfairness. Emotional turmoil, discontent, and outrage result. Spoiling impulses are reflexively instigated.

The anxiety generated by unconstrained envy, however, is so intolerable that the envy-laden ego insidiously seeks to spoil in the intrapsychic arena of the envier all that it believes incites and thus provokes it in both the target of envy and *the envier*. This contrasts with love, which comprises a dual sense consisting of both self-love and object-love. *One of envy's profound paradoxes is that it is sparked initially not by frustration but by a first taste of honey—a glimmer of perfection seen by loving and expectant eyes—whose goodness seems to promise satisfaction.*

This promise, however, is repeatedly broken. Instead, a dismantling of the arrangement of goodness follows when the shock of not getting what one feels one wants is felt in full force. Although this paradoxical attack on something wonderful—perceived as desirable—is illogical, it is emblematic of envy's irrational core. This attack, together with experiential anxiety, constitutes the mental expression of the biomental death instinct. Envy is the mechanism that compels one to deny himself, in repeated fashion, opportunities for satisfactions that reality, in fact, offers or may offer.

For example, to be envious of another person's advantages does not denote that the envier, at least at first, desires those assets for himself. The core of the envy dynamic is the envier's instantaneous wish to see the perceived other deprived, perhaps robbed, of those assets, and then simultaneously to see those assets spoiled and destroyed. Envy is threatened by the very existence of value and goodness. Unopposed envy as "antivalue" cannot tolerate any model to be admired or emulated. This intolerance is experienced as repugnance, perceived resentment, grudging, and ill will—all of which carry hostility and destructive intent.

Primary unconscious envy refers to the envier's attacking aspects of, and meaningful *relations* to, an ideal object sensed to be so perfect that it arouses the hopeful anticipation of yielding a share in that perfect excellence. Primary envy, moreover, is an attack on this arrangement of perceived goodness—not badness. It is *not* an attack secondary or defensive to a sense of the object being intentionally withholding, frustrating, and consequently sensed as bad and malevolent. It is an attack on an object phantasied as self-sufficiently independent. Envy sees the envied as a wall of inaccessibility. This paradoxical spoiling activity on inchoately fused perceptions of goodness becomes an important source of the eventual hopelessness and confusion that the envier comes to experience.

## Primordial Envy

All varieties of envious states, conscious and nonconscious, are founded on *nuclear envy*. The *clinical expressions of envy* have *both principal and secondary features*. *Developed* envy usually contains reactive features of frustration—disappointment of expectations and perceived needs that have acted as secondary reinforcements of its principal, unconscious base. Innate and reactive elements are so fused that distinguishing them in the entire constellation of envy is merely an academic exercise, often impossible.

*Nuclear envy*, moreover, is innate, constitutional, endogenous, elemental, virtually irreducible, primitive, and primordially based. For Klein, primary envy is primal breast envy.

*Envy theory* in its microanalysis of *nuclear envy* sees primordial *envy* as its nuclear core. This primitive heart of envy is operative at the start of life. In metapsychological terms, it emanates first from the relation between id and ego. The impact of this relational dynamic abides forever in the core of the self and always continues to exert its power. It is always at the center of *nuclear envy*. The origins of envy derive from its matrix in an individual's genetic endowment and perinatal constitution. The combined biological and emotional context of the actual mother-infant dyad organizes this.

The psychological birth of envy is ontogenetically contemporaneous with the infant's first experience of hunger and its first cry. This is the infant's isolation call. It signals to mother a state of loneliness and need for help. This describes the empirically observable scene of the infant-mother relationship. These experiential states of crying and squirming reflect the earliest observable expression of privation, hurt, and pain.

## Narcissistic Wound, Isolation, and Narcissistic States

In metapsychological terms, this denotes a narcissistic wound—sense of existential privation—and implies feeling passive/vulnerable/threatened. A globally diffuse awareness attributes the source of this threat to some dimly sensed other—the intrapsychic primal part-object, which is the correlate of the environmental breast. In other words, one's narcissism, whose default state is a feeling of comfortable, pleasant self-sufficiency/confidence, becomes threatened the moment need, the cry of unaddressed pain, is experienced. At rock bottom, it is a primordial, elemental, intrapsychic reminder of a need only satisfiable by the goodness/nurturance felt to be present in the phantasy-laden id, and absent in the ego. *Envy theory* sees this taproot as the principal source of later developed forms of unmodified adult narcissism, where people feel that they are undeniably and organically special—self-righteous vanity. It is the smugness of a tenuous self-sufficiency.

*Envy theory* positions the most explicit expressions of isolation both at its developmental inception—the beginning of life—and as aging proceeds—toward the end of life. The dynamics of envy, especially feeling lonely, isolated, distressed, and ineffectual, are pronounced at the start and last days of life.

Intense feelings of isolation elicit the narcissistic desire for some sort of contact to relieve the distress produced by such lonely feelings. Narcissistic desire, in this sense, mobilizes deeply intrapsychic defenses. Splitting and projective identification arise to create and fuse with a precarious safe haven—the internal ideal part-object. This deeply internal retreat may be one of the most primitive defenses used to mute profound anxiety and deep distress, and produce temporary states of self-soothing in the face of feeling alone. It is the prototype of *narcissistic states of the ego*. These are self-induced, dreamy, autistic-like states of pseudoautonomous removal from real people to internal phantasies.

For example, genital masturbatory activity both induces and is induced/reinforced by narcissistic states of the ego, in an attempt to ward off anxiety by defensively retreating to an interaction with an internalized, ideal part-object. The pleasure derived from this libidinal and excessive idealization is intense and profound. It comes to act as an attractor state, a magnet toward which the ego orients. Thumb sucking in infancy and rocking in regressed emotional states are outward behaviors reflecting narcissistic withdrawal or narcissistic ego states. The euphoria produced by addictions of all kinds likewise involves retreats to such narcissistic states of self-soothing—forced and tenuous states of pseudosecurity and reduced anxiety.

## Envy's Attention Jumps from Id, to Breast, to Mother

The unfolding of envy has a distinct trajectory. On deepest unconscious levels (nonconscious affective and cognitive information processing), primordial envy originates in the relation between ego and its id. Rapidly and perhaps simultaneously, this primitive inner template resonates with real people experience to emerge as a primary envy of the primal part-object, the feeding breast of early infancy. Very quickly it jumps to the primary whole object, the mother when she is felt as a separate individual toward the latter part of the first year.

This threefold constellation becomes a resplendent attractor, which remains in mental functioning as a primary reference point for all aspects of information processing. It acts as a constitutional preference system, a blueprint for selecting particular experiences. For example, some babies appear to prefer and do well in overactive environments, while others seem to thrive in more quiet surroundings. In later life, one's sexual orientation, for example, may be part of a constitutionally based preference circuitry. One's constitution, when meeting the environment, selects aspects (cues, prompts, props) of that environment that then act to reinforce already established innate traits, which in turn endure as compelling dispositions. This reinforcement cycle is strong but not absolute. Primordial envy significantly prefigures all subsequently developed manifestations of envy.

## The Illogic of the Unconscious: The Primary Process

A heavy load of primary processes (illogic and irrationality) governs unconscious situations. They operate by principles of confused information processing, not by logic and reason. Hence, etiological descriptions of the origins of *nuclear envy* may appear paradoxical and contradictory. This is what makes *nuclear envy* an idiosyncratic and, in many ways, irrational phenomenon difficult to both comprehend and explain. *Nuclear envy is sui generis* at its primordial core. It gives birth to itself. Together with this autoconception and its primal and primary components, acquired secondary features rapidly develop and flesh out envy's experiential psychodynamic pathways and varied expressions in everyday life. Envy's displays in words, gestures, and behavior are the calling cards to its access and therapeutic exploration.

## Envious Spoiling Contrasts with Hateful Aggression

Spoiling resulting from envy is different in quality from the aggressive assaults accompanying hate. Spoiling devaluations spurred by *nuclear envy* are evoked by a perceived goodness sensed as unattainable. A sort of furious disappointment and shock engenders these rueful storms. In sharp contrast, *hostile frustration felt secondary to the perceived badness* of an object provokes a hostile attack on such a hated object precisely because *the object is sensed as bad*. Typically, this badness correlates with the object's construed intentional and malicious withholding and, by implication, being threateningly harmful. The scenario characterized by such hate, in sharp contrast to that of envy, involves aggressive assaults whose primary aim is disarming a threatening enemy. The intent is to subdue, dominate, and forcefully control the source of sinister, menacing badness by quelling its malicious threat through force or by imprisoning it through containment.

Envy, on the other hand, aims to spoil, devalue, and, at least provisionally, put mental distance (denial and repression) between itself and the idealized object, which in phantasy is sensed as an independent self-sufficient entity. Envy seeks to nullify any semblance of goodness.

Often, both (1) hostile attacks on a bad, withholding object that is frustrating, and (2) envious spoiling attacks on a good but unattainable object that provokes shock occur simultaneously. Separating these is probably not possible. Hostility and envy usually coexist as aggressive attitudes toward the object. Envy and hate, in a circular way, reinforce one another.

Klein (1955) in her paper "On Identification" analyzes a novel whose central figure is a character named Fabian and alludes to this by saying:

Greed, envy, and hatred, the prime movers of aggressive phantasies, are dominant features in Fabian's character, and the author shows us that these emotions urge Fabian to get hold of other people's possessions, both material and spiritual; they drive him irresistibly toward what I describe as projective identification. (154–155)

Envy is affected, though not necessarily caused, by frustration, disappointment, and deprivation. Real deprivation, in fact, may not stimulate envy although it can facilitate its emergence if excessive envy is already present. Envy and privation, however, are directly correlated. *The roles that privation, disappointment, and frustration play during development weigh heavily in the formation of personality. Impulse control and one's reality sense are shaped by the way nongratification and the absence of satisfaction are experienced and managed.* How the mind, personality, and relationships develop over time directly results from the way the infant and, for that matter, child and adult experience and manage privation, disappointment of expectations and perceived needs, frustration, and nonsatisfaction of desire. Innate feelings of omnipotence and their projection correlate heavily with this.

The capacity to tolerate frustration in a healthy and adaptive fashion is crucial to understanding how the mind develops. For example, the innate quality of hopeful expectation may be robust enough to enable one to feel states of temporary nongratification as mere discouragement. If the capacity for innate hopefulness is weak, then frustrations may be experienced as a sense of creeping cynicism, furious disappointment, and distrust resulting in more lasting trauma. These traumas, if cumulatively experienced, may become misinterpreted as intentional persecution from a maliciously perceived, withholding, yet potentially generous, benefactor. Over the course of development, reactions to envy grow in complexity. The sense of deservedness and unfairness take shape and compound themselves adding to the hostile and resentful manifestations of envy. Hopelessness and despair are also rooted in this. *How nongratification of need and desire is experienced and coped with, therefore, heavily determines the course of normal and psychopathological personality development.* Envy, in part, directs and, in turn, is modified by all these evolving factors.

Last, some brief comments on *the healthy maturation of envy* will be discussed. The literature on envy is relatively modest and largely undeveloped concerning its *positive, healthy maturation*. This is true for both theory and providing clinically useful language.

When envy undergoes a healthy development, it may express itself as a drive hallmarked by noticing differences, discrepancies, inequalities, and personal shortcomings in more realistic rather than exaggerated ways. It may also express itself in the context of recognizing valuable and desirable traits in others. Conscious attitudes that include silently attentive pauses, respect, admiration, emulation, empathy, gratitude, cooperative sharing, and helping prevail in this context. These enhance positive emotional sensitivity. When unrefined splitting processes transform into healthy processes of adaptive diversification, especially through reality-oriented epistemological mechanisms, the ground is laid for enhanced opportunities for further growth and developmental advances. Risk factors for the instigation of idealization are thus diminished. The feeling of having options, choices, and preferences that are positively motivating and consciously discretionary rather than commanding and impulsively imposing marks *the healthy maturation of envy*. *The healthy maturation of envy*, in the broadest sense, aids in the cultivation of the mind.

## The Primary Life Instinct: Love/Libidinal Processes

Clarifying the conceptual positioning and meaning of the term "primary" and "instinct" requires a brief discussion of psychoanalytic psychology. The term "primary" suggests fundamental, unlearned, virtually irreducible, and having a privileged elemental status. *Envy theory* adheres to the archetypical constructs, however imperfect these hypotheses may be, of a life instinct and a death instinct, both of which are primary and complementary, not antagonistic. Both are essential for survival. These concepts refer to pulsatile, waxing and waning, biomental energetic forces prompting arousal, activation, orientation, motivation, and directedness toward a goal ("conation"). These goals are intimately related to interpersonal attraction and repulsion. They are more than merely affective discharges; they influence all cognitive processes (active and passive information processing) in positive and negative ways. Their biological component presumes their neurophysiologic and somatic base as well as degrees of their neuroplasticity and somaticplasticity. Only by their effects are these instincts inferred and used to consolidate trends in mental functioning.

*Envy theory* maintains that a person is a biomental self with a developmental history that increases in complexity from birth onward. The primary instincts are biomental forces that act to arouse biomental awareness of biomental imbalances and distress. This, in turn, spurs mental and behavioral directedness toward achieving the adaptive aims of meaningful survival.

In other words, physiological needs, emotional needs, and cognitive needs coalesce in complex ways to cause arousal and searching. The goal is to find and engage with objects/persons, actions, and activities that will function to balance and reregulate biomental needs thus enhancing quality of life, meaningful survival.

The primary life instinct is the inherent biomental impulse toward survival and the development of meaningfulness by efforts toward expansion. This denotes all biomental impulses and trends toward imparting qualities of "vivifyingness." The primary death instinct is the inherent biomental impulse toward destruction, disintegration, devaluation, and meaninglessness. It includes notions such as reduction, trimming, pruning, shearing, cutting, trash-producing, shaping, and so forth. These primary instincts are innate, irreducible *biomental* formations having both somatic/biological and psychological/mental aspects.

From the primary life instinct, love and all libidinal strivings arise as positive *mental* processes. These become complex, multidetermined pulsions toward obligatory survival, seeking, affiliation, expansion of connectivity, creation, integration, and self-coherence. Libidinal processes denote these unconscious energetic forces. They express themselves on all unconscious and conscious experiential levels in one's subjective sense of self and take expression as feelings, thoughts, and corporeal awareness. Their outward expression is observable in concrete behaviors that are positive, constructive, attachment-seeking, good, helpful, and loving. Although these libidinal processes are multifaceted, it is reasonable to group them operationally into a fundamental or "primary" category—love—upon which subsequently developed varieties of mental and behavioral phenomena can be functionally positioned and differentiated.

The centrifugal force of libido is its extroversion, which denotes its active aim of scanning and inducing continuous self-reconfigurations. The life instinct in the ego is *libido*, which has directional, organizing, and expansive aim-orienting properties. Libido is the life force—the energy of the life instinct stored in the ego—that acts to transform and reconfigure both ego and object in the binding/meaning imbuing action called *cathexis*. The ego's libido and its investment in meaningful objects—ego *cathexis*—is the psychoanalytic concept that correlates positively with the concept of *information processing* in cognitive science and *construals* in cognitive psychology.

For example, the energies of the life instinct reflected in strivings toward adaptation and survival underlie *normal idealization*, a principal feature of all information processing. In the neonatal period, ego and its superego organize together to develop a significant function: valuation of experience. Ego mediates and orchestrates attraction and repulsion; superego mediates the goodness/safety and badness/punishment values that guide the ego as executor. Normal idealization imbues attention with a transitory exaggeration of both the perception and meaning (beneficial excitement) of seemingly isolated experiences. In typical development, these cognitive and emotional expansions are soothingly stimulating events experienced as good.

In the paranoid-schizoid developmental era, such goodness is felt as elemental idealization that floods both ego and part-object experience. All experience is felt in extreme ways. When the depressive position emerges in the second quarter of the first year, the energies of the life instinct, acting as normal idealization and love, imbue experience with positive anticipatory expectancy and hope. This energetic charge fuels normative processes of reparation and feelings of gratitude. These ultimately reinforce the ego's capacity to feel normative separation from an object felt to be beneficial. The object is sensed as intermittently withholding but not malicious. As the early ego separates from an object, it increasingly learns to tolerate the object's delayed responsivity and, at times, absence.

In summary, in the paranoid-schizoid position, normal love is experienced as raw love or elemental idealization; in the depressive position, normal love is experienced in a less primitive fashion—namely, in a much less idealized form as "love proper" toward a whole object, a real person. *Early or raw love is elemental idealization; depressive-position love is love proper.*

Libido, it is to be emphasized, is more than merely a biologically preordained drive. It is a biomental force having somatic, appetitive, cognitive, affectively charged, and expansive object-seeking components. In its complex expression as love, it has superordinate status (with envy and hate) in the axiomatic makeup of the self. Love and hate appear to stand out more boldly as expressive behaviors than does envy, which is more interiorized.

The emotional, instinctive, and dispositional attitude of love derives from the life instinct. During the course of development and maturation, this universally shared, primary impulse of love comes to act as a commitment leading to the empirically observable performance of acts of loving-kindness. Broadly speaking, this sense of love is a mental state characterized by charitable and helping sentiments tending to have unconditional qualities. The instinctive spontaneity of this innate tendency is reflected when it activates in the absence of any conditioned stimuli. This is in contrast to the loving qualities of *the healthy maturation of envy*, which are conditioned by a wide variety of causative factors that have a complex development. Love and loving in this broad sense, together, make up the singular, overarching ethical axiom or principal beacon impelling all moral performance.

The expression of *the healthy maturation of envy* constitutes both a state of mind and, more observably, practices derived from dispositional, primary love as a state of mind. When destructive impulses are sufficiently contained by the force of primary love, *nuclear love* establishes itself as a nidus of ever-increasing integration and intensifying goodness in the ego. This refines the conduit for receiving and assimilating experience that promotes awe, pause, wonder, admiration, empathy, and gratitude. This healthy matura-tion is a positive achievement that undergoes development over a lifetime by intensive and deliberately focused psychological work. It is primary love conditioned by a wide variety of parameters over time. It takes shape in real life in forms contained under such rubrics as justice, righteousness, equitable fairness, charitable sharing, and helping.

*The healthy maturation of envy*, in these ways, functions as a complex array of ethical imperatives enacted as moral practices. *The healthy maturation of envy* is the mental state of love translating itself into behavior. It reflects the mean-ingfulness in relationships. Such a denotation, in fact, can be found in ancient traditions such as Buddhism and Hinduism. It is embodied, for example, in the concept of *dharma*, the major axiomatic proposition of these Eastern traditions, which connotes lawfulness, justice, fairness, righteousness, and moral conduct.

## The Primary Death Instinct: Anxiety, Envy, Spoiling, and Destructiveness

The primary death instinct, another psychoanalytic construct, denotes primary, unmotivated innate destructiveness. It is an internally generated autodisintegration. Its principal arena is in the unconscious dimensions of the self. From the primary death instinct, anxiety, envious spoiling, vitiation, hate, and phantasies of aggression and destructiveness arise. These emerge as destructive *mental* processes and may also express themselves in conscious and observable destructive behaviors. The energetic forces of the death instinct are always unconscious as are the libidinal forces driving attraction and affiliation.

Melanie Klein (1957) advanced the idea that the prime activity of the ego is the fundamental defense against the death instinct and that the ego is possibly even called into operation by the life instinct. If "purpose" is to be attributed to these instincts, Klein suggested their primordial aims in her conceptualizations.

The manifestations of the death instinct present themselves as anxiety, envy, hate, and outwardly deflected aggression. Some degree of life instinct always accompanies these expressions. Neither death instinct nor life instinct can manifest in pure culture, in a singular, unmixed, and isolated way. Anxiety, envy, and forms of aggression cover the experiential range from being nonconscious to being conscious, and everything in between. Emotional hate, behavioral aggression, and physical violence are conscious. Destructiveness on all levels aims toward a devaluation of the vital, positive meaningfulness sensed to be present. Meaning is "trashed" and becomes meaningless refuse.

Unconscious envy is unique since it holds center stage among all forms of destructiveness. It may act as the node around which all these other forms of destructiveness organize. Given this assumption, it is reasonable to operationally group envious expressions into a fundamental or primary category—envy—as a counterpoint to their opposite: namely, the libidinal processes characterizing love. It is always crucial to remember that both the life and death instincts operate in various states of fusion and defusion; they cannot exist or act in isolation, especially without the positive and negative constraints that the ego provides.

Although termed "primary," love and envy in their subsequent complex development as clinical and experiential phenomena clearly possess composite features. Nonetheless, with this acknowledgment, *envy theory* regards envy and love (as elemental idealization) as prototypical inception forms. As such, they are virtually irreducible and deemed "primary."

## The *Epistemophilia* within the Self

The *epistemophilia* within the self denotes impulses that promote the complex phenomena of meaning and meaningfulness in human experience. This innate impulse is also primary in human nature. Its principal aims are to seek, to know, and to meaningfully understand. This proceeds from the dialectical interaction of the impulses of the life and death instincts. Its organization is orchestrated by unconscious phantasy taking shape from the infantile ego's primary object relations to the mother's total self. For the infant, mother is a primary body-mind unity. This unique relation motivates and is motivated by anticipation, expectation, and attention, all of which create interest in perceptual explorations aimed at successful survival.

The *epistemophilia* within the self functions as a containing entity. It further organizes as ego integration proceeds. In the matrix of the entire self, its aims are meaningful survival and a sustainable quality of life. This capacity for continuous organization and reorganization across life's chronological thresholds contributes to the moment-to-moment meaningful and orienting updating of the experiential self as a whole, *self-signature updating*. It is a repeating cycle of self-identity reconfiguring itself throughout development.

## A Phenomenological Approach to the Theory of Envy

*Envy theory* attempts to convey the phenomenological expressions of envy in the subject who envies. Such an experiential focus denotes a decidedly intrapsychic perspective. The term "intrapsychic" is the historically older version of the more current term "intrasubjective."

Mental reality is both intrasubjective and intersubjective depending on the perspective taken. Intersubjective reality has its accent on interpersonally shared experience. It is an intermind dialogue. Intrapsychic reality accents the individual's own idiosyncratic inner world. It is an intramind dialogue. Both perspectives highlight the importance of an inner world that is experientially central to self-relevance—perceptions that others share similar traits and qualities.

Using more classical psychoanalytic terminology, *envy theory* holds that various degrees of narcissism (healthy and pathological construals of self) and object relations (how an individual idiosyncratically construes the animate environment) simultaneously coexist at every point in development. In these personality domains, the dynamic tensions, mixtures, and fusions of envy and love contribute to affect, thought, motivation, conflict, and behavior. In addition, envy is named *the missing theoretical and clinical link* in treatment-resistant psychiatric cases. Using insights about how an individual experiences himself in relation to others may serve not only a deeper theoretical understanding but as a bridge to enhance treatment success.

The broad dynamic that unconscious envy encompasses is a ubiquitous, underlying, and primary phenomenon. The envy dynamic consists of the ever-changing, conflictual interplay of opposing mental forces. In essence, this dialectic results from the relentless interaction of both libido and the destructive instinct and from conscious experience and its pull toward becoming unconscious. In this matrix, mental functioning maneuvers the mind to attain dynamic, ever-changing states of equilibrium. Consequently, specific anxieties, defenses, conflicts, psychopathological signs and symptoms, and compromise formations, as well as other conscious and unconscious cognitive, affective, and behavioral impairments, emerge and develop. It is to be emphasized that, in the Kleinian perspective, the universal affect of anxiety—signaling danger, fear, and conflict—always has a concrete content. This phenomenological content is called unconscious phantasy.

The theoretical framework outlined here introduces and uses phenomenologically descriptive language with meaningful application both diagnostically and in clinical dialogue—the delivery system for addressing envy. Nowadays, contact and treatment in clinical practice is brief. Diagnostic assessments are brief. Longer-term planning strategies, to be effective, are crucial to good care. *Envy theory* significantly adds to a clinician's effective diagnostic armamentarium. The clinically palpable language in this book focuses on the inferred mental phenomenology that accompanies the operations of the envy dynamic. To this end, a new lexicon of metaphors and concrete images is brought forth to suggest processes that otherwise might remain impersonal, excessively intellectualized, and abstract theoretical paradigms with stale connotations from the past (Kuhn 1996).

This phenomenologically oriented language attempts to approximate the active preconscious states of mind that animate the experiential sense of self. The content of these states of mind are composed of unconscious phantasy—abstract and ephemeral. Metaphorical approximations characterized by terms such as images, symbols, and concrete pictures are part of a language used to point to the meanings surrounding such unconscious processes. The anthropomorphic and spatial connotations used are figurative, not literal, allusions. This tighter correlation between theory and practice—clinically recognizable words, attitudes, and envious scenarios—may help streamline clinical assessments.

Plausible and useful clinical concepts are often based on empirical observations. However, for purposes of conceptual clarification, conjectured correlations to more abstract metapsychological and psychoanalytic hypotheses are included in *envy theory*. It is a premise of this book that metapsychological propositions are metaphorical similes residing on a level of abstraction and inference qualitatively different from scientific assertion and clear-cut fact.

Models of mental functioning that invoke illustrative metaphors often use artistic and concrete indicators in an attempt to paint pictures that reflect complex and elusive subjective meanings. For example, the Freudian model of psychic structure as id, ego, and superego is a shorthand way of denoting groups of intricate and complex psychic organizations and functions. These stylized forms are metaphorical approximations. They imply cognitive strategies used in a heuristic and creative spirit to suggest explanations regarding mental processes whose precise nature remains open to continuing investigation. The use of categorical statements in this book has been kept to a minimum, since statements about the detailed workings of the mind require continuing consideration, interpretation, and revision over time.

By using a phenomenological approach, *envy theory* advances the proposition that envy, foundational and nuclear, embodies itself as a psychodynamic amalgam with conscious and unconscious properties. It organizes and expresses itself by means of the experience-sensitive, object-related, and interpersonal engagements encountered at every point in development. These result in intricate and multidimensional mental states, uniquely individual and at the root of all varieties of human experience. Unconscious phantasy, unique among these states, is profoundly subjective. When recognized, it reflects the way the mind experiences itself.

Envy is foundational as it exists alongside, in interaction with, and fused with its inextricable companions, love and love's derivatives. The broad concept of envy is equated with the phenomenological experience of self-inflicted suffering. The concept of love subsumes a spectrum of affiliative relations that range from narcissism, "self-love," to "object-love" or love of the other. Self-love/esteem and object-love/caring are the phenomenologically experienced intrasubjective correlates of their concretely manifested expressions—self-caring and love behaviors toward others (for example, sharing, affection, and helping), respectively.

Juxtaposing and contrasting envy with love may appear to presume a polarized dualism that reductionistically explains intricate and complex psychological processes. The unconsidered use of such polarized constructs is perilous. Such use risks the danger of proposing a simplified clarity at the expense of underestimating the immense complexity of these issues. It is with these provisos that *envy theory* uses, in a deliberate yet cautious manner, schematic simplifications; these simplifications only suggest and approximate rather than exhaustively define features of *envy theory*.

## Human Cognition as a Binary-Processing System

An underlying epistemological supposition of this book is the principle that all cognitive and emotional awareness operates by binary-processing systems. This "base two" compass is an integral part of the phenomenology of mind. The mind has a normal, innate predilection for establishing pairs, emerging as dynamic opposites, and then using these to discover meaningful relationships and to establish values.

This innate template of constructing contradicting pairs in conjunction is a syzygy-like trend in human cognitive processes. These trends are the mind's innate orienting mechanisms. Concepts such as dualism, conflict, "the one and the many," contrast, and polarity correlate with this perspective of nature's binary template, especially from the view of epistemology—the mechanics of knowing.

Such a constitutional preference system may correlate with the natural bilateralism of the biological organism. Both sensory perception (exteroception) and motor activity have stereoscopic, stereoauditory, and left-right manual and ambulatory coordinated interaction patterns, respectively. This may reflect, as well as reinforce, binary and dualistically based adaptive functioning. A further extension of this idea is the importance of sexual dimorphism within species for both individual and species survival. Another correlation of these ideas about orientation is the faculty of proprioception. This denotes the innate mechanisms responsible for the perception of the location or position of limbs, trunk, and head in relation to one another and in space. Most of this information is nonconsciously based and mediated by the dorsal spinocerebellar tract to the cerebellum.

The perception of contrasting pairs stimulates the mind to sense distinctions and formulate comparisons. The links that fill the gaps between opposites reflect the mind's capacity for synthesis, the assemblage of meaning, and subsequent understanding. Attention to these binary, at times dualistically appearing, tendencies, therefore, is not a superfluous or reductionistic simplification. Rather, it acknowledges the valuable and pragmatic operation of inbuilt modes of ordering experience. This binary mode makes up the mind's fundamental manner of ordering information. Discrepancy is unstable and anxiety provoking; mental processes aim toward achieving fair and equitable resolutions, however tenuous these equilibriums.

The innate dependence of opposites ("unequals") on each other is presumed part of the hardwired though mutable template indigenous to mind. Sets of contraries or polar opposites may exist in a state of conflation or peculiar fusion in the dynamic unconscious. While the spectrum of these valences has roots in irrational unconscious processes (normatively typical), polar tendencies only begin to arise when the ego's preconscious and conscious mind attempts to formulate knowledge rationally. The spectrum of qualitative and quantitative distinctions that emerges from this is the matrix out of which meaning and knowledge arises. Such a proposed innate program is the nucleus that generates the universal triggering of value-laden appraisals, in other words, the inevitable launching pad arousing envy.

Although this view may connote an emphasis on dualisms and dichotomies, the functional dependence of the mind on opposites also implies an intrinsic ontological unity driving this. The need for unification acts to overarch and synthesize subsidiary dualistic elements. *Envy theory* maintains an active awareness of how dichotomous thinking emerges and is used for synthetic integration both adaptively and defensively throughout life. Dichotomous and dualistic conceptions are potential preludes to more fully developed synthetic and integrative views, ones more realistically inclusive. In other words, conflict may lead the way toward reconciliation and greater levels of complex integration.

In this sense, *envy theory* presumes all perception and conception to be based on perceived dichotomies, especially unequal opposites—awareness of split, unrelated contrasts. *The healthy maturation of envy* as discussed in this book concludes that actual equality is a necessary fiction. As envy's force softens, however, views of the self and others include a benign recognition and acceptance of the reality of unequals. When envy is modulated sufficiently (through depressive-position ascendancy), the syllogism of split, unrelated contrasts transforms into reconciled and more synthetically perceived resolutions. In this way, theories of justice and fair distribution in diverse circumstances become ego-syntonic and less conflictual.

For these reasons, in addition to assuming the binary nature of experiential information processing, a major premise of this book is that love and envy are the two primary dimensions of human experience. "Love" correlates with unity and "envy" with spoiling toward negation. Deeply intertwined and profoundly dynamic, these companions are bound together in complex and intricate ways. They constitute a dynamic oscillation more unified than split and neither truly polar nor mutually exclusive. In a sense, love and envy can be viewed as different domains that develop partly in parallel but also in interdigitated fashion. Love and its derivatives tend to be more conscious whereas envy's roots are always unconscious. That they are both essential and transformative to one another cannot be overemphasized.

Envy, itself, is not ambivalent; it cannot apprehend the positive and negative aspects of a situation. Rather it is a *preambivalent* state characterized by proclivities toward splitting and polarization. Envy has phases, chiefly excessive idealization then de-idealization and spoiling. They are in sequence, not in simultaneity. Only when envy is excessive does its proclivity to instigate intensely wide splitting become prominent in an isolated way. Thus, unless the inevitable mitigating factors around envy (love, reparation, and trends toward envy's healthy maturation) are given due consideration, the erroneous impression that envy is always the irreconcilable polar opposite of love might arise.

## Envy and the Developmental Point of View

*Envy theory* is grounded in a developmental perspective. This psychogenetic point of view denotes that mental processes have infantile origins (chronological markers) that undergo a complex genesis of growth, maturation, and development (ongoing mediation) in an interpersonal environment.

Human development, notably mental development, is the continuing product of the interplay between innate, constitutional factors and experience over the course of a lifetime. Chronological growth, biological maturation, and psychosocial development proceed by organismic growth, transactional development between nature and nurture, and environmental tutoring. The latter denotes the accentuation or inhibition of levels of innate potential through environment influences. Instinctual pressures and the *epistemophilia* within the self energize the forward thrust of the ego's development. Adaptation to inner and outer reality—including managing conflict—is a continuous, dynamic process. These are the elements that build and structure mental ontogeny.

Freud (1916–1917, 362) addressed this issue with his conception of a complemental series of factors contributing to the development of psychological disorders. He described three such leading factors: (1) inherited constitution, (2) infantile experience, and (3) accidental environmental experience—that is, trauma that occurs after infancy.

Both "a priori" and "a posteriori" factors as a whole, therefore, create personality. Inextricable mixtures of growth and maturation—contextualized, suffused, and driven by varying degrees of conflict on biopsychological levels—contribute to development. The self remains a biomental unity from birth onward and all human processes are platformed on this *biomental corporeality*. As this biomental scaffolding changes, the nuances of the experience of envy change.

In using a combined phenomenological and object relations perspective, real explanatory power emerges. For example, the mental/functional and physical/organic are seen as various ways of viewing the individual who is, in essence, one entity. This entity—the *biomental self*—is ordinarily perceived through various levels of analysis, often using a more split mind-body model. By contrast, *envy theory* regards the self as a biomental unity. In other words, mentation is the psychological side of biological neural networks. These physiological structures are organizational and functional systems formed by the connective, associative, and linking capacities of neurons. Mental and neural linkages acting in conjunction are fundamental properties of brain and person. From an experiential perspective, for example, there is an undeniably close association between the perceived way the physical body feels and how this influences emotional states of pleasurable well-being or pain and suffering.

A realistic understanding of the meaning of the self in health and psychopathology may best be approached by using measures inherent in a perspective that embraces explanatory pluralism both descriptively and etiologically. The range of explanations, therefore, spans basic, lower-order elements in conjunction with more abstract, higher-order organizing considerations. These include, for example, subjects' reports about how they feel, joined with metapsychological propositions that may explain the nature of these attitudes. Causal processes operating at several levels of explanatory abstraction influence mental processes. Patterns of "many to many" causal links between basic etiologies and their complex outcomes, especially in felt, first-person experience, are understood as typical ways the mind works (Kendler 2005).

*Envy theory*, however, opts to stress the mental dimension of this fleshy base. To emphasize the integral nature of psychological life and the physical body, the phrase *biomental self* is used. The *biomental self* always develops in an adaptive context. For example, the connection of envy with the physical body, particularly vision, is unmistakable. The term "envy" derives from the Latin words *invidia* and *invidere* meaning "to see into"; the connotation is to regard with malice. The eyes and the functions of seeing and looking are integral aspects of envy. Visual systems are exquisitely highlighted in the absence of language, both in the preverbal period and later when silence accompanies infantile gazes and stares.

Conflict organizes itself dynamically as it is created by the action of opposing forces. On a physiological level, for example, the dialectical actions of anabolism (cellular buildup) and catabolism (cellular breakdown) can be viewed as creative conflict between the buildup and deterioration of vital matter ultimately yielding metabolic homeostasis. On emotional and cognitive levels, conflict begins as recognition of discrepancies or opposites. The emergence of impulses toward reconciling these contrasts then arises and aims toward equitable resolutions. In this sense, all development both normal and disordered draws its impetus and content from the dynamisms that conflict provides.

By comparison, the Chinese Taoist notion of "yin-yang" illustrates the interaction of envy and love in mental life. An example of this would be the existence of one mountain with the simultaneous and noncontradictory coexistence of both a sunny side and side in shadow. These complementary systems in dialectical tension, in fact, make up one overall unity. In this example, the dialectic resides in the ever-changing relationship of the sun to the mountain and the observer's changing perception and interpretation of what is seen.

This use of a developmental perspective includes being cognizant of "the child within." Clinical work with children and adolescents unmistakably shows that infantile traits persist in the older child. Work with adults, as well, demonstrates the equally prevalent modes of childhood traits that persist and influence preferences and behaviors in adult life.

Infantile experience remains alive and active throughout development. These early experiences reside in the dynamically unconscious realms that are deep sources of motivation in everyday life. At all chronological periods, unconscious processes play a large part in determining attitudes, motivations, preferences, likes, dislikes, and so forth. The intimate association between the somatic self and the mental id, as repository of the dynamic unconscious, reminds us repeatedly that no mental experience can escape its fleshy footing and childhood ancestry. All experience from birth onward becomes housed as unconscious phantasy and is carried forward throughout life.

The roots of adult life always remain our childhood beginnings. The concept of a psychogenetic continuity and *envy theory's self-signature updating* denote that one's beginnings never evaporate. These archaic origins persist alongside and in dynamic interaction with newer developments. The developmental perspective recognizes that chronological growth, maturation, and development occur in linear fashion, but that everything that precedes what follows is also contained in that new production. The past becomes present in the future.

Changes in functioning do not neutralize, in toto, what preceded their newer forms. The imprint of all past experience remains alive at all times in the dynamic unconscious. These contents reside in nonconscious memory systems. Recognizing the inferred consolidations of these infantile and childhood traits expressed in observable ways in the adult mind and behavior yields deeper insights into the origins of adult preferences and psychopathology.

*Self* and its development are defined here in experiential and phenomenological terms. Self connotes the entire composite of biological/somatic and psychological/mental components that contribute to unconscious and conscious self-awareness at every chronological and developmental period. The biomental subject is the domain of the self. Figuratively, it is understood as a mercurial field of infinite dimensions of a constantly evolving ego. This idea suggests that aspects of the self are always normatively split and dissociated (nonconscious) from one another yet dynamically interactive. The course of human life is a progression from states of less developed mental coordination toward more unified, dynamic overall integration with progressively enduring stability.

The classical Freudian paradigm of psychic structure, as a whole, refers to the one self in technical terms. As mentioned previously, the terms "id," "ego," and "superego" denote shorthand metaphors referring to broad groupings constituting a team of psychological organizations and functions. All these aspects of psychic structure have both somatic and mental elements, exist in prototypical ways at birth, and quickly develop into more organized and complex forms from the neonatal period onward.

The *ego* as the core of information processing always remains virtually unconscious with both its mechanisms (primary and secondary processes that establish and maintain affective and cognitive associations) and its states of consciousness (inability and ability to be awake, alert, and to periodically demonstrate conscious awareness). The broadest ego functions are attraction and repulsion. The highly specialized dimension of the ego—the superego—structures good/assuring versus bad/punishing appraisals. It imparts a moral tone to all experience. As growth, maturation, and development proceed, the secondary processes of greater conscious awareness, rationality, and logical thought take shape and exert a stronger influence on mental functioning. Their base in the nonconscious primary processes, however, is never eliminated. As Ulric Neisser (1967, 279) has said:

> The products of the crude, wholistic, and parallel "primary processes" are usually elaborated by the "secondary processes," which include deliberate manipulation of information by an active agent. An analogy with the "executive routines" of computer programs shows that an agent need not be a *homunculus*. However, motivation clearly enters at several points in these processes to determine their outcome. Thus, an integration of cognitive and dynamic psychology is necessary to the understanding of higher mental processes.

All these contribute to continuous, dynamic self-regulation at every developmental period. That portion of ego responsible for perception and conscious awareness makes up an individual's conscious center of attention. It has great significance since it makes conscious awareness and intentional adaptation possible. This conscious or wakeful aspect of the ego (phenomenal consciousness) represents a relatively minuscule percentage of the total ego, as well as of the entire self, which largely remains actively, descriptively, and operatively nonconscious. A large portion of the ego always rests in a preattentive or preconscious state, which can easily become conscious. Most of the ego, however, exists in a state of countercathexis—that is, tenacious repression. This repressed information is unavailable to the ego's conscious awareness. It is dynamically repressed and functions according to the principles of primary process cognition.

The aforementioned is a backdrop to the use of the phrases *ego center of gravity*, *dynamic spot psyche*, and *self-signature updating*. These phrases indicate the degree of organizational integration of psychic structure and functioning inferred to exist at any chronological age. They reflect the developmental framework of *envy theory*, which emphasizes plasticity and biomental reorganization.

*Ego center of gravity* connotes a dynamically organizing structure that reflects the way the ego experiences itself in the entire self-system at any particular moment. It is an inner view of the overall status in which an individual finds himself at any point in development. The *self-signature updating* concept reflects the continually changing face of this inner, continuous mental repositioning. An outside observer recognizes this as that individual's identity. The concept of the *dynamic spot psyche* suggests a cross-sectional profile of the mind in developmental flux. It can be likened to the pulse of the mind at any given time. It is more labile and fluctuating, and represents the immediate state (equilibrium-disequilibrium, conflict, adaptation) of the psyche.

One's subjective sense of self correlates with these three more technically termed theoretical phrases. They indicate the ego's conscious, preconscious, and preattentive awareness of itself described from various perspectives. These concepts represent individual identity—in an experiential sense—at any given moment. This intrasubjective and intersubjective sense of self is the "me" to whatever extent language can adequately articulate this phenomenological fact. From the developmental conception of the ego-object positions that Melanie Klein has proposed, each of these three phrases corresponds to points on the dynamic, oscillating spectrum of the paranoid-schizoid← →depressive positions where the self may be positioned at any given experiential point.

The developmental point of view, accordingly, apprehends the individual as product of an intricate developmental process organized and integrated over time. Instinctual pressures spur development within the self, notably of the life instinct and, *envy theory* would add, the *epistemophilia*. In infancy, what is innate transacts with both a caregiving environment of safety and containment and the absence of inordinate infantile stressors to maintain forward developmental movement. Equally, it denotes an individual who is simultaneously infant, child, adolescent, and adult in varying proportion *at once in the here and now*.

Automatic *self-signature updating* produces what in clinical situations can be described as an individual's *dynamic spot psyche*. This means that, at every point in life, the individual is not only just that person, but, as well, all that has gone before. Each strata of chronological development, while partly integrated in the current whole, also remains available and active, somehow, in its archaic form and original model. Phenomenologically, this composite identity or spot self experienced in the immediate moment is an individual's *ego center of gravity* or *dynamic spot psyche*.

Recognizing earlier states and traits in an older individual may be easier than the reverse. On the other hand, seeing an infant as a future child, for example, involves a speculative view with potentials for eventual expression in the fluidly malleable course of development. Guidance, for instance, can provide opportunities for the fruition of anticipated potential achievements. Inspired guidance deriving from this sensed "shadow of the future," of course, is more properly the role of parents and educators who anticipate, guide, and optimistically encourage a youngster's ongoing positive accomplishments. It may also apply to one person's own early recognition of burgeoning values, aspirations, ambitions, and future goals.

In many ways, the course of psychological development over time resembles the development of a dream. Dreams are complex formations beginning with a base of latent dream thoughts—raw neural arousal—elicited by masses of biological and experiential stimuli. The goal of the dream is to resolve conflict—uncomfortable dichotomies—and to reorganize information processing toward less confusion, by either re-presenting chaotic data or merely evacuating it into concrete clumps that must remain unintelligible. The reorganizations resulting from the dream process may also function as the raw data prompting creative endeavors. Dreams often function as experimental training grounds for future problem solving in the waking state.

Primary, less organized elements, therefore, undergo a secondary revision to produce an organization that can manifest itself experientially in a way that is more intelligible. The final product then becomes a screened re-presentation, which appears as a quasi-rational dream tenuously acceptable to the secondary, more conscious processes of the rational ego. In a sense, the manifest dream is a rationalization. It is the result of making more primitive emotional states appear more plausible by justifying them using strategies proper to the conscious, awake state—namely, seemingly rational and reality-based adaptive motivations. The primitive, absurd, incoherent, sexual, and destructive aspects of nonconscious information processing, thereby, are muted and sanitized often to the point of distortion. A major aim of such processes is to reduce and contain anxiety.

Infantile and childhood experience, in a manner similar to this dream-work, revises itself over the course of time so that, in adolescence and by adulthood, those early mental facts are only remembered in disguised camouflages characteristic of adult experience. Not only are the adult memories of one's own childhood euphemized in this way but also conventional views about children in general become replete with beliefs that omit their raw and distasteful sexual and destructive components.

As development progresses, people identify with their psychological "body armor" made up of idiosyncratically erected defense mechanisms. The necessary development of defense mechanisms throughout psychological development amounts to self-defense or the containment and modulation of anxiety. These accretions are felt as one's experiential sense of self. Excessive defenses are likely to produce a sanitized, overedited end product characterized by an effete state of mind, one overrefined to the point of being ineffectual. This sense of self reflects the net result of a compounded agglomeration of misrepresentations and rationalizations over time.

The demands of civilization, often felt with malaise in an atmosphere of discontent, reinforce an individual's emotional body armor. The ever-present pressure of the social context has a major impact since the ego is always acutely aware of and affected by both its own perception of how others see it and the actual demands that others make. This situation, in part referred to as "impression management," reflects the continuing struggle between the individual and society's mandates to conform.

Last, all development is viewed as a continuous and dynamic process, active and creative at all points. Processes such as those that characterize the two fundamental developmental units (discussed at length in chapter 4)—namely, the paranoid-schizoid and depressive positions—are dynamic and not merely chronological operations restricted to the first year of life. Although the paranoid-schizoid position is developmentally prior to the depressive position, there is *considerable overlap*. They are developmental challenges that continue across all life's chronological thresholds. Their recurrent oscillation is axiomatically invariant. Together, they make up the principal psychodynamic configurations of mental life at all points after early infancy.

Both the paranoid-schizoid and depressive positions are principal and equal in importance because one requires the other to be present in some form for the other to operate. *Their overlapping is real and significant.* In some sense, the depressive position is the paranoid-schizoid position qualitatively reconfigured. In *envy theory*, descriptions of psychodynamic processes frequently invoke the mechanisms and maneuvers characteristic of these positions—*as if they were occurring anew in the here and now. They, in fact, are always freshly activating and reconfiguring the personality.*

## The Developmental Point of View and Psychotherapeutic Technique

*Envy theory* and propositions about *nuclear envy* provide fertile lines of investigation in the cognitive sciences, the political sciences, anthropology, and the humanities. An important pragmatic contribution is in the broad range of psychotherapies including psychoeducation.

The developmental or psychogenetic point of view has great value in psychotherapeutic technique. For example, this is an important emphasis in intensive, psychodynamic psychotherapies. The establishment of an intimate dyadic relationship simulates the early mother-child relationship and may facilitate the reemergence—in the here and now—of feelings and conflicts first experienced at that formative time, especially regarding envy. Other psychotherapies with different modalities may also be useful if attention is paid to emotional and interpersonal factors along with the cognitive and behavioral.

Paused, sensitive, responsive, and intuitive listening is the therapist's principal technique in beginning to achieve mutually effective communication. To the extent that this is accomplished, such a therapeutic equipoise establishes the therapist's capacity to make contact with and integratively contain the patient's conflictual projections. This creates conditions whereby the patient is more open to expressing what is being experienced.

This mutuality creates the groundwork for future cognitive-affective reorganization, linking, and understandability both for patient and therapist. Quality psychotherapy, in effect, aims to refine information processing in a shared communicative dialogue. In adults experiencing serious life crises, a sense of jaded negativity rooted in unconscious conditioning can stymie positive change. Quality psychotherapy identifies such attitudes and counters the insidiously creeping cynicism that may erode the integrity of the therapeutic relationship since envy inevitably affects both participants.

Explaining the psychotherapy of envy in detail is beyond the scope of this book. The details of envy and guidelines toward a philosophy of therapy, however, run throughout this text. Classical analytic protocols such as interpretation of affect, defense, and impulse using proper tact and timing may be too academic and constraining. In fact, effective therapeutic interpretations often elucidate whole situations. Artificially isolating affect, defense, or impulse out of context offers a partial knowledge that risks obfuscating understanding, if not increasing resistance.

The psychotherapy of envy is making contact with the emotional center of both participants. It requires a deep honesty and wish to participate in helping, though avoiding control and manipulation. For the most part, language is the chief vehicle although gesture and silence play important roles. The aforementioned approach may arouse the epistemophilic impulses in both parties and enhance the search for the psychological truth of the patient's experience.

One of the chief technical tools used in psychodynamically informed treatments is called "interpretation." This technique denotes the therapist's perceptive understanding of and communication to the patient of the unconscious meaning and overall significance of subjective experience both articulated and unarticulated. It includes understanding the spectrum of unconscious wishes embodied as unconscious phantasy underlying emotional and cognitive attitudes. Calling attention to these using therapeutic language and gesture denotes interpretation—articulating in explicit terms what is implicit and maintains problematic thinking, feeling, and behaviors.

Melanie Klein gave unique status to the interpretation of transference in treatments. It underlies the mutative action of therapy through its capacity to create conditions that promote the patient's progressive experiencing of insight. *Transference* denotes the unconscious transfer of mental contents, total experiential situations, from patient to therapist. These mental contents contain both unorganized affects and impulses together with more organized unconscious phantasies that include structured, though primitive, object relations configurations.

These action sequences contain emotions, defenses, attitudes, and much more. They often take the form of concrete narratives reflecting life experiences. They also may be expressed as apparently random thoughts, free associations, and dreams. The play sequences of children reflect expressions of unconscious phantasy. Unconscious object relations inform how the patient behaves in language, gesture, and action with the therapist.

Splitting, projection, introjection, identification, and projective identification are among the principal mental processes that occur both intrapsychically and interpersonally to establish transference. In psychodynamically oriented settings, transference emerges as it gradually deepens in intensity over time. It is a compass that orients the therapist to the position of the patient's inner world. The patient's *dynamic spot psyche*, current *ego center of gravity*, and *self-signature* are emblematic of this inner world.

Verbal constructions formulated by therapist and imparted to patient denote consciously articulated descriptions and interpretations of affect, defense, and transference in the here and now—as they are expressed between the two participants. These instance-specific statements point to, clarify, and reveal the unconscious significance of discrete aspects of the patient's current experience and communications. Constructions, in this sense, may be elemental interpretations of simple or more complex emotions and defenses, or more elaborate statements that connect previously unlinked issues that are relatively current. The therapist can glean the status of transference phenomena at any given moment when he or she asks the question: Who am I now in the patient's transference experience?

In intensive psychodynamic treatments, greater interpretive elaboration takes the form of "reconstructions." These denote genetic interpretations that *link* here and now interpretations of the transference with the patient's past memories and unconscious phantasies. Although the here and now interpretation of transference reflects the way the patient is responding to the therapist at that moment, it remains a partial reflection of how the patient is relating to his infantile objects on the level of unconscious phantasy. Once this basic level of the transference is articulated, it may then be associatively linked with postinfancy object relations of childhood and adolescence. The latter include the patient's reported and retrieved early memories of perceived interactions with childhood figures. Therapeutically effective reconstructions such as this require extensive and long-lasting treatment in order for memories, feelings, and insights to grow and coalesce into understandable convictions.

The preceding discussion only sketchily outlines psychodynamic technique, the technique most suitable to the therapy of unconscious envy. Certainly, ample time is required to achieve a depth of understanding. Time is necessary for the mutative consolidation of cumulative insights to evolve and develop. In general, briefer and less intensive therapeutic situations make the use of the aforementioned techniques less likely. Logistical factors including a patient's needs, preferences, finances, and so forth may preclude long-term treatment. Briefer treatments, in fact, do have utility and often may be the norm. Their value should not be underestimated. Hence, a realistic orientation to the therapy of envy necessarily frames it in contexts of time, frequency of contact, and level of depth aspired to by the patient. Skill, a deft, light touch, and sensitivity characterize good technique. Envy, however, is exceedingly obstinate. Change requires unflagging motivation and sufficient time.

## The Value of Recognizing the Role of Envy in Everyday Life

Both the recognition of envy and its therapeutic management have value. A premise of *envy theory* is that the maturation, amelioration, and soften-ing of envy may substantially raise one's quality of life. Quality of life refers to successful adaptation to reality, less mental suffering, deepening insight, broader range of self-understanding, improved interpersonal relationships, and real-life accomplishments. Psychological insight, in effect, a quantum broadening of conscious awareness, denotes incrementally increasing levels of understanding one's own enduring dispositions. Knowledge and skill de-velopment in this area afford the potential to adapt to weaknesses in natural inclinations as well as strengthen undeveloped assets.

Mental pain and emotional suffering in part result from experiences per-ceived as inordinately stressful. Included in this are severe forms of conflict, fear, anxiety, envy, depression, and guilt. Interpersonal relations, accord-ingly, also suffer. The operation of unmanaged, excessive envy plays a major role in producing and perpetuating a compromised quality of life. *Envy management skills training* (chapter 9), for example, is especially useful as part of child and adolescent psychoeducation. It significantly aids in fostering self-management abilities. Therapeutic interventions coupled with an intro-spective examination of the role of experiential envy are valuable assets that can promote self-understanding and improved social relations.

## Envy and Insight: Mutative Treatment Issues

Melanie Klein (1928) and Wilfred Bion (1962a, 1962b) were aware of envy's strictures on cognition. They indicated this understanding in formulating their concepts of the "epistemophilic impulse" and the "K" link, respectively.

Bion's expansion, especially from a cognitive perspective, of Klein's discoveries has considerably added to the further development of her findings. K link denotes the acquisition and consolidation of knowledge as meaning; epistemophilic impulse denotes the desire and search for knowledge and meaning.

Bion equates the minus K link (-K)—thwarting of the acquisition and consolidation of knowledge—with the action of envy. The spoiling of K or the "epistemophilic impulse" confounds the drive toward comprehending meaning on all levels. The need to discover and uncover meaning—that is, the "epistemophilic impulse"—is inherent in the matrix of life. It is central to relatedness both intrapsychically (object relations) and interpersonally (person-to-person contact). With the many other instinctual impulses (trends toward affiliation, connectedness, a "to and fro" proximity, making distinctions, and destructiveness), the epistemophilic impulse drives the mind in its quest for experience. Every search for truth is the search for personal truth, the meaning of one's own life. An understanding-based therapy orientation with a psychodynamic component in an intimate interpersonal context, therefore, is the principal mutative mode for achieving the insights necessary to effectively and substantively treat envy.

Insight—looking into one's world of unconscious psychic reality and discovering meaningful connections—can be seen as the contradistinction to "outsight." Outsight is looking outside of oneself to attribute accountability to things externally located. When they are unowned, such attitudes and behaviors are negative and socially undesirable. By contrast, when people emphasize outer accomplishments, this may imply trivializing inner or self-development. Outsight strongly correlates with "extrospection." It may take the form, for example, of idealizing the merits of science, in the pursuit of discovering objective truth through the accumulation of measurable, observable data in research studies about mental phenomena. Outsight may then attribute primary meaning to this body of knowledge, one having privileged reality status. Exclusive reliance on such an overvalued point of view may reflect a defensive avoidance of the examination of introspective experience, data less objectively observable and measureable.

Outsight, in this sense, is the counterpoint to insight. Although the term "outsight" is awkward, it accents a relative *under*emphasis on a balanced focus that sufficiently includes looking into one's inner world and situating reasonable accountability for impulse origination and motivated action there—a personal locus of control. This "outsight," attributional orientation, is a common situation. It is seen in those who feel that others largely determine the good and bad consequences in their lives. In such a passive state of mind, people grossly underestimate the effects their own thinking, feeling, intentions, and behavior have on themselves and, in turn, on others. Judgments of the causes of outcomes are passively attributed to others and, in turn, the "outsighted" individual feels passive and powerless.

Children and adolescents, for example, have great difficulty with issues of personal responsibility. Largely, this is normative and an expectable feature of phase-specific development. By contrast, adults with personality or character disorders regularly attribute personal distress, not to their motivations and choices, but to others. The other pole of "outsight" is excessive emphasis on outer accomplishments or successes. Often, this correlates with an underestimation of the value of psychological development, whose intangibility may be seen as implying unimportance.

The mechanism behind "outsight" is the subject's defensive use of projective identification. Often, internal psychic material (anxiety, affect, conflict, wishes, phantasies, and so forth) becomes excessively unmanageable and cannot be contained in even rudimentary cognitive structures. This experience becomes so unbearably painful both nonconsciously and consciously that it reflexively mobilizes packets of this raw information and relocates them outside the self in another, or in the material conditions of the environment. Such recognition falls short of taking ownership. Outsight correlates with passive mental states and diminished self-efficacy and feelings of self-agency. Volition becomes impaired and varying degrees of abulia result.

Mental distress, therefore, is often attributed to feeling overburdened by "stressors" in the environment, usually the demands of others—one's parents, spouse, and employers, for example. Such an externally positioned locus of control attributes power and authority to outside influences and, in turn, strongly connotes a personal sense of passivity and ineffectance. Volition and actionable intentionality become disabled. A sense of the capacity to change in actively motivated ways is muted or absent. To the extent that envy blinds insight, the ability to reflect on and take ownership of one's thoughts, feelings, attitudes, and phantasies is also muted.

Insight, the therapeutic and reparative counterpoint to envy, denotes that moment of discovery by the self about previously unknown aspects of itself. Insight denotes the awakened conscious awareness of previously unrecognized *relationships*. This denotes the linking of experiential relationships. The therapeutic examination of both internal object relations and external interpersonal relationships brings this about. To the degree that this is achieved, unconscious phantasies, the subtext of these inner world relationships, are reconfigured, and psychic structure is changed.

The discovery of insights is, in mental fact, an expression of personal creativeness. It cannot be imparted by another but must originate as an intrasubjective creation, the flowering of previously unrecognized linkages. It is the moment when meaning intensifies. This galvanizes the integration of previously scattered fragments so that they coalesce into more organized wholes. This newfound coherence then changes the meaning of one's experience. Personal agency, a sense of being able to take responsibility for one's experience and successfully act on the world, becomes self-empowering.

Insight and conviction based on "lived" experience go hand-in-hand. An understanding of "ego relations" and the *epistemophilia* within the self is crucial to this. Meaning is meaningful to the extent that it goes beyond the moment of its inception and, in a startlingly silent manner, insinuates something intuitively profound. In this way, insight has an invitational quality that evokes the promise of more to unfold in the future.

Insight denotes processes more than those included in intellectual and rational cognition. It is both a multidimensional and continuous construct that connotes much more than mere awareness of illness. Insight may be the more conscious cognitive connotation of the experience of intuition; it has an inwardly sensual, preconscious connotation, one characterized by emotional conviction.

Insight fosters integrative psychological refinements. These are brought about by repeated experiences of self-observation, mainly introspection and self-analysis. Psychotherapies enhance this. This mental growth broadens the experiential scope of one's inner world and is an incentive toward further exploration. In this sense, insight has inspirational, motivational, and self-perpetuating features that encourage personality growth and development. Insight counters personal anonymity. An individual comes to know himself more clearly both emotionally and intellectually. In many ways, insight correlates with a sense of unequivocal commitment to, or at least a flash of, rational and intelligent self-assurance.

The relationship between insight and learning is complex. Insight consists of a series of infinitely repeating end points that signal the discovery of novel relations between and among previously disparate elements of information. This includes recognition of both innate predispositions and environmentally acquired incentives. In complex ways, these contribute to motivation and behavior. Insight is an amalgam of integrated affective and intellectual linkages among modes of understanding. It is usually the outcome of intentionally focused psychological work that gleans from both the past and the "here and now." It has "gestalt-like" qualities, an integrating recognition transcendental and all encompassing. On empirical levels, the expression of wit—clever observations with elements of insight—reflects this.

Insight, as proposed here, should be distinguished from that type of learning that is more intellectual and deals primarily with conscious data as, for example, the learning of mathematics, chemistry, or physics. Another form of learning is the Socratic method. It consists of guidance and suggestion toward a series of understandings about material less than overtly conscious *but not "absolutely" unconscious, as is unconscious envy*, the subject of this book.

The Socratic method involves what has been called a "skills-based" approach and is used in active cognitive psychotherapies that aim to uncover the maladaptive preconscious assumptions inferred to underlie distressing symptoms and unwanted behaviors. In addition, there is the learning that occurs on a primarily behavioral level through stimulus-response training. Combinations of these types of learning are used in a range of cognitive and behavioral therapies. Modality-specific clinical indications for these important tools range from unsafe behaviors to consciously perceived, unwanted attitudes that cause distress and are impairing. Discrete and clear-cut signs and symptoms are targeted in those treatments.

In contrast, the types of psychotherapeutic interventions most aptly geared toward the realization of insight are those that include psychodynamic orientations. Insight, in this sense, results from the internal self-modulation achieved by the patient, himself. The therapist does not impart it actively. Psychodynamically oriented interpretations that acknowledge the complex interplay of internal forces in loving and hating act to facilitate this sort of modulation. They especially address the destructively omnipotent aspects of envy and its unconscious mental geometry. In contemporary treatments, however, therapists use interventions that include elements from many of these orientations to the extent deemed suitable for a particular patient's varied and changing needs. Theoretical and clinical pluralism constitutes the largest sector of practice in current treatment strategies.

A working familiarity with the theory of envy, moreover, may have value as a practical diagnostic tool rather than only as a treatment technique. Reasons for this are the obstinate nature of envy and what is viewed in contemporary times as the impracticality of longer-lasting, psychodynamic approaches and psychotherapeutic techniques that aim at "deep analysis." They are not preferred because they are time consuming, not instantaneous, and they are costly.

The therapy of envy is intensive and requires time in order for insight skills to develop. Using the Kleinian paradigm, insight may also be understood as that momentary flash of the realization of new meaning that hierarchically restructures the "depressive position" (discussed in chapters 4 and 9). This occurs by a dip into the realm of nameless, unconscious processes in the service of achieving more transcendent mental configurations of consciousness, characterized by increased self-knowledge and greater emotional stability. It is an ultrasensory, ultraperceptual, and ultraconceptual excursion into the "id."

Expeditions toward this end are turbulent and inevitably evoke intense anxieties usually related to fears of uncovering the normative psychotic aspects that inescapably lurk in the hidden recesses of the mind. The vivid experience of strong emotions that often accompanies perceptive realizations and notable insights is an abreaction of affect that adds to the conviction produced by insight. It is only by mustering the courage to "blow off one's tenuous mask of sanity" that a brutal face-to-face encounter with one's inner world of psychic reality may be discovered. In these momentary states of insight, a greater awareness of relations and gestalts of meaning may emerge.

Again, in Kleinian terms, insight sparks further integration of aspects of the primal elements that comprise the "paranoid-schizoid position" (discussed in chapter 4). An advance from disjointedness to wholeness, extreme to integrated, occurs. The primal and elemental constituents of the mind galvanize into primary and secondary organizations with symbolic meaning. Further advances of reparation in the depressive position occur. Hostility and sorrow are traversed. More compassionate and refined experiential states characterized by a deeper self-understanding follow. The entire experiential self-system undergoes a shift from harshness to a softening characterized by more relaxedness, cheerfulness, and humor.

In effective therapeutic situations, empathy and compassion facilitate emergent understandability. These resources reflect the therapist's ability to use normalized projective identification and introjective receptivity, the foundations for empathy and intuition. The use of empathy in the therapeutic situation is part of the active process of intuitive listening. It is active listening achieved in a state of mental equipoise. It is mental receptivity rather than motoric expression in either directive language or action. It empowers the effective interpretation of conflict and thus the mutative organization of insight. All this counters the creeping cynicism that the subtle and "ununderstandable" dynamics of envy may stimulate in the therapist's attitude.

Therapeutic compassion acts as the capacity to sensitively bear the anxiety and suffering that the patient's material conveys. Appropriate therapeutic interventions offer the patient the opportunity to generate the insights that may extend his conscious knowledge of himself, his self-understanding, and achieve a greater capacity for self-analysis. The patient, therefore, achieves both insight and a new relation of empathy and compassion both in himself and toward his objects. These objects include subjective construals from the past as well as real people in the here-and-now. This enhancement of the *epistemophilia* within the self acts to gradually organize and link seemingly incongruent communications into meaningful realizations. Both active and passive information processing on conscious and nonconscious levels is refined.

Insight and an overall emotional and intellectual restructuring—personality growth and development—go hand-in-hand. This implies that memory has produced a change that is lasting and will affect future experience. Insight, inspiration, and intuition are related to this. Insight shapes outsight and so acts to improve conditions in both the inner world and the outer social environment.

## Summary

Using Melanie Klein's discovery of primary envy, I have attempted to rethink and develop it in detail by using the conceptualization *nuclear envy*. I have broadened the idea of envy by adding a novel construct—*the healthy maturation of envy*. This hopeful emphasis underscores self-development and an improved quality of life.

*Ego relations* denote the intrapsychic dynamics of aspects of the *biomental self* interrelating with each other intramurally (within the self). The ego's own self-awareness becomes the crucible in which love (self-love and object-love) and destructiveness (envy, hate, and aggression) take expression. Ego as experiencer, and object as experienced, coexist at birth. The actual mother-infant relationship is the reality scene in which this subjective drama begins and develops. The nascent ego at this time grasps an experiential object, however partial or featural this may be.

Both ego and its objects, present from the start of life, develop over time. The ontogenesis of this developmental process is driven by the inherent *epistemophilia* of the self. This epistemophilic wish to understand proceeds from the natural interaction of libidinal/reparative and destructive/vitiating forces. These drive anticipation, expectation, attention, and interest in, and the ego's exploratory use of, a survival-based meaningful attachment to an object. This attachment denotes a relation of expansiveness hallmarked by loving, hateful, and envious affective attitudes. *Envy theory* puts equal emphasis on the dual components of these—the intrapsychic and interpersonal.

*Object relations* here denote the infant's meaningful connection to the mother's body and mind. This correlates with prototypical and primary information processing and affective self-structuring. These object relations grow, mature, and develop over time yet remain foundational reference points throughout life. Creativeness, destructiveness, and self-understanding impel the individual toward the goal of meaningful survival in the interpersonal world.

An outline of the essential elements of *nuclear envy* is presented. Its primary denotation highlights its virtually irreducible status and primacy, together with love, in building the personality. Love or libidinal processes are the mental expressions of the primary, unconscious biomental life instincts.

The life instinct is a broad abstract construct—a shorthand concept— that denotes the urge to expand on all levels from the somatic through the cognitive and emotional. In the paranoid-schizoid position, primitive love toward the part-object (featural aspects of the mother that are necessarily incomplete and aspiring toward some manner of completion) takes the form of *elemental idealization*; in the depressive position, love toward the whole object (the mother as person in entirety felt as a separate individual) takes the form of *love proper*.

When destructive impulses are superseded by internal loving attitudes, primary love facilitates the introjection of the internal good object. This focal point of *nuclear love* becomes firmly established, to some extent, and is the conduit for the effective internalization of development-promoting nurturance—food, love, and understanding. The infant can accept what mother generously gives to the extent that envy and greed are not excessive.

Vitiating (envy) and destructive (hate) processes are the mental expressions of the primary, unconscious biomental death instinct—another broad emblematic designation. Destructiveness manifests differently in the two fundamental developmental units. *Spoiling envy* characterizes the paranoid-schizoid position; *aggressive hate* characterizes the depressive position.

The experiential qualities of love and envy are also described phenomenologically. In the context of a developmental perspective, the postinfancy individual is an experiential self existing simultaneously as infant, child, and adult in unconscious phantasy. In other words, the paranoid-schizoid and depressive positions are alive and well and active. This theoretical conjecture has utility in clinical work, especially since it draws on the living psychological past that always plays a significant part in creating the mental here-and-now. Automatic *self-signature updating* reflects this coherence of past and present at every experiential moment.

The elucidation and articulation of the experiential inner world at any moment is a window into unconscious phantasy. Some issues related to psychotherapies have been discussed. The instance-specific pulse of the mind is called the *dynamic spot psyche*. Insight as a multidimensional and continuous process is named as the principal vehicle that galvanizes the integration of the ego. This acts to facilitate *the healthy maturation of envy* expressing itself as admiration, gratitude, generosity, realistic appreciation, interdependence, mutuality, sharing, and a genuine willingness to help. It also expresses itself in other forms of normal self-love and love behaviors. Individual consciousness, in effect, steadily reconfigures itself toward more alert states of insightful self-awareness as unmodulated envy recedes.

The relation of envy to insight is discussed. Insight, a form of epistemophilic integration, coherence, and containment, is a self-modulation achieved by the patient, himself. The therapist's perceptive understanding of the complex interplay between the patient's unconscious and conscious life is communicated by verbal clarifications and interpretations in treatment situations. Calling attention to this interplay creates conditions whereby the patient, himself, may integrate previously unassociated experiential relationships. Information processing both conscious and nonconscious is refined.

Insight goes beyond mere awareness of psychological distress and its causation. It increases the patient's conscious knowledge of greater portions of his total personality, self-understanding, and capacity for self-analysis. It is intellectual self-understanding accompanied by profound emotional conviction. Insight and a new relation to both the self and its objects are characterized by an improved capacity for empathy and compassion. All these act as mutative factors in reparation and personality change. Insight and learning occur in tandem. Insight and healthy "outsight" go hand in hand to improve inner and outer conditions: namely, the inner world of experiential reality and the outer world of interpersonal and social relations—outer accomplishments.

# CHAPTER FOUR

# Human Psychological Development: Theoretical Underpinnings

## Introduction

Human psychological development and character formation are driven by the dialectically intertwined attitudes of love, hate, and envy. Organized, subliminal structures that embody these attitudes are configured in the preconscious aspects of the ego as unconscious phantasy. Ego encompasses all structures and functions responsible for information processing and storage.

*Envy theory*, in part, relies on formulations comprising the lived aspects of psychodynamic paradigms to elucidate inferred nonconscious processes, substrata behind conscious experiential states. These constructs include aspects of both conceptual and operational definitions. Some familiarity with the classical ideas in psychoanalytic psychology is essential to understanding how envy operates. By setting parameters around a range of specific concepts, *envy theory* attempts to distinguish and describe by intellectual assessment and measurement the processes behind the patient's reported narrative. This illustrates how the subject experiences himself, his mentally intended actions, and their effects on others.

*Unconscious phantasy* is the drama played out in the inner world, the unconscious dimensions of mind. It denotes internalized part- and whole-object *relations* with their particular, accompanying anxieties, conflicts, and defenses. More precisely, part-object relations principally govern unconscious phantasy. Unconscious phantasy constitutes the elemental meaning-laden units of mental activity. Its correlate in cognitive science terms is the neural net profile. It underlies all attitudes—positive and negative evaluative responses of an individual in the experience of self, others, and world.

Unconscious phantasies are dynamic units, the mentalized precipitates of biomental instinctual drives. This mentalization process describes the way the biological organism develops into an experiencing psyche. Animated depictions of various aspects of the ego (experiencer) interacting with its objects (idiosyncratic perceptions of persons experienced) portray these unconscious events; this is how unconscious phantasy registers mentally. These units motivate, organize, and structure the ego's relations to its objects in primarily unconscious ways.

Such dramatic scenarios are not typical visual images, although they may manifest as visually appearing dream sequences in the sleep state. The spontaneous and creative playfulness of children is an example of the externalization of unconscious phantasy. In child therapies, play becomes a vehicle for the exploration and understanding of unconscious processes in a way similar to the use of dreams in adults. After puberty, unconscious phantasy comes closest to consciously awake experience in sexual preferences and the sexual fantasies that accompany sexual self-stimulation and sexual activity.

Unconscious phantasy may be correlated with neural network information-processing systems structured and modified by environmental and emotional stimuli. These experiential imprints have memory-like functions and significantly influence all states of mind—attitudes, moods, and displayed behaviors. They do not depend on conscious thinking, and may participate in procedural and associative memory registration. These are intimately allied with constructs such as corporeal intelligence. This fleshy store of information contains both unmentalized (corporeal body) and mentalizing (psychological id) elements infusing the preattentive points of view of consciousness. The psychodynamic descriptions of mind used here aim to convey the vividness of the inner world, especially its role as the unconscious subtext of conscious experience.

The essence of unconscious phantasy is its *omnipotence*, a mock, false illusion of completeness, might, and self-sufficiency. This phantasied self-dependency makes it *felt* in a strikingly powerful way as a concrete subjective experience, and drives its virtual disregard of reality. It denotes the irrational components in information processing. Omnipotence denotes that unconscious phantasies are *experienced as having taken, are taking, and will take effect*. In other words, at this deepest level of unconscious processes, the very emergence of an impulse takes shape as an unconscious phantasy virtually fulfilling itself. The structures, pressures, and forces in unconscious phantasy are imbued with this quality of unlimited power drawn from the dynamic unconscious.

While having important distinguishing nuances, the phantasy of omnipotence (a state) and construct of primary process nonconscious thinking (a functional process) are virtually synonymous. Since all this is virtual (more mental simulation than real), no real substantive and lasting change occurs. Cycles of unconscious phantasy's efflorescence vacillate with their disappearance. Disappointment and frustration are potent triggers for this.

After infancy, the secondary processes of reality testing and rationality expand. What was almost exclusively virtual is now beginning to transition into the material world of more permanence and actuality. Through the ego, these higher mental processes act to modify omnipotence, but not eliminate its persistent and overriding influence on feeling and thinking. In general, omnipotence shapes/contains two basic aims: (1) the subject's drive to control or possess the overvalued (idealized or demonized) object to the ultimate point of identifying/fusing with it, and (2) the subject's attempt to control the overvalued object by domination and subjugation to the point of humiliation and torture. The latter is preeminently the vehicle of real, manic aggression, while envy in the former is accompanied by unbearable ego pain and autosuffering. Omnipotence, power, and control always go hand-in-hand.

Envy, for example, in its attempt to control the envied, partially gratifying object by spoiling it, simultaneously inflates both further omnipotence and excessive narcissism (pathological narcissism) in the subject. While envious spoiling is destructive in this way, in the end, it becomes a self-inflicted and self-directed attack.

In contrast to and not sharply distinct from envious destructiveness, aggression is a more object- (not self-) directed attack on a dangerously perceived, nongratifying object. Envy's narcissistic omnipotence seeks to spoil the hated ideal object, whereas aggressive omnipotence seeks to dominate and subjugate the hated bad object. Envious destructiveness has an offensive and spoiling quality in contrast to the more defensive and controlling quality of aggressive force. Both center on issues of aggressive control using mechanisms of projective identification. The overall destructiveness resulting from envy and aggression, however, forms admixtures that are exceedingly difficult to differentiate.

Considering shifts in the psychic economy of libidinal and destructive energies is an abstract way of describing the motivating circuitry behind envy.

Excessive narcissism, for example, denotes an unbalanced excess of libidinal stores within the ego. Libido seeks expansion; excess libidinal stores denote lavish aggrandizement. Emphasis is on an inflated ego. This is a libidinal omnipotence taking the phenomenological form of excessive experiential self-idealization. In vernacular terms, it is arrogance, pride, and vanity. Its counterpart in the experience of the object is excessive idealization, an object seen as "strikingly" perfect. Both of these are corollaries of and defenses against excessive envy. These are paranoid-schizoid configurations, which, when excessively consolidated, may result in various types of psychopathology. For example, when destructive forces are heightened, reversals occur. Libidinal omnipotence in the self diminishes as envious devaluation of the object ultimately reverses into a spoiling devaluation of the self—a self-induced, undermining self-defeat.

This section specifically deals with intrapsychic, mostly nonconscious, processes. It must be remembered, however, that these psychodynamic operations are the inferred underbelly of real behaviors carried out in real time. For example, acts of violence such as theft, assault, rape, murder, and war have complex antecedents, many of which may include the unconscious phantasy scenarios of wished-for omnipotence and control mentioned here.

In contrast, when the ego in the depressive position puts a qualitative or quantitative excess of libidinal energy into itself, the condition of manic grandiosity and excessive overvaluation of self is expressed. Maniacally frenzied behaviors express this. Unlike the insular narcissism of envy, manic aggrandizement typically requires a real target—another person to intimidate and control. A libidinal inverse, the object deflated to contemptuous proportions along with the ego's glee of *schadenfreude*, matches this. This negative correlation is a haughty contempt for an object deemed inferior, not superior. This excess has pathological status and is usually a defensive flight away from sufficiently facing and working through the psychodynamic, functional intricacies of the depressive position—real concern for the other: empathy, caring, sparing the object harm, and reparation.

Furthermore, it may be a defensive distraction hiding its roots in unintegrated, split-off, and excess envy. Split-off envy, when projected into the object to devalue it, may at first cause states of hyperidealization. The manic subject sees the object in overly inflated ways, an ambivalently feared and awed object with attributes of brutal power over life and death. In effect, such severe pathological states reflect the ego's negative idealizations of objects: that is, a highly destructive object becomes idealized. Object relations are felt to exist in an atmosphere of menacing grandiosity that is threateningly explosive. Such conditions show how pathological depressive-position dynamics become superimposed on pathological paranoid-schizoid dynamics. Brutal dictators and autocrats are viewed in this way.

In other words, narcissism/omnipotence (paranoid-schizoid position) and mania/grandiosity (possible in the depressive position) are concordant states in terms of the self's exaggerated psychological energies; they are inverse correlations in terms of ego-object configurations. Usually, only one pole of the inverse equation becomes manifest depending on individual constitution, defensive makeup, and current center of gravity within the developmental positions. All these psychodynamic operations are organized as unconscious phantasy—how people experience themselves. States of excessive narcissism may manifest as inordinate vanity, smug self-confidence, and lack of empathy. States of mania and grandiosity manifest as pressured and excessive thinking and speaking and nonadaptive extremes of behavior such as spending money recklessly and sleeping only a few hours.

Unconscious phantasy (content), in technical terms, is the direct correlate of the construct of "mental mechanism" (process). Unconscious phantasy connotes subjective, personalized, affectively charged experience subliminally sensed. It underlies mood, motivation, and the attribution of meaning to experience. In contrast, the phrase "mental mechanism" denotes the identical set of forces and devices but with an impersonal and descriptively mechanistic connotation.

In modern cognitive science, for example, unconscious phantasy would be a form of "hot cognition." In *envy theory*, the existence of any type of "cold cognition" devoid of affectively personalized coloring is suspect. What have been referred to historically in psychoanalytic literature as the "mechanisms of defense" are here called unconscious phantasy configurations. Unconscious phantasy or mental mechanisms signify the animated operational matrix of all mental functioning. This includes the structural formations, energetic circuitry, and defense mechanisms that compose the mind. Defense in this sense suggests processes of containment and regulation of dissonance, conflict, and anxiety management, both in normal and distressed mental functioning.

## The Unconscious as a System: Nonconscious Information Processing

This section discusses psychodynamic conjectures and hypotheses as background elements for a deeper understanding of *envy theory*. They include classical psychoanalytic postulates, hypotheses, and theories, and their implications. Some of these propositions are extremely abstract; as such, they are referred to as "metapsychological" conjectures.

*The unconscious proper—the unconscious as a system*—is a primitive array of impersonal, omnipotent forces that developmentally, in a figurative sense, takes on a mind, a subjective personality that loves and hates. Mind is presumed to be the psychological dimension of the body and so has somatic interpenetration. Mind as id, ego, and its objects (foremost of which is the internal superego) expresses itself as one's inner world. It is a universe of dramatic animations that develops by relations with others, including aspects of intrapsychic self and interpersonal figures subjectively perceived. *Music rather than logic or mathematics describes the unconscious.* From a cognitive science perspective, the unconscious denotes implicit information processing.

In this figurative sense, *envy theory* imagines the structure of the inner world composed of id, ego, and superego having a central structural-functional nucleus that radiates out forming a virtual space. For example, the range of ego as a nonconscious and partly conscious experiential entity may be pictured as emanating a nuclear hub—the id at its center. From this, spokes or concentric circles extend out in a way similar to three-dimensional orbits around a sun. The ego's projections or concentric waves arising from the center and traveling toward the periphery form mentalized precipitates along the way leaving multiple "internal objects" (the "mental models" or "schemata" of cognitive science) in their wake. Close to the center of this system, consciousness (information processing) exists in a state of nonconscious repression. The concentric circles that emanate have progressively more preconscious and conscious status the further out they extend. The measured use of metaphor in this way adds to *envy theory*'s aim of describing theory as experience-near with an affectively charged understandability.

The functionally discrete subsystems (id, ego, and superego) making up the mental self as a system have intersystemic relationships that pervade one another. Having trained together since birth, they act as a team. Within the subsystems of ego and superego, intrasystemic activity operates especially by the psychodynamic forces of primary processes (nonconscious information processing) and preconscious-conscious secondary processes (conscious information processing).

The term *id* is a shorthand way of denoting the *unconscious as a system*. Id connotes a *mental structure*, and suggests the overarching aspect of the entire self, primarily containing the nucleus of the biomental instincts. The phrase *"unconscious as a system"* suggests a more *dynamic exchange of mental forces, energies, and regulatory principles of operation—in other words, process and functioning.* However, it is worth emphasizing that id forces permeate all the mind's discrete structural aspects—id itself, ego, and superego.

The *unconscious as a system* (the topographical unconscious) includes *the life-and-death instincts, the primary process, the pleasure-unpleasure principle,* and *timelessness.* These inferred forces reflect the irrational illogic of this nonconscious mental substrata. Included in this are unconscious mental contents, for example, tenacious states of omnipotence that organize and present themselves as unconscious phantasy—structural units of primitive information processing. There are no mathematics or logic here; only unconscious melodies resound.

The nuclear core of the id issues from what *envy theory* hypothesizes as a biomental *preprimary process* dimension of the self. This construct reflects the earliest disorganization of information processing and contains somatic, cognitive, and affective elements. Preprimary process connotes inferred, unknowable, protoorganization.

*Envy theory*'s deliberate choice of using the term "id" (Latin term meaning an impersonal "it") is a reminder that most of the mind's biological and psychological profile—its source—remains unmapped, perhaps unknowable. Thus, a pregnant and provisional term such as id covers a multitude of yet undiscovered factors open to conjecture and testing. As a psychophilosophical construct, for example, it refers to the hypothesis of an unknowable primordial base. It is related to what Bion (1970) calls "O," defined as subjective-objective transcendence at the core of being.

The innermost area of the id is composed of death instinct. This construct suggests the nonconscious processes active in the transitional areas between soma and psyche. This primordial entity connotes both forceful *disorganization* and chaos—that is, primary innate destructiveness. It can be understood as the catabolic side of the biomental self.

The more peripheral areas of the id, so to speak, contain some life instinct, whose energy exists as *unorganized* life instinct libido. The exact nature of these areas remains obscure and characteristically hallmarked by qualities of confusion. To be sure, the construct of an "unconscious"—a nonconscious source behind all mental functioning—connotes intrinsic unknowability.

Out of the nuclear core of the absolutely nonconscious id, the extended id (containing some ego-*organizing* libidinal energies that may enable degrees of unconscious and preconscious functioning—substantive information processing), the primary process proper, emerges. It comprises those freely mobile energies that make up *the unconscious as a system* or, in other words, the area of the state of the "repressed." From here, omnipotent and irresistible instinctual urges (vying for expression in the awake state through the

information-processing and data-collecting ego) repeatedly seek both pleasure and destruction while ignoring or hating aspects of reality that act as
limitations and impediments toward instant gratification.

The phrase *the dynamic unconscious* technically refers to all unconscious
mental contents held in that unconscious state by the action of repression.
Nonconscious information processing in this condition is always an active
and dynamic phenomenon.

*Primary process* mental activity, therefore, is *primitive mental activity*. It
connotes immediate, almost spontaneous, instinctual energetic discharges
whose actions are to both form and break linkages of meaning on all levels
of knowing—perceptual, preconceptual, conceptual, affective, and object-
related. In essence, primary process denotes confused/disorganizing information processing. As psychic energy becomes bound, organized, and less
mobile, it precipitates out forming psychic structure. This structure possesses
a mode of functioning with principles of operation that tend toward stability
and are slow to change.

The primary process domain of the unconscious transcends understandable correspondences (reason and logic) since splitting and projective identification, which cause fusing and conflation, are among its chief operations.
Such *confused* information processing is both nonconceptually symbolic and
presemantic. It is characterized by primitive mental mechanisms: projection,
introjection, splitting, denial, omnipotence, excessive idealization, and identification. These have a distinctly concrete quality and action-oriented mode
when they structuralize themselves (for example, dream images, unconscious
phantasy).

These mechanisms regulate primitive degrees of internalization (nonconscious encoding, storage, memory) and contrast qualitatively with the identifications and internalizations occurring in the secondary process operations
characteristic of logic and reason.

The primary processes pervade the secondary processes, and so partially
distort thinking in the awake state. Unassimilated internal objects are sensed
as fluctuating ego states and rapidly changing affective and cognitive attitudes. Empirically, these unstable mental models manifest as an inability to
make up one's mind, or as forms of dissociation. More assimilated, internalized psychic content manifests as ego traits and characterological styles seen
as clear thinking, single-mindedness, and consistent mental stability.

*Envy theory* regards the *unconscious as a system* as comprising the largest
part of the whole personality. In other words, at any point in development,

whether awake or asleep, unconscious processes govern the self in leading ways. These always pervade the entire ego and superego. Although appearing paradoxical, *envy theory* regards typical human consciousness as virtually unconscious; glimmers of conscious awareness are intermittently interspersed.

The id imputes hedonic, felt value to experience. By contrast, the ego, which equates with experience and time, has both conscious and unconscious dimensions. It functions to scan, witness, search, register, and respond to what is safe while avoiding what it perceives as unsafe. This process, in part, is made possible by the ego's innate capacity for *projective internalization*.

*Projective internalization* reflects the basic way the psyche functions. This core cognitive mechanism makes contact with, or is aware of, the environment through combinations of sensory, perceptual, affective, and other cognitional faculties. It includes both nonconscious and conscious information processing. The ego's drive toward extroversion manifests in its continuous exploration of both itself and its environment. The ego autorecognizes aspects of itself in the environment. This promotes and establishes expanding degrees of complex self-identity. Both the innate points of view of the ego and the fresh experiences it registers contribute to ego buildup.

The *superego* functions as a sphincter to both allow and reject information. Together with the ego, this gating function positions data within the overall experience of the entire self. The superego functions in value-based decision-making. It influences the ego to choose between alternatives, selecting or rejecting options based on its evaluative and moral judgments. This function very closely correlates with the course behavior takes.

From a metapsychological perspective, the superego has an absorbent quality that attracts and stores excess libidinal energies. This absorbent function is even more active in the attraction and containment of envy-laden accruals. The sphincter function of the superego has as a core activity, or has responsibility within the ego for, regulating the pulsed, selective access (yes/good) and blocking (no/bad) of input—the flow of experiential information. These pulsations are fueled by the id's energies that take the form of the psychodynamic construct termed "the repetition compulsion."

A note on the concept of the "*repetition compulsion*" is in order. On a clinical and observable level, the phenomena of the compulsion to repeat include irresistibly recurring thoughts, feelings, and behaviors. When these impair functioning, they manifest as symptoms of psychopathology. Sigmund Freud (1914b, 1920, 1926) sought to explain such symptomatic occurrences, especially since these recurring, entrenched symptoms acted as strong resistances to conflict resolution and forward progress in treatment. He postulated an unconscious primary need for repetition, the "repetition compulsion."

The repetition compulsion was understood as an id-based motoric principle governing mental processes. For Freud, it is the unconscious drive behind desires, filling them with characteristic anticipatory, often unpleasant, tensions. True to their instinctual origins, the aims of the repetition compulsion are to rework and eliminate the very desires that they fueled. This includes repetitive opportunities to resolve conflict, remaster trauma, and enhance adaptive skills. During these reemerging events, anxiety and tension are temporarily reduced. Such resistance to resolution was attributed by Freud to the ascendant operation of the death instinct. This was inferred to fuel the seemingly blind and mindless repetition of self-destructive mental and behavioral activity. Obsessive-compulsive disorders are empirical examples of repetition compulsion phenomena.

Since no mental process is governed entirely by a pure culture of a single positive or negative instinctual force, the operation of the life instinct (the search for new experience and its *expansion*) plays an integral part in this cycle of experiential repetition. Clinically, the strength of repetitive occurrences that seem irresistible and compulsive connotes the mark of everything that emanates from the unconscious, especially the instincts. For example, as will be discussed in chapter 5, desire, love, hate, and envy have outstanding repetitive characteristics.

Only intermittently, in the waking state, do the latently conscious aspects of the ego become alert and consciously attentive. This highly restrictive spotlight of consciousness in the alert and awake state reflects the operation of the secondary processes—conscious information processing. These include the higher mental functions of logic, reason, and memories, which have accrued and been refined by learning. The influence of the primary process (omnipotence and the id), moreover, presses to become known in experience. It does this only very dimly in the shadow of the secondary processes of the ego. In other words, the eyes of the ego can only dimly perceive the brilliance of the id. In a figurative sense, the conscious points of view of the ego are at the apogee of the id, points farthest away from the irrevocably nonconscious nuclear core of the id.

Although a relatively minuscule aspect of the entire self, the conscious ego's *inestimable importance* rests on its being the primary contact point of self with reality (conscious awareness in the waking state). This primary orienting function of the ego, which includes attention and adaptive assessment of safe pursuits, ensures survival and is essential to life. Both the ego's perception of the outside world and its introspection of its inner world afford opportunities for the information processing, understanding, and insight necessary for psychic development to proceed. Furthermore, it is through the ego that self-understanding, achievement of a self-analyzing function, and emergent insights arise. From these, subjective adaptations to one's own nature and objective adaptations to the interpersonal and social environments proceed. Properly developed attention minimizes the mind's inevitable drifts toward boredom.

*Libido* with its biomental roots is the psychic energy of the life instinct used by the ego in the process termed *cathexis*. Cathexis is the transformative action of the libido. It is the verb that connects the subject with its object. It is an attachment of interest and meaning. Cathexis is an action used by the ego to construct a predicate, an assertion about the nature of the subject. It is emotional and cognitive information processing; on the more physical side, the quality of appetitiveness characterizes it. When the ego cathects a part-object (primitive ego in partial fusion with the other) or a whole object (ego directing its attention to an object felt as separate), the ego imprints itself with its own interpretive understanding of what it just did.

Cathexis denotes the ego's *binding and linking* processes, whose work includes an *investment of meaning* that has mental structure-building, organizing, and function-promoting properties. The concept of "binding" denotes the experiential establishment and discovery of linkages that have affective and cognitive subjective meaning. Phenomenologically, the conscious and unconscious awareness of significance at any chronological age arises by the ego's investiture of libidinal connections. These linkages take the form of experiential meaning. They are also the basis of the affiliative attractions behind all expressions of love.

Cathexis and repression correlate with one another. Dynamically, the *unconscious as a system* (primarily the nonconscious id governed by the primary processes) operates in a state of repression. *Repression* refers to the condition of relatively obdurate, tenacious unconsciousness, which characterizes those areas of mental functioning that are widely split apart and kept split apart from conscious awareness—the conscious points of view of the ego governed by the secondary processes.

Repression has two aspects: countercathexis and anticathexis. Part of the unconscious pull downward that maintains repression emanates from the constitutional condition of "countercathexis." This bottom-up repression is a primal repression of material that was never conscious. It maintains a continuing lock on the unconscious state. Its contents remain impervious to awareness. This primal repression functions as an attractor state or magnet that continuously aims to ensure an overall unconscious quality to experience.

Another part of the steady action of repression is its push toward perpetuating and newly increasing the scope of unconsciousness through the action of acquired defense mechanisms. This process is a secondary, highly active repression called "anticathexis." In other words, experience that was once within conscious or preconscious awareness is forgotten and becomes unconscious. The ego's defense mechanisms used to manage the anxiety caused by intolerable conflict ordinarily bring this about. It is a top-down repression. It is the motivated forgetting of unwanted, once conscious experience. Current studies in cognitive science (Anderson et al. 2004) have used functional magnetic resonance imaging to identify the neural systems involved in the processes associated with nonconscious states of mind.

The *unconscious as a system* is dominated by the forces of the death instinct. This suggests trends aiming to approximate a state of primitive, primordial voidness. However, there is sufficient life instinct present in this system to spur the dynamisms needed for living, notably through preconscious ego activity. For example, a physiological analogy that suggests the idea of such voidness is similar to an experiential event in the living organism: the gap of apparent voidness that punctuates the space between the two poles of respiration—inhalation and exhalation.

To reiterate: *The unconscious as a system, the topographical unconscious, the primary process rules of unconscious operations (confused information processing), and the id as a mental structure are roughly synonymous.* In the nuanced conceptualization of these entities, the death instinct (*unorganization*) predominates, yet there is sufficient life instinct (organizing information processing) present to spark the dynamic dialectic that drives the mind to activity on all levels. The id is that which is primitive and acts as an empire of omnipotence. Furthermore, the id may also be understood as the normally constituted "psychotic part of the personality" in all individuals despite the presence or absence of actual mental disorders. Normal dream experience is an example.

The construct *the id's paradox* denotes the presumption that, while the id is inimical to reality, it also presses to express itself in reality through its ego. In a manner of speaking, this upward drive toward entering conscious experience is a mock excursion since the id's ultimate aim is total self-extinguishment. In the process, it attempts to extinguish the ego as well. The id is ruled principally by the death instinct. The ego, by contrast, is impelled to explore the real world by detour after detour. Yet its final destination becomes the very origin from which it began its developmental journey—its id. This in essence is a primal attraction, a return to mindless diffusion.

In the adaptive context of reality, the *ego* acts as the ambassador and transitional representative of its id, its fatherland. While the id as the normatively constituted psychotic (unorganizing) part of the personality seeks reckless satisfaction in an omnipotently unbridled fashion, the ego pursues safe and modest satisfactions according to the reality principle in order to ensure survival. *Figuratively speaking, the ego regards the id's intrusions as insurgent attacks, while the id, by contrast, believes that it acts as a freedom fighter.*

Such detailed differentiations of aspects of the self are clearly metaphorical and advisedly speculative. These distinctions and nuances, however, have pragmatic value since they attempt to depict the psychodynamic phenomenology of self-experience. Ego, then, in relation to id, operates in various roles: scout, envoy, and ambassador. In a figurative sense, as scout, the ego is sent out to perceive and gather information about the unknown environment. As envoy, it is a representative or messenger. As ambassador, the ego gradually assumes a relatively more independent position from its id. It functions in a diplomatic way to tactfully avoid appearing offensive while attempting to mediate and win goodwill—cooperation in the social environment.

Another principal wish of the ego is to enjoy its biomental sensuality, especially the corporeality of the flesh it feels, its somatic platform. The reality principle reflects the operation of the secondary processes in preconscious and conscious ego cognitive information processing. This rational capability fosters a reality sense that strives toward constructive adaptation and a more reality-oriented equilibration of the inner world as it transacts with the environment. Omnipotent impulses, and their projection-coloring judgment and misassessments of reality, are thereby constrained.

For these reasons, the two most general functions of the ego are (1) setting up defensive barriers against the anxiety generated in it by the id's inevitable path toward ultimate self-destruction, and (2) perception aimed at adaptive maneuvers (cognitive and behavioral) toward meaningful survival in the external world. The ego is equipped with faculties for the assessment of safety and unsafety/danger. As the life instinct diffuses within and sustains the ego, it gives the ego an ability to assesses the hedonic (pleasurable versus painful) value of experience.

Successful adaptation to both internal reality and the external world reflects a general dominance of life instinct forces. In effect, therefore, the ego is the principal manifestation of the life instinct and its libidinal aims: attraction, integration, pleasurable affiliation, and adaptation. In *envy theory*, this denotes love in the broadest sense.

These libidinal aims, however, are brushed with the overwhelming influence of the id, where the death instinct naturally holds an ascendant position. Envy is the principal, organized representative of the death instinct in the ego. *Envy theory* proposes that everything that can be described in negative ways—destructiveness, spoiling, hate, and aggression, for example—is based in some measure on the dynamics of unconscious envy.

## Narcissism, Idealization, and Omnipotence

A distinction among the terms "narcissism," "idealization," and "omnipotence" is useful. These three key concepts make up a large part of the envy concept and are the foundational dynamics of the paranoid-schizoid configuration. Their meanings overlap and shade into one another. Each term, however, describes a different facet of the mind's structure and functioning. Especially in early development in infancy, these three states are not necessarily pathological. They all have special functions in normally organizing and structuring the mind. After infancy, however, if these states dominate mental functioning in a persistent, unabated fashion, they take on a psychopathological defensive function.

In *envy theory*, these terms denote psychodynamic dimensions of all mental functioning—typical and atypical. They do not necessarily denote circumscribed defense mechanisms. All three concepts refer to primitive paranoid-schizoid functioning (extremely polarized states of mind) either directly or underlying more developmentally advanced depressive-position functioning (characterized by greater integration and balance). All individuals have this makeup; it is not restricted to any particular class, ethnicity, group culture, or personality makeup.

In metapsychological terms, the distribution of psychic energies, principally the libido of the life instinct, largely defines these dynamic concepts. An important reason for positing the inferred instinct concept is so that effects, as will be described, can be categorized and differentiated. Defining concepts using different levels of analysis and description (phenomenological, metapsychological, and so forth) adds to their theoretical and clinical usefulness. From a metapsychological point of view—one highlighting psychic structure and object relations—narcissism is a state of the ego where the ego centers its attention on (*cathects*) an internalized ideal part-object. This inner-directed self-reference inflates self-relevant feelings.

*Narcissism* is the energetic dimension of the ego, a function of its life instinct quota. It is also a structural configuration *experienced* as the state of self-love in all its forms. Narcissism is the state of the ego enriched with life instinct. It is the ego's largesse and wealth of vital energy whose source is the id. When normal, this becomes the phenomenological experience of normal self-love, self-admiration, self-regard, and self-confidence. The motor behind universal self-relevance strivings, especially maintaining a reasonably coherent sense of self and self-identity, is narcissism.

When abnormal and excessive, it is expressed as arrogance, egocentric pride, and vanity. The diagnostic condition "narcissistic personality disorder," for example, is a clinical example found in adulthood. Empirically and characterologically, excessive narcissism is "feeling special." This implies a belief that one is objectively different from others in a unique way and able to have unique or extraordinary experiences unlike average people. This vain and smug attitude may expand into feelings of entitlement resulting from belief in having privileged status.

If early forms of narcissism are not modified, especially by empathy and compassion arising in *the healthy maturation of envy*, adults continue feeling "special"—qualitatively distinct and, in some fundamental way, superior to other people. Others are regarded as "outsiders." This reinforces seeing them as foreign and strangers. Underlying fear, suspiciousness, and mistrust lead to emotional distancing, heightened distinctions, and experiential alienation. This narcissism provokes feelings of envy; it also stimulates feelings of uncomfortable and unwanted dependence on others.

*Idealization* as a nonconscious cognitive/affective mental dynamic refers to the energy of the life instinct that flows into both the ego and the object thereby enriching their positions and elevating their meaning for the experiential self. It is the innate disposition toward expecting something much greater than is presently experienced. In a manner similar to the diverse range of most aspects of mental functioning, *idealization occurs on a spectrum from normative to excessive, the latter of which is its defensive dimension.*

Idealization ordinarily connotes an *object made ideal*. This overvaluation usually takes the form of a positive or libidinal idealization. It may also take the form of a negative and omnipotent idealization, in effect, a hypnotically attractive demon-like figure. This is encountered typically in the delusions and hallucinations of persons who are psychotic. Whether the idealized object has overvalued positive or negative features, it typically is felt as so extreme that this *unbearable intensity* forces the experiencer to alter contact by devaluing, distorting, or leaving the field of such an experience.

Another way of describing idealization is using the construct of perfectionism. From an information-processing perspective, perfectionistic cognition at first tends to grasp data in small increments, as partial, featural, and incomplete points of a larger global entity. This partiality makes up an imperfect cognitive module that inherently and actively strives to complete or perfect itself. Hence, at all developmental epochs from infancy to adulthood, there is an underlying drive to make what is experienced as incomplete, imperfect, or partial into something more complete and perfect. In perfectionism, cognition exaggerates partial details into unrealistic, idealized entities. *The psychodynamic concept of idealization correlates with the construct of perfectionism but with an emphasis on affective appeal.*

Aspects of the ego, such as the "ego ideal" (values and aspirations), can also undergo idealization. The ego ideal represents a privileged gradient in the ego that functions as part—the positive pole—of the superego. A normative experiential core of positive expectancy and hope derives from *normal and normalized idealization* within the self. Such states of anticipatory hopefulness are generated both from the self's idealization of aspects of its ego and its objects. This is an important metapsychological proposition that will be discussed at length in further chapters.

The genesis of idealization naturally arises from the infant's survival-based attraction—infantile primitive love—to the mother. The mother, in turn, has a complementary, instinctively based idealized attraction to the baby. These are normal forms of idealization. They are rooted in *nuclear love*. This maternal side aimed at infant survival is experienced, for example, in perceptions of and irresistible feelings of perceived "cuteness" and "adorableness." It results in strong urges to be close to and interact with the infant. This survival-based reciprocity includes a nuclear core of meaningfulness. A meaning-seeking and generative aim characterizes what I call *mothercraft*. As much as mother does not completely meet the infant's needs and expectations, the infant mobilizes its own instinctive capacity for idealization to fill in these experientially felt gaps.

Hence, each infant idealizes specific aspects of mother, her corporeal parts, and her emotional functions in idiosyncratically determined ways. Neither infant nor mother is ontologically or objectively ideal. The individual and conjoint needs of each, however, result in the psychologically determined push for normal idealization to enhance survival chances. These are mediated though sensation, perception, feeling, and other cognitional modes. The core mechanism underlying this process is subsumed in the psychodynamic construct "projective identification."

*Envy theory*, moreover, emphasizes that *idealization has a significant role in normal development*, as it does in anxiety states as a defense mechanism. *Normal idealization* in its primitive form in earliest development (the paranoid-schizoid position) is *raw love*. To the extent that this *elemental idealization* does not become excessive, this raw love helps to establish the infant's positive attachment of trust to mother. *Envy theory's* aim is to elucidate the role of envy in development and to underline, in the strongest way possible, the incomparable role of love and positive nurturance in promoting healthy development.

In all situations, however, idealization is such a powerful state of mind driven by an intensification of nonconscious mental processes that it is unstable and short-lived. *Idealization in all circumstances is tenuous.* It deflates rapidly, just as it inflates rapidly when elicited. Persistent states of idealization (for example, mania and delusions) are pathological.

*Omnipotence* is a fundamental concept about unconscious processes in psychodynamic psychology. Its nuanced denotations are varied: power; force to do work; ability to control, influence, and coerce others, resources, and environment; and capacity to effect change in order to achieve an outcome that alters relationships.

It is a generalized existential, experiential mental state in which instinctual forces and primary process regulatory principles operate in ascendancy over all other conscious mental processes. In this sense, it is the fundamental dimension of all unconscious processes in all people. In adulthood, when omnipotence consolidates as a defense mechanism, it is termed "grandiosity," "hypomania," "mania," and "megalomania."

The drive to excessively inflate the ego arises from the *power of the id*. This inflation is excessive narcissism. Omnipotence characterizes narcissism. It is a false sense of power, self-sufficiency, completeness, authority, and unlimited self-dependence. Terms such as "almighty" and "potentate" signify omnipotence. Along with narcissism and idealization, omnipotence is a pillar upholding paranoid-schizoid dynamics at all periods in life. It is the premier defensive response to states of real helplessness and emotionally augmented feelings of primordial dependency and states of passivity, whether real or imagined.

Omnipotence typically characterizes all nonconscious cognitive and affective processes at all developmental eras, but is the leading state of mind in the preverbal period of infancy. Here, its psychotic-like (lack of sufficient reality sense) influence may be viewed as expectable and normative. Omnipotence as an experiential state acts to maintain in tenuous fashion emotional and cognitive phantasies of maximal power and control. This is a concerted attempt—on subliminal and unconscious levels—to disregard, undo, ward off, and defend against anxieties generated by primordial ego-id relations: separateness, helplessness, powerlessness, dependence, and the distress of intolerable envy. The strivings of omnipotence at all developmental periods act to deny personal shortcomings in a tenuously ad hoc manner.

For example, unconscious phantasies are hallmarked by omnipotence, which denotes that they are experienced as having taken, are taking, or will take effect. This occurs in infancy because secondary processes of conceptualization, reasoning, and reality testing are fragile and not yet sufficiently developed. After infancy, states of omnipotence match the strength and intensity of the *unconscious as a system* in its impact on mental functioning to the extent they are not constrained by normal reality testing. When not realistically modulated, they can reach true psychotic proportions found, for example, in manic states, schizophrenic decompensation, or severe character pathology and personality disorders.

Omnipotence as a state of mind is ordinarily configured in the structured form of unconscious phantasy, which is the form of primitive mental content. Omnipotence and envy go hand-in-hand. Omnipotent unconscious phantasies are organized complexes of id impulses and ego defense mechanisms that act to bind and contain anxiety. Omnipotence always implies that defensive control is operative.

In a manner of speaking, the omnipotent forces of the id existing in the self desperately strive to maintain their powerful hold on experience, motivation, and behavior. The aggressive and sexual impulses in these forces aim for control in all sectors of the personality. They spur the ego's need to regulate these drives so that some level of survival may prevail. The enormous importance that omnipotent processes implies for self-defense and survival in human psychology and clinical work cannot be overemphasized.

In summary, in *envy theory*, libidinal omnipotence (a defense against envy) is expressed in the process of excessive idealization, a powerful inflation of value and desirability. After this, envy-driven destructive omnipotence (envy's spoiling aim) manifests itself in its impulse toward powerful, destructive spoiling. This spoiling renders the object impotent, and, in turn, becomes autodestructive for the ego. Excessive narcissism imbued with omnipotence is also a typical defensive response to feelings of envy. Understanding the role of unconscious omnipotence is crucial to any consideration of unconscious envy. An illustrative example is the famous statement of King Louis XIV: "L'État, c'est moi." Saying that "the state is me" encapsulates concepts of narcissism, omnipotence, and self-idealization.

Developmental processes are clearly apparent early in life, especially in infancy, childhood, and adolescence. In later life, however, development (biological and psychological) is still a significant, dynamic force adding to personal change and to significantly changing adaptations in changing life circumstances. In other words, growth, maturation, and development change the complexion of how narcissism, idealization, and omnipotence is experienced and managed.

## The Bidirectional Loop of Nature and Nurture

Innate factors—inborn sets of genetic and neurophysiological equipment—form the matrix out of which *biopsychological predispositions and preferences* emerge. These dispositional sets, to some extent, direct growth, maturation, and the assimilation of *selectively preferred* environmental stimuli, especially relations with caregiving persons. "Relations" denotes the subject's interpretation and meaningful understanding of the experience of material and psychological contact with another. These construals eventually become an internalized part of the self; they are laid down in nonconscious memory.

No inborn trait merely unfolds, in toto, at any point in development. As each ability, faculty, and capacity traverses the course of one's life, that trait stamps and is stamped by its particular "here and now" expression in the present moment. Reciprocal modifications occur bringing about both constraints and new capabilities. This bidirectional journey over time progressively develops to become the distinguishing signature of one's unique personality and emblematic character. That signature, in some indefinable way, is always the same, but remains flexibly malleable, perhaps, not qualitatively, but quantitatively. Its face changes over time.

This developing constitutional and temperamental matrix is configured at birth in biomental transactions with the animate and inanimate environments. All expressed aspects of life and behavior, including the expression of envy, are contextualized. The mark of the environment configures and stamps them with its distinctive features.

The mind as intrasubjective arena makes up the experiential inner world. *Envy theory* takes the position that the individual comes into the world with preferences both innate and even elicited by the environment. Klein (1963b) in one of her last contributions alluded to such a consideration. She says:

> In this way the picture of the external world—represented first by the mother, and particularly her breast, and based on actual good and bad experiences in relation to her—is coloured by internal factors. By introjection, this picture of

the external world affects the internal one. However, it is not only that the infant's feelings about the external world are coloured by his projection, but *the mother's actual relation to her child is in indirect and subtle ways, influenced by the infant's response to her.* (Klein 1963b, 312; emphasis added)

For example, contemporary studies on parenting styles and practices have demonstrated that there is significant and demonstrable reciprocity existing within the changes on children produced by parents and the changes in parents produced by their children (Collins et al. 2000; Swain 2008).

Not only the baby, but also the child and adult, moreover, become "agent influencing" in, as well as "object influenced" by, the external milieu. This underscores the inescapable transactional quality of all experience. Experience is always bidirectional with causal feedback loops. The emphasis here is not control; rather it is an adaptive regulation-seeking expansion—growth, maturation, unfolding, and development of latent and new abilities.

Hence, no absolute solipsism or existence independent and isolated from the influence of its context is possible since mind is an inevitable outgrowth of the very object of its subjective attention. In other words, an individual simultaneously structures and is structured by the environment, especially the world of animate relationships.

The cognitive aspect of *projective internalization* exemplifies this bidirectional loop. This point is crucial in *envy theory* because envy emerges in and always resonates with paranoid-schizoid dynamics, which are primitive and narcissistically based. As is reiterated throughout this book, the paranoid-schizoid position (that I also refer to as the "narcissistic position of envy") is not autistically insulated. It is receptive to and configures itself according to its *projective internalization* of the object world by its inner subjective and outer social attachments.

## Self-Signature Updating and the Consolidation of Self

The developmental perspective regards the individual at every chronological age as having a unique signature that can be equated with his or her conscious and unconscious "self-identity." Its character is updated on a "minute-to-minute" basis continuously throughout life. *Self-signature updating* reflects a continuous and steady overarching unity defining who a person is. It encompasses the hierarchical progression of cumulative development by maturation and experience over time. It is an essential part of the repeating cycle of lived development—experience in a historical context.

The layering and hierarchical nature of development during one's lifetime is an essential consideration in the narration of human nature. However, attention to what is inferred to be largely constitutional gives greater depth of understanding to the richness and complexity of the stratifications that make up the accrued inner world of subjective experience. In addition, these insights may explain the infinitely varied yet similar expression of displayed interpersonal behaviors among individuals.

Individual differences, in part, result from multiple causes. These include one's innate love-envy disposition, how it transacts with the social environment, and its culturally conditioned acquisitions. Inborn and primary constitutional endowments are the wheels upon which ride the whole of one's preferences. This complex process dynamically acts to configure and reconfigure lived experience continuously and with a steady freshness from moment to moment.

The ego at birth rapidly progresses from a state of relative disorganization with weaker neural connectivity and mental integration toward increasingly more durable states of unity. This reflects the way all information processing develops. The concept of domain specificity, the modularity of mind, suggesting separate subsystems that are relatively independent and having separate functions, each of which is dissociable, is a commonly held tenet in cognitive science (Fodor 1983). This, in part, reflects the idea of compartmentalizations within mental functioning. *Envy theory* adds to this by emphasizing that incremental integration of these subsystems is not only possible but a developmental value.

A normative, mercurial condition of multiple experiential ego states (unintegrated points of view of one ego) existing in parallel continues to exist to some extent throughout life. These multiple "I" experiences are often contradictory and promote conflict. The earliest forms of perceptual processing characterized by featural, part-by-part, and incomplete recognition—mere appearance—continue to exist together with more integrated patterned forms of holistic, configural recognition—cognition with significance.

The ego's unified coherence or dissociation/confusion depends on the overall integration of the personality over time. Inchoate detailed cognitive elements gradually become experienced as meaningful patterns in normal development.

At every developmental period and continuing in adult life, however, there is a relative consciousness of self, which, in many respects, can be described as an "illusion of unity." An individual's singular and consistently present physical body and consistent personal name, for example, reinforce this state of seeming self-unification, being one person. The accretion of mechanical, repetitive habits played out both mentally and behaviorally over time adds to this. Inflexible patterns of thinking, feeling, behaving, and reacting reinforce such a mercurial state of the self and constrain change.

Such tenuous self-unity, however, may be a prelude to a potentially more singular state of stability if intentional work on self-development is pursued and fosters internal accomplishments—greater ego integration. Differing experiential versions of the self (the self's multiple modules or subsystems) diminish to the extent that brain-mind integration over time occurs.

The overall sense of self perpetually reconfigures its identity—*self-signature updating*.

## Unconscious Phantasy:
## The Currency of the Mind

*Unconscious phantasies*, as Klein (1925, 1958) and Susan Isaacs (1948) originally described, are the underlying impulses, motivations, anxieties, conflicts, and defenses structured as personalized object-related configurations in the nonconscious mind. These primary mental contents are given idiosyncratic meaning through individual experience. They are affectively charged, vivid anticipatory mental structures that make up the psychological geometry of mind.

Unconscious phantasies are unconscious organizational structures akin to mental models that influence the interpretation of sensory data, shape the encoding of information into long-term memory, bias the retrieval of stored memories, and influence the direction that behavior takes. They are characterized by a subjunctive mood—namely, anticipatory "if-then" expectations.

The universal experience of anxiety signaling mental dissonance, for example, is always accompanied by unconscious mental contents—unconscious phantasy. This mental architecture (form and contents) is a design and arrangement reflecting the subjective makeup of an individual. It is an inner model, the plan that informs lived self-experience. It is the unconscious strata motivating behavior.

Unconscious *phantasy* is distinct from *conscious fantasy*, which denotes, by contrast, the more conscious material of daydreams and imagination. Daydreams, for instance, are products of the awake state motivated by degrees of defensive denial of reality and the conscious creation of a temporary illusory world. Night dreams, on the other hand, occur in the sleeping state and are prompted by a psychic pressure to reflect and attempt the working out of conflicts. Scenarios in the night dream are reflections of unconscious phantasies, but are less disguised by intentional denial. Dreams reflect the characteristic distortion by conscious standards of the dream process—condensation and displacement, the illogical rearrangements driven by primary, unconscious processes.

Art, different from the aforementioned, is close to unconscious phantasy but also close to the conscious techniques that reality provides to make it an organized configuration of symbols that are concrete, explicit, and available for social communication in the real world.

For example, all expressions of art—visual, auditory, and architectural—reflect the interface of the conscious ego with its primitive id impulses as they seek manifest expression, containment, organization, and reworking in repetitive and adaptive ways. Unconscious phantasies provide the inner models or blueprints for conscious and tangible form in the expression of art.

Artistic production is driven by the need to externalize wishes, relationships, and situations of conflict in a manner that has mysterious, emotive, and compelling attractiveness. It is rooted in the need to restore damaged aspects of one's internal psychic reality. This is a core feature of the mind's psychodynamic working through its deepest sorrows and conflicts. Working out these central dilemmas with some degree of conscious intentionality is part of the depressive position, the humanization process.

Art's attractiveness, accordingly, combines both beauty and ugliness often in subtle and inexplicable ways. "Qualia," the idiosyncratic meaning and partially indeterminate feeling that gives color and nuanced interpretation to experience, arises from unconscious phantasy.

In psychoanalytic terms, as id impulses arise, they emerge as instinctual drives having physiological and mental tensions. When the agitating pulsions of these instinctual needs are felt, ego mechanisms are instantaneously elicited to structure and manage them in adaptive ways. The chief aim of these mechanisms is to unconsciously fulfill the wish or defensively bind the anxiety issuing from conflictual instinctual desires. This mix of instinct in the ego's defensive response takes the form of an internal object-related structure referred to as unconscious phantasy.

These mental precipitates are the id's refraction though the structuring, interpretive, and sense-making prisms of the ego. Unconscious phantasies are the language that instinctual impulses use for nonconscious information processing. These are the currency with which mental structure accumulates and all psychological processes are negotiated; hence, they are the ultimate reference points of experience.

These mental models or elemental schemata are descriptively and functionally unconscious—that is, not readily accessible to conscious awareness. They may have preconceptual, conceptual, and emotional components—all of which are richly saturated by their somatic underpinnings. The intrapsychic experiential world, a world of unconscious phantasy, is what has historically been referred to as the "*inner world.*" What have been traditionally described as the mechanisms of defense are what Melanie Klein has understood in her conception of unconscious phantasy.

For example, in infancy, when in a twilight state, the hungry infant may desire sucking on the nipple to receive nourishment. This desire is the biomental instinct with its physiological and mental components. In the absence of an actual feeding, he will conjure up a transitory experiential scenario of sucking and feeling satisfied. On an observable level, one might see the infant's lips enacting sucking motions. This is normative "hallucinatory wish fulfillment." It also is an example of unconscious phantasy in which the instinctual desire to feed not meeting with an expected environmental response employs an experiential makeshift ego mechanism/unconscious phantasy to temporarily satisfy its need. Biomental unity is reflected in this.

An adult male reported the following dream. He saw the automobile of his business competitor as only having three wheels, unable to move forward, stuck in traffic on a major highway, and repetitively hit by passing trucks. He saw himself on a bicycle but unable to ride it properly because of a broken leg. When commenting on this, the patient said he frequently wished his rival would go out of business, secretly wished him ill fortune, and, at these times, felt guilty about being so hostile and selfish. The dream suggested unconscious phantasies of seeing his competitor disabled and attacked (projective destructive wish), but also seeing himself punished with a broken leg and also unable to move forward (turning against the self, reversal into the opposite, and displacement as defenses against the anxiety of aggressive intentions).

Unconscious phantasy is the preverbal language of instinctual impulses. Instinctual impulses are at once both biological stimuli (the "somatic" aspect: somesthetic sensation and tension) and intrasubjective experiential entities (the "mental" aspect: various feelings of dissonance, anxiety, and attraction).

Although imprecise, it would not be incorrect to say that unconscious phantasy is *descriptively unconscious and subliminally preconscious "affective" thinking*. In this sense, unconscious phantasy is the mental reflection in the ego of the biomental instincts that exist in the id, the larger scope of the entire self.

The primary process mechanisms characteristic of the paranoid-schizoid position imbue unconscious phantasy with primitive qualities of confusion, conflations in information processing. *Distinguishing impulse (instinctual force) from its defenses (reactive processes producing content—for example, idiosyncratic attitudes, images, subliminal preferences) is imprecise. Such distinctions can only be accomplished hypothetically since both impulse and defense of impulse appear in conjoint fashion as unconscious phantasy.*

Unconscious phantasy configurations are functional, psychodynamic units having both affective and cognitive/ideational components. They consist of featural rather than configural whole complexes. Their format takes the form of structured, primitive mental images that are concrete, animated, fluid, and dynamically interactive. The older psychoanalytic term "imago" connotes this.

Unconscious phantasy is primitive and built around the mentalizing of bodily experience, particularly the functional aspects of anatomical parts. The specific meaning of this intrapsychic construct of *mentalization* and *mentalizing* is unique to *envy theory*. Somesthetic sensations in infancy and later life comprise the physiological source of these human instincts, which Freud called "Triebe." Unconscious phantasies are forever grounded in corporeality as their mental action patterns, in the flesh and blood of the body. This is the unyielding basis for their concrete quality.

Introjection and projection, for example, are mental mechanisms that reflect and emerge out of the somatic matrix of organ modes of functioning (eating, swallowing, vomiting, spitting, breathing, seeing, urinating, defecating, and so forth). Early infantile experience, in part, encodes itself in nonconscious memory systems by using this fleshy base of sensory and motor responsiveness. Although it may be an inexact description, unconscious phantasies are nonconceptually symbolic, largely part-object, localized component configurations of contesting internal forces, whose principal axes include action-oriented states of love, hate, and envy. These states are relations, connections of primitive meaning, between subject and its objects.

Conscious thinking (the secondary process), by contrast, comprised of conceptual entities in various syllogistic combinations uses verbal language, and has a distinct developmental history that unfolds and develops over time from infancy into adulthood (Piaget and Inhelder 1969). Unconscious phantasy is primary process, concrete mental content. Consciously experienced logic, reason, and language are secondary process, abstract mental activities.

❖

*The experience of "meaning" and "meaningfulness" derives from the nature of the dynamic, interactive relationship between unconscious phantasy and conscious thought. Insight is the meaning that comes from the search for the personal truth of one's life. Insight emerges as unconscious experience becomes more consciously integrated and lived. Ultimately, insight is driven by the impulse to search for genetically programmed anticipated rewards, the goal of meaningfulness. This is the mind's hidden treasure or longing for "booty" in all its connotations.*

Using the backdrop of a developmental perspective, *envy theory* regards the following as fundamental to its presuppositions: somatic and mental processes have an inseparable unity; from the start of life, unconscious phantasies are formed largely out of concrete bodily sensations; and they are constituted from the mental perception of bodily processes. These sense data are innate, the genetically programmed part of the inherent survival resource system with which people are equipped. The aims of survival are twofold: (1) to remain alive under life threatening circumstances, and (2) one whose nuclear aim is meaning seeking.

Environmental influences activate or leave dormant these innate sets of preferences, to varying degrees. The *epistemophilia* within the self, which proceeds from the creative union of the life instinct and the death instinct, is a meaning-seeking impulse. Personal meaning precipitates out as the object relation. It becomes mentalized and registered in meaningful ways as dynamic unconscious phantasy. In the broadest sense, the link between ego and object is motivated by the life and death instincts. Viewed from an interpersonal perspective, these complex *links saturated with meaning* establish the quality of attachment between infant and mother early on and also underlie all interpersonal intimate relationships.

Unconscious phantasy operates continuously. It is the mental dimension of its physiological counterpart, the body. The entire body participates and becomes centrated in brain processes. It is a *virtual information stream* operating intrapsychically and intrasubjectively. This inner world is also open to the interpersonal-intersubjective field of communication, which can modify and change its content and how it operates. In this way, it can significantly alter mental processes and personality. In a sense, unconscious phantasy acts as a "shared dream" between and among individuals. This may be an important basis for understanding group psychology, especially its unconscious motivations. The intrapsychic geometry of unconscious phantasy becomes restructured by extrapsychic reality, especially interpersonal and social transactions.

In any consideration of unconscious processes, it may be more precise to understand them as ontological and phenomenological entities that are "subjective" rather than "objective," notwithstanding any attempt to objectify them conceptually by using linguistic descriptions, which are only approximations.

Misnaming what is subjective by considering it "objective" would constitute an error in critical thinking. The *unconscious as a system*, as such, is "objectless." In this view, the mind is conceptualized as a sea of virtual subjectivity that encompasses and comprises a dynamically fluid, centrated sphere of being that includes material ordinarily appearing outside itself—that is, its objects. These objects exist in states of fusion with and in the ego; they are created and maintained by the ego's projective identification. This conception is virtually synonymous with the way the paranoid-schizoid position operates in the mind—without logic and with an asynchronous melody.

The origins of unconscious phantasy are equally both *sui generis* and the product of an interaction with the inescapable human environment. In *envy theory*, this is neither a contradiction nor a logical paradox but an ontological reality. It best describes the origins and structure of the experiencing self, personalized ego, and uniqueness of each individual.

The subliminal information exchanged between two people continually reconfigures unconscious phantasy. It organizes itself below the threshold of conscious awareness and only gradually filters into explicit communications in this intersubjective rapport. Its overall communicational impact is far greater than the spoken word. The intelligence within preverbal and nonverbal aspects of human communication far exceeds that communicated through verbal language. The *transference/countertransference* phenomenon in psychodynamic therapies (and also observable in different ways in everyday relationships) reflects the interpersonal, intercommunicative arc of this information stream.

Mental processes, mostly nonconscious by nature, are the milieu out of which more matured thinking—conscious concept formation, symbols, and abstract reasoning—develops. Meaning and the quest for knowledge are inseparable. Envy operates primarily in the realm of unconscious phantasy and colors what eventually emerges in conscious cognition. These conscious thought processes have a chronological, developmental history that expands from infancy to adulthood. Unconscious envy, however, always remains influential and makes a significant impact on the intellect throughout life. Excessive envy, moreover, is a leading factor behind intellectual inhibitions of all kinds.

*Envy theory*'s emphasis on primacy of unconscious phantasy derives from an underlying linguistic supposition. Unlike proponents who largely center meaning in words, *envy theory* emphasizes that the center of meaning resides principally in the ontological existence of a self that progressively unifies, integrates, and experiences meaning and value—the intelligence behind and driving language.

Yet language, important as it is for subjective and objective communication in human culture, is only marginally adequate to describe unconscious processes that constitute the very core of human psychology and their expression in behavior. Artistic productions, for example, often convey information that words alone cannot. Language-based expositions such as this book are mere approximations that hint at their signified meanings, which are latent, buried, hidden, and primarily unconscious. Yet words and language are needed and clearly useful, especially when viewed as what they are—articulated, concretized *approximations* referring to infinite sets of abstract, experiential meaning.

Unconscious phantasy, the vehicle housing these energetically enlivened informational units, dynamically consolidates the fluid inner world. Unconscious phantasy is the format that the sense of meaningful survival uses to reinforce itself. All mental and behavioral change results from alterations in the structure, functioning, and dynamic organization of unconscious phantasy. These units of psychic life do change naturalistically by growth, maturation, and typical development through experiences of all kinds. They are not static.

Accelerated, more intentionally sought after personality change may also occur through the psychotherapeutic process. The verbal dialogues that make up psychotherapy are a major route toward bringing the more silent mental dialogues of unconscious phantasy to light.

The conscious discovery of aspects of unconscious phantasy is ordinarily referred to as "insight." Moreover, insight produces and reflects a vital reduction of personal confusion—for example, uncomfortable dichotomies in feelings, thoughts, attitudes, decision-making, and resolve. The sudden awareness of hitherto unrealized meaning, however, requires further consolidation and integration through repeated "working through" over time in order for these reorganized states of mind to endure. However, complete and permanent insight is never achieved since unconscious phantasy always exists as infinite sets of yet-to-be-developed meaning.

The verbal dialogues that occur in psychotherapy, for example, can create conditions in which psychological and behavioral change may occur. These sorts of changes, including *the healthy maturation of envy*, may also occur in a more elementary way, and perhaps far more commonly in everyday life, by the *"instinctive resourcefulness"* (Ninivaggi 2005, 2009) that ordinarily remains mentally latent. This is an adaptive capacity consisting of implicitly based understanding and procedural reaction patterns. It emerges out of the silent assessment of the meaning of a situation and the preconscious, almost automatic deployment of actions to reinstate—correctively—an equilibrium after stressors have disrupted it.

Such *instinctive resourcefulness* occurs both naturalistically and intermittently as a normal part of everyday living. This speculative hypothesis may be far from lending itself to proof other than by the anecdotal narratives found in disciplines such as philosophy and religion. Take for example the cultural organization known as Zoroastrianism developed in ancient Persia in the sixth century BC and the cultural mandates formulated in the Vedas, the scriptural texts of ancient India (chapter 10). In these early times, for example, envy was identified "instinctively" and recognized as troublesome. The problem of envy was addressed by a variety of formalized management strategies in these cultures (Ninivaggi 2008). Such *instinctive resourcefulness* characterizes the development of cultures and civilizations.

## The Paranoid-Schizoid and the Depressive Positions

### The Biomental Birth of the Human Infant: Birth, Breath, and Breast

The human infant coming into the world faces an array of novel experiences. The three most pressing are birth, breathing, and feeding.

In *envy theory*, feeding and the term *breast* are synonymous. In a conflated way, they constitute the infant's urgent focus. Both connote the source of food, actual contact by infant lips-mouth-body, and the cycling of pleasure, unpleasure, presence, and absence. Thus, birth, breath, and breast act as major provocateurs that challenge the infant to respond in ways felt as either meeting needs or increasing frustration. Such contact is the infrastructure and prototype of mental attention.

When sensation and perception activate, degrees of unintegrated ego are prompted to begin integrating and start organizing experience. The periodic, rhythmical, and flowing interactions between infant and mother together with the rhythmical experiences of breathing and heartbeat begin to stabilize dissonance and introduce glimmers of integration. This is the founding moment of mind. The subjective awareness of this biological aliveness is *the experience* of experience. Experience here denotes a lived configuration of both the awareness of and response to an experiential event. In the first few months, this cognition constitutes an awareness mostly of "appearance"; very soon, the experience of "significance" arises.

*Envy theory equates experience with ego.* Broadly speaking, experience is the subjective side of being alive. When awake, experience sweeps along a spectrum with three nodes: alert conscious awareness, preattentive conscious awareness, and unconscious awareness. When asleep, experience is more restricted to low fidelity, descriptively unconscious awareness as in dream states.

The preverbal experiential state of infancy is primordial, primal, and primary. It is a mercurial field of aliveness fluctuating between both maelstrom and dynamic quiescence. Sensorimotor neurophysiological immaturity and active psychodynamic functioning influence it. As development proceeds in the first three months of life—*early paranoid-schizoid psychological position*— these extremes are followed, and to some extent superseded, by the *depressive psychological position* (Klein 1935, 1945, 1957). Its onset is about the fourth month through the end of the first year of life. *The real overlap, to some extent, of these positions must be emphasized to prevent understanding them as too sharply divided and their dynamics as absolutely distinct from one another.*

Klein's seminal discoveries in this regard remain of inestimable importance to developmental psychology. These normative developmental configurations constitute the infantile onset and first patterning of ego-object experiences, which persist and are repeatedly restructured throughout life; they are never resolved to conclusion. They remain repeating cycles that elaborate and expand mental development. It is to be emphasized in as strong a way possible that Melanie Klein never viewed all the complexity of human development as compressed or completed within the first year of life.

Although both Klein's contributions and *envy theory* emphasize the crucial influence of emotional development on cognition and behavior, information-processing constructs are embedded in these in subtle ways. The constructs of the paranoid-schizoid and depressive positions, for example, are based on dynamic relations between part-objects (cognitively as "appearance only") and whole objects (realistic perceptions having significance associated with real people felt as separate from the self).

From a cognitive science perspective, the term *part-object* refers to the earliest form of cognitive recognition—featural, local, component, part-by-part, partial, incomplete, and piecemeal. This characterizes all paranoid-schizoid operations and their emotional attributions and construals, typically extreme and unmodulated. The experience of *absence* vacillates with impressions of *presence*. Ego and its objects are felt as partially fused and not distinct. From an emotional point of view, the paranoid-schizoid position is *impersonal*, in other words, part-objects are close, though not entirely, to somatic and reflexive operations.

The term *whole object* refers to the more integrated processes of perceptual recognition—holistic, configural, approximating completeness, and global. This characterizes all depressive-position dynamics with its less primitive construal of emotional salience and meaning. Ego in this position feels that its objects are separate from itself. The depressive position is *personal*; in other words, actual persons are recognized and feelings are becoming more empathetic. Experience, accordingly, vacillates between feelings and perceptions of *full* versus *empty*, with emphasis on the gradations and nuances of these. While both forms of recognition have a developmental timeline, they always retain some influence, in varying ways, on cognition throughout life. Both are core features of the way envy operates.

Melanie Klein (1946, 1957) described the paranoid-schizoid position as the first developmental configuration that the awakening mind draws on to generate and order experience at birth. Although the terms "paranoid" and "schizoid" suggest psychopathology, it is to be emphasized that the mental status of the infant so designated was understood as normal and typical. The terms "paranoid," "schizoid," and "depressive" were chosen to indicate *normative* anxieties and mental operations *typical* of both the earliest periods in infancy, and also unconscious processes at all ages. If, however, there is a biological (genetic or constitutional) predisposition/vulnerability for psychopathology, then the developmentally expectable paranoid-schizoid position would be influenced by these distorting elements besides also proceeding in typical though modified fashion. Environmental traumas significantly influence the risk of developing mental disorders.

In fact, *envy theory* emphasizes that paranoid-schizoid-position psychodynamic operations often become developmentally entrenched and stagnant. Hence, they make any substantive supersession by the depressive position tenuous. The depressive position, however, always holds unique status in its exquisitely humanizing adroitness to the extent it is achieved. Some degree of matured depressive-position functioning—significance, salience, and meaning—typically takes shape in all persons. Stated poetically, the music defining the depressive-position can never be known definitively. One can only become familiar with its melodies repeatedly and so reach another level of more encompassing tonal mastery.

These two positions are the hardwired/innate modes that the mind uses to make sense out of the broad range of its overall subjective and interpersonal experience. To reduce them to or view them as linear stages is less precise than to regard them as interactive configurations that have an onset at birth and an abiding presence throughout life.

These normative developmental positions have a quality of indolence because they are intrinsically slow to reconfigure. Yet their interfaced oscillation remains invariant. The drive toward successful adaptation and meaningful survival oscillates with the id's insistence on the repetition compulsion, which acts as a deep-rooted resistance to unimpeded progressive advancement. These are the invariant factors characterizing the psychodynamics of mental functioning.

Newly emerging tasks, particularly stimulating social engagements, arise across the life span. For example, toddlers work on self-control and "yes and no" choices; preschoolers ask "why," explore, and imitate rather than initiate; school-age children engage with peers and develop self-worth by refining skills; adolescents form identities using newly emerging sexual impulses and concerns in peer and social contexts; young adults begin new affiliations outside the home in work and intimate partner settings; and the long course of adulthood presents opportunities for greater freedom in self-motivated productivity, generativity, value implementation, and self-actualization.

*All developmental psychosocial configurations, early and later, are significant achievements whose richness and newness influence each other over a lifetime.*

Melanie Klein held these views, especially concerning early infantile development. She understood these positions as valid theoretical models that also had status as typical experiential states of mind originating in infancy and continuing thereafter as emotional frames of psychological reference. These normal and expectable mental orientations were much more than retrospectively constructed speculations about a "hypothetical infant." In effect, since she never qualified or deviated from this perspective, it suggests that she viewed the positions as essentially true. Whether they can be understood as literally true or, in fact, as clinically true theoretical models is an open question. *Envy theory* regards them as contextually valid ideas that truly approximate experiential states of mind. Moreover, they transcend their actual linear chronology because of their indestructible mental presence and influence throughout life.

### The Developmental Positions in Infancy: The Normative Paranoid-Schizoid Position and the Depressive Position

In the chronological and normative *paranoid-schizoid position* of the first quarter of the first year of infancy, the immature and rudimentary ego experiences the object in an incomplete way. This is termed a "part-object" relation. This developing affiliation is primitive, raw, extreme, inchoate, and tends to be more impersonal. *Envy theory* strongly emphasizes that although *the paranoid-schizoid position is hallmarked by part-object experience, adumbrations of whole-object experience are present and exert real effects in a variety of ways.*

The hallmark of all paranoid-schizoid experience is the experiencing of part-objects and partial aspects of objects, which denotes an experiential emphasis on constituent, featural, and incomplete elements and not the composite, patterned, interrelated whole. This developmental state of perceptual incompleteness also reflects the ego's experience of itself as incomplete in whatever primitive way it can have this experience. *Envy theory* refers, at times, to the paranoid-schizoid ego as a "part-ego." Cognition and emotion, which is nascent, primitive, and still developing, typically experiences extremes: *absence versus presence, ideal versus horribly imperfect.*

While perceptual systems in infancy are multimodally interactive, their constituent features are experientially dissociable and are apprehended and felt as unintegrated, at times, disintegrating parts. In other words, attention is a fixation, a restricted glimpse of only one aspect or feature of a larger experiential picture whose configural entirety is not apprehended in stable ways.

Part-object experience is accompanied by affectively charged, polarized extremes of emotional recognition, extremely bad (persecutory/demonized and the spoiled, imperfect object of envy) versus ideal. This part-object may even be sensed as independent and self-sufficient, an eerily removed yet juxtaposed presence. As alluded to earlier, this naked cognitive partiality in information processing inherently and actively strives to "fill in the gaps" by frail attempts to induce experiential completeness to what it experiences as incomplete.

At this very early cognitive and emotional developmental period, successful adaptation necessitates making what is imperfect and painful into an experience "more" perfect and so less dissonant and distressing.

At this period of the paranoid-schizoid position, there is active but un-unified, intersensorial synthesis. Perception of spatial relationships has a concrete quality. Permanent cognitive, intellectual structures are yet undeveloped. It is a preverbal, presemantic era of linguistic silence and somatic-affective preeminence. Yet infancy is an exquisitely communicative period.

For example, it is generally recognized that the frequency of crying peaks at about six weeks and only gradually downregulates, often to disappear, by about four months. Typically, this apparent distress is marked by the absence of any measurable physical abnormality. It is referred to as "functional colic." *Envy theory* infers that this period reflects the experiential presence of many, though not all, disturbing unconscious phantasies.

Memories are registered by procedural and conditioned responses that are presemantic and silent. They are the imprints derived from the ego's ever-vigilant scanning and silent witnessing. The ego's modus operandi for knowing, especially for encoding relationships on every level, is its capacity for *projective internalization*, which is also concomitant with the ego's witnessing at all later periods in development. *Projective internalization* denotes experiential simultaneity: being both within an experience and also aware of an experience. Conscious and nonconscious cognitive systems underlie this. In earliest infancy, awareness is shadowy and ephemeral.

Intelligence in the infantile period is more corporeal than conceptual. Since perception plays a leading part in measuring reality, the early infantile perceptual grasp of the entire object with all its details is instance-specific, concrete, and partial. In this sense, it is locked into the experiential moment. The actual contact, for example, between infant lips and nipple produces more of an experience of fused physical action rather than one of distinct, discrete, and separate parts that are interacting. The life-sustaining activity of sucking/feeding is embodied in the construct of breast as the prototypical first object of vital significance.

It is also worth emphasizing that, as the nuclear paranoid-schizoid position naturally progresses, the unintegrated but integrating ego can begin to sense links of meaning between aspects of objects (part-object linked to part-object). These configurations are fused amalgamations rather than distinct whole entities. This primitive state of virtually silent corporeal consciousness, however partial and nonintegrated, nevertheless imprints itself experientially. These early experiences stored in flesh-colored forms may express themselves in corporeal sensations and other ways throughout life. Melanie Klein (1957) often referred to this nonconscious retention as "memories in feelings."

The outcome of negotiating the paranoid-schizoid position always has healthy and unhealthy features. Healthy outcomes are characterized by greater ego integration, a reduction in impulsivity, less cognitive dissonance, the shift from partial to holistic perception, the sense of patient expectation, and anticipatory enthusiasm. If *nuclear envy* is not excessive, *nuclear love* facilitates to varying degrees the introjection of the internal good object as the focal point in the ego from which further expansions and healthy developments proceed. It acts as an attractor state for all further beneficial identifications. The particular balance of these mixtures influences the structure, content, and course of the next chronological, developmental configuration, the depressive position.

The normative and expectable *depressive position* is reached at about the second quarter of the first year. It gradually consolidates over time. It is both a marker of *qualitative psychological change*, and a mediator for all further mental development. The developing ego transforms itself from a state of partiality to a condition of greater wholeness. Cognition and emotions now are enabled with a sense of full versus empty and the gradations between. This implies that the ego functions more as a cohesive container with organizing boundaries. Object relations are whole-object relations that are personal and emotionally nuanced.

At this time, the infantile ego begins the long process of grasping and synthesizing the object in an increasingly whole and complete manner. As development proceeds throughout the first year, primitive, raw, and naked experiential capabilities become more integrated and competent. Sensory perception becomes sharper and greater integration in cognition and memory qualitatively advance toward increasing semantic fluency. Silence now begins to fuse in words; it becomes overlaid and expressed by linguistic sound. Communicative silence, however, remains as an inaudible hum, the background upon which language becomes written.

Although this period of infantile cognition is still comparatively rudimentary, it has a significantly more reality-based operating framework than previously. In other words, whereas the part-object (in a state of mentalizing) is experienced more idiosyncratically, the mental whole object is imbued with characteristics that make it relatively more realistically understood. Configural recognition and processing become prominent. Analysis of small differences in details and spatial relations of features within prototypical neurocognitive organization tend to dominate information processing. Gradually over time, experience can be tested and measured by the ego using more reality-based parameters. The sense of reality slowly comes on line.

Emotionally, the beginnings of normal feeling states correlated with mental anguish and distress shape themselves at this time. The sense of time correlates with the gradual consolidation of the ego and its constancy—resistance to disorganization. The phenomenon of sorrow, for example, spans a complex spectrum from normal grief as a reaction to a loss, to transient sadness, to infantile depressions such as found in failure-to-thrive conditions. These form the basis for later states of mourning, bereavement, and complex clinical depressions. In these adult conditions, all the characteristics of time—memory of the past and future and abrupt disruptions in the normal flow of acceptable change—challenge the capacity to cope. The anhedonia found in clinical depression connotes a belief that no pleasure is possible, either now or in the future. Time stands still.

A marker of the onset of the depressive position is the social smile in early infancy. This may suggest that the capacity for humor (antithetical to envy) is beginning to develop. Healthy outcomes are multiple but are marked by a secure rather than raw sensitivity, greater cognitive receptivity, a wider scope of memory configurations, and deepening feelings of love and empathy.

The paranoid-schizoid position fuses into the depressive position. Each position, however, retains some functional independence. The early patterning of these two positions establishes the neural circuitry—bias signals—of emotion and cognitive processing along pathways that tie and integrate inputs, inner states, and outputs in both subjective experience and behavioral performance.

### Dependency and the Developmental Positions

Dependency denotes the ego's experiential position in relation to a perceived other. In both the paranoid-schizoid and depressive positions, the dependence of ego is its orientation to its construed objects. These objects are created by ego's apprehension of nonself. This positional primacy is central although emphasis in each position is *qualitatively* different. The "ego-object" perspective rests on outward interest and perception. By contrast, yet in simultaneity, the ego's fundamental dependence on its "inwardly" existing id—nonconscious and somatic self—is a virtually unchanging anaclitic dependence, the backdrop orientation for all ego-object relations.

Paranoid-schizoid dependency in terms of "objects" is characterized by unconscious phantasies of concrete fusion, which are created and maintained by projective identification. The elided or merged mental entities that result from such fusion are primordial, primal, and elemental in nature. They are nonconceptually symbolic, prelinguistic configurations of part-objects—namely, parts of ego in primitive relation to partial apprehensions of objects. These experiences are much more determined by phantasy than objective reality.

The extreme *paranoid-schizoid neediness*, a combination of real and phantasied need, normal to the paranoid-schizoid position is accompanied by feelings of virtual absence beyond merely feeling empty. The state of experiencing *absence* is more primal whereas the state of *emptiness* suggests that differentiation is occurring and implies a contrast between empty and full. This correlates with the transition from the paranoid-schizoid position (sense of absence) to the depressive position (sense of emptiness where fullness had been) configuration of self and other, where ego boundaries are beginning to form. Accordingly, in the paranoid-schizoid position with virtually no ego boundaries, primitive projective identification automatically fills the just forming ego shell by introjectively absorbing and fusing with the material experienced.

*Depressive-position dependency/neediness*, by contrast, is hallmarked by burgeoning differentiation and a sense of separateness. This qualitatively distinct dependence is between ego as gradually unifying self (whole ego) and primary whole object—mother as real person. This denotes whole-object relations and the ego's development of functional configural cognitive expansions.

The results of depressive-position advancement are multiple: a relatively more conscious awareness of dependency proper, aggression, more intentionality (especially an awareness of the potential to harm, often felt in phantasy), cause and effect associations, and the developing capacity for separation out of the phantasy of paranoid-schizoid–based absolutely fused dependency. Depressive-position functioning goes hand-in-hand with the development of conceptual symbol formation and linguistic fluency, cognitive abstraction, and the "secondary process" nature of rational thinking.

In the paranoid-schizoid position, feelings of maximal neediness—states widely split apart from what may satisfy needs—denote *incipient* dependency, in fact, the state of protodependency. These extreme states of mind are stridently frustrating and filled with fear and vulnerability. It is worthwhile to reiterate that the effects of the "death instinct" reflected in unmatured, unintegrated biomental unorganization are paramount in the paranoid-schizoid position. Fear, anxiety, and envy are the principal, negative forces operating in raw, undeveloped ways in this period. Resentful hostility, moreover, arises in diffuse ways. The paranoid-schizoid position is one of maximal helplessness, especially real motoric experiential passivity, because of unmatured neuromuscular systems in early infancy. Ego passivity and disabled volition correlate with the paranoid-schizoid position.

The profound and typically protracted course of this normative state of helplessness becomes etched in the mind. It remains as the deep, seemingly inexplicable sense of passivity affecting and significantly influencing later expressions of thought, feeling, and complex forms of motivation. Impairments in volition—ego states of intentional and actionable aims—are rooted in this. This altricial—helpless at birth—passivity is a major source of later inhibitions—states of mental "stalling."

In passing, mention should be made of the phrase "comfort zone." Although this conventionally suggests an attitude and feeling state of low or manageable anxiety where stressors are kept at bay, it is a condition that maintains a status quo, a course of life "on autopilot." *Envy theory* sees an important root of this default motivational-amotivational condition in states of passivity that date to and have become entrenched in early infancy.

*Envy theory* postulates this root of passivity to reside in the inevitable awareness of fusion that comingles with unconscious phantasies of merger with an idealized object at the start of life. *At rock bottom, as envy theory stresses, lies the unconscious awareness of the ego's dependent and amorphous fusion with its id, the primordial part-object.* This *primordial anaclitic dependency* is the core of the sense of an "elemental other," the intrapsychic chaperone. It is not true dependency. An underlying tone of amorphous fusion of ego and id and the overlay of partial ego relation with part-object comprises the protodependency constellation of unconscious envy characteristic of this primitive period.

The nascent sense of burgeoning differentiation and becoming separate is also accompanied by the envy-laden feelings that are instigated by privation. This is reflected in the protodependency issues inherent in envy and envy's omnipotently based offensive responsivity. In the paranoid-schizoid position, the part-object may be sensed at times as removed, self-sufficient, and "independent." Nongratification is sensed by the part-ego in the paranoid-schizoid position as this sort of withholding, in fact, an existential, privating inaccessibility.

Depressive-position dependency, in sharp contrast, is characterized by an active awareness of incremental degrees of separateness and difference. The capacity for more realistic perceptions of the external world is expanding. Objects perceived as whole entities, as such, and as whole entities linked with one another can now be perceived. Whole objects are identified with actual interpersonal figures. This imparts a feeling that observations are more complete rather than incomplete. The locus of perceived control shifts inward and the ego senses itself as more consciously competent and effectual. Nascent impulses of intentionality and volition begin to emerge.

For example, the ego can now feel that it has lost what it once had—be it the object itself or something that the object had once given it. This results in a sense of *true deprivation* and resulting frustration. This is a frustration secondary to perceived intentional withholding. Both act to reinforce—not cause—the underlying foundation of *nuclear envy* within the paranoid-schizoid position—perpetually felt as a deeply hidden sense of unconscious privation, the emptiness of never having had what is desired.

Depressive-position dependency, therefore, is a secondary or more differentiated sense of earlier protodependency. It may be called "separateness proper." More precisely, it is a secondary (complexly developed over time) dependency fueled by mixtures of phantasy and actual environmental absences or separations that are felt as not wanted and unacceptable. In its phantasy proportions, defensive attempts at omnipotent control, even to the extent of domination of and holding onto the whole object, characterize it.

Yet, in sharp contrast to the paranoid-schizoid position, the experience of depressive-position dependency contains a softer, expectant hopefulness of regaining what was lost. This positive expectation vacillates in simultaneity (unlike in envy) with sadness and despondent despair. *Ambivalence and the depressive position go hand-in-hand.* This reflects the relatively more lovingly colored dependency issues that arise from the depressive position. These ordinarily appear in forms such as jealous, greedy, and aggressive possessiveness. All are triggered by events characterized by disappointment.

*Depressive-position aggressivity* strongly correlates with developed forms of *hate.* True hate unlike envy is a destructively negative, yet ambivalent, feeling toward a bad object. The ambivalence arises from some degree of attraction and admiration—felt in simultaneity—for the object as a whole entity. Depressive-position hate takes the form of sadism, greed, and various forms of manic domination: subjugation, humiliation, and torture. Infantile hate is elemental; its seeds take definable shape only gradually.

Holding on and the inability to let go, especially of emotional attachments and memories, are essential features of depressive-position dependency, disappointment, frustration, hate, aggressivity, violence, and cruelty. Omnipotence in the depressive position fuels its unconscious drive for power and control over the object. Various forms of hate constitute the negative side of depressive-position dynamics.

Hence, *the love-hate paradigm is the true hallmark of and belongs to the depressive position.* It reflects a relatively whole ego having the capacity to properly love, become disappointed, hate, feel consequences, and make reparation to repair and restore self-inflicted damages both intrapsychically and interpersonally.

To reiterate: paranoid-schizoid part-object relations are raw, primitive, extreme, and characterized by feelings of privation/absence. Such feelings are further characterized by partial object awareness sensed as the presence of the other as eerily self-sufficient and largely inaccessible more so than withholding. Fear and utter passivity are foremost.

The depressive position, by contrast, launches awareness of whole-object/whole-person recognition, truly dependent relations, the capacity for feeling deprivation from an, at times, intentionally withholding object, and a burgeoning yet still unmatured sense of volition. Disappointment leads to frustration, anguish, anger, hate, destructiveness, empathy, sorrow, and the benevolent wish to repair. Whereas in the paranoid-schizoid position *nuclear envy* took ascendancy, in the depressive position *nuclear love* is dominant. In contrast to the cacophony of the paranoid-schizoid position, the music of the depressive position is sweet not bitter, alluring not repulsing, poignant not cold hearted, and dramatic, if not melodramatic.

### The Depressive Position: Humanization of the Id

The *normal depressive position* of early infancy is a typical developmental occurrence launched at about three months of age and extending to about one year. It accompanies the onset and gradual development of abstract symbol formation. This reinforces the healthy intellectual and cognitive understanding of the meaning and memory of experience.

A crucial qualitative shift occurs at this developmental juncture. Dyadic relations of part-ego to part-object hallmarked the earlier paranoid-schizoid position. In the depressive position, this is partiality superseded by perceptions and apprehensions that are less split and more complete and whole. The ego feels whole in relation to an object grasped as whole. In other words, triangularity in relationships on all levels emerges. In analytic theory, this formalization of triangularity is the hallmark of the Oedipus complex. What must be reiterated again is the idea that, in fact, no absolute states of mind actually occur. For academic purposes, schematic divisions are made to merely approximate their referents. For example, within earlier dyadic relations, elements of triadic relations are present, probably in some sort of unorganized conflation.

The normative depressive position is the infant's mounting capability to creatively manage primitive experiences of absence, unintegration, incompleteness, and confusion. From a metapsychological perspective, the balanced interaction of the life instinct and the death instinct in the ego enhances the *epistemophilia* of the self. In real-world time, this is further enhanced by the material, emotional, and mental caregiving (the safe and regulatory experience and modeling of nurturant containment) of the mothering person, and the absence of inordinate infantile stressors.

From a cognitive and emotional perspective, the ego develops an organizing inner focus with more intentionality and conscientiousness. The nuclear status of love asserts itself as part of developing configurations of nascent empathy, concern, caring, tolerance, and reparative trends, all of which are set in motion in the depressive position. This gradual refinement of *intelligent* love amplifies the formation and meaningfulness of developing object relations whose overall aim is both self- *and object survival.*

In other words, the depressive position ushers in a more accurate apprehension of reality—namely, a relatively more solid *reality sense.* It promotes the burgeoning capacity to differentiate more realistically the internal world of psychic reality from the perceived and actual world of external, real objects and environmental events.

The paranoid-schizoid underlayer of singularly perceived part-objects becomes *overlaid with the depressive-position dynamics of multiple whole-object relations— closer approximations toward completeness, however imprecise, on all cognitive and emotional levels.* This normative "depressive" level of developing organization is characterized by less splitting, less fragmentation, and more constrained omnipotent impulses, especially those prompting aggressive control.

In other words, the transition from a paranoid-schizoid psychological configuration to healthy depressive-position functioning involves the following: (1) a burgeoning realization of intentionally felt aggression toward an ideal, (2) the perceived absence of this previously felt ideal due to its personally caused loss, and (3) recovery of that ambivalently loved object, but now felt not as ideal—but rather as "very good." Renunciation of ideal construals and sublimation toward perceptions of experiential goodness—experiencing self and other as basically good—underlie this transformation.

This increasing capacity to sense wholeness, greater degrees of completeness, and integrated containment among real perceptions of multiplicities brings about a grasp of objects, which now can be felt in more complex and ambivalent ways. Whole objects are apprehended (for example, the actual mother and father) and primary and secondary object relations are more firmly laid down (for example, primary relation to mother, and secondary relation to father as the first new object to explore after mother). The term "new object" strongly implies the developing infant's capacity to explore (become aware of and interact with) the entire extended environment beyond just the primary mothering person and relation.

In earliest infancy, *the psychic presence of father* has real meaning. The father is present for the infant in many important ways. First, from the start of life, the indirect impact of father exerts influence through the primary caregiver, the mother, as an image in her mind. Bion's (1962b) concept of mother's "reverie"—empathetically understanding and transforming the infant's mental states—assumes the presence of "father" in her mind, and the infant's participation, in some way, in this is substantial.

How the maternal experience of the baby's father is held and how it is commingled with her sense of her perceptions of her father as well as her baby deeply affect the infant (boy and girl, as well as growing child) in a variety of ways, especially through mother's affectively modulated caregiving. Second, father plays an important role for the infant as an interactive, *physical bodily presence*, or, for that matter, by periods of his material absence. Of course, this presence reflects the significant qualities of male parenting, love, and nurturance underlying the meaningful impact of father for child.

The role of father as the premier secondary object emerges. Both theoretically and in real life, the colossal importance of father as part-object (penis) and as whole object (person) in relation to the breast and the mother—in effect, the *Oedipus complex*—takes center stage. All these constructs exist as unconscious phantasy on nonconscious levels of information and affective processing.

As the depressive position begins to supersede the paranoid-schizoid position (both chronologically and in later life), the rawness and primitive quality of one's unmodulated id becomes transformed. This id transformation denotes the id's blending more with and becoming more in alignment with the conscious ego. *What had been experienced concretely and dominated more by corporeal drives morphs, in part, into a more reflective and empathetic frame of reference.* This is reflected in behaviors and implies an attenuation of the exclusive dominance of unmodulated unconscious phantasy.

In summary, the depressive position and the Oedipus complex jointly provide a leap into the humanization of the individual psyche: social competence and enculturation. Mental looping occurs, which opens an ever-greater capacity for receptivity, inclusion of new persons and events, the synthesis of polarities, and an intrinsic trend toward adaptive rhythmic cycling and maturity, in other words, forward movement rather than the blind repetition and stalling characteristic of the paranoid-schizoid position.

Once the depressive position has been reached, it replays itself throughout life in a cyclic, rhythmic, recurrent, and episodic fashion to attain ever more refinement. Primitive destructive impulses, in particular the omnipotent, unbridled power of unconscious id impulses, are reconfigured by the continual achievement of empathy and compassion. Moreover, the renunciation of developmentally primitive patterns of mental processing enhances intelligent creativeness on all levels, as in, for example, cognitive symbol formation and emotionally charged aesthetic productions. Since, however, the decided focus of the present work is to highlight envy, these later constituents of mental life, undeniably important as they are, will not be addressed at length in the fine detail they require.

### Infantile Unconscious Phantasy/Mental Schemata: Sexual Body Part and Sexual Relationship Images with Meaning

Klein emphasized two principal developmental events in earliest infancy with strong social repercussions: (1) the "combined parent figure" (1923, 1929, 1932, 1957), which is a paranoid-schizoid, part-object early oedipal configuration; and (2) the depressive-position reparative elements that go into the resolution of the more fully developed Oedipus complex in the context of a triangular relation to two whole objects, the actual mother and father.

Klein conjectured that the infant's envious impulse to intrude into and rob the breast of its contents correlated with the unconscious phantasy of a breast merged with a penis in mutual gratification. This conflation of part-objects locked in wild, pulsating excitement continued in nonconscious processes throughout childhood and was suggested as the cause of nightmares of ugly, monstrous, and tormenting creatures. If excessive envy prevails, fear, paranoid persecutory anxieties, and confusional states persist. Parenthetically, it can be speculated that fascination with orgies and wild sexual debauchery depicted in some classical works of art and also in people's behaviors may have a tie in with such unconscious phantasies.

If envy is not excessive, *jealousy*—which may act as a defense against envy—in the oedipal situation is a major means of working it through. The latter permits a diffusion from almost exclusive attention on mother toward inclusion of father and other whole objects.

Empirically, nursing at the breast or bottle-feeding from birth to about the second year is observably an intimate biomental experience for both members of the infant-mother dyad. Infants become accustomed to nourishment and comfort from food, warmth, physical protection, love, understanding, and language—whatever the level of quality and quantity. The experience of weaning (Klein 1936) toward the end of the first year and into the second year also typically instigates a significant loss of a vital experience felt as *disappointment* connected with the feeding mother. *The constellation of these early losses may be the prototype for all later disappointments.* It influences how loss is experienced in the Oedipus complex and how jealousy plays in when three persons are involved.

Weaning naturally shifts attention to other objects in the environment. Although mother is the primary object used by the infant for exploration on all levels, the onset of the depressive position, weaning, and the inevitable Oedipus complex naturally introduce the crucial significance of father. Interest in father as a person, who is different from mother, correlates with newfound novel activity, action, and more robust physical interaction.

This tends to shift attention outward, and these reality components help shape and modify *unconscious phantasy* life as it becomes acquainted with and modified by these reality features. Primitive unconscious phantasy changes and contributes to the formation of *mental schemas* that function as subliminal templates for conscious attitudes and preferences.

A reference can be made at this point to the construct of "absent penis" and of "no penis." Both of these are contributions of *envy theory* and corollaries of Bion's constructs of "absent breast" and "no breast." They are, however, on different levels of reference: "absent breast" is on the earliest pregenital level of nurturance—paranoid-schizoid position; "absent penis" is on the early depressive position, pregenital level. It is the primitive root of the later more organized phallic level of genital awareness (around age three).

I have proposed the "absent penis" and the "no penis" conceptions as significant depressive-position constructs that have incipient genital and oedipal significance for developing sexual orientation. They are metapsychological constructs relating to unconscious phantasies and primary process unconscious cognition. Genetic, constitutional, and experiential factors contribute to their makeup.

Some situations of male homosexuality, for example, are associated with complex unconscious phantasies wherein the part-object breast is so excessively idealized that a developmentally fuller appreciation of the significance of the part-object penis has been eclipsed. The part-object penis, in effect, is buried in the part-object breast or deeply within the mother's vagina/body. Its emotional invisibility in unconscious phantasy is felt to be an "absent penis." Thus, the male infant/child identifies with the maternal figure.

Conversely, if in the paranoid-schizoid position, the breast is excessively *de*idealized, it may be felt as a positive absence or void. Idealization of the part-object penis may occur prematurely and become a fixation point that influences sexual orientation and sexual object choice in later development. In this case, the male infant/child excessively becomes attracted to the male figure, who is then overly idealized. *Envy theory* does not assign psychopathology to these possible configurations but regards them as conjectures having some explanatory value.

In these cases, the male infant and child has an insufficient or skewed identificatory experience with maleness: absence of the unconscious phantasy of a positive penis or father. This may result from a perceived emotional absence, an actual absence of a real environmental father, or an overidealization of what signifies maleness.

As a result, in the fully genitalized era of adolescence, the child is inordinately attracted to the penis and to males in general in an excessively idealized fashion. This is prompted by a primitively based paranoid-schizoid and depressive-position unresolved conflict. Only later is it augmented by the unfolding of fuller and more mature genital expression. Homosexual object choice may develop. This may be an attempt to restore what was felt lost through privation (male penis envy). This may be felt as ego-syntonic and a preferred choice in thinking and behavior. It may also reflect a defensive attempt to manically aggrandize the penis (manic idealization) that was felt to be destroyed aggressively because of the male infant's anger instigated by the perceived deprivation and withholding of father.

Short of overt homosexuality, males who idealize the part-object penis or whole object father may develop an empirical bias toward males accompanied by a devaluation of females. Adult sexist and chauvinistic attitudes that extol maleness and *perceived* male qualities such as power, prowess, and action-oriented accomplishments may be driven by such underlying phantasies.

### The Conscious Experience of Sexual Attraction

The above mentioned unconscious phantasy configurations having sexualized meaning actually do express themselves experientially in adolescent and adult life. An individual's seemingly instinctive and idiosyncratic attraction to another person—heterosexual, homosexual, or bisexual—reflects these unconscious proclivities. The clearest examples correlate with sexual dimorphism.

Whereas primary sexual characteristics, namely the reproductive organs, themselves, typically reference the conscious object of sexual preference, the particular secondary sexual characteristics a male or female finds most appealing have roots in how idiosyncratic infantile phantasies emerge, develop, and become reinforced. How natural inclinations and preferences are shaped by the way envy is experienced and managed plays a leading role in the outcome of adult sexual attraction and preferences.

Moreover, *unconscious phantasies are constructed largely of "part-objects," cognitive and affective partial apprehensions magnified out of context that remain static reference points in the unconscious.* Leading universal examples applicable to both sexes are: the breast, the penis, the buttocks, and the lips, to mention only a few.

However, male secondary sexual characteristics such as beard, hairy chest, broad shoulders, bushy eyebrows, and muscular arms, for example, are also experienced as "part-objects" in unconscious phantasy. They are singled out and excessively libidinalized (infused with inordinate amounts of life instinct sexual energy). If these are idealized in infancy because of their idiosyncratically imputed significance (for example, power, force, domination, submission, and control), in adult life they become conscious sexual attractors. These formulations, *mutatis mutandis*, also apply to female secondary sexual characteristics in their role as adult sexual attractors—for example, prominent lips, shapely pelvis. In addition, body parts in both sexes that are apparently nonsexual may become overly libidinalized—for example, tongue, legs, feet, anus. Sometimes these phantasy attractors and clothing associated with them become the focus of attention in fetishism.

## Infancy: The First Pass Structuring
## of the Developmental Positions
## as Lifetime Prototypes of Object Relations

How the paranoid-schizoid and depressive positions are handled early on establishes the ego's enduring orientation to itself and its objects throughout life. The ego's fidelity to reality is thus refined in ever-increasing measure. There is always a dynamic balance of healthy and unhealthy outcomes.

If the infant is able to feel sufficient gratification while feeding at "the breast" without envy and greed interfering too much, the reception and assimilation of nurturance—being loved and understood—is enhanced with loving, enjoyment, and gratitude toward mother. These establish a securely organized attachment of trust.

In particular, *the introjection of the "good part-object breast" in the normal paranoid-schizoid position galvanizes ego integration and acts as the focal point and vital core of the stabilizing ego. In the developmentally advanced era of the depressive position, the qualitatively more empathetic introjection of the "good whole object mother," achieved by means of reparation, further consolidates ego integrity and coherence, advances biomental reorganization, and modulates extreme states of mind.*

*Reparation, however, is made up of much more than mere expiation; it is empowered by the unique charge of the creativeness of the id. It organizes mental homeostasis through the reparative and creative libidinal forces at work in the ego.*

*This healing of splits in ego and splits projected into object enables the ego to love and care for the good whole object as it exists in relation to the integrating ego.* A further elaboration of the depressive position is found in chapter 9.

In summary, the ego in the paranoid-schizoid position is experienced as a passive entity acted on by outside influences; it is needy, insecure, and unstable. Ego and object boundaries are blurred. Whatever object awareness exists is felt as omnipotently possessed and virtually indistinct from the ego; paradoxical blurring/fusing of boundaries and feelings of isolation collide. The part-object is constructed both emotionally and also determined by the infant's immature cognitive apparatus. Part-objects are partly fused objects that are confused primarily with aspects of the infant's own body. Survival in the paranoid-schizoid position is principally the ego's survival at all costs.

Paranoid-like persecutory anxiety, indignation, grievance, and persecutory guilt are retaliatory-based responses to intermittent perceptions of part-object malevolence. Persecutory anxiety occurs when the ego feels immensely passive, vulnerable, and acted upon by hostile outside forces. If the part-object breast is excessively idealized, by contrast, the ego feels diminished and envious anxiety arises. *Nuclear envy* dominates.

In the *normal paranoid-schizoid position*, the part-object breast is incorporated in an *undamaged*, contained manner into the structure of the ego. Thus, it acts as a "good breast," one that is *normally idealized*. This decisively furthers ego integration and the normal building up of the ego. During these normal developmental sequences, the ego experiences a respectful, *paused awe* for the goodness it perceives. The normal paranoid-schizoid position is characterized by consistent ego attitudes of agreeableness and flexible, adaptive accommodation in response to perceptions of benevolence rather than perceptions of fear. This is a "proto" self-regulation characterized by a developing capacity for *paused anticipation*. Normal idealization is akin to a state of wonder and awe, the nucleus for all further developments of love. *Nuclear love* asserts itself more boldly.

Hence, healthy outcomes in the paranoid-schizoid position have both affective and cognitive dimensions. As the part-object becomes regarded with admiration, awe, and respect, it becomes loved and sensed as basically good. From a cognitive perspective, this indicates that idealization has normalized and that healthy valuation has become an established parameter for measuring experience. This capacity for a balanced valuation of experience is the primary precursor to the progressive establishment of the meaningfulness that becomes attributed to experience.

In contrast, when excessive persecutory or excessive envious anxiety (feelings of fear, hostility, and confusion) predominate, the part-object is experienced as both malevolent and fragmented, a significantly disorganized morass. It is incorporated as sorely less than optimal: as an impotent, barren, and bad breast. Excessive envy is accompanied by the incorporation of a deidealized spoiled breast. This perpetuates internal disorder and weakened ego states: intolerance, impulsivity, and proclivity to disintegration. It is worthwhile to reiterate and underscore that the course of average development includes elements within the range of what is normal but may also include some elements of the extremes of both ends of the normal-abnormal spectrum.

The *ego in the depressive position* is whole enough to begin feeling separate from the object now felt as whole, complete, and distinct. The ego, experiencing a newfound sense of activity and effectance—empowerment to bring about desired results in more competent ways—implicitly realizes its actual capacity for forceful aggression and true hate. This connotes the realization of possessing the malefic power to intentionally harm and weaken a separate, ambivalently loved object.

A sense of activity begins to supervene over feelings of passivity. The ego thus comes to feel a sense of *normal remorse, culpability, self-reproach, and guilt* at its capacity for and phantasied attempts to enact this targeted object destruction. In the chronological period of infancy, these developments are unmatured, rudimentary, primitive, and virtually nonconscious. These anlagen are the seeds that give rise to their more complex forms that only develop more completely during a lifetime.

Profound sorrow releases reparative urges to spare the object. Survival in the depressive position denotes a twofold phenomenon: (1) the ego's release of the object from the ego's capacity to harm it, and (2) the ego's effort to survive both the devastating depressive agony that follows harmful assaults (perceived and real) and loss of the omnipotently felt possession of the ambivalently loved object. This is the conflictual framework behind *separation anxiety*.

Patience, tolerance, and the *roots of empathy* inaugurate further ego integration and object consolidation. This is accompanied by a developing capacity for waiting ("impulse control") with a greater sense of expectant security in the face of glaring ambiguities. When reparative urges culminate and the ego experiences the object as the good, unharmed, and unfeared "other," the resulting internalized identification with this "good breast" consolidates and promotes further self-regulation.

A secure identification denotes a felt experience of union with the deeper dimensions of oneself (the ego's core of its id, the *primordial object*) and with the *primal* (*part-object breast*) and *primary objects* (*whole object mother*) of desire and knowledge. This more secure twofold ego-object relation remains the ultimate point of all subsequent psychological self-referencing.

The creativeness and fertility issuing from the experience of the whole object now becomes the focal point in the ego for all further integration, growth, and development. Once excessive envy in the paranoid-schizoid position has been sufficiently mitigated, the mixture of hate and destructiveness (sadism and manic domination) in the depressive position may begin its own journey toward progressive resolution.

Hateful feelings as self-reproaches for intentional harm to the object transform into states of respect, positive regard, admiration, and gratitude. This dominance of *nuclear love* encompasses a more secure recognition of the goodness of self and other. This becomes the wellspring of all creativity and sublimated forms of creativity on both mental and genital (sexual potency and capacity for healthy adult intimacy) levels as development proceeds. From a cognitive point of view, this enhances the exponentially developing capacity for meaningful valuation of all experience. The rational mind develops.

It is worthwhile to mention that, when a *successful transition from the paranoid-schizoid to the depressive position fails* for some reason (and this includes an actual genetic, neurological, physiological, structural, or constitutional cause along with experiential emotional trauma), an *obsessive-compulsive disorder*, for example, may arise. Obsessional mechanisms reflect mental functioning that is stuck and slowed in its transitioning out of the paranoid-schizoid position. Tremendous anxiety is generated and compulsive responses, however precarious, are instigated to reduce these tensions. In contrast, a manic constellation of defenses and disorders may arise. These represent a psychological flight away from depressive conflicts when the ego is already sufficiently within, but unable to work through elements of, the depressive position.

Obsessional conditions are characterized by primitive mechanisms such as splitting and projective identification rather than ambivalence proper (a more developed and conscious emotional state). Splitting here expresses itself as doing-undoing, a preoccupation with separation, keeping things widely apart and isolated, and a compelling need for precision and exactness. Obsessional paranoia is seen in preoccupations with contamination, germs, uncleanness (implied paranoid-schizoid fears), and other anally related issues.

In projective identification, unwanted, conflictual, and "dirty" aspects of the self are split off and relocated outside the self. In turn, they become the object of identification. Such connectivity reflects tenacious but unsuccess-ful repetitive attempts to control what was dislodged from the self, but is ironically still felt to be a part, in absentia, of the self that still needs to be reworked somehow.

The role of the *sadistic superego* is prominent in these situations. It is a conscience saturated with envy. In addition, as such, it relentlessly persecutes the ego with barrages of self-doubt, confusion, uncertainty, shame, embar-rassment, secrecy, and a need for repetitive reassurances—all stemming from perceived transgressions of fairness and equity. *Envy theory* recognizes the importance of this moral tone in experience and how envy drives it. A great deal of what is sensed as fair and equitable has innate, phylogenetic roots.

Envy, hoarding, and secrecy are found together in such clinical presen-tations. All these emotions (doubt, shame, embarrassment) and behaviors (hoarding, secrecy) are compounded over time and appear well after the first year of life. In fact, they often are reactions to and defenses against uncon-scious envy though not invariably.

In later childhood, adolescence, and adulthood, the conscious awareness of envious attitudes often triggers secrecy and a need to hide such hostile inclinations. Various mechanisms of defense are used to mask envious at-titudes. Appearing indifferent is a socially adaptive and defensive strategy when idealized comparisons and raw competitive urges are aroused. In addi-tion, the action of the inferred death instinct expressed as obsessional repeti-tion reflects continual, intermittent retreats toward further paranoid-schizoid mechanisms. Perhaps, the malignancy of this inferred etiology is plausible since *hoarding behaviors* as part of obsessive-compulsive disorders are *often intransient and seemingly unmodifiable.*

## Self-Signature Updating: The Developmental Positions Reconfiguring Over Time

Although the initial critical period for negotiating each position occurs in infancy, resolution in infancy is never complete. A continual and oscillating psychodynamic configuration of challenges and adaptations automatically attempts to update itself on a steady basis. The two basic developmental positions are states of mind that regularly occur, recur, and oscillate at all chronological ages.

Normalcy denotes adequate ego integration. It also reflects the mitigation of destructive impulses: envy in the paranoid-schizoid position, and hate in the depressive position. When envy and hate can be sufficiently managed, depressive-position configurations further act to spur reparation, a sense of gratitude, and refinements in emotional and conceptual self-consolidation. These self-signature updating processes secure and support continuing mental health.

In summary, the tie between Melanie Klein's theory of the positions and *envy theory* is the following. *In the nuclear paranoid-schizoid position, raw love, especially in its form as elemental idealization, and envy, the most primitive form of incipient raw hate, are the driving tensions that establish mental functioning through part-object relations.* These are cognitive and affective mental states having characteristics of "presentation" rather than "representation." As much as this primitive configuration of confusion is resolved, attitudes of awe, wonder, and admiration modulate raw fear. Positive self-regard and object concern/regard in concert begin to organize and take hold. *Nuclear envy is contained and qualitatively modulated by nuclear love.*

Crossing this threshold sufficiently ushers in the depressive position. Love and hate toward whole objects—real people—now superimpose themselves and act as the principal coordinates regulating self and object experience, as well as influencing interpersonal attachment behaviors. The representability and cognitive dimensions of these mental states become more conscious and measurable over time. To the extent that the depressive position advances by using momentum provided by burgeoning guilt and reparative love, gratitude both self-directed and in object relations prevails.

The nucleus of hate is envy; the nucleus of love is idealization. While the nuclear configuration of the matured personality has its center of gravity in the depressive position, the core of the depressive position is always centrated in a underlying matrix of primitive paranoid-schizoid dynamics.

## Primary Envy of the Primal Part-Object, the "Mother's Feeding Breast," as the Prototypical, Object Relations Model of Envy: A Recapitulation of the Envy Dynamic

In earliest infancy, when envy is incited in the imagined, expected, or actual presence of another, automatic comparisons naturally arise. A perceived sense—to some extent realistic yet also colored by subjective interpretation—of something *missing in the perceiver but possessed by the envied object* is strongly felt. Karl Abraham (1919, 1921) suggested this aspect of the envy dynamic when he referred to the envier as seeing the envied object as a "privileged proprietor."

Idiosyncratic interpretations of experience attributable to primitive and unmatured cognitive faculties heavily contribute to the phantasy points of view of early envy, its idiosyncratic grasp of experience, and the internalization of interpersonal relationships. Experience is the experience of partial aspects of the world—part-objects. Inner mental processes and outer environmental realities are always dynamically synchronizing one another.

*Idealization in part aims to attribute maximal creativeness, a self-dependent autonomy, to its targeted object.* The more pronounced the subject's perceived sense of having a missing feature, the more inordinately enhanced by extreme forms of *idealization* such a feature becomes. Such *defensive* idealization is the unconscious process of excessively enriching the meaning of an experience to the point of unrealistic perfection.

In the paranoid-schizoid position, the major experiential form that this vicarious projection assumes is shaped by the ego's state of omnipotence. The envier's unbearable sense of partiality, inadequacy, and vulnerability motivates this. In contrast, the dynamics of the depressive position imbue experiential creativeness with relatively more secondary process qualities of fertility, creative productivity, and wholeness. This considerably lessens egocentric states—the unmitigated omnipotence of unmodulated unconscious impulses and their unconscious phantasy states.

The aggrandizing value appraisal brought about by idealization (maximized in the paranoid-schizoid position) inflates the ego's defensive sense of omnipotence to counteract feelings of being poor, helpless, passive, and little. Envy stimulates an awareness of deep feelings of the *absence* of what is sensed as desirable, advantageous, and beneficial. The envier feels the personal presence of passive, ineffectual, and unwanted weaknesses: vulnerability, disability, flaw, deficit, and limitation. This autistic-like state of confusion and disillusionment elicits a rage that aims at destroying all aspects of both the evoked, unbearable distress and the intolerable anxiety that always accompanies envy. Excessive surges of narcissism accompanied by the need for omnipotent control are elicited to counter envious anxieties.

Melanie Klein (1957) described the origins of envy as emerging in the first relation that the infant experiences—that is, mouth to breast. This longing for the ideal breast includes a craving for food, libidinal desires for love, and wanting relief from anxiety. Anxiety in this state of mind is primarily envious. Its additionally associated hostile and aggressive features are characterized by fearful and persecutory responses to a sensed bad object, which, in part, reinforces the defensive presence (needed to counter anxiety) of the idealized part-object of envy.

*These dual anxieties, both persecutory and envious, significantly enhance an innate readiness for entrainment with something significant to induce stability and achieve some degree of equilibratory resonance.* All these factors are necessary for survival. *In the neonatal period, only a relation with the breast may fulfill these needs.* This enables the infant to recognize the breast with the characteristic value and meaning innate to and released by the *epistemophilia* of the self. Sight, sound, smell, touch, and taste are biomentally coordinated to receive and interact with the breast at the moment of birth.

In the neonatal period and for a long time afterward, the mouth is dominant in sensory, motor, and affective experience. Tactile, temperature, pain, pressure, smooth muscle, and extended motor responsiveness reflect the very high degree of developed sensory, motor, and affective pathways operating at this early time. This constellation reflects the substantive biomental nature of early infancy.

Klein described this longing for the breast as a primitive object relation; she stated that it materialized and was anchored in the concrete lips-to-nipple sucking activity of the infant. All this is also emblematic of *envy theory*'s proposition of the earliest primordial, dyadic, anaclitic mental relation: ego to id as the enduring subtext on which the ego builds all subsequent relations to objects. This remains the nonconscious urgent focus of attention upon which is layered further relationships to highly significant others, the first of whom is mother.

Of note from a neuroanatomical perspective is the extensive mapping and representation of the lips in the somatosensory portions of the central nervous system. In addition to hand and face cortical representation in the brain, the lips show virtually massive neuronal circuitry from the start of life (Berlucci and Aglioti 1997).

The Kleinian conceptualization of *the breast* denotes the infant's interaction with a *feeding breast*, which is inclusive of the biological fact of this feeding interaction with its mental and affective concomitants: experiential nurturance, satisfaction, loving affiliation, pleasure, relief from anxiety, feeling understood, and, in general, a surge of creativeness.

All these features of the breast—the first perception of enduring importance—characterize the primal object needed for survival on all levels. The breast is unconsciously felt to be the prototype of creativeness; its feeding function and its milk are experienced as the source of life. On experiential and material levels, therefore, *the "breast" is the instantiation of vivifyingness.*

Unconscious envy arises when the subject who wishes to receive nurturance does not feel the adequacy of any sort of received nurturance whether real or imagined. *This sense of privation is reinforced when the subject believes that the nurturer is feeding itself. Envy is the sense of privation coupled with feelings that "the other" is endowed with the self-dependent capacity of feeding itself.* This construct of the significance of the breast and complex construals of it, for example, even supersedes the significance of face recognition in early infancy. The relation to the breast has not only psychogenetic primacy, but also indestructible psychodynamic primacy in mental development.

At any developmental or chronological period, *envy of the mother* is a profound and shocking realization because ordinarily it is unthinkable. It seems irrational and counterproductive to resent and turn against the very figure who has given birth to and fed her child, and continues to help her child to survive.

The paranoid-schizoid position denotes a part-object relation that includes not only anxieties, phantasies, and defensive maneuvers, but also *normal developmental adaptation and personality integration facilitated by love and the search for meaning.* This ego-object configuration is developmentally superseded, but not absolutely replaced, by the normative depression position. The paradigmatic depressive-position model consists of a triadic set of object relations intimately related to early oedipal dynamics. *Neither position is ever fully or entirely completed or mastered. Both persist in the unconscious and are reworked as a normal part of everyday life.*

This point is critical to underscore. Klein (1957, 1959) stressed that the greater the degree of *ego integration* and capacity for empathy and compassion, the greater the ability to recognize one's own destructive potential. Consequently, there is a greater ability to *spare the self and the other intentional harm.* The extent to which these reparative developments are achieved reflects the degree of mental health achieved in the depressive position. It highlights the leading roles that love and attempts to establish meaningful relations play.

The experience of envy of the mother's potent creativeness is unique. On the deepest unconscious level, *envy theory* equates the power that this exerts, *mutatis mutandis,* with the ego's primordial envy of its id. Accordingly, upon this bedrock of primordially based envy—an unconsciously rooted envy of the mother—is the formal basis of primary envy. Recognition of this thesis requires open-mindedness, courage, and fortitude. Realizing that one can and, in fact, does envy one's own mother and even one's self in part (id) or in its entirety are startling shocks. It may be more profound a shock than acknowledging one's unconscious incestuous wishes. It is defended against by everything that is emotionally and intellectually available to cover it up, if not negate and summarily dismiss it.

## Primary Love of the Primal Part-Object: Paused Awe, Silent Wonder, Admiration, Hopeful Anticipation, Reverence, and Compassion

*Envy theory* regards the earliest developmental configuration—the paranoid-schizoid position—to be the principal primitive state of the developing psyche. At the start of life, primary love exists as a *raw love* chiefly composed of normal *elemental idealization*.

Primary libidinal/loving experiences toward the primal part-object breast and, in effect, the mother as primary whole object expand and are elaborated when the paranoid-schizoid position sufficiently resolves in early infantile development and repeatedly becomes refined thereafter. *Envy theory* emphasizes that *whole-object experience is foreshadowed in the paranoid-schizoid position where part-object experience is dominant*.

These loving feelings are real and substantive. They modulate primitive fear and hate in qualitative ways. Unmodulated fear, which signals danger, gradually sublimates aspects of itself into the emotion of surprise. *Surprise*, a healthy achievement in the chronological paranoid-schizoid position, reflects the increased vigilance and vividness accompanying an unexpected event. This harkens the canalization of receptivity to novel experience, which, in itself, reflects an enhancement of cognitive and learning processes. Experiences of astonishment and amazement in later life derive from early infantile experiences of awe, surprise, and wonder. When normal and not marked by excess, these healthy outcomes become the orienting foundation for all later mental development. They can be characterized as states of *paused awe, admiration, silent wonder, deep respect, hopeful anticipation, and a burgeoning sense of reverence*.

The chronologically primary love of the primal part-object (breast) denotes normal idealization typical of the normal paranoid-schizoid position. Developmentally normal idealization, the elemental and raw love engendered by the life instinct, infuses both the nascent ego and its sense of the elemental goodness of the object.

Idealization of the primal part-object normalizes, stabilizes, and becomes a healthy sense of valuation. These ego-centered epiphanies reflect attitudes of adaptive accommodation and agreeableness. They signal burgeoning differentiation and less confusion and lead to successful adaptation and self-integration. Feelings of admiration quickly become sensed as feelings of appreciation. All these elemental nonconscious paranoid-schizoid states pave the way for and partially transmute into the gradually emerging, more conscious depressive-position constellation characterized by less omnipotence, greater empathy, gratitude, compassion, wholeness, and clarity of resolve toward less impulsive action.

Successful mourning or working through these positions, especially the reparative climax of the depressive position, is reflected by ever-deepening degrees of ego integration and recognition of one's real potential to harm. This is an acknowledgment marked by conviction of the psychic fact that one has really harmed the loved object.

The sorrow and mourning that accompany a progressively less aggressive and more compassionate relation to both self and one's objects are startling epiphanies. The poignancy of these feelings rises to a pitch that becomes arresting and compelling. An indication that a successful outcome occurred is measured when one sees the self and the object in their more realistic, mixed roles as *both good and sometimes bad*. In a novel way, the capacity for such *ambivalence* may now be used to spare them the hatefulness and harm that previously had been targeted at them.

This process of maturation and integration *begins* its long journey toward refinement first in the chronological period of infancy. At each subsequent childhood developmental level and with increasingly greater emotional and cognitive development, further work on refining the depressive position and aspects of the paranoid-schizoid position always occurs.

In adulthood, with greater emotional maturity and cognitive development (abstraction, symbolization, memory, and the expansion of meaningfulness), the depressive position becomes reworked repeatedly, especially when significant relationships are punctuated by disappointment or are lost through separation or death. The poignancy of each renewed experience of depressive sorrow deepens.

The *capacity for realistic mourning* becomes a ballast insuring discrimination of the real from the unreal. This enhances the ability to embrace the transitory quality of experience with more acceptance and securely based expectant hopefulness. Complete and permanent resolution is never achieved. *In adulthood, it is by allowing depressive pain and suffering to occur—in full measure—that one is exposed to one's inner world, especially what had been split off, denied, and repressed—in other words, experienced as previously unconscious.*

Struggling through depressive-position sorrow is akin to feeling that one is and will die from the crisis of inexorable pain that emerges. Suffering depressive anxiety and guilt amounts to a feeling of dying on multiple experiential levels. If one can endure this, survival heralds a psychic transfiguration—the awakening of feelings and realizations that hallmark the essence of the human condition. Complete mastery of the depressive position is never achieved, nor can it be. The enrichment that depressive-position dynamics imparts to one's life is virtually unending; it remains a lifelong affair, a dynamic process of becoming. The capacity for a sense of authentic love—unequivocal commitment—develops in this way.

*These dynamic ego-object relations in the "positions" are states of mind that are continuously worked through as part of all development—normal and abnormal—during the course of all life's chronological thresholds yet in differing ways. Growth with its maturation of cognition and developing emotional refinement influences these iterations over time and life's chronological thresholds. Experiencing aspects of each, especially their interplay, is part of the universal experience of the core developmental process, both normal and pathological. This concept of continual development over a lifetime highlights the possibility of deepening the capacity for both the continuing enrichment of character and the development of ever-greater integrative refinement in one's quality of life.*

Klein (1957) explicitly understood the envy dynamic as central to the paranoid-schizoid position. This primal footing beneath all aspects of mental functioning is and remains rooted in primary nonconscious processes and the dynamic unconscious. It is housed there as unconscious phantasy, which acts in template fashion for all later, more highly complex states of anxiety, defense, and adaptation to reality.

Klein maintained that the prototypical model of envy was the infantile ego's envy of its first part-object, the feeding breast, which transmuted into and rapidly oscillated with a primary envy of the whole object, the primary caregiver, the mother.

*Envy theory* adds to this *nuclear envy's* hidden subtext: the *primordial envy of ego toward id as the irreducible bedrock of all primary envy.* In simultaneity, envy and love interact and mutually influence one another. When the grievance and hostile indignation stimulated by envy are mitigated by love, feelings of paused, respectful awe, wonder, and hopeful anticipation—that is, basic trust—toward the primary object needed for survival become increasingly established. The substratum of hopeful anticipation becomes normalized unconscious phantasy.

The earliest object relations may be described in a dual way: the infant's relation to the *mother-breast* (*primal part-object*) of the paranoid-schizoid position, and to the *breast mother* (*primary whole object*) of the depressive position.

These are real experiential configurations, which persist in unconscious phantasy and underlie all states of mind after the period of infancy. Perhaps the central point to emphasize here is that the first prototypical ego relation is to the mother's feeding breast. This is a relation *of love as well as hate, especially in the primitive form of primary envy.*

The introjective encoding of this first object lays the foundation for all subsequent internalizing cognitive-affective processes, which implies emotional development and adaptive learning from experience. The relational ballast of this interactive association of ego and object cannot be emphasized enough. It is given meaning by the inherent *epistemophilia* within the self. After infancy and in adulthood, the capacity to develop, respect, and revere values and standards of conduct, both personal and social, derives according to the degree that envy has undergone a healthy maturation.

Last, the preverbal period that includes both the paranoid-schizoid and depressive positions in the first year of life has exceedingly significant importance since it also is the time when the skills necessary for the development of *empathy* and *intuition* are laid down. The presemantic infant with limited functional motor abilities must optimize the use of its sensory faculties to experience the world in which it finds itself. It is an experience of relative silence, without language. The sensations of receptivity—sight, sound, smell, touch, and taste—are maximized to the extent that they are constitutionally endowed as well as fueled by internal motivation, seeking, and the elicitations of an attentive, responsive caregiver.

Hence, the infant develops and hones its nonverbal skills through the highly sensitive reception of stimuli, especially from the interactive and reinforcing personal environment. This intersubjectively shared, interpersonal, and affectively charged experience canalizes pathways for unconscious communications. This leads to more refinement of the capacity for transient participatory identifications forged and reinforced by highly charged emotional states. Maturing intelligence adds organizing cognitive richness and meaning to affective and intellectual cognition.

For example, recent contributions in psychodynamic psychology have referred to what *envy theory* describes as developing self-awareness, reflectivity, and empathy in the depressive position in theoretical terms by a special use of the term "mentalizations," qualitatively different from this term's denotation in *envy theory* (Sharp, Fonagy, and Goodyer 2008; Allen, Fonagy, and Bateman 2008). Moreover, treatment protocols using this specialized perspective are being tested in psychotherapies for conditions such as borderline personality disorder and the autistic spectrum of disorders.

In conclusion, the ego as information-processing witness to both itself and the object of love, hate, and envy enriches its neural connectivity and interpersonal attachments in these active ways. Burgeoning *intuitive capacities* become instrumental in all forms of communication at this early period, and underlie the communicational fidelity that later occurs when expressive language becomes dominant. Nonverbal communication and a wealth of nonconscious processes lie beneath both empathy and intuition.

## Summary

A broad view of human psychological development is presented. Constructs from classical psychoanalysis are used as the building blocks of this framework since they have an experience-near and phenomenological appeal. Besides, they are fundamental elements in understanding envy.

To position and elucidate the *nuclear envy* concept, *envy theory* focuses on the ego's modus operandi for knowing and active information processing—a capacity I term *projective internalization*. It is concomitant with the ego's faculty for witnessing—nonconscious and conscious experiencing—at all periods in development. *Projective internalization* denotes simultaneously being in an experience and being aware of an experience. It has conscious and nonconscious components.

The construct of the *unconscious as a system*—the id—is advanced. What I term the *id's paradox* is explained. It is the nonconscious mental id's drive to express itself and live in reality through the exploratory capacity of the preconscious and conscious ego, especially by sensory and motoric activity, in relentless pulsions whose final aim paradoxically is ultimate extinction.

Unconscious phantasy—how the mind experiences itself—is the object-related, organized mental content that embodies primitive units of meaning in the unconscious mind. Omnipotence as the illusory sense of self-dependence and completeness is one of the chief characteristics of the unconscious at all developmental periods. Lived experience, especially by unconscious phantasy guiding conscious awareness, is the matrix of psychic reality. Unconscious phantasies are the mind's information-processing units, subunits, and modules.

This radical object relations proposition emphasizes the poignant, experiential significance of personalized meaning rather than the operation of mechanistic mental functions. The individual is equipped at birth and thereafter with biopsychological preferences. Hence, idiosyncratically preferred experiences reinforce innate predispositions and are actively sought.

Biomental expectation pathways unfold and consolidate. Along with these, the monumentally important role of the actual external environment is also emphasized in *envy theory*.

The experiential subject throughout life exists in a state of continuous self-reconfiguration termed *self-signature updating*. The subjective inner world is the expression of unconscious phantasy, the way the mind perceives itself, especially its primitive, nonconscious substratum. This functional psychological geometry operates in a bidirectional loop. It both structures and is structured by transactions between itself and other subjects—"ego-object relations."

Melanie Klein's discovery of the developmental configurations, the "paranoid-schizoid" and "depressive" positions, is outlined. Movement and change in mental life is always referable to the dynamic and invariant oscillations between these ego-object positionings.

Her central proposition that primary envy, in an object relations perspective, is the primary envy of the primal part-object—the mother's feeding breast—is underscored. It is at once a comprehensive apprehension and a relation.

*Envy theory* characterizes as the nuclear relation of the infant its relation to the *mother-breast* (as *primal part-object*) in the paranoid-schizoid position and its relation to the *breast mother* (as *primary whole object*) in the depressive position.

Primary envy is always based on what *envy theory* advances as *primordial envy*: the ego's relation to its id. Envy and love, spoiling and idealization in all their permutations, are experienced mentally as part-objects and dynamic part-object relations. They persist in the transition to, within, and at the nuclear core of all whole-object relations. I regard these two configurations (primal envy and primary envy) as actual and real phenomenological experiences in infancy. They endure as forms of unconscious phantasy thereafter. These are forever grounded in paranoid-schizoid dynamics.

The counterpoint to Klein's idea of primary (technically in *envy theory* "primal") envy ("raw hate") of the *mother-breast* is primary (technically in *envy theory* "primal") love ("raw love or elemental idealization") of the primal part-object, the *mother-breast*. Excessive primary envy is destructive and abnormal. Primary love is constructive and normal. These part-object configurations are primitive paranoid-schizoid relations.

This earliest paranoid-schizoid form of primitive love is an impulse of normal idealization characterized by paused awe, silent wonder, deepening respect, hopeful anticipation, and a burgeoning sense of reverence. Admiration and emulation flow from this healthy maturation, valuation, and normalized idealization, all of which are significantly less omnipotent than their raw antecedents. When *nuclear envy* is sufficiently modulated by *nuclear love*, destructive impulses decline and the introjection of an internal good object forming the core of the ego can be established. This becomes the nidus for developmental progress and the emergence of the depressive position.

Depressive-position libidinal counterpoints to aggression and hate toward the whole object *breast mother* are empathy, compassion, gratitude, and meaningful understanding. These humanizing and mentally representable qualities arise out of the depressive position, which acts to reconfigure the omnipotent power of primitive id impulses, especially prominent in raw paranoid-schizoid operations.

In other words, in mental health, paranoid-schizoid dynamics should be more transient phenomena that are substantively—not totally—reconciled in early infancy by a successful advance to the healthy depressive position. Throughout the rest of development, these dynamics live forever in the active nonconscious dimensions of emotional life. To the extent that the biomental self is sufficiently integrated, depressive-position dynamics should be in ascendancy and comprise more of one's conscious concerns—namely, empathy, compassion, self-reflection, and helpfulness.

Object relations with mother together with father become the premier standards of creativeness that are recognized as both external realities and internal states of mind in infancy. The meaningfulness of these linkages resides in and emerges out of the inherent *epistemophilia*—impulse to know and feel in a meaningful way—within the entire self.

*All developmental psychosocial configurations* in infancy, childhood, adolescence, and adulthood are significant developmental achievements whose richness and newness influence each other over a lifetime. As growth, maturation, and development proceed, interpersonally developed affective sensitivity refines the capacity for participatory empathy. In turn, progressive intellectual enrichment over time reinforces both nonverbal intuition and the eventual emergence of linguistically based insight and understandability—the cultivation of mind.

# CHAPTER FIVE

# The Subjective, Intrapsychic, and Phenomenological Experience of Envy: Envy and Related States of Mind

Consciously experienced features of envy typically appear in those who view themselves or are viewed by others as insecure. Insecurity and feelings of inadequacy are often accompanied by looking outward and noticing or perceiving features in others felt to be superior or ideal. In addition, when envy is activated on unconscious or conscious levels, it is experienced as painful, distressing, and unsatisfying.

Difficulties arise in attempts to describe—in rational terms—material believed primarily unconscious, in other words unconscious envy. Particular theoretical perspectives shape different conceptions. *Envy theory* uses language and tools provided by phenomenology, psychoanalysis, and cognitive science. Defining unconscious processes may even appear contradictory with paradoxical implications. To avoid circular reasoning, some of the discussions presented may appear to beg the questions at issue. With these caveats, the following descriptions regarding envy and related states of mind are proposed.

In psychoanalytic terms, envy and its operations are deeply rooted in nonconscious primary processes, cognition devoid of logic and reason. This primitive mental activity comprises the basal system of id-based regulatory principles whose topography makes up the dynamic *unconscious as a system*. The phrase "dynamic unconscious" denotes the domain of fundamental operating principles regulating the substrata of mental functioning. These act to maintain opposing, contradictory unconscious processes, affective and cognitive, in dialectical tension.

*Nuclear envy* is not a simple, discrete emotion or state of mind. It is a diverse set of urges, emotions, and cognitions. *Primordial envy*, ego's unconscious envy of its id, is born of and remains in a state of primary repression. This is the nuclear, inaccessible domain closest to the core of the entire unconscious. Primary repression and all that subsequently becomes repressed, in joint action, suffuse the entire psyche.

As with all such unconscious operations, their buoyant derivatives filter into preconscious and conscious spheres of awareness as they gradually manifest themselves in disguised ways in both experience and behavior. The manifest content of experience is the obvious side of its latent understructure. *Both the direct action of envy and the psychological defenses against it typically appear together.*

The direct spoiling action of envy and defenses against this process interfere with ego integration and successful forward emotional development at all points in life.

In broad psychological terms, any discussion of envy is also a discussion of emotional processing. Emotions, affects, and feelings are biomental responses to changing stimuli and conditions both inside and outside the individual. They are alerting signals that inform the subject of a perception, idea, or object requiring attention. Emotions help regulate an individual's biomental homeostasis, ensure survival, and, in addition, act as signals of expression for social communication. Subjectively experienced feeling states are communicated through words and facial expressions. The perception of nonconscious subtle emotion by an outside observer is derived from seeing or hearing such emotional signals ordinarily denoted by the term "feelings." Manifestations of feelings are both brain-based and culturally determined. They have both innate and universally shared genetic substrates and the shaping imposed by cultural constraints.

Emotional processing is complex activity involving stimuli that elicit nonconscious physiological arousal termed "emotion," which, in turn, mentalizes into psychological "affects" or the unconsciously experienced platform out of which arise consciously identified "feelings." *Envy theory* defines *mentalization* as the way the biological organism develops into an experiencing psychological self. In other words, it suggests corporeal experience morphing into mental experience.

Using classical psychoanalytic constructs, *envy theory* precisely denotes *mentalization* in a unique way. It is one of the principal actions of the psychological id. In this intrapsychic process, *the id draws on the biological aspect of the life and death instincts and transmutes them into mental phenomena.* The chief psychological precipitates of this mentalizing process are the ideational and affective structures called unconscious phantasy. Out of this dynamic unconscious process, preconscious and conscious thoughts and feelings arise. This conception of mentalization must be distinguished from the more commonly used interpersonal conception that defines it as "the way humans make sense of their social world by imagining the mental states (for example, beliefs, motives, emotions, desires, and needs) that underpin their own and other's behaviors in interpersonal interactions" (Choi-Kain and Gunderson 2008, 1127).

Language and characteristic facial expressions reflect feelings. So-called "social emotions" such as guilt, shame, and affectionate love, for example, have explicit functions as social communication. By contrast, *envy theory* does not understand unconscious envy primarily as a social emotion since more mature, complex social emotions typically develop after the first year of life (unlike envy) and have strong, usually prominent, conscious components. Societal values and processes of enculturation structure social emotions; learning plays an enormous role in their acquisition.

Real social situations, however, do affect the rise, fall, and management of envy since, in *envy theory*, envy's third root is its reactive, socially sensitive response to real and perceived comparisons, deprivations, and injustices. These are consciously felt and often are reactions to and defenses against unconscious envy. The psychodynamics of envy, besides its plethora of unconscious roots, draws from emotion, affects, feelings, and the thought processes that accrue around these in childhood, adolescence, and adulthood. These basic processes function to increase attention, organize motivational preferences, structure interpretive construals about meaning, and influence volitional behavior, especially on interpersonal and social levels.

## Anxiety, Guilt, and Mental Suffering

Suffering and mental pain are direct experiential states of mind; they have complex etiologies. Both signal distress, discomfort, and dysphoria. While a comprehensive examination of anxiety and guilt, markers of mental pain and suffering, is beyond the scope of this book, some general perspectives, especially relating to envy, will be discussed.

The concept of mental suffering is one of the most general ways to describe significant states of relatively persistent emotional discomfort, a dissonance associated with conflict whether consciously perceived or unconsciously sensed. Suffering connotes feeling tortured, secondary to something specific rather than nebulous. Emotional suffering connotes a long-term dysphoric mood, while the phrase "mental pain" suggests a more acute experience of distress, one having sharper intensity.

Anxiety and guilt comprise the underpinnings of all mental suffering. *Anxiety* is the painful feeling, at bottom engendered by fears of impending annihilation, of the threat of self-destruction. As Melanie Klein (1948, 1957) proposed, the impetus for this internal fear of annihilation is the operation of the death instinct in the ego. She described the operation of the death instinct in the ego as the "primordial anxiety."

One of the leading anxieties characteristic of the paranoid-schizoid position is persecutory anxiety centered on paranoid fears of retaliatory attack by a bad, hostile, feared, and hated object. Extreme vulnerability and passivity are foremost. Although attack on the object is initiated offensively by the ego in the first instance of the persecutory sequence, fears of being attacked in retaliation dominate. The ego is thus beleaguered in feeling passively acted upon in a destructive manner. Anxiety, moreover, as the mental expression of the inherent biomental death instinct, may be felt at any point in development. This sense of danger to one's survival operates as the diffuse background upon which varied forms of persecution and guilt supervene and play themselves out. Anxiety and guilt are more than merely conscious feelings. Characteristic mental contents—unconscious phantasies—always accompany these dysphoric states.

*Guilt* is the form of mental suffering accompanied by agonizing and protracted feelings of being tortured or punished for having committed a wrong or imagined violation. This infraction may take the form of a crime, harmful offense, or having failed to meet an imposed obligation. Guilt involves aftermath feelings resulting from being or doing something incorrect. It must contain conflict over self-appraisals, self-worth, and self-value that include connotations of good and bad. Guilt is more organized than anxiety, which is diffuse. It is an integral part of the Oedipus complex. A normal sense of guilt is the conscious feeling of remorse. Abnormal forms of guilt have both conscious and unconscious dimensions that include excessive self-blame and self-reproach. Often, an obsessional quality characterizes such pathological guilt-ridden distress. This incessant cyclicity makes guilt particularly painful and difficult to resolve.

While the content of anxiety, like envy, expresses itself in a contextualized fashion with nuances and variations, it always is more diffuse and less organized structurally than guilt. The organization of guilt may take two distinct forms related to the two developmental positions originally outlined by Melanie Klein (1935, 1940, 1946).

In the paranoid-schizoid position of early infancy as well as later, envy operates by first recognizing the goodness, potency, and creativeness of an object, more precisely, a part-object. To the extent that envy is dominant, the ego cannot tolerate this recognition of brilliance. It feels unhappy, distressed, and resentful. Envy is felt as indignant displeasure, an annoyance at the perception of discrepant unfairness. It then proceeds to destructively spoil that goodness in an effort to attenuate unbearable envious anxieties resulting from such contact. These anxieties emanate from envy of what is felt to be a most powerful, life-giving fecundity. As this occurs, the ego's spoiling of the object elicits a form of *primitive or premature guilt* subsequent to this perceived vitiation of goodness. This guilt is hallmarked by distress over damage done through the attempts of the ego to rob and disfigure the ideal object. In turn, fears of subsequent retaliation by that spoiled object are engendered. Guilt about this destructive envy of the mother is liable to be experienced as persecution. In the paranoid-schizoid position, where conflations abound, the infant does not have capacity to experience separately guilt and persecution.

This dreaded state of mixed anxiety, fear, and premature guilt is what *envy theory* calls *persecutory guilt.* This earliest experience of guilt regarding the object is virtually egocentric and centered on fears of self-destruction and, in fact, the very survival of the ego, itself. Persecutory, premature guilt is intense, profound, primitive, and raw. It contains the paradoxically piercing anxiety that makes envy so exquisitely unbearable, intolerable, and difficult to work through. *Persecutory guilt is strong enough to freeze developmental processes by inhibiting, and preventing adequate entry into and work in, the depressive position.* It is indolent, gnawing biomental pain. From a neuroscience perspective, studies show that there exists a predisposition to such anticipatory dread as measured by fMRI responses in the amygdala and anterior cingulate cortex (Carter and Krug 2009).

Klein (1957, 1958, 1960) discussed this concept as a "premature guilt." *Premature guilt is synonymous with persecutory guilt* and part of split-off envy, which maintains an undercurrent of unconscious guilt throughout development. It also increases an individual's vulnerability toward regression—risk of psychotic decompensations. This correlates with the irreducible pressure emanating from the negative dimension of the id whose hedonic expression in the ego is a dangerous sense of terrifying destructiveness and foreboding functional breakdown. Whether persecutory guilt is a part of all early development is unclear. It may be an important factor in both the genesis of mental disorders and their obstinacy to change.

In contrast to the aforementioned primitive form of guilt and during the course of the more highly refined depressive position after the paranoid-schizoid position, the ego senses itself as more distinct from the object, now perceived as a whole object. A sense of *nascent* empathy and concern is achieved that qualitatively goes beyond egocentric needs for survival. The ego's concern is centered on the survival of the object together with the ego's fears of its capacity to hurt this ambivalently loved figure.

*Depressive-position guilt* is *guilt proper* or *true guilt*. It comes about because of the subject's aggression felt in full force toward the ambivalently loved object. Reparative impulses stimulated by caring are creative attempts to spare the object any further harm, and restore and recreate the object's vitality on many levels. The ego passionately wishes to affectionately retain and heal the good object it has harmed. *Reparation* is a deeply empathetic concern for damage done in phantasy or in reality to a loved figure. Primitive splitting processes underlie the urge to damage and break apart. Care for the loved object significantly mitigates splitting and destructive urges. It provokes remorse, regret, and a release of the urge for reparation. This guilt proper is the basis for all later forms of mature feelings of sorrow and remorse.

*Envy theory proposes that the intensity and obstinacy of primitive envious persecutory guilt acts as a major roadblock, perhaps the principal impediment, to advancement into the depressive position with its potentially more salutary experience of true guilt and reparation, both of which are needed to propel envy toward its healthy maturation.*

## Envious Anxiety

A principal operative mechanism of envy is the maintenance of its unconscious status by active masking. Recognizing envy through its derivatives and conscious effects, therefore, is essential. Envy presents itself as psychological alloys having *anxiety* as an outstanding dimension.

Identifying envy in therapeutic situations is elusive because it is cloaked amid a contextualized narrative in which it does not declare itself directly. Its manifestation appears in inadvertent and incidental features in both clinical and everyday presentations. These transformations are blends of healthy reactions, sublimations, coping, and defenses. Other more clearly recognizable matters take center stage: separation anxiety, dependency conflicts, defensive pride, pseudo self-dependency, angry resentment of perceived injustice, resentment over perceived inequitable and unfair distributions, seeing envy or jealousy in others, aggressive outbursts, academic and occupational inhibitions and failures, apparent depressions, hoarding, stealing, and marital problems. In both children and adults, the need to be first may signal underlying envy.

Justified resentment or indignation, by contrast to envious begrudges, denotes anger provoked by an objectively real wrong or offence. Yet split-off, unconscious envy is often a significant root cause of these and other commonly encountered clinical and everyday problems.

Anxiety connotes the unsettling detection of pain from a perceived noxious stimulus. It signals a threat that might or actually will result in damage or destruction. Envy issues from what I have termed *contact anxiety* (see chapter 6). It is qualitatively distinct from the separation anxiety proper to dependency, whole-object relations, and the depressive position. Contact with, rather than separation from, the object is the stage upon which envy's circuitry unfolds since it is reminiscent of the earliest states of primitive cognitive and affective fusion (paranoid-schizoid position) characterizing the inception of envy.

Envious anxiety is a signal, which sounds an alert and connotes the danger issuing from the impulse for destructive spoiling (to ego and object) impelled by the activity of the death instinct in the ego. Envy breeds plurality, a dissonant splitting into incoherent bits. Whatever ego is present at a particular developmental era tends to experience this massive profusion of multiplicities in a manner that is chaotic and frightening.

The following is a list of the phenomenological variations of anxiety states that correlate with primitive envy. Subjective awareness of them ranges from unconscious through preconscious toward more conscious feelings. They all include conditions of distress. They are need, aching hunger, wish, emptiness, privation, isolation, aloneness, passivity, helplessness, inferiority, anergic powerlessness, loss of a sense of perfection, inadequacy, feeling poor, frustration, pain and suffering, irritability, dysphoria, grievance, resentment, feeling persecuted, bitterness, rage, disgust, humorlessness, and unhappiness at the good fortune of others.

Envious anxiety is a state of unsettling restlessness, agitation, and hostile intolerance marked by ambiguity in the form of confusion. The elemental sense of inferiority, a perceived incompetence at any developmental level, correlates with negative self-appraisals and dysphoric anxiety, not true clinical depression. In many ways, envy is a state of demoralization in which the foundations of what is considered meaningful are shaken.

The foremost subliminal experience of envy, however, takes the form of an undercurrent of compelling anxiety that has gnawing, tormenting, confusing, aching, and unremitting qualities. Envious anxiety is narcissistic, self-persecutory, and self-destructive anxiety, often exacerbated in the *perceived presence of the object* (intrapsychic and interpersonal).

The concept of "aphanisis" introduced by Ernest Jones in 1927 suggested such a fundamental anxiety, more profound than the fear of castration. It is an anxiety marked by a sense of impending extinction, particularly by the disappearance of sexual desire. Envious anxiety may begin as an unnoticed creeping cynicism, a jaded negativity that escalates to levels of dread and despair that approach such a sense of nameless terror. The intensity of the destructive forces in envy can elicit this sense of ambiguous, impending doom connoting primordial voidness.

*Envious anxiety is an anxiety of self-destruction. It is the anxiety in primary masochism where the aim of the death instinct has become self-attractive, reflexive, and implosive. The anxiety generated by the action of the death instinct acts upon the very actor who generated it.*

Thus, the experiential impact of envy, at root, is the anxiety of self-destruction. Klein (1957) attributes this denotation to envy. Klein has said that "primordial anxiety" is the anxiety generated in the ego by the death instinct, even bringing the ego into activity from birth onwards. Similarly, Bion (1962a, 1962b) equates envy and the death instinct and describes it as "the fear of dying," which he says is the essential infantile experience in its struggle for emotional and material survival. This experience remains the background of all mental life and the anlagen of mental disorders henceforth. *Envy theory* endorses both Klein's and Bion's views.

Envious anxiety is a sense of anticipation ultimately heralding fragmentation into a state of experiential void. This may refer to the primordially based emptiness that one might conjecture to exist even before narcissistic states of the ego have arisen in the neonatal period. These primitive states can be reexperienced later in life. The ontological or real status of these nameless mental states forged in the prelinguistic era, if they exist, might even precede the primary process, itself, and reside within the most elemental strata of the *unconscious as a system*, the core of the id. Bion (1962b) has termed such states of primordial anxiety—"nameless dread." These considerations make the experience of envious anxiety virtually intolerable. This compelling characteristic contributes to the challenge of understanding and adequately articulating *envy theory*.

## Envy as More Than a Simple Emotion or Complex, Subliminal Mood

Although often viewed as an emotion or sometimes only an impulse, unconscious envy is more complex. Although some psychologists may refer to envy as a "social emotion," it is, in *envy theory*, distinctly contra- and antisocial in origin and function.

Envy is basic excitation, movement, direction, and orientation filled with meaningful content and rooted in unconscious processes. In this sense, it may be more akin to a mood—that is, a long-lasting, pervasive affective state rather than a momentary, brief, episodic affect. As a mood, envy imparts dense emotional coloring to perception.

Envy, however, is far more complex than merely an emotional, affective, or feeling state. It is not a simple unitary phenomenon. It is similar to a pleiotropic conception, like the construct of the instinctual drive (*Triebe*) coined by Freud. Such an idea makes up a broad and overarching category that subsumes specific subcomponents and derivatives that express themselves in a variety of ways. Such inferred archetypal constructs are known chiefly by their effects. Envy, however, is much more than merely a naked impulse or a drive. Understanding this requires description using extensive theoretical and phenomenological levels of abstraction.

The developed expressions of envy have cognitive, affective, motivational, and goal-directed conative dimensions. Envy, therefore, is a complex mixture containing instinct, ego, and superego constituents. A myriad of mental maneuvers is set in motion. It is a dynamic state of the ego marked by characteristic anxieties, defenses, and object relations. In terms of the structural theory of the psyche, envy most often is an expression of the combined actions of id, ego, and superego, as this team exists experientially in the personality. Envy, therefore, is a configuration of impulses that are amalgamated with the structures of the ego and its objects, especially the superego.

Envy, by nature, remains concealed in these operations. It tends to split itself off from simple identification with aspects of the ego or the entire self of the envier. It projects itself outward, away from any experience that is more conscious. Split-off enclaves of envy embed themselves deeply in the self and often remain cloaked. Split-off envy ordinarily conceals itself so well that it remains elusive and seemingly nonexistent in interpersonal dialogues and behaviors. Inwardly, envy sequesters itself, largely though not completely, within the superego. Envy, therefore, cannot be clinically apprehended in pure culture, as an isolate. It manifests more as a climate in which precipitates of past and current issues, conflicts, attitudes, object relations, and concrete interpersonal behaviors express themselves.

Envy, therefore, especially in its root forms, is not empirically accessible. As unconscious envy deploys and evolves, it always allies with more blatant configurations of derivative compromise formations that signal anxiety, danger, conflict, and defense. Envy's accompaniments that are more tangible are recognizable in therapeutic settings. For example, conflict related to separation anxiety, dependency, pathological ambition, greed, jealousy, inordinate pride, failure, biting criticism, and some paranoid states are often envy's "calling cards."

Personality styles that are querulous—that is, irritable and paranoid—and those that are excessively prone to noticing inequalities in life have a strong disposition in envy. The surface difficulties of these presentations so deeply interwoven with envy seem to beg for direct therapeutic attention. Envy offers one (usually a psychotherapist) who is sensitive to its hidden presence an opportunity to unmask it. When this uncovering is successful, envy in its more complex, amorphous, and underlying dynamic configurations becomes clearer.

Envy can be understood as more a general state of mind, a diffuse subliminal attitude. It is an inherent dimension of the whole personality and, together with love and hate, operates to define temperament and character throughout life. Envy is not a sign, symptom, or discrete and specific indicator of a circumscribed condition. It is a conceptualization on a different level of abstraction than, for instance, the symptoms or diagnoses of depression, anxiety, obsessions, compulsions, bulimia, panic states, personality disorders, psychosis, and so forth.

The experience of envy arises out of a primordial and elemental base that takes compound forms as it unfolds in complex, contextualized expressions. Simple and understandable envy, for example, can result from clearly conscious feelings of inferiority compared to another who is regarded as superior. *Simple envy is conscious, not malignantly spoiling, and does not have the indolent, recurrent, and resistant qualities that unconscious envy has.*

The envier, in the throes of unconscious envy, intermittently sees the world and others as negative, empty, unsatisfying, bitter, unjust, and unattainable. *Envy corrupts the sense of beauty* and the world appears etiolated and ugly. The envier both creates and exists in a state of self-imposed suffering that is embittered, persecutory, bleak, and unsatisfying.

*Envy theory* contends that envy represents a massive, psychodynamic collision of love and hate. This not only produces conflict in a general sense, but when managed properly can also provide the mind with opportunities for advancement. Within envy can be found a creative spark that when discovered and cultivated may be used to spur its healthy maturation.

## Envy and Desire

*Desire* may be likened to an ocean of energy-craving endless expansion. In the mind, desire seeks objects. It would not be incorrect to equate unconscious envy, in part and in a general sense, with desire. Envy, like desire, is an important causative factor stimulating alertness, attraction, longing, and intention, especially the wish to expand. The psychoanalytic meaning of wish connotes it to be a current in the mind issuing from unpleasure and aiming toward pleasure, the pleasure of satisfaction. The satisfaction of desire implies emotional and affective gratification, a reduction of tension. From a cognitive perspective, the quelling of desire is accompanied by a reduction of uncertainty of attaining such realization.

Desire denotes wanting. It connotes affectively charged degrees of a voracious need to expand itself, especially by contact, acquisition, eating, and containment. Desire as excitement, feeling alive, and the experience of pleasurable exhilaration is reflexive in that it is self-reinforcing. Desire as such is an endlessly recurring drive that seeks repeated fulfillment. It is a cyclic, repetitive hankering for expansion and satisfaction.

Just as physical and mental maturation and development proceed over time and accrue complexity, so too primitive, unmatured envy begins as desire and evolves in complexity. It issues forth as a state of longing that senses perfection and richness and seeks some satisfying share of it. However, unlike pure desire, this wish remains only a near satisfaction quickly thwarted by feelings of privation and the subsequent development of unhappiness, resentment, and a blatant impulse to spoil.

There are, however, significant differences between desire and unconscious envy. The qualities of desire include passion, enthusiasm, fervor, fierceness, and ardency. In contrast, envy is minimalist, austere, cold, bitter, and implosive. A hallmark of desire, in contrast to envy, is the anticipation and expectation of fulfillment, which often may actually be achieved. Sentient desire is a biomental orientation that positions itself with the aim of securing more and more experience—of any kind. Each perception, in effect, anticipates the onset of another perception. Each desire anticipates the next. Desire and expansion go hand-in-hand. By contrast, the concept of "need" in a more specific way denotes a basic, innate requirement for survival. Whereas the concept of need has a physiological connotation, desire has a more affective, pleasure-seeking quality. The repetition compulsion (chapter 4)—the need for the repetition of desire—is an intrinsic part of both love and envy.

While always retaining its nuclear and elemental identity, envy also amalgamates, in part, within an individual's daily experience and becomes part of affective attitudes; it both influences and, in turn, is reshaped by them. Elements of desire are indigenous in envy. Envy exists in a hierarchy of forms. These range from those that are more primitive and unhealthy to forms that are transitional and potentially constructive. Envy cannot exist alone or in isolation since it is part of the whole personality. It is suffused within complex, mental stratifications. The embeddedness of envy in many aspects of the entire personality underscores its different expressions along the developmental course. The different expressions arising from deeply stratified envy reflect the changes that occur in the gradually maturing ego as it becomes contextualized both interpersonally and by adaptations to the real world.

Envy, like desire and wish, is ubiquitous, exerts a constant though fluctuating pressure, and is ultimately unquenchable. However, unlike simple craving or complex states of desire (which anticipate and can experience temporary satisfaction), envy *never* achieves even partial or temporary satisfaction because of its *self-imposed autoblocking of fulfillment*, which is initiated and reinforced by its persistent tendency to spoil.

Envy contains an element of possessiveness that demands attention and exhibits a strong desire to own and an unwillingness to share. Envy, in part, is the wish to possess what one believes one does not already have. It is incited by the perceived recognition in another of a fuller, richer, or more excellent version of what in oneself is sensed as not developed or not actualized, in effect, a missing part. Since envy senses it can never possess the envied object, it rapidly seeks to spoil it.

Whereas envy implies the unconscious sense of privation and missing parts in the makeup of the personality, jealousy implies a more conscious sense of not having some possession of another person or that person's love. What is desired in jealousy is not a part possessed in another, but an entire whole—a third entity that the jealous one treasures and does not seek to spoil.

Terms that imply possessiveness, taking, and acquisition and that suggest or may incite underlying envy include covetousness, avidity, avarice, greed, and hoarding. These states of mind correlate with the subjective sense of "mine" and "I own it." Although the focus in these concepts appears to be an external piece of property or possession, *envy theory* emphasizes that the external reference is merely a pawn. Possessions and their acquisition, on nonconscious stratas of meaning, are instruments for defining—typically by control—the relation between two or more people. In addition, the material props typically are symbolic of significant bodily parts (for example, breast, penis, interior bodily cavity) of one or both of them.

The archaic term "covet" is closer in meaning to the concepts "to desire" or "to lust after" than the concept of envy. To covet denotes the greedy desire to take or steal the possessions of another. There is an emphasis on yearning, craving, and excessive acquisition, but there is no destructive intent associated with the concept of covetous desire. Obsessive-compulsive disorders are characterized by obviously irrational hoarding behaviors, especially compulsive hoarding, whose base is in unconscious envy and greed. The uncertainty and doubt about ever having enough triggers precarious compulsive attempts to reduce the dysphoric anxiety that repetitively builds up.

The term "avidity" denotes a strong, enthusiastic desire to obtain something. It connotes an enduring, persistent, restless hankering. The emphasis here is on eagerness to procure rather than greed. The term "avarice," in contrast, is usually synonymous with that of greed. The terms "avidity," "avarice," and "greed" connote desire and craving driven by feelings of not having enough while perpetually wanting more. For example, in eating disorders, rapacious patients frequently state that "food tastes too good" and say "I can't resist because the temptation is too inviting." All these attitudes suggesting irresistibility imply underlying excessive idealization and problems of self-regulation, both of which are motors driving unconscious envy.

The term "hoarding" denotes the collection of and failure to discard possessions, which appear worthless or of no value to others. Hoarding connotes irrational, often blindly driven accumulation of items not necessarily having objective value. The person who hoards may be aware of the irrationality of these behaviors yet they take on almost automatic responsiveness short of highly calculated forethought. Such hoarding may reflect pathologically inflexible behavior patterns.

By contrast, greed connotes the conscious, premeditated, and willful accumulation, often to irrational degrees, of materials that have ostensible value. Greed is insidious and leads to the feverish pursuit of that which one feels is insufficiently possessed—material goods, money, food, ideas, and so forth. Greed is irrational robbing. Greed can cross boundaries into unlawful acquisition.

Whether hoarding is subclassified as compulsive or noncompulsive, envy and greed remain as nonconscious motivators. The term "hoarding" connotes greed in action, the actual gathering up of material goods. Less commonly used terms include esurience and rapaciousness. Esurience is an archaic word denoting strong hunger accompanied by greed. Rapaciousness denotes a greedy swooping up of goods with a strong connotation of robbing, plundering, and ruthlessly exploiting. Further distinctions between envy, greed, and jealousy will be discussed later.

## Envy, Cheating, Stealing, and Acquisition by Aggression

Envy operates on unconscious levels, and its effects are chiefly intrapsychic. Empirical effects can also be described. The principal endpoint of envy's action is an ultimate self-destructiveness in mental and behavioral sectors of the personality. Since envy does not operate in isolation, it usually compounds itself with other complex emotions—for example, jealousy. Envy, in this way, may take on manic and grandiose proportions that typically extend beyond the individual into interpersonal and social realms. These complex forms reflect the typical overlay of defensive depressive-position dynamics on an unresolved paranoid-schizoid base of envy.

When envy fuses with experiential overlays such as jealousy, rivalry, and competitiveness, it may express itself in *complex behavioral forms* such as cheating, stealing, and acquisition by forceful aggression. These behaviors are characterized by the wish to dominate and subdue. They also include strong features of dishonesty. These envy-based impulses become observable in their enacted demonstrations and obvious effects on others. Noncooperativeness, competition, rivalry, a "win-lose mentality," and zero-sum strategies may range from small-scale cheating and stealing to larger-scale aggressions such as those that manifest in wars. Petty criminal acts and those on larger scales, such as occurs with malfeasance in financial institutions, have bases in envy. The implications of *envy theory* for social psychology and law are plentiful.

## Envy, Love, Hate, Fear, Anger, Aggression, Hostility, and Lust

A theoretical distinction between envy, love, hate, fear, anger, aggression, hostility, and lust may further clarify the nature of each, especially in relation to and contrast with one another.

*Love*, as well as sexual desire emanating primarily from the conjectured life instinct, is correlated with libido (pleasure-seeking attraction and affiliation) stored in the ego. It acts as the primary affiliative, energetic, and vital force in the psyche. It is the search for a good object; it aims toward beneficence, to participate in the experience of pleasurable goodness. The rewards that love brings are felt as treasures that expand one's sense of largesse, fullness, and completion, at least temporarily. Love is an emotion easily recognizable.

*Libido* is the technical term signifying the metapsychological concept referring to this vital psychic energy of the life instincts that underlie love in the entire self. The ego's use of sublimation derives from highly refined impulses of transformed sexuality. These are libidinalized or affectionately redirected aims manifesting as pursuits hallmarked by creativity. One of love's counterpoints is hate, which issues from the hypothetical death instinct, and is embodied in destructive mental forces, which are actively annihilative, not merely apathetic.

While recognizing the theoretical and clinical value of coupling love and hate, especially as the *conspicuous* manifestations of the life and death instincts, as previously emphasized, *envy theory* proposes an addition to this.

The new paradigm *love and envy* emphasizes a wider frame of mental functioning, advancing a broader scope of dialectical, orienting polarities in the infinite dimensions of experience. Love and envy are primary counterparts just as love and hate. Whereas love and hate are ordinarily conscious and conspicuous in their varied expressions, envy is *unconscious and inconspicuous* in its nuclear form. More accurately, love and envy are *natural companions* to one another. This view does not contradict nor replace the more usual juxtaposition of love and hate. It is an expansion that highlights an additional and more specific dimension of the role that destructiveness plays in mental functioning.

*Hate* emanating primarily from the conjectured death instinct denotes a destructive mental mode that tends toward breaking apart, subduing, and downgrading the quality of interpersonal contact on emotional and behavioral levels. Hate also expresses itself by attempting to decrease degrees of conscious awareness through its use of aversion, splitting, and repression in mental functioning. In these negative ways, hate aims to constrain an object perceived as bad. Its aim is malice: to forcefully control, subdue, or destroy. Withdrawal and avoidance ultimately characterize hate. *Hate is a depressive position–based destructiveness toward a whole object.*

The principal emphases in the experience of hate are *negative perceptions* regarding an outside other seen as essentially hostile, strange, sinister, menacing, having threatening intentions, and needing to be controlled, sometimes by forceful means, and usually at a distance. Intense dislike, strong aversion, fear, and hostile ill will mark attitudes of hate. Hate as an emotion and destructiveness as its aim have correlates that are more directly expressed in conscious awareness than does envy, whose center of gravity is virtually unconscious.

Often, hateful attitudes and destructive intentions are felt as fear. *Fear* is a hallmark of anxiety. Hate, fear, and anxiety often coexist. They are clearly demonstrated in observable behaviors described as aggressive and characterized by emotional forms of hatefulness, hatred, and animosity. Hateful states of mind are usually associated with strong fear, a sense of threat, menacing, and harm. The object of hate is regarded as an enemy needing to be actively and aggressively contained. Fears of retaliatory attack and a sense of persecution accompany such hate-filled states of mind. Empirically and in clinical situations, affective and narrative expressions that involve hate and hateful emotions often act in a complicated defensive fashion to mask underlying primary envy.

Whereas hate is a deeply felt aggressive dislike, the term "hatred" connotes a more enduring, complex aggressive emotional state characterized by chronic development over time. *Anger*, in contrast, is an acute, momentary offensive and defensive emotional reaction to a perceived attack, injury, or threat. Anger begins as a sense of annoyance and may escalate to a hostile show of indignation and furious irritation usually accompanied by physiological changes. Rage is an extreme form of out-of-control anger.

*Aggression* is consciously recognizable ideational, verbal, or physical forcefulness accompanied by violent content. Aggression often refers to a conspicuous behavioral mode of enacted violence. Ordinarily, it is aimed outwardly, directed away from the self. In contrast to envy—a more silent, internal state of mind—aggression ordinarily describes concrete behaviors and disruptive conduct. Its presence in mental functioning and observable behaviors, therefore, is undeniable. It may include bullying, intimidation, threatening, verbal hostility, theft, destruction of property, fighting, combat, war, and so forth. Bullying and intimidation, for example, are clearly seen in children and male adolescents in their forceful strivings for hierarchical dominance. The fear elicited in victims by such threatening behaviors is powerful, and its disruptive influence both personally and socially cannot be ignored.

Aggression, in general, refers to any form of forceful control or inflicted cruelty causing pain and suffering both psychological and physical. A vigorous and hostile intent to weaken, harm, control, or appropriate characterizes its aim. Sadistic aggression, in particular, expresses itself as manic domination whose aim is subjugation, torture, or humiliation. Sadism, moreover, has a strong pleasurable component that accompanies its destructive action. Sadism and greed are aggressive aspects of depressive-position psychodynamics and are hallmarked by strong ambivalence—simultaneous mixtures of loving and of hating.

For example, when an idealized object is projectively attacked because it is envied (a paranoid-schizoid operation), the net result is a destructive introjection, the accumulation of spoiled and damaged objects in the inner world of the envier. To offset this malevolent situation, depressive-position greed may be activated in a defensive manner. The experiential state that results is phenomenologically felt as an insatiable hunger for new good objects. *Envy theory* hypothesizes that this greedy emotional voraciousness is defensively triggered so that new unharmed introjected objects will act to protect the ego against the persecution exerted by the original objects the ego has spoiled and subsequently stored in itself.

Two common forms of observable human aggression that have a strong though not exclusive base in paranoid-schizoid dynamics are (1) defensive aggression, and (2) offensive aggression. Defensive aggression is self-protective. It is a reaction to a perceived bad, persecuting, and feared object—an enemy. Defensive aggression is usually affective, impulsive, and protective. It can be either unpremeditated or premeditated. Such socially observable aggression is expressed in forms such as intramale, territorial, and maternal aggression and the irritable aggression, for example, seen in overcrowded circumstances. From a physiological perspective, defensive aggression has been correlated with high blood levels of cortisol.

Offensive aggression is usually premeditated. It is the "cold" aggression characteristic of the predator-prey situation. It is an offensive attack. From a physiological perspective, offensive aggression has been correlated with low cortisol, high testosterone, and low serotonin blood levels. It is the type of aggression seen in animals engaged in food acquisition to satisfy the need for survival.

When offensive aggression is accompanied by malicious intent in human beings, however, it is fueled by the mechanisms of envy. Since envy may contain multiple offensive and defensive aggressive features, however, no clear-cut and regularly occurring associations can be made in a simple way.

Envy and greed often result in aggression of different sorts. Envy instigates subtle autodestruction; insidious disorganization from within propagates; and greed often incidentally destroys what it seeks to accumulate. Envy and greed as internal states of mind combine to motivate the outward expression of aggression. Whereas envy is unconscious, greed has more conscious components.

Hostility and paranoid states go hand-in-hand; their coordinated operation illustrates intrapsychic psychodynamics. *Hostility* is noticing a bad object, an "enemy" felt to be a threat who potentially may harm, destroy, or kill—a real or phantasied threat to survival. Hostility is enmity, the ill will that resists and opposes something perceived unacceptable and threatening. Aggressive actions are used defensively to protect the self from this threatened destructiveness. When unrealistic paranoid processes (excessive projection) are at play, the following mental mechanisms arise. The ego splits off its own bad, hostile, and malevolent aspects whose aims are felt to threaten the coexisting intrapsychic good aspects that constitute the self. Good and bad internal objects battle each other. To ease the inner turmoil of such contrasting and conflicting mental schemata, defensive projection occurs. These bad objects are then projected away from the self, and typically are perceived as located in an outside other, an enemy in the environment.

The nuances of hostility in the paranoid-schizoid position and hate in the depressive position are the following. In the primitive paranoid-schizoid position, aspects of destructiveness and malevolence are projected outward to ensure survival of the fragile ego. The ego, then, in this state of extreme vulnerability thus feels itself to be helplessly passive and at the mercy of outside malevolent, part-object forces. These have a strong *impersonal quality*. Paranoid-schizoid anxiety generates fearful and persecutory hostile aversion toward these part-objects. This aversive state of tremor is the feeling of being helpless, feeble, and threatened. It is an amorphous and chaotic condition where extremes of and contrasts in sensation and perception occur. The capacity for adaptation and defense become mercurial and unstable.

The extremely hostile part-objects perceived to be bad attackers in the paranoid-schizoid position are constructed in this fashion through the primitive ego's capacity for negative idealization (extreme featural aspect aggrandizement). Negatively idealized part-objects are felt to be malevolent and are feared and hated, yet envied in a perverse way. When the accent within idealization is positive, envy rather than hate is the leading dynamic. When the accent within idealization is negative, fear, paranoia, and persecution predominate.

In the depressive position, the ego, to varying degrees, accepts its own internal destructive impulses, and in a relatively more active way becomes the acknowledged agent of destructive intent. The ego now can actively hate and wish to harm, in addition to its more developed capacity to love, the whole object. This has a strongly *personal quality*. Depressive-position hate is directed to a mostly bad (but partially admired) *whole object. Hate together with love (rather than idealization) are hallmark emotions of the depressive position.* It is only by the healthy working through of the depressive position that illusory persecutors may be realistically differentiated from real and actual enemies.

Hateful emotions at all periods in development arise as this process takes on a very interpersonal dimension. This usually becomes concrete and tangibly experienced as an actual figure (the hated bad enemy) in the social environment. Hateful emotions tend to dehumanize the object of hate. *This downgrading is a paranoid-schizoid attempt to devalue and make impersonal.* The aim of hate (whether realistic or delusional) and paranoia (always delusional) is to control the negatively perceived, external enemy so it does not attack the subject.

In contrast, envy perceives its object as ideal, which, in turn, provokes unbearable intolerance and subsequent self-destructive anxiety. To stop this pain, envy aims to delete the positively perceived privileged figure. Envy's locus is principally intrapsychic and unconscious. Envied figures in the social environment are initially noticed in a bright light. Quickly, this light dims. They are either spoiled or dismissed; in effect, ultimately voided.

Love, in contrast to hate and aggression, is an affiliative, cohesive force resulting in linking, union, creativity, integration, and more complex levels of biomental reorganization. Love increases self-consciousness and intensifies meaning. The affective dimension of this is the experience of pleasure, well-being, and happiness.

*Lust,* by contrast, is that dimension of love that has strong appetitive and sexual features. Lust is characterized by the expectation of intense pleasure, which is somatically felt in sensual ways. Lust has passionate, addicting, and compulsive qualities. It may suggest some degree of underlying sadistic, excessive idealization. Whereas love is impulsive, novelty-seeking, and aiming to gain pleasure, lust has compulsive qualities aimed at (momentarily) reducing tension and anxiety. Love and lust are felt directly in conscious awareness and are clearly recognizable from empirical observations of their characteristically related behaviors.

Love and hate are also consciously felt. Each, in effect, is accompanied by loud, glaring, and palpable features. In contrast to this, unconscious envy reflects broad groupings of mental forces, including unconscious phantasies, which are nonconscious combinations of both love and destructive impulses.

*Envy* is a complex psychodynamic process made up of both love as excessive idealization and hate having a persecutory leaning. Unconscious envy remains a state of mind. It engenders a nuclear plexus of feeling states, motivations, ideas, and impulses that propels an individual toward envy-derived behaviors. It begins with a charmed attraction whose first allure gradually becomes transformed into an anxious unhappiness. Subsequently, hatred develops that manifests itself as envious spoiling. In subtle and subliminal ways, envy initially perceives the object as intensely attractive and pleasing rather than as hostile. Envy's first emphasis is on *positive, idealized perceptions.*

Envy, however, is predominantly under the sway of destructive and spoiling aims since the envier cannot tolerate accepting the initial perceptions of attractiveness, abundance, perfection, and creativeness in another.

The initial excitement stimulated by envy cannot be endured or sustained because the envier is largely constitutionally incapable of processing this affectively charged information. The envier cannot withstand the decompensating effects of envy. This hostile intolerance coupled with a sense of being persecuted correlates with the basal sense of perceived injustice and unfairness always arising out of envy. Once stimulated, envy rapidly spoils its first glance of perfection. This vitiation is then accompanied by an affective state of intense, often unbearable, anxiety, which is both an unconscious and partially conscious intolerance at the sight of goodness in another. Envy is experienced as an enormously unpleasurable, self-centered preoccupation. Envy spoils the ideal object by robbing it of its creativeness as it puts badness into it in a variety of ways.

## Envy and Jealousy

"Thinking of you having fun with somebody else makes me feel bad." This sentiment encapsulates an often-encountered statement reflecting the conscious experience of jealousy. The distinction between envy and jealousy will be briefly discussed here and more fully elaborated in chapter 8.

Envy and jealousy are complex and usually intertwined intrapsychic states. They are distinct both qualitatively and in the contexts in which they arise. Envy is developmentally primary and is the matrix that fuses into more complexly developed jealousy-based configurations. Distinguishing them is difficult, especially since less obvious states of envy lie beneath more glaring states of the jealousy that overshadows underlying envy. Jealousy is always accompanied by some degree of envy. Envy, in contrast, may occur in the absence of jealousy. A rough schematic serves to illustrate important differences.

*Envy* is an attitude elicited in the subject by the perceived presence of another with whom the envier is not necessarily in love or strongly attached. The envier sees only partial aspects of the other as initially ideal and desirable, hence, superior. Feelings of gnawing privation arise. Although resentment builds at the realization of not possessing these idealized and desired qualities, a greater desire to deprive the other and destroy what is perceived to be advantageous becomes the overriding impulse. There is an attempt to spoil the envy-provoking object in some partial or more extensive way to mute envious dysphoria, which is usually quietly persistent. Destructive envy always acts to break social bonds. Envy promotes distance.

*Jealousy*, by contrast, is not dyadic but triadic. It is an attitude of the subject in the context of two additional subjects, one of whom is ambivalently loved and desired; the other is regarded in a hateful way because that other, perceived as more attractive, is thought to possess, or be in the process of taking away, the desired one. The jealous one's passionate fury is made intense because he believes he once did possess both the love and loved one he prizes, but now has lost both to a rival. He or she feels dismissed and excluded within a complex interpersonal and social context but continues to seek proximity.

In jealousy, loss provokes depression, which until resolved may elicit strong defensive responses approaching states of hypomania or mania. Feelings of dependency, guilt, exclusion, ambivalence, uncertainty, loss, and deprivation characterize jealousy. Split-off unconscious envy, a major root of jealousy, is the force behind confusion-producing doubt and uncertainty in jealousy. It is an *emotional protest of nonacceptance. There is no primary wish to damage or spoil the desired object, only to eliminate the hated rival believed to be a threat.*

Underlying envy of the rival fuels jealousy in the triadic situation. The object of jealousy continues to be overvalued and held onto. Jealousy seeks to maintain social bonds. In contrast to envy, jealousy fears to lose what it has or once had. Jealousy is the pain of loss; it is the agony of seeing that another is now in the process of enjoying what once was possessed. It begins with a protest of unacceptance, and ends with hopeless despair. Jealousy often serves as a more ego-syntonic defense against underlying envy, which can be detected in the destructive relation to the rival in a jealousy triangle.

Last, one may differentiate between normal and pathological jealousy. Both are heterogeneous and may be characterized by an outstanding measurable feature such as obsessionality, depression, separation anxiety, paranoia, or hypomania-mania. Nonpathological forms of jealousy may be part of normal personality styles. Jealousy becomes psychopathological when significant impairments are accompanied by distress and other clinical signs and symptoms.

## Envy and Loneliness

Although envy is far from being a simple state of mind, a frequently encountered, generalized, and typical manifestation of underlying envy is the feeling of loneliness. *Loneliness* is the unpleasant experience of discomfort resulting from an inner sense of being incomplete—namely, missing something that, if present, would undo the sense of loneliness. It is the despondent feeling of being split apart and separate from something desired. Loneliness is associated with a desire for what is perceived to be at the moment unavailable, even inaccessible. The sense of loneliness occurs in quietude and along a spectrum of intensities; the more painful the sense of loneliness, the closer is its association with envy. Loneliness and the problem of isolation are most pronounced at both ends of the life spectrum, birth and older age.

Loneliness, at its unconscious base, is the unsettling awareness (primordial envy) of the ego's estrangement from its id, which is felt to be ideal, the superlative source of everything perfect and satisfying. During earliest development, as the ego differentiates from its id matrix, it always retains a longing for reunion with this phantasied state of completion. This pining for the id, in part, is the elemental basis from which the ego is propelled to look outside itself to find new objects to satisfy its inner need for completion. The ego searches for new objects to compensate for its primordial sense of privation—being split apart from its id.

One of the many paradoxical features of envy is that it creates loneliness. Those states of loneliness are often the outcome of the envier's own distancing of himself from others and what he senses might possibly complete him. The envier instantly mentally kills all potential models, heroes, and heroines that may serve as inspirational companions. This maneuver represents a major defensive attempt to assuage envious anxiety. On a deeper unconscious level, this anxiety is felt as intolerable, becomes unbearable, and drives a pressing need in the ego to seek to mute envious anxiety. The envier thus attempts to leave the interpersonal field because contact with and attention to the desired object is too unbearable. *Envy theory* refers to this paradoxical envy dynamic as *contact anxiety*.

For example, one who is overwhelmed by envy may appear angry or display angry outbursts. Anger is an acute response to perceived pain and emotional hurt. The origin of this hurt, at bottom, is the envier's own self-disparagement believed, however, to be provoked by someone else. Hence, this angry emotional response results in a self-protective distancing. This then may be felt as a form of disgruntled loneliness. As has been reiterated throughout this book, such clinical presentations are complex. They defy simple analysis since they always include many context-specific etiologies besides envy.

A sense of inner loneliness, isolation, and feeling impoverished are telling features of envy. There is no greater poverty than the emptiness produced by envious self-imposed restrictions.

## Consumed With Envy versus Falling in Love

Envy of the object and object-love have similarities and clear qualitative differences. Envy and love resemble each other in their initial stages of development. Both begin with a similar experiential sequence: idealization, longing, a sense of privation, and emptiness. These arise together with the nonfulfillment of the aim of their desire.

*Romantic love*, on the one hand, begins with a noticed (initially nonconscious) attraction to one who gradually is perceived to possess highly desirable, virtually perfect features both physically and psychologically. These features tend to be extravagantly overrated and produce a feeling of elation and novel surprise. The loved one is regarded with feelings of amazement.

As a conscious overestimation of the goodness of the object of love increases, it reaches ideal proportions as Freud (1914a, 1924) has described. When this quota of idealization is neither pathologically excessive nor exclusively prompted by inordinate feelings of inadequacy, fear, or persecution, it is normal and adaptive. The one falling in love experiences a strong, almost irresistible need for proximity to the other. The other's attractiveness becomes overwhelming and compelling. This has some lustful and many pleasurable qualities since the expectation in romantic love, unlike in envy, is that some actual satisfaction may eventually be achieved.

Romantic love may be successful when excessive envy is absent in the subject and when the object of desire, in fact, wishes to reciprocate. In the state of romantic love, dependency needs become sufficiently met, at least for a while, with a mutually shared bonding that reinforces closeness. Infatuation transforms itself into reasoned intimacy, and idealization takes on less extreme proportions.

Only when romantic love is initially unrequited, in the process of ending, or terminated does a state of numbing and trauma possibly set in. The glaring face of jealousy and possessiveness often accompanies this. It is at this point that jealousy and its underlying envy may surface in extreme ways. Eventually, lost love ends in a depressive state with prominent features of guilt and unrequited pining. In contrast, envious states of nongratification have no predominant qualities of sadness. Remorse and true guilt are largely undeveloped in envy. Yet they are typically seen in the disappointments of expectations accompanying conflicts in romantic love.

*Envy* of the object, in contrast to love of the object, begins with an initial idealization *of omnipotent proportions* that produces a transitory elation. However, it *rapidly deteriorates* into the realization of overwhelming emptiness. This inevitably progresses to feelings of isolation, being frozen, being unable to give or receive, and numbing, which in the normal course of falling in love do not occur.

A sense of emptiness and loneliness follows. This is associated with and caused by the envier's damaging, spoiling, and destructive attacks on the desired object in an effort to mute its attractiveness since this once-exciting stimulus now is felt to be the cause of mental pain. In parallel fashion, these initially object-directed assaults from the ego now become centripetally experienced by the ego and are felt as attacks on parts of the ego itself. Subsequently, the ego is self-traumatized and, in a paradoxical way, becomes numbed "by its own hand."

## Envy and Disgust

As discussed in an earlier chapter, one explanation for the existence of envy lies in envy's potential value to enhance survival. In this regard, *envy theory* sees a fundamental function served by envy to be that of *exploration*. Envy impels experiential excursions characterized by strong impulses toward recognition of aspects of the environment; simultaneously, self-orientation also organizes itself in adaptive ways. Both processes act to mutually enhance survival.

These forays operate, in part, by scanning the environment for survival advantages, for example, resulting in attempted interpersonal contacts and associated intrapsychic object awareness and registration. This is spurred by the innate inclination that anticipates and expects to find an object and establish a meaningful experience, an object relation. The expectation of finding and establishing an object relation is an inherent instinctual proclivity. This impulse "to indulge" is characterized by features that include both attraction and anticipation of pleasure.

I refer, in a metaphorical way, to this process of exploratory indulgence as *reality tasting*. It exists on a continuum. When in normative ranges, it acts to enrich experience. When excessive envy is present, however, it paradoxically makes the proper mental and emotional digestion of experience impossible.

When tasted through the medium of excessive envy, experience is perceived as "too rich" because it is too ideal, superlative, excellent, and perfect. Excessive envy robs nourishment of its intrinsic value and spoils it. In a figurative sense, this results in the tasted food of experience being apprehended as "too sweet, too rich, too strong," and so forth. It thus becomes regarded as unsuitable for consumption. Assimilation in a pleasant and enjoyable way is spoiled; an impasse is reached. Further spoiling of this partially experienced perfection is then set in motion.

*Envy theory* proposes that the fundamental emotion of *disgust* is called into action in this way as part of a broad range of defense mechanisms marked by strong affective responses, ones mobilized to ensure further survival. When envy spoils what it had initially idealized, the spoiled perfection becomes flawed. It is turned, figuratively speaking, into poison. Recognizing the potential for further contamination by continuing to take in perceived noxious material, multiple aspects of the spoiled experience are rejected and forcefully expelled. The latter is accomplished by mental mechanisms that employ *projective identification* (chapter 6).

*Disgust* is one of the affective components of the biopsychological self-defense mechanisms used for ridding oneself of any internally possessed food, goods, or mental contents felt to be damaged or damaging. Disgust is the mental counterpart of physiological processes of nausea. Both disgust and nausea signal a potential for autointoxication and elicit mechanisms to counter this threat to survival. Disgust is also part of the motivating affect that drives the projective attacks on the perceived source eliciting the harm. *Disgust and envy go hand-in-hand.*

Disgust is to be differentiated from contempt, disdain, and scorn. Whereas disgust signifies an effort to expel and distance oneself from undesirable and noxious material that, at first, seemed attractive, *contempt* is the feeling of personal superiority and haughty distain in the perceived presence of an inferior (never having been ideal) object with the implied aim of dominating it for one's own benefit. If excessive ill will accompanies contempt, feelings of *schadenfreude*, derision, and disdain are stimulated.

Disgust implies repulsion and ejection; it is a paranoid-schizoid-position phenomenon. Material once ideal has now been spoiled and is repugnant. Contempt implies possession and control of material found to be already flawed but nonetheless possibly unusable, often by exploitation; it is a depressive-position phenomenon.

From a neuroscience perspective, the role of disgust can also be seen in evolutionary terms. The insular cortex of the central nervous system plays a critical role in the bodily experience of emotion and autonomic nervous system regulation. The anterior insular cortex is important for processing taste information and for the emotional experience of disgust. Strong disgust is perceived in complex ways through the brain's cortico-striatal-thalamic circuitry (Phillips et al. 1997).

Ensuring survival of individuals and the species has strong predicates on how food is recognized and on aspects of its suitability for ingestion. In evolutionary theory, *smell and taste replaced vision as dominant senses with the advent of mammals* reputedly about 180 million years ago. At that time, limbic system structures in the brain superseded automatic, instinctual reflexes, the so-called reptilian brain. In other words, emotions supplying salience and evaluative information came into prominence. Besides containing the olfactory tubercle, the ventral striatum houses the nucleus accumbens. Its function has been demonstrably associated with reward reinforcement and motivational enhancement. Smell and taste pathways laid down mammalian limbic circuitry. Today, combined with higher cortical and subcortical neural inputs, the functioning of these brain structures underlies the way all experience is processed and how the assessment of meaning on various levels of specificity is formulated.

## Envy and the Lie

Some conjectures about envy and cognitive processes will be advanced. The development of thinking, especially its idiosyncratic interpretive slant, is rooted to a significant extent in the way emotional sensitivities shape thought. Emotional stressors—perceived as unpredictable—resulting from true privation, absences, loss, deprivations, frustrations, and disappointments (perceived and real) experienced in infancy play leading roles influencing these sensitivities.

*Envy theory* postulates that these infantile stressors are suffused with and also shaped by the envy dynamic. Bion's (1962a, 1962b) contributions to *envy theory*, particularly his proposition of a minus K link (chaotic information processing), previously discussed, directly relate to these developments. Envy and the action of minus K are intimately connected. Envy spoils and destroys the linking between any two things, especially animate objects. In effect, envy deletes the mind's learning program. This begins in infancy and continuously reconfigures itself throughout life.

When the aforementioned constellation of "dis-stressors" becomes excessive, unbearable, and intolerable, psychological defense mechanisms are set up and unconscious object-related phantasies arise. When not excessive, these act as guardians that attempt to support emotional stability and prevent adaptive deterioration due to overwhelming emotional stressors. In trying to accomplish this, the resulting emotional attitudes are often admixed with *cognitive misformulations*. These are constructed to evade the pain inevitably evoked by contact with the "truth experience" of psychic reality (especially limitations in one's resources to cope). Evasion barriers—global, diffuse emotional, and corporeal protective responses—against pain thus arise. These early attempts to regulate the inevitable fear and pain accompanying uncertainty are primitive and precarious.

As cognitive processes develop, thinking reflects the distorting influence of psychogenetically older mental barriers previously used to handle and lessen earlier emotional upheaval and physical pain. They take on forms, in part, that can be described in experiential terms as "*lies*." These falsifications act to mask and thus distort more direct and accurate contact with the reality of the inner psychic world, especially those infantile encounters that had been naturally raw, primitive, and felt as intolerable, especially since coping strategies were naturally limited.

These affect-laden "lies" are perpetuated as self-deceptions and become cumulative throughout development. They may eventually appear as habitual cognitive strategies that operate as recognizable intellectual blocks. In this sense, they are fraudulent misrepresentations that may develop into distorted cognitive interpretations and styles of interpreting experience in later life. Envy blinds insight on all intellectual and emotional levels.

As will be described in chapter 9 regarding *the healthy maturation of envy*, at any developmental level, moving toward direct contact with psychic reality inevitably stirs complex emotional tremor and the threat of catastrophic upheaval. Such recognition is always accompanied by a powerful sense of impending change. In the process of regulating such change, the gradually formed and accreted defense mechanisms, lies, cognitive misformulations, cognitive-emotional misconstruals, and evasion barriers become stratified and embedded within the ego's view of itself (ego relations), its objects (object relations), and the world (adaptive learning from experience).

These split-off, dissociated, and unintegrated garrisons of precarious self-defense act as fortresses perpetuating and reinforcing estrangement of aspects of the self from the self as a whole. This is the basis for existential and psychological notions of inauthenticity, alienation, personality rifts, and self-falseness. Lies as self-deception are the antithesis of honest self-appraisal. Persons whose self-image and presentation to others is based on a less than genuine interpersonal relatedness are said to be "poseurs." They intentionally create a more ideal or wished-for characterization of themselves. This correlates with a heavy armor of defense mechanisms erected to cover massive conflict.

A fundamental thesis of *envy theory* is that *envy spoils truth*. If truth is an understanding in accord with and corresponding accurately with fact and reality, *envy of truth produces lies*. Lies are untrue, deceptive statements that evade, rather than reflect, reality both internal and external. Lies may use corporeal, affective, and cognitive constructions. Not only do they act as self-deceptions, they also distort interpersonal communication.

## Envy and Psychosis

Envy's center of gravity primarily resides in unconscious mental processes. By its very nature, envy exists in split-off enclaves that remain deeply buried, inaccessible, and unnoticed. Because the typical surfaces of ego function-ing—ordinary awareness—tend to float on levels that appear more governed by reason, logic, and propriety, the underlying presence and influence of unconscious envy tends to remain obscure.

*Envy theory* reminds us that the id, the *unconscious as a system*, and the primary processes that govern its operation are defined as primitive, omnipo-tent, and psychotic principally by the conscious, rational mind of the ego. This reflects the perceived mutually exclusive split between the two, and reinforces the alienation of and forceful adamancy of the *un*consciousness of the *unconscious as a system*.

Just as envy is a regular part of mental functioning, so too the psychotic process—namely, primary process psychological functioning—is intrinsic to the mind. Primary process mental functioning uses no data from percep-tions of reality; it operates autistically, in isolation. The id functions as the *normative* psychotic part or aspect of the entire self in every human being. Mental health and normalcy denote that id, ego, and superego are reason-ably integrated and thus function in a balanced and coordinately adaptive fashion. Ego with its secondary processes of reason constrain irrational and psychotic intrusions.

When in harmony with ego and superego, primary processes contribute importantly to normal conscious functioning as, for example, in the parts they play in dreams, humor, and creativity. Envy, when not excessive, can be a motivating force spurring constructive curiosity, exploration, ambition, and emulation. Envy, however, may approach levels that are more exces-sive but just short of inducing actual psychosis. These levels can be part of a constellation of impairing neurotic and characterological conditions, for example, in anxiety, mood disorders, and narcissistic and borderline person-ality disorders.

When envy is excessive to extremes, primitive processes dominate men-tal functioning. Id and superego overrule the more conscious dimensions of the ego's information processing and self-regulation. When id processes dominate, paranoid-schizoid and psychotic mechanisms abound. In these cases, they are unopposed by the forces behind *the healthy maturation of envy* including adequate reality testing, empathy, and emotional stability. In es-sence, this imbalance denotes that destructive forces prevail. Several general trends result: an intolerance of frustration, and a destructive hatred of all aspects of conscious awareness, especially perception of the external world and insight into subjective reality. All the aforementioned denote the nature of psychosis.

Since the premier mechanism behind the envy dynamic is projective identification (itself also a primitive, paranoid-schizoid mental operation), excessive envy plays a large part in more severe mental disorders such as psychotic states and vulnerability to psychotic episodes. Although normal projective identification is an important part of mental development and everyday functioning, excessive and unmodified projective identification and envy are risk factors that may lead to psychopathology.

This is attributable to the action of projective identification that produces massive fusion among discrete mental entities, especially by spoiling and deleting their meaning-laden linkages. *Unrealistic confusion, especially between what is good and what is bad, results.* Excessive envy not only causes unbearable emotional confusion, but its capacity to distort thinking also acts to disorganize normal conceptual processes. Boundaries and distinctions on all levels break down. Linguistic functioning also decompensates. A stifling of resolve to action correlating with behavioral change accompanies this.

One principal defensive response to excessive envy is the mobilization of *"narcissistic states of the ego."* In psychotic conditions, the ego so beleaguered feels an experiential morass that includes passivity, smallness, inadequacy, powerlessness, weakness, avolition, and vulnerability to harm and being attacked. To defend against these overwhelming feelings of anxiety and dysphoria, the ego retreats to and dialogues with an internally constituted idealized part-object. External reality and adaptation, functioning through the rational mind, are intermittently abandoned. The boundaries between discriminating what is interior from knowing what is exterior are enormously blurred.

In many cases of malignant psychosis, however, the retreat to this internal part-object is not experienced as soothing. It becomes felt as a potential persecutor. To manage this, a psychotic idealization is employed. It is pathological excessive libidinalization. In effect, this idealization is an *idealization of destructiveness.* Destructiveness is elevated to highly enriched proportions and both extolled and envied.

From a metapsychological point of view, it takes shape as unconscious phantasies of paranoid-schizoid part-objects imbued with excessive death instinct. These are experienced as demon-like, all-powerful figures with irresistible hypnotic-like controlling power. Images of demons, devils, monsters, diabolical spirits, and so forth are the phenomenological forms that hallucinations and psychotic delusions take. These destructive figures are enormously seductive, alluring, and persuasive. They misrepresent their malignancy, and offer the psychotic patient refuge in a purportedly better inner world. In fact, this is a withdrawal from reality to an internal world of confusion and deterioration. Parenthetically, large parts of the therapy of psychosis are showing the patient repeatedly and in great detail this gross distortion of reality. Even in the face of such disturbing psychosis, the therapist must manage his own fear and distress, and continue to communicate with clarity his understanding of the patient's experience of psychosis.

Clinically, psychotic states express themselves when a patient presents with excessively woolly language and hazy thinking—that is, confused information processing. Auditory hallucinations or demon-like visual hallucinations may be present. These malignantly destructive figures may command the patient to harm or kill himself or others. The patient has a perverse attraction to these destructive voices. He may even feel that, in some paradoxical way, they are his only friends and protectors.

Often, the psychotic individual will relate to environmental figures that correlate with, simulate, and reinforce this internal drama. For instance, such patients may idealize notorious criminals, murderers, and serial killers. In addition, an attraction to figures that have destructive and violent characteristics is common. For example, there may be an attraction to dogs perceived as highly aggressive: pit bulls, Rottweilers, Dobermans, and Akitas. The psychotic individual riddled with these paranoid-schizoid preoccupations may relate to real but destructive figures in the environment, persons that have manic-like features of powerfulness, grandiosity, and forceful manipulativeness—for example, dictators and tyrants. This reflects a complex depressive-position defensive covering that is tenuously attempting to manage paranoid-schizoid passivity and weakness.

### Envy and *Schadenfreude*

The concept of *schadenfreude* (pleasure at the misfortune of others) often is used in sociological and psychological literature to denote a synonym of envy. *Envy theory*, however, denotes this experience of glee at the misfortune of another as a distinct expression of a manic defense mechanism, which is a flight away from perceived sorrow caused by intentional harm. This psychodynamic consideration strongly connotes that *schadenfreude is qualitatively distinct from envy*.

The derision reflected in *schadenfreude* is not envy. Such manic reactions typically counter normative responses intimately associated with depressive reactions and sorrow—aspects of the construct of the developmental configuration termed "the depressive position." The misfortune of others normally elicits feelings of concern and pity—the antithesis of *schadenfreude*, pleasure at the misfortune of others.

From a theoretical perspective, the pathology of *schadenfreude* is consistent with the psychopathology of the depressive position. Moreover, recent fMRI studies (Takahashi et al. 2009) demonstrate that different brain areas (ventral striatum including the nucleus accumbens) are activated when *schadenfreude* is explicitly experienced in contrast to those brain areas activated in envy (anterior cingulate cortex). Moreover, as in all later developmental processes, earlier factors (in this case, envy) reside on the nonconscious platform from which later derivatives (for example, *schadenfreude*) arise.

Such manic pleasure in inflicting or witnessing torture or suffering in another involves psychodynamics that are basic to the depressive position, not the paranoid-schizoid position in which envy operates. Elements of control, triumph, and contempt for the object characterize this sneering mania. Rather than arising out of earliest paranoid-schizoid mechanisms like envy, *schadenfreude* arises out of later depressive-position psychodynamics as will be discussed in depth later. This important distinction sharply differentiates *schadenfreude* from envy.

## Envy as a Major Root of Motivation, Volition, and Inhibition

Envy is a central dynamic driving the mind into operation and stimulating its continual, dynamic reconfiguration over time. Envy has both adaptive and nonadaptive dimensions and is an essential feature of mechanisms contributing to survival. Envy, for example, provides the ego with recognition of distinctions and contrasts and so stimulates interest, which reinforces exploration and challenge. When not excessive, this offers an endless array of potential opportunities for healthy, adaptive reality testing.

Motivation, volition, and inhibition as played out in behavior are complex and intertwined. Values, personal needs, social considerations, and cultural conditioning contribute to decision-making on unconscious and conscious levels. One's perceived locus of control and sense of self-agency are affected by envy and how it is modulated.

What is commonly recognized as the "competitive push" is an example of the spur toward ambition and drive to win. If excessive envy remains unmodulated, it can stultify exploration, investigation, and the drive promoting creative contact. Depending on the innate intensity of envy, competitive contact—*contact anxiety*—might exacerbate envy's intensity. The unbearable anxiety it produces can result in the inhibitions that halt accomplishments and engender "fear of success." Such inhibition dampens healthy ambition and prevents successful and productive interpersonal work. Impairments along the lines of the motivational-volitional spectrum result. Envy puts a stranglehold on resolve to action.

In other words, when one's dispositional envy is low or when envy is managed in healthy ways, flexible, adaptive ego functioning may occur. In childhood, an example of this is reflected in developmentally appropriate play. In adults, when envy is low and modulated in healthy ways, thinking, attitudes, and behavior are also marked by qualities of *playfulness, humor, and cheerful spontaneity*. Thinking processes are more fluid and creative, emotions are softer and more resilient, and behavior is adaptively exploratory. Learning, moreover, is enhanced.

The unhealthy effects of envy are seen in extremes ranging from rigidity, inhibition, mental costiveness, and nonspontaneity to excess silliness, disorganized behavior, and intemperate, unsafe playfulness bordering on trickery. These extremes interfere with attention, concentration, and learning, which prevents the intentional work function of the conscious ego from asserting itself in unobstructed ways. The nature of the superego (a repository of unstable envy), its healthy flexibility or constraining rigidity, is directly related to these considerations. It is discussed in later chapters.

## Envy as Narcissistic Self-Destruction

Envy is both psychological violence and paradoxical by nature. It sets up disturbing polarities characterized by perceptions ranging from attributions of superiority to ascriptions of inferiority. For example, the self is felt inferior, and the object is excessively idealized; then the object is spoiled and the self excessively idealized. In states of envy, the ego traverses a kaleidoscope of multiple and fluctuating versions of this in which both ego and object assume these roles in confusingly fractal and inverse ways. The outcome is spoiling the idealization first in the object, then inevitably in the self—a lose-lose situation.

For example, for purposes of illustration, if only one of these dimensions is temporarily frozen for it to be examined, it would reveal that the ego, in a narcissistic state of omnipotence, is assuming a superior role. When envy is examined from this isolated perspective, the ego could be described in a state of pride and arrogance. This denotes a self that has an excessively high estimation of its value, importance, and power. Such an exaggeration is an experiential self-idealization. This self-aggrandizement, however, is only a fleeting aspect of the envious condition. *Pride and envy always go together hand-in-hand.*

Envy, however, incessantly tends to focus its idealizing perception not on the self but on the object. As this reverberating vacillation between self-idealization and idealization of the object continues, anxiety and confusion increase and produce unbearable states of turbulence. When excessive, the ego attempts to manage these anxiety-provoking scenarios by spoiling the targeted object of envy that holds the excessive idealization. Psychological violence ensues as the idealized object is slammed with spoiling and devaluation.

The ultimate thrust of these spoiling assaults, however, results in a boomerang effect—spoiling of the self. This self-spoiling then acts as a shock and becomes inhibiting. *Adaptive collapse* is set in motion. This autodestruction becomes a narcissistic self-destruction. *Adaptive collapse*, which results from the cataclysmic violence of envy-laden emotional states, includes freezing of all mental operations, stifling of emotional responsiveness, inhibitions in thinking, and breakdown of the proper recognition of reality.

## Summary

The material in this chapter reflects the phenomenological and experiential perspective upon which the *nuclear envy* concept rests. How unconscious envy is inferred to be immediately sensed, perceived, and experienced by an individual makes up the phenomenological basis for a comprehensive examination of envy. Envy is a nuclear part of human psychology. Its elaboration in *envy theory* is a prelude to its applicability in diverse research settings and clinical situations.

Envy presents itself in relationship to many experiential states, emotions, and moods: anxiety, guilt, suffering, desire, love, lust, jealousy, hate, resentment, loneliness, disgust, psychosis, motivation, inhibition, impaired volition, and self-destruction. In an attempt to broaden the scope of insight into mental functioning, *envy theory* has advanced a love-envy dialectical model. Rather than replace the love-hate model, an accent on the role of envy and its relationship to primitive love/elemental idealization and other important emotional attitudes is offered. This emphasis, therefore, suggests the pervasive presence of envy in vast areas of human psychological functioning, both personally and socially as well as in normalcy and psychopathology.

Envy is unique in that it unfolds in the context of *contact anxiety*. This connotes a proximity, juxtaposition, and fusion of ego with object (part-object) that launches feelings of privation, excessive idealization, and envious spoiling. From an interpersonal and social perspective, physical proximity elicits local comparisons that reinforce envy. In effect, this is an attempt at destructive deletion, a negation of the object relation since closeness generates such unbearable distress. This intrapsychic process radiates into interpersonal and social relationships.

Envy, when unmodulated by sufficient libidinal/affectionate strivings, is an intolerable experience that acts as a self-destructive implosion, an *adaptive collapse*. Aggression conversely is destructive explosiveness diverted outwardly.

# CHAPTER SIX

# The Nuclear Genesis of Envy

The nuclear genesis of envy describes the way envy arises. Two perspectives are used to outline the hypothetical why and how behind envy's emergence: (1) its earliest developmental origins, and (2) its emergence when activated thereafter.

As has been a recurring theme in *envy theory*, the activation of most psychological phenomena typically arises in this twofold way: emergence from its earliest prototypes, and also in real time with content from acquired experience.

Nuclear genesis connotes developmental origins since this earliest infantile patterning, genetically and constitutionally endowed, remains so influential. This origin makes up a large part of envy's nonconscious pathways whose cognitive and affective blueprints—bias signals—elicit and guide how envy operates.

## The First Prototypical Mental Object

To understand the dyadically based emergence of envy, considerations of self and other—namely, ego and object—are important to review. At all chronological ages, perception has two different features—partiality and a gestalt quality. In the neonatal period, perceptual ability is characterized by a dominance of featural, partial, and incomplete recognition. The normal infant is aware of the real presence of the caregiving figure, typically mother, as a part-object in the first few months and as a whole object—an appearance *with significance*—shortly thereafter. Part-object awareness has a distinctly less personalized and more concrete quality whereas whole-object awareness is truly personal.

*Envy theory*, drawing on a psychoanalytic framework, considers mental development to reflect self-emergence as a reflection of the functional agencies—id, ego, and superego—gradually coming online. At birth, the mental agency, id, is fully present. The *id* has been described as the psychological way that the physiological and anatomical body is experienced as a mental phenomenon. In other words, the id is the body in the mind. As soon as the infant experiences itself and the environment, *ego* functioning begins. The hedonic components based on attraction (good-bad), pleasure, and satisfactions derive from and go toward developing *superego* capability from the start of life.

Sensing the presence of another correlates with the capacity of the ego to experience or "witness." In *envy theory*, how the awareness of "the other" comes about is crucial. These impressions make up part of the scaffolding of and are the birthplace of all envious experience.

*The inception of this primordial sense of "other" is conjectured to be the infantile ego's experience of its own id.* This is primordial envy. The first and ceaselessly primordial experience of this elemental "other" is the ego's subliminal awareness of its *primordial anaclitic dependency on its id*. This indestructible platform rests at the base of all dynamic unconscious processes. This "dependency" is a fused cohesion, an adhesive juxtaposition, not a distinct separation. The discrepancies, comparisons, and dualisms between experiencing "wealth versus absence" that forever beset the ego's executive functioning are rooted in this nuclear template—the seemingly irreconcilable dynamic of the one (self) and the many (ego and its id).

This primordial awareness of "the other" functions in the background of nonconscious information processing from infancy and thereafter in the sense of a *chaperone* that forever attends all additional experiential transactions. Subliminal as this "other" is, it acts as a commanding presence that crucially influences all information processing and the way meaning is constructed.

In earliest infancy, the primary prototypical mental object—a vague experiential awareness—takes shape in an atmosphere of this background primordial *chaperone*. Words and concepts used here are hypothetical approximations of prelinguistically experienced awareness.

How experience organizes itself results in producing the form of a *primary object* (mothering/nurturing figure) from two component parts: *part-object (breast)* first and later on top of this is *whole object (mother as a person)*. The primary object composite is the result of the infant's own compelling projections, inwardly felt sensations, and whatever endogenous perceptual equipment is open to grasping environmental stimuli.

*The very earliest prototypical mental object (primordial object) is the basal experience of the ego's own primordial ancestor—the id. Superimposed on this primordial object, the ego establishes an experience of its primary object—the dual recognition of a part-object breast (primal object) somehow linked to a whole object (primary object)—mother as a person.*

An inherent equilibratory resonance underlies the infant's preattentive sensory and perceptual readiness to recognize a suitable environmental figure—mother. This entrainment contributes to states of self-regulation, soothing, stability, survival, and laying down elemental meaning. These processes are driven by and regulate the ego's inherent sense of incompleteness.

Hence, the infant's primary grasp of caregiving—mothercraft in the actual interpersonal environment/the breast and the mother—becomes shaped and superimposed on its primordial grasp of its own felt core reality—its id. *The id is the chaperone that remains the ego's primordial companion for life.*

Studies in neuroscience, for example, attest to the salience of significant persons in the interpersonal milieu. These relationships, especially the figure of mother, embed themselves cognitively in nonconscious ways. They significantly contribute to the abiding influence of nonconscious motivational components including goals, needs, and mental plans or goal pursuits concerning these primary relationships. They often transfer to other figures in the interpersonal environment (Fitzsimons and Bargh 2003).

As growth, maturation, and development proceed, the ego inevitably comes to "disregard" its early nonconscious preoccupation with its id. *Focus is normally redirected toward the novel features of the external environment.* Perceptual and conceptual expansions accompany and give rise to greater periods of alertness and conscious awareness. Emotionally, however, the ego's emergence from its previous state of closeness to its id (narcissism and omnipotence) ushers in feelings of loss, deflation, and increased helplessness. This sense of lost perfection is reinforced by the ever-present subliminal recognition of its id in the form of primordial envy.

The ego's core sense of loss of perfection may be likened to a state of deflated infatuation, however inchoate this amalgamation of feelings may be. Such an unremitting pining for once having been part of the id, in mental fact, remains as the unconscious base of the self, as an empire of omnipotent influence. This is the infantile experience of *primordial anaclitic dependency.* This loss is the felt experience of *true privation.*

The sense of true privation is, in effect, a feeling of basal impotence. It is idiopathic true privation, a state of absence. *Primordial anaclitic dependency* and states of *true privation* are primordial, organic, and irreducible. They are the deepest cause of envy from the *id relations* point of view. They are reinforced by the partial sense of privation stimulated by dependence on, periodic absence of, and intermittent nonsatisfaction by the first prototypical mental and material object—the nurturing, creative breast experienced in infancy.

The first prototypical object outside the ego in the real world is the breast as a part-object; it is also felt to be an aspect of the whole object, the mother. The experience of the breast as a *part-object relation* is the experience of what *envy theory* terms the *mother-breast*. As much as normalcy and balance prevail in the infant's relation to the caregiving figure, this *mother-breast* is felt in a vacillating way: normatively ideal or good and normatively withholding/self-sufficient or bad. In both these configurations, the *mother-breast* is enviable.

Klein reiterated her hypothesis that "the infant has an innate unconscious awareness of the existence of the mother" (1959, 248) and also "the mother's breast, both in its good and bad aspects, also seems to merge for him with her bodily presence; and the relation to her as a person is thus gradually built up from the earliest stage onward" (1952a, 63).

This deepest cause of envy from the object relations perspective, therefore, is envy of the vivifying richness and creativeness of the *breast mother*, a phrase I use to denote the infant's *total yet primitive grasp of the entire mother*. This denotes the experience of the part-object breast (*mother-breast*) in the context of a whole-object relation. Envy is experienced as a part-object relation but persists into whole-object relations, where it is always found at their core.

The sense of lost perfection associated with the phenomenon of defensive narcissism has its origins in earliest infancy. It issues from the sense of true privation (*id relations and primordial envy*), which becomes reinforced by the periodic, actual absence of the nurturant figure (object relations amplified by perceptions of real-world interpersonal relations). The sense of lost perfection arises and is reinforced when envy is stimulated.

Envy, in this way, acts as a threat to both sustaining phantasies of narcissism and to maintaining states of omnipotence. The ego wants to retain and regain its sense of power, control, and self-dependence yet envy acts to deflate the ego's omnipotence, stimulate dependency needs, and remind the ego of its littleness, inferiority, and helplessness. This again reflects the delicate balance among three of the ego's principal energetic centers of gravity/attention: narcissism, object-love, and object envy.

## Primordial *Anaclitic Dependency*:
## Ego Depends on Id Forever

The *primordial dependency of ego on its id is elemental. It is the earliest prototype of all other relations that evolve into dependency.* It is the relational prototype of the cognitive and emotional sense of discrepancy, asymmetry, dissonance, and privation. This is the basis for the inception of envy in its primordial root form.

All later and more complex states of "dependency proper," such as the ego's dependency on the mental object and the infant's dependency on the actual mother, become superimposed on this substrate of primordial dependency on the id. The latter, secondary dependency of ego on its objects is characterized by separateness, difference, and frustration, all of which provoke a sequence of envy-laden psychodynamics reinforced by the *ego's underlying primordial anaclitic dependency on its id.*

*Anaclitic means amorphously fused dependence on, leaning on, and having a characteristic intimate contiguity, closeness, adhesiveness, and immanence with. This conception of intimate clinging is the essence of what I term "id relations," which are indestructible and persist throughout life. The ego is forever beholden to its id.*

At the moment the ego senses separation, "betweenness," and distance from its id, a gradually unfolding awareness occurs consequent to this previously shared but now shattered *pseudosymmetry.* Mental space, a universe of mental objects, becomes a psychological reality. Ego, I maintain, perceives itself as the center of its emerging mindfulness and as an agency set against its id—the original "other."

With this disenfranchisement, the ego senses the id as something else, foreign, alien, mysterious, strange, unknown, outside, and uncanny. The primitive ego is confronted with an inchoate sense of self-sufficient independence sensed in the "other"—the id.

This is the nuclear root of all future feelings of withholding ascribed to an entity sensed as strangely self-sufficient to the point of being independent. The mind's default state of experiential asymmetry, discrepancy, dissonance, privation, and conflict rests on feeling the need to come to grips with this collision—one (single self) becoming many (ego and id). The epistemological and adaptational ramifications of this are enormous.

Very shortly after this epiphany, the ego as the eye ("I") of the self gradually comes to focus on the outer environment, forgets it origins, and becomes radically estranged from its primordial mother—its id. Intrasubjective separation processes such as described are central and serve as the core of the nuclear genesis of envy. Primordial envy of ego toward its id is always at the core of more complex forms of primary envy.

*The paradox in this illustrative scenario is that the same one entity—the self— along the course of its progressive differentiation and development in chronological time inevitably experiences an uncanny sense of asymmetry, noncorrespondence, and estrangement between its own parts. During the course of development, what becomes experientially more conscious is felt as separate from what remains more unavailable, nonconscious, and often irretrievable—id awareness.*

At any point in life, feelings of loneliness, separation, and existential alien‑ ation, not being part of a social system or group, for example, reflect this core estrangement. Although often attributed to some outside situation or social context, experiences of estrangement originate from their ancestry in earliest infantile development according to *envy theory*. They are rooted in the primor‑ dial splitting that inevitably occurs between ego and its ancestral id at birth.

For example, alienation, seeing others as "alien," "outsider," and "enemy," is the inevitable extension of this primordial intrapsychic estrangement, the background upon which all experience is interpreted. Two elements are con‑ tained in this: (1) fear of a potentially threatening unknown, partly absent enemy (persecutory hostility), and (2) a conflicted attraction to such an alluring and partly absent mystery (envy dynamic). While both attitudes usu‑ ally coexist, either envy or hostility takes precedence in mental functioning, depending on predispositional endowment and environmentally experienced contextual situations.

Over time, the gradual development of thinking and memory reinforces a belief in the centralized primacy of the consciously experienced aspects of the ego. The awake state, conscious awareness, and the outer environment come to be regarded as the only real features of all experience, especially since they are perceived as regular, consistent, and recurring. In this developed belief resides the source of the epistemological and ontological questions central to, and inescapably recurring in, philosophy and psychology: the problem of "the one and the many" and of "monism versus dualism" as previously men‑ tioned. *Envy theory* formulates these considerations as problems arising from the ontogenesis of cognitive and emotional boundaries—both intrapsychic and interpersonal.

From the perspective of the ego and its *id relations*, this first state of depen‑ dency arises from the developing potential space between id and its ego. It is a state of dynamic fusion in the process of differentiating into separateness— one into many. It is the blurry mind-body experience that relocalizes as the sense of a separate, subjective self. The individual, in reality a codependent group of functions, learns to spotlight only a limited, select few of these and identify with them as if they were the entire range composing its being.

Parenthetically, *envy theory* suggests that this psychic reality has been recognized in a displaced way culturally—for example, in philosophical and religious traditions. Using different terminology, it has come to be named the ontological problem of "the one and the many," one world of only one substance or a multiverse of differing dimensions not only quantitatively different but also qualitatively distinct.

Additionally, this has been a central concern in the study of human psychology and can be understood as "the problem of boundaries." Such boundaries take the form of mental distinctions and emotionally experienced distinctions between one individual and another. Asymmetry, discrepancy, dissonance, and conflict are the scaffolding in this template of how consciousness operates. Furthermore, most epistemological mechanisms may be explored using these models.

## Adhesiveness in the Paranoid-Schizoid Position: Why Envious States Are So Persistent

*Envy theory* sees envy as nuclear to all information processing, mental health, and deviations resulting in psychopathology. This emphasizes the persistence of envy dynamics that arise in earliest infancy in the paranoid-schizoid position. The level of persistence of envy in any individual is a result of its constitutional endowment and how development, nurturance, and conflict resolution have successfully or unsuccessfully negotiated envy's mitigation.

Normal development advances by attempting to transcend ontogenetically earlier, more primitive mental operations. *Envy theory* goes to great lengths to point out that these earliest configurations are laid down so powerfully that they remain imperishable reference points. In other words, envy, narcissism, omnipotence, and irrational information processing adhere as the indestructible platform upon which more rational cognitive and affective experience later develops. Intransigence is an apt designation characterizing this persisting configuration of primary processes underneath secondary processes of reality-based cognitive development.

From the perspective of the ego's object relations, ego awareness is launched at the start of life in the paranoid-schizoid position where envy reigns supreme. Schizoid object relations are narcissistic object relations. They reflect the immature ego's incorporation or autoimprinting of its frail awareness of aspects of objects it has grasped. The object is recognized, but only incompletely as partial, featural, or part-object.

In typical and expectable fashion, envy intermittently acts to defensively spoil the ideal part-object. Less envy stimulates less spoiling and optimizes successful resolution. Excessive envy fosters greater spoiling and tends to reinforce itself.

The once ideal part-object that has now become damaged and in a state of ruin provokes intense feelings. Rapidly, primitive feelings of persecution as well as a sense of protoguilt arise. *Both persecutory feelings and premature feelings of guilt amalgamate and tend to cement the ego in the paranoid-schizoid position.* The conflicts and dissonant experiences so generated are experienced as enormous, taxing cognitive processing, and also resisting easy resolution.

When premature guilt is excessive, envy perpetuates itself and halts normal development. Envious spoiling targets creativeness on all levels. In these situations, in unconscious phantasy, the primal object breast is spoiled, especially its creative capacity to generate and provide love, nurturance, and understanding. Since envy also spoils the envier's own capacity to receive love and nurturance and to understand, in effect, the ego is in a state of emotional starvation. No goodness is being received and no healthy reassurance that goodness exists is felt. *Since little or no pleasure and enjoyment are felt, there is no glimmer of gratitude experienced to mitigate destructive impulses, envy, and greed.* This standstill correlates with the persistence, intransigence, and adhesiveness that envy propagates.

Excessive envy and pathological projective identification act to blur distinctions between persecution and true guilt in both phantasy and reality. In infancy, this prolongs developmental immaturity and retards the advancement of adequate ego integration. This prevents a normative diminishment of persecutory experience and the subsequent development of distinct self and object differentiation. This also impedes the emergence of the capacity for concern, empathy, and guilt—all of which make a more manageable resolution available.

Only in the depressive position can the individual experience the healthier dynamics of true dependency, separation, true deprivation, aggression, and conflict around these. Learning, remembering, and repeating occur and cyclically reinforce themselves. The relation between greed and jealousy, for example, emerges out of the complexities of the depressive position. In this position, the ego fervently wishes to hold the ambivalently loved but harmed object. The whole object is needed and depended upon.

Complex emotional relations of separateness, holding on, dependence, and so forth can only be experienced when objects are experienced as whole entities in complex multiple relationships with each other. Only in the developmentally advanced depressive position where reality holds sway over phantasy can true dependency, holding on, and *the capacity for letting go and moving forward* occur. This capability is essential to normal development and mental health in childhood, adolescence, and adult life.

## One Self Having an Ego as the Beacon Illuminating the Sea of Its Id

The question then becomes, "Is reality—outer world and inner world— essentially unified or does it exist in a disparate, randomly, nonconnected way?"

*Envy theory* proposes that the radical estrangement of aspects of the consciously developing self from the primordially based unconscious self is the nuclear genesis of envy, as well as of later experiences of separateness. As ego gradually splits away from id, the ego comes to regard id as outside, "not-me," and "the other." What was originally one becomes felt as a complex amalgamation of many parts. The ego develops perceptual capacities; one's sense of self then restricts its experiential locus to this consciously aware but truncated ego portion of the entire self-system, thereby excluding proper recognition of id.

Experientially, the one self consistently remains aware of only a small portion of its entire self, the majority of which remains nonconscious and unremembered. What is apparently outside awareness is either preattentive and can be recalled, or remains in a state of more consolidated repression ("dynamic unconscious"), in effect, a state of absentia.

This *miniscule cognitive spotlight*—the *preconscious ego*—then establishes itself as the dimly lit beacon that only periodically illuminates itself sufficiently enough to become more fully conscious—a state of focused attention. Underlying this, unconscious splitting processes in primary process cognition typically cause information processing to revert back to its default state of polarized differentiation in binary-like fashion. This is the experiential template for all preattentive and wakeful perception and cognition.

*The ego, moreover, operates as the perceptual beacon of the self. It holds the privileged status of being the unique spotlight in consciousness that has the potential ability to effect change in the entire psychological system of the self. Such changes are intermittent achievements that come about, for example, when insights into motivations and self-understanding arise, especially through self-inquiry, self-development, and in therapeutic situations.*

All defense mechanisms, especially denial, splitting, repression, dissociation, and intellectualization, reinforce a sense of distance between aspects of the self. They are mental "body armor" fostering imperviousness and the ego's insensitivity to feeling the exquisite pulsations of its id. When excessive, this amounts to a rigid, inflexible experiential sense of splits, separateness, and missing parts in all aspects of the perceptual sense of self as a whole.

The modulation of overwhelming anxieties—unbridled id emanations into the ego—by the ego's use of excessive defense mechanisms often results in an ego that is hypertrophied, excessively overgrown, and, in a sense, calcified. This notion underlies the concept of *resistance to insight*. It is one of the main reasons that psychological change is so difficult and that sincere self-development strategies and psychotherapies require sufficient time to achieve a sustainable effectiveness. Resistance—mental body armor—acts as a blockage. It shields adequate and healthy awareness from direct contact with disturbing nonconscious processes: deep anxieties, defenses, and complex sources of unconscious conflicts. This serves adaptive purposes in small doses, but can be lethal and impairing when excessive.

In a manner of speaking, *resistance denotes remaining aware of conscious, safe, and nonthreatening issues in one's psychological world while simultaneously denying one's primordial mother—the id. This, at rock bottom in unconscious phantasy, is a repression of the recognition of the elemental primordial object relation at the core of the ego—the id as the primordially based breast feeding its very offspring, the ego. It reflects the unconscious process of splitting and the mental state of maintaining information in a rigid condition of unconsciousness—namely, repression.*

## Envy's Three Causative Roots: Why *Nuclear Envy* Activates

*Nuclear envy*, or the inception of envy, activates for many reasons. Although precisely understood explanations may be far from adequately understood, nonetheless, three leading reasons are postulated. Envy's roots are its biomental triggers. Envy's core scaffolding or structure is composed of its three roots. Each root is described by outlining its structure and the circumstances around its activation. The origin of envy's inception—its nuclear genesis—centers on the ego's differing senses of *privation*—feeling experiential gaps—and *attempts to extinguish* this intolerable experience.

On the most abstract theoretical level of *envy theory*, privation sensed in the ego arises from the life instinct's clash with the innate death instinct's blind, unflagging, and unrelenting push toward nullity. All this operates through the ego's nonconscious information processing and registration systems on the most primitive levels of cognition and emotion. The activation of privation occurs almost simultaneously with idealization processes that inevitably lead to spoiling and ultimate deletion. The intolerable senses of privation and idealization in whatever form they take (for example, phantasy of ideal breast) constitute the targets of deletion. In other words, envy seeks to extinguish any hint of privation and idealization as a glimmer of creativeness and vivifyingness on all levels (roots one, two, and three) of their unconscious and conscious arising.

The prime mover of envy is its preexperiential, innate schema—that is, its constitutional template. A fuller unfolding and development from this nonconscious nucleus occurs over time by the significant contributions of experience and the real social environment. One's envy load and constitutional endowment ultimately drive why and how envy arises. This platform is reflected in the intensity of envy's robbing and spoiling attacks aimed at deleting all senses of privation and idealization, and in the duration of each in real time. Constitutional envy load—the degree of envy experienced—is a principal risk factor for upsetting healthy development and predisposing to psychological disturbance.

*Envy theory* proposes that *nuclear envy* at each moment of its inception activates from a combination of three root causes. Each root cause is activated by differing degrees of the sense of *privation* and its sequellae, intolerance of this trajectory, and efforts to eliminate it. Since *envy theory* is intrinsically a developmental theory, each of the three root causes has a developmental arising and context. In other words, root one or primordial envy is basal and ever-present. Root two has two parts: part one is primal envy that arises in the paranoid-schizoid position chronologically (first three months of life) and remains active thereafter; part two is primary envy that comes into being during the depressive position (about four months to twelve months) and, similar to part one, remains active uninterruptedly in the unconscious strata of consciousness. Root three is activated to the extent that sufficient perceptual competence and conscious awareness has been achieved (typically in the second year of life).

Three roots activate unconscious envy: (1) a spontaneous root, (2) a root with two parts: peremptive and preemptive, and (3) a reactive root. These three dimensions of envy constitute *nuclear envy*, especially when etiological emphasis is placed on envy's spontaneous (primordial) and preemptive (primary) activation. *All three arousal stimuli typically work in concert—almost in simultaneity—with root three acting as an amplifier of the others.*

First Root: *Primordial envy* spontaneously activates. Out of a primeval base in the dynamically unconscious primary processes of primal repression, envy activates when any innate impulse, need, desire, or wish *spontaneously* arises. This is, in essence, automatic and immanent—that is, without any apparent stimulus. It is unmotivated, unlearned, and not reducible to any cause beside its own axiomatic existence. This spontaneous quality correlates with genetic endowments in human neural networks. This *autonomous root* of the organic arousal of envy cannot be underrated since it is the undiluted essence of envy's irrational, virtually omnipotent, impermeable, and resistant core. It is part of the impervious scaffolding of the primordial unconscious.

This first root activation is de novo and paroxysmal. It is an unconditioned event without provocation. This idiopathic activation needs no preceding stimulus, and is not reactive or secondary. In other words, it is not a reaction to frustration or disappointment. It may occur in states of satisfaction and in quiescence. This imperative and absolute *autoactivation is envy's first cause that, in itself, is uncaused.* The nuclear id-ego state (id relations) is the infrastructure out of which this *nuclear envy* erupts. Primordial envy outranks all other aspects of envy in power since it is closest to id relations: the *primordial anaclitic dependency* of ego on its id.

Second Root: The second root of envy has two parts: *primal envy* of the primal part-object breast, and *primary envy* proper of the primary whole object, mother. The first part, primal envy, emerges out of a primordial foundation in the inherent libidinal (infatuation)–destructive (spoiling) dialectic: the nuclear protodyad-based (id-ego) relation—*primordial envy.*

Similar to the behavior of instinctual wishes in the dynamic unconscious, *primal envy has a peremptory quality* that impels toward activation at all costs. The ego's primal envy is an unorganized, minimally libidinized, and deeply unconscious envy. It is dominated by destructive forces originating in the id that come to infuse the ego, and, along with the extroversion of libido, cue the ego to progressively seek out three prop-like objectives with which to reestablish lost entrainment. The first objective is the id, the second is the part-object, breast, and the third is the whole object, mother.

The first part of the second root of envy, *primal envy*, arises at the start of life in the paranoid-schizoid position where information processing remains uninterruptedly nonconscious throughout life. Primary process illogic and unconscious phantasy reign supreme. Primal envy's declaration is the *organic anticipation of and partial, burgeoning awareness of idealized goodness, potency, creativeness, and vivifyingness*—the ideal object. As the sense of privation and idealization escalate, primal envy activates as a *peremptive*, decree for absolute extinguishment. This is a deletion by fiat elicited by the hint of a provocateur. Primal envy's declaration is the *organic anticipation of and partial, burgeoning awareness of idealized goodness, potency, and creativeness*—the ideal object. This partially libidinalized envy—the short-lived infatuation phase—is projected primal envy. The pressures of instinctual endowment and innate readiness for object awareness as an inherent preconceptual potential drives this peremptive motor both to notice and to react to this nonconsciously perceived part-object breast. This expectation pathway is a prewired readiness to anticipate, seek, and notice an object. This inherent object bias is the inchoate, species-specific sensory and perceptual preattentive ability that empirically and behaviorally expresses itself as the conspicuously social nature characterizing human culture. Previous actual experience with satisfaction associated with a real external caregiver is certainly a large and significantly reinforcing part of this already inherent object expectation.

Envy theory maintains that id relations refer to the primordial anaclitic dependency of the ego on its id. It is a primitive relationship of liege. This primordial foundation of unconscious envy is concentrated in envy's root one and overlaps into the transition from envy's spontaneous first root to its second root. This is the primary process (illogical and "unrational") basis for both the inherent, peremptive activation of envy (primal envy) and envy (primary envy) arising in a preemptive way when, in the presence of the object, envy's spoiling trajectory arises in advance of any other possible nonenvious response. Primary envy attempts to forestall envy's deleterious experience of intolerable privation and its painful consequences. These elements—explosive extinguishment (primal envy) and first strike (primary envy)—establish the self's position of readiness for the inevitable full deployment of envy—that is, the complex and reinforcing interactions of all three of envy's roots.

The primordial "other" in envy theory is the idealized perfection, excellence, and richness of the id, the empire of omnipotence. It ultimately finds expression/instantiation/reemergence in the ideal breast, the ego's first, primal part-object. This state represents what in adult life is a sense of unreasoned infatuation.

Thus, the second root that triggers envy's activation is the dual impact of primal breast awareness (primal envy) and primary ideal whole-object awareness, mother (primary envy). Both always exist as an inextricably conflated experiential unit accompanying envy's activation. This second root (primal and primary) holds a transitional position between envy's first (primordial) and third (reactive) roots.

These ego-object configurations of envy along with their numerous complex instinctual energies ultimately become sequestered in the superego. The superego is the repository containing standards composed of idealized valences that act as imperative impulses toward attraction/prescription and avoidance/proscription. This influences decision-making, choosing between alternatives. In concert with contributions from the entire ego, behavioral actions are chosen and carried out. The superego functions like a mental sphincter that permits and regulates uniquely pulsed, varying combinations of open and closed flow between the unconscious, preconscious, and conscious aspects of the mind. The primordial id-ego matrix provides an indestructible priming to envy's operation. It facilitates the ability to detect and identify all of envy's triggers. In the wake of envy's "un-understandable" primitive activation, all the rest of its psychodynamic circuitry proceeds.

Third Root: The least hypothetical reason for the arousal of envy, its third root, is *secondary envy*. It is the *reactive, secondary response to the awareness of idealized goodness in the primary object—the mother.* This is the more organized, concrete experience of the primary object sensed in a dual way: (1) as part-object in the paranoid-schizoid position and (2) as whole object in the depressive position. In concert, these dual perspectives contribute to a relatively integrated self that feels sufficiently distinct from its perceived whole object. *This occurs on the concrete level of real person to real person.*

The ego aspect of the self thus can feel dependency on and hunger for the goodness of the other whole object. Likewise it can feel separation and disappointment when perceived losses occur or personal resources are lacking or inferior to those of another. This level of whole-object awareness correlates with the actual perception of a real interpersonal figure in the social environment. Typically, by the second year of life, sufficient memory is consolidated so that the ministrations of real people are grasped, remembered, and more clearly understood as present or absent. When the ego is thwarted from experiencing pleasure from the object, *deprivation* is felt. Deprivations experienced later in life are often exaggerated by the earliest sense of primordial absence as a basal sense of emptiness.

The envier may feel deprivation in another way as well—that is, when another person is perceived as *not* being envious. The perception of the absence of envy in another implies that the envier is deprived of being envy-free. This cause of envy, in essence, is an envy of peace of mind and mental health.

This constellation of partial separateness, reliance, and unsettled vulnerability reflects typical or *secondary dependency—dependence proper*. It denotes the ego's feeling of helplessly being unable to achieve sufficient satisfaction in an autonomous, self-dependent manner, free from the object's influence. Real, social situations involving comparisons ("upward social comparisons"), deprivations, inequities, and perceived injustices—for example, "haves and have nots"—contribute heavily to this third root. This dependent helplessness is experienced after real episodes of satiation and satisfaction, along with repetitive feelings of disappointment of the expectation of possible gratification, of deprivation of what was or could be had, and of perceived intentional withholding. These reactions reinforce themselves and are reinforced by the perpetual physiological, emotional, and cognitive needs that *begin in infancy and recur throughout life*. It makes the object's perpetual appeal a reinforcing and irresistible experience that is constantly anticipated, wished for, and sought after. In this cycle, learning, remembering, and repeating play themselves out.

*Envy theory*, however, emphasizes that the third, reactive root of envy is its weakest trigger although the one most clearly recognized and described since it is closest to conscious awareness. The conscious form of envy that may be so provoked is typically less malignant depending on the intensity of its components, roots one and two.

The risk factor prompted by root three is palpable and empirical. In other words, envy's first root takes precedence over and supersedes its second root; and the second root, in turn, supersedes the third root in strength and dominance. Root three, typically empirically measurable, is envy's principal amplifier. It is the currency of scholarly research into envy, especially because it is testable.

Once envy is set off, the ego, inevitably confronted with its own dependency, inferiority, helplessness, and vulnerability, has no choice but to conform to envy's protocol. To adapt to this and regulate the disrupted psychic equilibrium (often triggered by feelings of disappointment), envy is elicited to demote the perceived superiority of the idealized object. This third component of envy is a *post hoc* response to disappointment and expectations not met. Its aim is to quell the distress of negative self-appraisals that include envious anxiety, resentment, and perceived unfairness.

This state of unhappiness is stirred when the inordinate magnificence of the object is felt as a threat to the empowerment that the ego's own narcissism and quota of libidinal energy tenuously provide it. The experiential self feels diminished in the face of the other's perceived completeness. In the wake of envy's activation, the ache accompanying this omnipotent idealization must undergo a temporary deletion—a deidealization best achieved only by destructive spoiling. The arousal of envy, moreover, always remains a typical constant in human psychology. Only when excessive narcissism and noxious environmental triggers flood it does envy devolve into spoiling and destructive psychopathology.

On an observable, interpersonal level, the *choice of envied object* is based on "lock and key" and "glove and hand" mechanisms. The envier scans the environment for some *hint of common ground* between himself and another. This

hint is based on *idiosyncratic phantasy* and may have little to do with real provocation from another person. An unconscious equation is established. This link
is an asymmetrical and inverse connection based on perceived absence in the
envier and presence in the envied one. When the envier sees a figure in the
environment that appears to possess what the envier lacks, that figure then
acts as a potential key to be identified with to enable the envier to unlock his
own wished-for potential. The hand of the envied one signals that a fit into the
empty glove of the envier would bring about satisfaction and completion. This
always remains a phantasied experience of anticipation and later disillusionment; hence, attraction, envy, and spoiling follow in sequence.

## Id Relations and True Privation, the Basis of all Envy

The psychoanalytic concepts of the object and the ego's relations to its objects (object relations) have a long history. Both ideas are frequently used to
describe mental processes in psychodynamic terms. The concepts of the id
and the ego's relations to its id (*id relations*), on the other hand, have been
addressed much less frequently (Schur 1966; Loewald 1980). These considerations have been relegated to obscurity since they are generally seen as
archaic metapsychological models with less practical applicability than more
focused considerations of adaptive ego functioning.

*Envy theory* brings a fresh look to the concepts of id and the id in relation
to ego. The concept of *id relations* is central to the *nuclear envy* thesis.

*Just as the early ego comes to an awareness of objects and develops object rela-
tions, so too the ego, from its inception at the beginning of life, has a distinct relation to its biopsychologically derived mental source, its id. Id relations consist of the
quality and quantity of the multifaceted connections that ego has and forms toward
its inescapable id.*

*Envy theory* postulates that *the ego becomes aware of its id as the first object/
presence in subjective experience*. This first experience is primordial and cannot be understood as the experience of an "object" in either the part-object
or whole-object sense. The term *"presence,"* perhaps, best describes this
first amorphous and inchoate experience. Loosely speaking, the id is the
nonconscious mental container of all that is unknowable, yet omnipotently
attractive and perpetually desired. The id as the ego's first objective could be
called, in a loose fashion, the ego's primordial object.

This defining moment—*ego's primordial awareness of its id*—is made possible since the very fabric of the ego initially consists of id instinctual forces
in process of transformation or what *envy theory* calls *mentalization*.

These id impulses can be described as diffuse groupings of life instincts together with aspects of the death instinct. Having this energetic id loading, the ego is compelled to experience a relational attraction as some splitting processes take shape between ego and id. Hence, some awareness of this experience arises. As the ego nonconsciously senses more and more the intensity of the instinctual forces and their disarmingly powerful attractiveness, a relation emerges and is discovered. The ego's *id relations* thus arise and develop. This has a chronological sequence starting at birth. Id relations continue to persist nonconsciously throughout life.

This primordial *id relation* is one of *primordial dependency. The ego is dependent on its id in a fundamental and elemental way.* This dependency is constitutionally set. It is a relationship bound forever by what I term "liege"—that is, a state of fundamental allegiance and obligatory service.

This dependency is the source of a primordial envy of ego toward id because of the unappeasable frustration that arises as ego senses its inferiority compared to an immense power, the omnipotence of its id. *The id becomes the ego's first "other" or "other presence."*

This lingering attendance is the nidus that contains everything the ego desires but can never sufficiently become or attain. This unflagging sense of longing is a state of amorphous near satisfaction that reflects the innate, constitutional, indestructible, and principal side of the constellation of *nuclear envy.* As mentioned previously, the ego, at every point in development, retains a primordial awareness of its id. This ever-present sense of "the other" is termed *the chaperone.* The silent chaperone never leaves. It is the ego's eternal companion. It remains the prototypical platform on which all other relations between the ego and its newfound other "objects" develop.

A simple illustration will be used to clarify the nature of *nuclear envy's* activating factors and dependency: the image of a coin. The one coin of envy can be viewed as having two sides: a first, front, face, obverse, or *principal side,* and a second, back, reverse, or *counterpart side.*

The *principal side* of nuclear envy, its true face, is its constitutional base. It has two parts: (1) primordial (root one), and (2) primal and primary (root two). The primordial root has been described as paroxysmally activating and uncaused. The primordial dependency of ego on its id—the ego's *id relations*—results from splitting and differentiation processes that occur at birth. This sets up the *ego's awareness of its incremental distinction from its id.* The long developmental course of ego organization both in relation to its id and to the external environment adds to the ego's slow unification as an individuating, relatively self-dependent, and substantial entity. The ego primarily continues to be subject to a primordial elemental dependency on its id. *Envy theory* views this as an immutable given.

As the ego grows, its center of attention becomes relocalized, centrated within itself, refocused, and not directed exclusively toward its id. As the ego comes to experience this gradual and apparently *partial* separation from its id, it begins to discriminate and sense qualitative and quantitative distinctions between itself and its id. *The ego, feeling that it is not and can never be or become its id*, arrives at this realization in a startling and uncanny manner. This shock—an elemental narcissistic wound—makes up the first experience of what I call *true privation*. It is a profound pain felt by a fragile self in the wake of sensing experiential dissolution and emptiness.

Primordial envy is prompted by a raw and primitive clash of dual libidinal/creative (idealizing) and destructive (spoiling) impulses within the fragile ego toward the very ancestral matrix from which it arises. *True privation* is the unbearable emotional sound that the ego hears amid this clash. This paradoxical, soundless dissonance is felt as an existential ache.

To survive, the ego must mute, through processes of further splitting and denial, its sense of maximal helplessness and dependency on its id. It must redirect its attention to a field that is less overwhelming and thus more manageable. The ego's *id relations* become less merged and less syntonic. As a progressively greater awareness of this alienation occurs, the ego's sense of the presence of its id becomes increasingly more dystonic and experienced as a major source of experiential anxiety. The primordial organization of primitive mental space—the presumed separation of ego from id—is thus engendered.

The ego's abdication occurring from the perspective of the principal or first side of envy represents the primordial experience of *true privation*: the ego never being able to be id. The ego feels little compared to an eternally omnipotent and inexorably superior id. *This principal side, especially the primordial component—the ego's id relations—becomes bedrock and an immutable given in the organization of mental life for both men and women*. It establishes a ceiling and a base whose parameters are rigid, fixed, and impermeable.

This amalgamation of the senses of asymmetry, discrepancy, dissonance, and conflict becomes the blueprint for all cognition, emotion, and construals of meaning and reality. In clinical situations, for example, it expresses itself as "therapeutic impasse" and is the basal root of "treatment resistance" and the "negative therapeutic reaction." Whether this primordial aspect of the envy template is analyzable or must remain un-understood both theoretically and clinically remains an open question.

From the perspective of the principal side of *nuclear envy*, the ego feels separate from, yet awed by, and dispossessed of the power of its primordial object, the id. Additionally, the principal side of *nuclear envy* also contains primal and primary envy, the inborn anticipation, recognition, and seeking of an object. At first, it is a figural grasp of a part-object; later, it is a configural, global apprehension of a whole object. Primary envy develops on the substrate of primal envy, which reinforces it. Primal and primary envy have strong transitional characteristics. This second root is part of envy's principal side but also participates in *envy's counterpart side—reactive envy secondary to felt deprivation.*

## The Ego's Object Relations: Mandatory About-Face from Id to Objects

The complement to the principal side of envy is its reactive, secondary dimension: its *counterpart side* involving the ego's relations to its objects; this is envy's third root. This backside of envy has its own complementary trajectory parallel to the ego's relations to its id. This occurs after the paranoid-schizoid position. Object relations are "at home" in the depressive position; technically, these are referred to as whole-object relations.

*This path of object recognition involves the ego's awareness of, need for, and dependency on objects, not its id.* It is this dimension of envy, its second side, composed mostly though not entirely of object relations, which is more understandable and therapeutically amenable to change. There are, however, considerable transitional features of part-object relations embedded in all whole-object relations.

*Nuclear envy*, it is to be remembered, is a large constellation composed of its two sides and three roots: (1) its principal side of spontaneous envy (root one) and peremptive primal envy and preemptive primary envy (root two), and (2) its counterpart side of reactive envy (root three).

The inception of this counterpart side of *nuclear envy* arises as partial affiliations with objects are sparked. These "objects" are secondary objects in contrast to the id—the singular, nameless primordial presence having nuclear omnipotence. The proclivity toward any object awareness (the ego's awareness of its id presence: primordial envy; or the ego's awareness of other objects: part-object in primal envy and whole object in primary envy) is always akin to a taste of perfection, an inducement to pursue a greater portion of this emerging promise of satisfaction.

Envy activates on its second side when the ego looks outside itself, so to speak, and becomes aware of (not-self) objects. The ego is compelled to do this because the id's arresting motto is as follows: "No man can look at my face and live." For this reason, projection is necessary. It is a survival reflex prompting a necessary turning outward toward objects. This process is the ego's relocation of its attention to a safer, more tolerable domain in contrast to the experiential chaos and blinding, intolerable brilliance of the id's nuclear energy at its original source. This refocusing tends to center on whole objects—real persons in the environment. Their construals in the mind are noticed secondarily.

In a manner of speaking, the id's motto connotes the id's partial bluff. This warning is strong enough to suggest that too close a contact may result in death of the ego or psychological madness. It is partial in that a courageous yet considered confrontation may result in insight and a renewed charge of creativity and life. The id, figuratively speaking, becomes a forbidden fruit. It forever remains the psychotic part of the personality, which may either become normatively managed (creativity, play, and humor) or involved in psychopathological developments.

If one could ascribe a motto to the ego, it would be, "My will is to deliberately live safely and rationally for as long as possible in the finite world of time." In response, the id instantaneously replies with another of its emblematic mottos: "Live free or die."

When id impulses are insufficiently integrated by the ego into the entire self, the ego experiences these id impulses as if they were terrorists from the outside seeking to overthrow the ego's stability. The id, however, always feels itself to be a freedom fighter, perhaps even an insurgent, trying to recapture what it regards as rightfully its own and so reestablish its primordial authority.

*The preceding discussion addresses theoretical aspects of the ego's turning its attention from its id to the outside world of real persons. As has been emphasized repeatedly, the indelible imprint of the id's influence on the ego is overwhelming and long lasting. This first taste of perfection and the envy generated by the memory of its absence inevitably affect all the ego's subsequent endeavors.*

To recapitulate: The principal side of *nuclear envy* is chiefly grounded in a base of ego-id relations. The counterpart side is its base of object relations, typically with whole objects whether intrapsychic or interpersonal in the real world.

## The Ego Tries to Discover Its Id in the Later Discovery of Objects/Persons

Toward the middle and end of infancy and thereafter, people in the social environment become the ego's major focus. This is the chronological era where depressive-position functioning supersedes paranoid-schizoid processes. Since *envy theory* highlights envy in its part-object configurations (paranoid-schizoid), using the term "ego" implies the principal part of the self undergoing changes. When this primitive era of partiality is overlaid with whole-object or whole-person awareness (depressive position), the self as a person operates and undergoes changes in more complex ways. Although, at this point, the self is becoming a person, when the term "ego" is used, it is *to emphasize how the person experiences self and the world of others.*

This experiential shift reflects the ego's turning from an inward, id-based attention or preoccupation to an outward, object-based awareness. People are grasped as interpersonal objects who are stored intrapsychically as whole objects. Persons are stored in memory as ego develops a sense of past, present, and future. This is a function of conscious awareness, the operation of reason and logic. In psychoanalytic psychology, it is referred to as the secondary process.

These newly perceived outside objects of attraction, moreover, remind the ego of its own lost perfection—its id with which it originally had an intimate affinity. The perfection attributed to this newfound ideal becomes "objectified" as an internal object, an amorphous bundle of sensation and affect, in a gradually expanding mental universe. Hence, mental models and cognitive schemata begin to form. At birth, experience is less personalized; during infancy, experiences takes on a more personal character; after infancy, personality forms.

Split off from the central aspect of the ego—its nuclear center—and projected outward toward its peripheral orbits, the created/constructed ideal object acts as a prompt for further splitting and the excessive idealization of other objects. As the infant encounters the interpersonal environment, external figures are imbued with projections that have these ideal or negative hedonic contrasts perceptually, cognitively, and affectively. In turn, these external figures are registered simultaneously as, or associated with, these already formed, internal mental objects.

*Envy is the mechanism that circuitously reminds the ego of its own lost perfection, power, richness, and creativeness.* It is an archaic revival that is *forever present in the here and now.* This prototype reflects the force behind the operation of the "return of the repressed" in the mind. The ego responds to envy by inflating its own narcissism, which acts as defensive omnipotence to counteract feelings of passivity, helplessness, powerlessness, and dependency. The unconscious phantasy of narcissistic self-dependence is a defense against feelings of maximal helplessness.

The second side of envy usually takes center stage in the life of the mind rapidly in chronological time. The infantile ego is immersed in ever-changing scenery with new dramas developing over time. Internal and interpersonal objects other than the primordial id now occupy most of the ego's attention and continue to perpetuate the processes of envy. Relations of secondary dependency on real people become reinforced. Primordial envy (ego-id), however, reinforces and is reinforced as the core of primal and primary envy (ego-objects).

The infantile ego has a further, complex dually dependent relationship with these objects depending on their perceived, different locations: (1) dependence on the *intrapsychic object* correlated with perceptions of an external figure, usually aspects of mother or primary caregiver, and (2) dependence on the *actual, external, concrete interpersonal figure*, itself. The ego, moreover, at all points in life retains this dual attitude to its objects. For every real interpersonal figure encountered, the ego grasps it jointly as a concrete environmental individual and as an interpreted, emotionally colored internal figure that the ego has construed with idiosyncratic meaning. These two levels of relationship, though distinct, typically appear fused.

This sense of mingled dual dependency is a "secondary dependency" in contrast to the primordial dependency of ego on its id. When the notion of "dependency" is ordinarily discussed, these secondary dependent ties are what is meant. Overt feelings of disappointment of expected satisfactions and recognizable frustration are discernible in these dependent interpersonal relationships.

Since dependency needs can never be fully satisfied, they inevitably instigate frustrations, which, in turn, reinforce excessive envy, narcissism, and omnipotence. Dependency needs, disappointment, and frustration are gross reflections of the activity of envy's second theoretical side—its object relations with real people. Envy's principal or subtle constitutional underside—primordial envy, the ego's primordial *id relations*, and the ego's primal envy of the primal part-object breast and its primary envy of the mother—always remains a subliminal orientation for relations with real people.

## Separation Anxiety of Dependency/Frustration and Contact Anxiety of Proximity/Envy

The primitive processes engendering separation and dependence also engender mental space and the developing universe of objects in the inner world. In infancy, the ego functions as witness/experiencer in the gradual course of its *biomental self*-differentiation. It incrementally comes to regard itself during its scanning/attending function as separate from both its mental objects and actual figures in the external environment. This is self-other differentiation, the formation of ego boundaries. It experiences a range of positive and negative feelings. Separateness and dependency are feelings that have crucial importance.

*Dependence* implies reliance on another for the satisfaction of those needs that are—in fact or perceived to be—able to be filled primarily by that other. Anxiety stemming from feared detachment from the other always accompanies feelings around dependency needs. Fears that the dysphoria of neediness will continue unattended and even escalate beyond what can be endured exacerbate this *separation anxiety*.

Frustrated dependency needs instigate anxiety, anger, hate, and retaliatory hostility, often a damaging cruelty. Separation anxiety is properly related to the depressive position in which dependency on, separation from, and feared separation from a whole object/real person are leading anxiety configurations. *In separation anxiety, there is a commanding wish for closeness to the other to reduce distress that arises when a needed object/person is felt to be disappearing.*

A more primitive counterpart to separation anxiety is a distress I have called *contact anxiety*. *Envy theory* postulates this as one of the premier forms that characterizes ego-object juxtaposition, the envy dynamic, and the paranoid-schizoid position.

In *envy theory*, when the ego experiences itself "in relation to" or "in contact with" another, some degree of envy is elicited. As a counterbalancing attempt to diminish the ego's envious sense of littleness and enhance the defensively instigated wish for self-dependence, narcissism rapidly inflates. These libidinal and structural shifts range from normal to excessive and pathological. Excessive narcissism, for example, in adolescence and adulthood may express itself as arrogant pride and unrealistic self-dependence, a veneer of independence. In this way, the sense of neediness is temporarily masked.

Excessive narcissism parallels excessive omnipotence. Both are defensive attempts to mute the unbearable *contact anxiety* of envy—namely, *feeling little and inferior to another who is in close proximity and imagined as more powerful and superior.*

From a developmental point of view, the earliest form of *contact anxiety* arises in the paranoid-schizoid position where partial aspects of the ego are projectively fused with partial aspects of the object—part-object relations. This is a primitive state of experiential fusion, amorphous attachment, and adhesive dependency. No true separateness and no truly developed dependency configurations have yet emerged. *This raw state of volatile anaclitic adhesion between ego and its id and ego and its primitive grasp of the external object sets the tone for the dynamic of envy.*

In *contact anxiety*, the ego's wish is for a spoiling deletion of the other to reduce distress stimulated by an object sensed as ideal and overwhelming. *Contact anxiety* is generated on multiple levels. Two important levels are the ego's contiguity with its id, and the ego's proximity to a tenuously apprehended object. *Contact anxiety* correlates with attentional shifts and the wish to deny what is being experienced. This is accomplished either through feeling bored or some other form of denial of attention to an experience.

Interpersonal relations in the external environment—people being with people—are empirical events also stimulating envious *contact anxiety*. This social reinforcement of envy is fueled by virtually reflexive comparisons of similarity, differences, status discrepancies, and so forth. Often, only a minor element of similarity and commonality is needed to trigger this process.

Separation anxiety characterizes depressive-position psychodynamic conflicts while *contact anxiety* characterizes paranoid-schizoid-position conflicts. *Contact anxiety* differs from persecutory anxiety since *contact anxiety* is a significant feature of envious processes. It is more subtle, subliminal, deeply rooted, and less conspicuous than attitudes of fearful aversion and persecutory anxieties. Another broad distinction, which, however, is not consistently characteristic of it, is that the *contact anxiety* of envy tends to be stimulated in concrete contexts where there is actual physical proximity to others or to inanimate objects (for example, desirable cars, works of art, jewelry, and so forth) that imply the success of others. The sensory functions of seeing and looking, specifically of attraction to, largely enhance *contact anxiety*.

Healthy dependency, on the other hand, rests on hope and some sense of trust coming from feelings of mutually exchanged, interdependent satisfactions. In situations of healthy dependency, superior-inferior polarizations do not arise to such asymmetrical proportions that become excessive and generate intolerable anxiety and convoluted defenses.

## Summary

The nuclear genesis of envy is approached from a novel perspective. A conception of *id relations* (ego's awareness of its id) that originates at the start of life and continues thereafter as the matrix of all experience is introduced. *Id relations* are primordial and indestructible. They are the blueprints for the structuring of the developing self.

Building on and reconsidering some of the propositions and conjectures in previous chapters, the ego's elemental state of dependency on its id is advanced as the inception of the nuclear genesis of envy. This provenance is the ego's *primordial anaclitic dependency on its id*. This primordial dependency remains experientially active throughout life. Mental space, the canalization of the self-system, arises from this primordial relation.

*Envy theory* proposes that *nuclear envy* at each moment of its inception activates from a combination of three root causes. Each root cause is activated by differing degrees of the sense of *privation*, intolerance of this, and further efforts to eliminate it. Since *envy theory* is intrinsically a developmental theory, each of the three root causes has a developmental context. In other words, root one, or primordial envy, is basal and ever-present. Root two has two parts: part one is primal envy and this is present in the paranoid-schizoid position chronologically (first three months of life) and thereafter; part two is primary envy and this comes into being during the depressive position (about four months to twelve months) and, similar to part one, remains forever active in the unconscious strata of consciousness.

The first root of the nuclear genesis of envy is envy's spontaneous, unprovoked autoactivation. This reflects its primordial and constitutional base. This is the organic intolerable sense of innate privation, and burgeoning aim to extinguish this basal sense of privation.

Following this, two additional events occur. A second root has two parts. Part one of root two is the primal envy of ego for the part-object ideal breast. This constitutes the unconscious anticipation of an ideal part-object breast, the accompanying intolerable anxiety, and developing wish to eliminate this experience. Primal envy elicits a peremptive—by fiat—urge to delete any hint of ideal goodness. Part two of root two is envy's preemptive, anticipatory unconscious and partly conscious sense of the existence of further creativeness in the ideal whole object, the idealized mother; this is followed by an anticipatory first strike to wipe out the perception of ideal goodness. Emphasis here is on offensive forestalling rather than defense. Delineating clear-cut defensive responses in the overall envy dynamic is difficult and often merely an academic exercise.

The third root of envy is its reactive, secondary response fueled by experiences of real and actual dependency, helplessness, and disappointment. This third root reinforces deeper feelings of primordial, primal, and primary envy. Unconscious phantasies about these events also reinforce *nuclear envy*. Envy's first root always drives and may be sensitized over time by envy's other two roots. Envy's first root is its most impersonal and mechanically reflexive. Envy's third root is its most personal. Root two occupies a transitional area between the first and third. All three roots converge to produce envy.

A series of axiomatic propositions is advanced: (1) envy emerges from the radical estrangement of ego from its id; (2) this is the fountainhead of the deepest longing, sense of primordial privation, and envious dysphoria intrinsic to the nature of man; and (3) at birth, this becomes attributed to, and incarnated in, the form of and relation to the ideal *mother-breast, and later the whole mother.* This last construct (3) is referable to both the first prototypical mental object and the caregiving environmental figure with which the infant has an innate readiness to resonate, entrain, and synchronize.

*Contact anxiety* is intolerance to proximity to the experience of goodness. It suggests the earliest states of primitive fusion with another greater and more powerful (principally id)—paranoid-schizoid configurations. The ego's self-constructed sense of an object experienced as overwhelmingly ideal is engendered by this. *Contact anxiety* further exacerbates envy and destructive spoiling, which is an attempt to mute it.

While the conception of object relations has a long history in psychoanalysis, *envy theory* advances and formulates the novel idea of *id relations.* This elemental and primordial sense of "the other"—the id—experienced by the ego in a discrepant, asymmetrical, and dissonant manner is the bedrock of all dependency and, I submit, of *nuclear envy.* This primordial, indestructible, and abiding subliminal awareness is termed *the chaperone.* It arises simultaneously with the first object relations, and acts as a commanding experiential presence on which all object relations—intrapsychic and interpersonal—become superimposed throughout life.

# CHAPTER SEVEN

# A Microscopic Analysis
# of Envy's Dedicated Pathways

### Envy's Developmental Triad:
### How Envy Unfolds

In the wake of the nuclear genesis or inception of envy, its unfolding psychodynamic trajectory arises. This stream takes root, expands, and inevitably deploys toward fruition largely on nonconscious levels of information processing. Fruition may take troublesome dimensions, usually the case, or may lead to more positive, healthy advances.

The nuclear genesis and circuitry of envy are present embryonically at birth. Over time, they unfold, develop, and consolidate, yet retain primitive forms. Envy's psychodynamic circuitry, the form of its propagation, is a dedicated constant. These ingrained activation patterns are attractor states with self-propelling impetus. They are part of the primary processes of primitive mental activity and principally operate by nonconscious cognitive and affective mechanisms. At any chronological age, envy's developmental triad is similar. As alluded to in previous chapters, environmental factors significantly influence the details of envy's specific contents, adaptive or psychopathological effects, and the way they manifest themselves in real life.

*Envy theory* refers to *the three-pronged basis of unfolding envy* as its *developmental triad*. Dynamic sequences that interpenetrate the ego's unconscious, preconscious, and conscious experiential dimensions characterize these three overlapping phases. All phases suffuse one another. They occur in simultaneity and as interdigitated feedback loops with reverberating circuitry. The aim of envy's development is dynamic reorganization of the mind—modifying unconscious phantasy and assimilating new data. Elements of this include cognitive exploration, expansion, pruning, emotional protection, and self-containment.

Primary process mental activity is filled with unconscious part-object relations. These are swiftly changeable, irrational mental contents. They permeate, at times to the point of distortion, secondary process rational thinking, its store of mental representations, and its affective currents on both nonconscious and conscious levels. Linguistic description, however, requires characterizing all these dynamically synchronous events as if they were linear steps. The description of primary process mental activity using secondary process terminology loses much in translation. Envy's *developmental triad*, the routes of its circuitry, travel concentrically from deeper states of nonconsciousness toward more conscious awareness and attention.

*Phase one*, *inception*, involves the *nuclear genesis of envy's three roots*: (1) the spontaneous awareness of sensations and primitive feelings of primordial privation, (2) a sense of primal peremptive and primary preemptive anticipatory privation, and (3) distress arising from feeling deprived. The ego suddenly senses experiential gaps that previously were filled with the abundant omnipotence of the id. This first phase—the prototypical narcissistic wound—is an amalgam of *nuclear envy*'s three causative roots and initiates the emergence of *nuclear envy* and feelings of absence.

*Phase two* has three parts, *idealization-deidealization-numbing*. It is a defensive attempt to reilluminate these black holes of privation by using omnipotent idealization to create ideal objects to fill in these gaps. This precarious maneuver rapidly collapses by deidealization, and again exposes the ego to states of painful absence. This overwhelming trauma induces a defensive numbing.

*Phase three*, *spoiling*, unfolds as an explosive attempt to arrest this numbing. While phase one and two are nonconscious, phase three, although rooted in unconscious processes, is closest to conscious experience, attention, and willfulness. Spoiling, in part, manifests itself in behaviors that can be observed. Its mode is a devaluation of what previously had been felt as ideal but is now perceived as blemished and falling apart.

Destructively spoiling the ideal object acts as an *inversion of values*, *attacking goodness not because it is bad but because it is good*. This paradoxical act shocks the mind and begins processes of decompensation. Destructive omnipotence on unconscious phantasy levels becomes increasingly amplified. An autoerosion is also now ignited since the object being dismantled is projectively imbued with parts of the ego. The container of mental space filled with objects is upheld by the ego. When objects are destroyed, parts of the ego are destroyed. Destruction of the object always weakens the ego and the entire self-system. Objects function as a prime dimension of the ego's vital organ systems; when these are attacked, the ego in turn suffers. Spoiling occurs both intrapsychically and interpersonally, spilling into actually manifested interpersonal realms. It appears as a hostile wrecking of some pleasure.

## Developmental Triad
## Phase One: Inception

Within the deepest layers of the unconscious, envy arises by a first sense of *innate privation*. This spontaneous inception was described in the previous chapter discussing the complex process of the nuclear genesis of envy, primordial envy. Activation of this first root suggests an approximation of events leading to the rock bottom, spontaneous emergence of envy, in a sense, why envy is born. The sense of innate privation—organic absence, nothingness, voidness—is the antithesis of the sense of omnipotence. This phase constitutes the essence of a narcissistic wound. It encompasses both an expression of envy and emerging defenses against envy. The greater the sense of privation, the greater does the defensive counterbalance of omnipotence erect itself.

Unconscious phantasies of the ego's inferiority in relation to a primitive sense of contiguous superiority (ego's id) simultaneously accompany this biomental first root activation, reflecting the ego in a state of massively confused attraction. The ego's *id relations* (primordial envy) thus activate jointly with the instantaneous, unconscious awareness of the primal part-object, *the mother-breast* (primal envy), and, shortly, the primary whole object, the mother (primary envy).

Primitive anticipatory infatuation and excessive idealization underlie why the "object" elicits such overwhelming excitement. The two aspects of this second root of the nuclear genesis of envy further bring forth the gnawing ache of privation. They function as the inherent priming of innate expectation pathways that charges and facilitates envy's circuitry. Both the mere hint and the anticipation of ideal goodness—not self-possessed—generates impulses leading to spoiling.

The third root of the nuclear genesis of envy is prompted by its reactive, secondary response of deprivation to whole-object loss (of ideal possessions of real people) acquired over time. This is realization of the loss of idealized goodness in the object experienced both as phantasy and in actual reality.

Such a sense of deprivation or feeling empty is reinforced in early infancy by real experiences. Its chronological onset occurs especially at the time of weaning and by the infant's experiences of mother's coming and going.

*Envy theory* presumes the endowment of an innate envy mechanism held in abeyance until triggered spontaneously and also by an outside stimulus. When mother satisfies infant, infant feels full. When infant feels empty, he attributes this withholding to mother and feels a sense of deprivation. When physiological needs signaling emptiness (hunger, cold, and so forth) are felt, envy is triggered. When these needs are met, envy may be quelled. When needs arise again and there is a lag in meeting them, the experience of envy becomes reinforced.

*Nuclear envy* arises from these three root arousal stimuli. Privation elicits feelings of absence that, in turn, elicit feelings of emptiness. These become organized, patterned in experience, and remembered.

## Developmental Triad Phase Two:
## Idealization-Deidealization-Numbing

Phase two has three mostly preconscious parts: (1) idealization, (2) deidealization, and (3) numbing. All these are modulations of how the ego experiences itself.

Part 1, *omnipotent idealization*, reformats the ego's own subliminally perceived negative or absent traits (privation) into idealized ones. This mode of idealization can be either adaptive *when not inordinately excessive* or defensive when wide splitting stirs intolerable anxiety. This defensive mode mobilizes *libidinal omnipotence*. It arises from unfulfilled expectations and acts to boost in tenuous fashion the ego's insecure and threatened narcissism, especially in the face of burgeoning primordial object (id) awareness. In so doing, the hearkening internal sense of partial deficit and subsequent disappointment becomes temporarily satisfied in a roundabout manner.

The ego mobilizes its reserve of libido, an anticipatory infatuation, to create its wished-for ideal fulfillment to counteract sensed absences in itself. Libido fills ego lacunae where the perfect brilliance of id had been and is no longer. This illuminates these gaps into seemingly ideal entities. This process is, at first, an idealization of self.

Instantaneously, this emerging ideal configuration becomes split off from the ego's central hub and projected toward its outer orbits creating internal objects—units of mental schemata making up unconscious phantasy. The exact character and phantasied scenarios of these are determined by combinations of innate preferences, real experiences, and context. Minimal integration during these processes makes for a universe of disparate elements. Projective identification, the chief mechanism underlying this, ushers in the return of the repressed contents of the id back into the ego. This is a concrescence, a melding together, of id impulses and ego defenses. They structure themselves under the sway of envy to form idealized object configurations, unconscious phantasies having attractor-like infatuation, governed by paranoid-schizoid part-object principles. Whereas, at first, idealization was aimed at inflating only the ego, it now differentiates and spills into the creation of other objects. In other words, direction changes. At this point, the first attempt at self-idealization is failing in its exclusivity and becoming diluted.

The ideals so created are projectively identified with and felt as or belonging to the "other." In this way, they become elevated in meaning to the status of idealized internal objects. Now, idealization is being transferred from only the ego to the ego's objects.

Since splitting is occurring between the ego as scanner/witness and its interpretive creations—internal objects—*these idealized mental models are experienced as far superior, perfect, abundantly rich, and powerful compared to their now perceived "un-ideal" absence in the envier.* One of the functions that idealization serves is providing the ego with a *temporary* state of basking in the reflection of an empowering presence felt initially to be highly desirable. This gossamer aggrandizement, however ephemeral, is an attempt to restore the now missing id back into the ego. The power of this wish-fulfilling process drives envy's circuitry.

This overestimation of the object leads to an overwhelming yet *short-lived attraction* to it. The intention is not merely possession but merging into the idealized creation. This attempted expansion reflects the ego's feeble attempt to regain its lost, projected, idealized perfection—the id. This temporarily inflated, unstable, and frail primary process ideal image—*an eidolon phantom*—is a *precarious* achievement since it has no conceptual or libidinal constancy. The ego becomes "blinded by the light" and stunned. The idealized image thus *degrades very rapidly—deidealization.*

Part 2, *deidealization,* robs the ideal object of its brilliance. As wider and wider splitting increases, the expanding magnification of *idealization becomes intolerable and begins to collapse.* This is the inevitable fate of envy's preliminary state of transient infatuation. Emphasis now centers on attempts to achieve a negation, an extreme deletion, of idealization. The ideal object is robbed of its ideal qualities, in essence, of its entire creativeness. This abnegation of the experience of the ideal is paradigmatic of envy's pulsions toward paradoxical self-denial, an inability to tolerate anything good. Envy's deidealization, as such, aims more toward temporary oblivion than enduring demonization. It is a graduated assault on experiential vivification.

The meager secondary processes of logic and reason (the reality principles of the ego) are too frail to handle such primary process id-based irrationality, especially as its buoyancy insidiously bubbles into preconscious awareness. In other words, the envier is feeling more and more distressed. Wide splitting processes and polarized dichotomies, preambivalent in nature, spread over mental functioning. These begin to rule the direction this dimming deidealization takes.

All these efflorescent processes further reinforce an already exacerbated sense of absence, deficit, privation, and emptiness—the hallmarks of envy. The envier realizes that this perceived yet unowned perfection is absent in himself, and ultimately can never be had. A profound sense of privation, inferiority, poverty, and a personal sense of littleness become overwhelming. When all attempts at any realization of satisfaction are finally thwarted, an enormous sense of unbearably numbing privation ensues. It is felt as a major narcissistic injury. It is an experience of not having, never being able to have, and not being part of what could make the envier feel fuller, ideal, and perfect.

Part 3, *numbing*, results from the trauma produced by this realization of stark unattainability, failing idealization, and deidealization resulting in the shock of contiguity with a blank screen.

This traumatic impact makes the ego profoundly unstable. Mental operations freeze. Projective as well as introjective processes temporarily cease. On an empirical level, there is a pronounced display of states characterized by pervasive withholding both automatic and intentional. Feelings of *isolation*, *being frozen*, *being unable to give or receive*, and *numbing* occur. A condition of frozen withholding is at the core of experiential envy. *Inhibitions in thinking, feeling, and acting accompany this numbing.* In other words, at any developmental level, cognitive, affective, and motoric functioning comes to a halt. This slowing reflects envy's costive constraint that is subjectively felt and observable to others, although the nonconscious causative factors prompting it remain obscure. The envier does not consciously know what this unsettling feeling is or why it is occurring; only that it feels dreadful.

Subjectively, a sense of the uncanny, the strange, and of alienation fills experience. This reflects a "narcissistic state" of the ego and is intimately allied with schizoid dynamics. Derealization, depersonalization, and dissociative mental states are also clinical manifestations of this. These psychic changes stir the very depths of envy's root anxiety, felt as a nameless, latent fear of deterioration and impending, catastrophic annihilation. The affective undercurrent of envy is felt as a menacing fear of evaporating into nothingness.

This uncanny implosion toward nothingness is the ego's confrontation with the death instinct as it wells up from the id. When such a tremendous amount of anxiety is felt, massive self-defense and object-directed offense mechanisms aiming to quell this emotional turbulence are brought into action. Their aim is to reestablish mental stability.

On an observable behavioral level, especially in adolescents and adults, the individual appears removed, preoccupied, distracted, unreachable, and self-absorbed. Comportment, routine functioning, and activities of daily living are slowed and impaired. The modulation of eating and speaking becomes disrupted. Often, people dominated by excessive envy are seen by others as withdrawn, isolative, nonsocial, tense, stingy, miserly, and "not connected."

This paralysis is so intense that actions to mute it are reflexively set into motion. At this juncture, envy then gradually manifests itself in progressively more consciously felt ways.

## Developmental Triad
## Phase Three: Spoiling

To defend itself against intolerable envy, an envy-driven inversion of values prompts the ego to act in irrational ways. This denotes *envy's paradoxical attack chiefly on the inner experience of the object, not because of its badness but because of its goodness.* Spoiling disfigures, mars, and blemishes ideally perceived beauty.

In addition to intrapsychic spoiling, ultimately an autoerosion, spoiling spills out into behaviors. The ego (the actual person) begins to *devalue and spoil* the entire experiential range of what it considers foreign and located outside itself. This spoiling phase is closest to conscious awareness. Behavior is influenced and can be observed and measured. Spoiling and devaluing at this point are directed typically toward an interpersonal figure in the environment. It may take the form of belittling. Spoiling of ideas as implied in the phrase "punching holes in these ideas" is also an outer-directed manifestation of envy. An empirical sign of envy is the withholding of helping. This is spoiling by omission.

The robbing quality of incrementally encompassing deidealization in phase two is now augmented by also putting badness into the envy experience. The envious person becomes aware of an attitude of unbearable unhappiness at the perceived good fortune of another. This boosts the fury of such envious spoiling. In a paradoxical fashion, envy's destructive attacks simultaneously highlight an already devastating sense of inner annihilation and emptiness. Disgust and repugnance increase the vehemence of this forceful spoiling.

Envy, when directed outwardly, intermittently boomerangs and turns against the envier. Since these abortive attacks are, in essence, attacks on projected aspects of the envier's own ego (projection and introjection operate simultaneously), these attacked self-aspects become damaged and partly destroyed. As the envier, in effect, turns on himself, inner annihilation is even more dramatically felt. Self-suffering follows the ego's self-imposed masochism. Absence, gaps, and emptiness are bitterly felt and continue to be reinforced as the depletion, starvation, and privations resulting from destructive spoiling further intensify. These attacks on goodness equal a negation of creativeness—envy's raison d'etre. They are ubiquitously felt both intrapsychically and interpersonally.

The shock of envy, now acting as *autoerosion and self-destruction*, splits itself off from all else and induces awareness to float in amorphous states of virtual oblivion. Narcissistic ego states reinforce themselves and are empirically observable. Vernacular expressions used to reflect these disintegrating states of mind include "spaced out," "zoned out," and "out of it." Psychic invisibility, impoverishment, and deterioration spread.

Psychosis, schizophrenia, and malignant personality disorders, for example, reflect chronic narcissistic states that have become habitual, impervious, and intractable. Their resistance to amelioration, in part, is attributable to the level of malignant, inflexible envy ruling them. Such narcissistic states may become permanently structured in the personality and maintained by projective identification. These are the narcissistic object relations or paranoid-schizoid object relations found in severe personality disorders and psychotic conditions.

## The Outcomes of Envy's Developmental Unfolding

Developmental triad phase three, spoiling, emblematic of envy's *destructive omnipotence*, is a pivotal juncture. Paradoxical spoiling produces an emotional stalemate. One of two paths can be taken to equilibrate mental experience and prevent total *adaptive collapse*. The ego's natural inclination is to reorganize itself to create fresh centers of gravity on a moment-to-moment basis. Hence, either strong defenses are mobilized, envy's more typical and pathological route, or a healthier, adaptive modulation with an advance toward empathy and admiration may occur.

The defensive and highly inflexible route, although unstable, is the path envy's propagation usually takes. Intransigent adhesiveness—stalling of forward advances—characterizes phase three, spoiling. This defensive tact is a default state of passive reflexivity, a habitual response to mute anxiety, confusion, and felt helplessness. In addition, outer-directed destructiveness—an offensive attack on the idealized goodness of the object—aims to extinguish the distressing states that envy's perceived injury and subsequent rage produce. It is here that spoiling attacks on the goodness of the object elicit paradoxical yet inescapable fears of retaliation. This correlates with other processes in the elemental genesis of all states of persecution.

Multiple causative factors determine the way envy is experienced and managed. How the ego interprets its experiences to create an interpretive inner world in negative (envious and persecutory) or more adaptive ways adds to later-acquired learning from experience. This can check and redirect envy's unbridled progression. *The healthy maturation of envy* involves its emotional and cognitive transmutation into more active states of patience, admiration, emulation, security, empathy, gratitude, helping, and sharing. Chapter 9 discusses these in detail.

## What Does Envy Really Aim to Spoil?

Envy is intrinsically spoiling and destructive when not modulated or superseded by positive strivings. Stealth characterizes envy's insidious, hostile corrosiveness. *It is an attack on meaning and creativity.* Envy denudes the circuitry of information processing—its faculties for active orientation and reality-based cognition. Consequences include retaliatory anxieties in the perpetrator. This occurs because envy used as an offense mechanism inevitably produces degradation, devaluation, denigration, and eventual disgust for the ideal object, the object so attacked. This "trashing," in turn, typically provokes the fear of revenge.

The self that initiated the offensive attack then becomes the victim of its own now retroverted attack by self-generated fears of retaliation. All aspects of the object are spoiled; in turn, one's inner world, of which the spoiled object is an integral part, is felt to become spoiled and subsequently further impoverished.

*Spoiling is both an extraction of creativeness and an infusion of destructiveness; both of these result in mutilation.* In unison, the object of envy and the subject who envies become spoiled. The three major areas of spoiling are creativity, the id, and the self as a whole.

## Creativity Spoiling

In envy, the aspect of the object felt superior and unattainable is hated on multiple levels because of the painfully frustrating, unrequited desire provoked. Envy makes the envier unbearably unhappy at the unattainable good fortune and perceived enjoyment of the envied object. Envious self-protective, offense mechanisms are attempts to devalue and spoil the object's desirability felt to be its goodness. Envy's aim is to lessen the desperate feelings of need for and dependency on this perceived goodness. As idealization wanes, feelings of disgust escalate.

*Creativity as such is the global target of envy.* Hate, attack, spoiling, and devaluation aim to destroy three dimensions of creativity: (1) the envied one as a *container* of goodness, perfection, wealth, resources, excellence, and creativity, (2) the idealized good, perfect, and rich *contents*, and (3) the *capacity* to produce, enjoy, and share this goodness. At rock bottom, what is envied is *creativeness on every level. Spoiling is the dual attempt to suck fecundity out of and to inject barrenness into the envied good object.*

Competent functioning—idealized, creative goodness—in giving, receiving, and sharing felt to exist in the one who is envied becomes the target of envious attacks. This state harkens back to envy's prototypical onset, the default blueprint of which is its innate expectation pathway in relation to the competent, feeding breast as object.

A persecutory state of anxiety, in turn, may result. The envier's pervasive sense of depletion, impoverishment, vulnerability, passivity, and helplessness weakens adequate guarding against the threat and danger of subsequent retaliatory attacks. Fear and further anxiety escalate.

## Id Spoiling

The insidious malignancy of "object destruction" extends into *id relations.* The ego paradoxically attacks its own id.

*Envy theory's thesis is that the core of envy lies in the primordial anaclitic relationship of liege. Its negative dimension connotes a bitter and resentful state of servitude of ego toward its own id.*

This resentment is indignant displeasure at the perception of unfairness, asymmetry, discrepancy, and dissonance. The abdication of ego from its primordial alignment with id demotes it to servant-like status. This foundational template consists of the ego's feeling little, inferior, and inadequate compared to the perfect, all powerful, and majestic id. To mute this unbearable and intolerable state, *the ego in reflex fashion attacks the id to the point of massively denying its very existence.* In other words, it is common to hear people either deny or minimize the dark side of human nature. Splitting body and mind with pejorative bias against the somatic self is another example of this denial.

While id spoiling occurs nonconsciously, numerous consciously held adult attitudes attest to attacks on the id. Included in this disavowal is the feeling of *repugnance and disgust at the very idea of the existence of primitive id instincts.* The suggestion of the existence of a majestic and all-powerful death instinct is viewed as fanciful. The proposition of a series of life instincts reeking of lustful, base, perverse, and sordid sexual passions is more conceivable but nonetheless distasteful. The concept of envy, itself, as primary in mental life has been reduced to the status of a mythological "tooth fairy" notion.

*Id spoiling* is the conscious ego's relentless attempt to sanitize the primordial dimensions that are the source and basis of its own existence. Figuratively speaking, it is akin to destroying the primeval rain forests to further the aims of civilization.

The prototypical model of envy's psychodynamic course is embodied in the following sequence: the ego's idealization of its id (positive dimension); its deidealized feeling of privation and emptiness of this id-laden power (negative dimension); and a subsequent state of numbing and trauma. The ego attempts to deny its own native primitiveness by clothing itself, especially its genitals and buttocks metaphorically and in fact, with the respectability of culture and civilization, using a language that is clean not dirty, superficial not deep, and speaking in a language ostensibly euphemizing to the point of triviality both sexuality and death.

To this end, the conscious ego tries to rob the id of its native creativeness. It attacks, spoils, devalues, and hates the id and everything the id stands for. This *"id bashing"* underlies all later forms of spoiling, devaluing, and debasing met with in everyday life. In so doing, the id is felt as alien, foreign, remote, distant, outsider, strange, and "the other." It is the undercurrent sense of danger, hate, and negative bias upon which everything felt as different, foreign, and enemy is superimposed. Fear of retaliation, persecutory anxiety, and paranoid states may take shape from this configuration.

The default state of nonconscious mental activity—repression—best describes the envious cloaking the ego exerts on its progenitor, the id. *The ego, in a manner of speaking, has "bit the breast" that has fed and continues to feed it.* Denial, repression, and forgetting characterize how the envious ego relates to its id. These primordial splits in consciousness, as such, act as fault lines for self-destruction and pervade all sectors of the sense of self and experience in the interpersonal world.

## Self-Spoiling

When envy becomes extreme, the very faculties of the envier become the object of hate. Envy attacks, spoils, and knocks them out of action. This self-directed spoiling is an attempt to downregulate and extinguish the capacities to both elicit envy and feel its pain. It becomes an abnegation and self-denial of also experiencing the pleasure of goodness. This sort of "cutting off one's nose to spite one's face" is enormously destructive since this self-undermining is a devastating personal trauma. It further damages, if not ablates, sensitive parts of the personality.

"Blinding oneself in only one eye" is also another emblematic metaphor for envy. Spite and vengeance, in all their manifestations, are indicators of envy's malicious intent. Mental processes become increasingly destabilized. For this reason, effective adaptation to inner and outer reality deranges and falters. Envy seemingly provoked by an outside object that is aggressively spoiled will paradoxically result in even more massive self-spoiling and *adaptive collapse*.

Not only the experience of envy, but also any possible enjoyment the envier may have been capable of, becomes muted. The inability to tolerate the envied object and the incapacity or unwillingness to receive what is experientially desirable—*even if it is offered*—attest to the self-destructive effects of excessive envy. Trauma, pain, and shock become self-reinforcing and lead to the decompensation of psychic reality. This further diminishes emotional stability and skews subsequent competent mental functioning.

*Malignant envy strongly blocks reception.* Envy's nature is inimical to realistically recognizing, let alone receiving, any perceived goodness in the environment. The perception of goodness and creativeness becomes intolerable. Envy reinforces the agonizing sense of futility and impasse brought about by self-imposed privation and the disturbance produced by subsequent feelings of isolation and emptiness. Hope and any impulses toward vivification start to wither. Envy's paradox resides in its spoiling component preventing the envier from identifying, in an enduring fashion, with the envied ideal. *The envier, therefore, does not and cannot recognize that the envied ideal is, in mental fact, an undeveloped part of himself.*

The irrational quality of envy stems from its pathological erection of communicative blockages, especially an inability to receive. It is a self-imposed, self-undermining incapacity to accept and take in anything good. This paradoxical inhibition is an expression of innate unconscious motivations that tend to activate despite environmental situations. This undermining pattern of self-endangerment by self-defeating choices, to be sure, is not understandable as an adaptive response to the need to survive. *Envy theory* does not view it in the same way as one would view an actual victim needing to survive by forced self-damaging behaviors in a truly harsh or objectively punishing environment.

The roots of all unconscious self-hatred, self-rejection, and self-denial emerge in the field of envy's self-imposed barrenness. Self-esteem becomes exquisitely vulnerable in this regard. This constellation of psychodynamic operations is the foundation for feelings of inferiority, inadequacy, vulnerability, poverty/impoverishment, and impotence. The dynamics of primary, unconscious envy solidly lay down these bedrock phenomena. If left unchecked, the malignantly destructive quality of envy—its intrinsic tendency to finally result in this sort of autoerosion, autointoxication, impoverishment, and emotional bankruptcy—devastates one's overall quality of life both personally and interpersonally. Fundamental creativity is blown apart as envy unleashes its fury.

## Projective Identification: The Premier Mode of Nonconscious Information Processing

Projective identification is an unconscious splitting off of unwanted attitudes, impulses, feelings, affects, thoughts, phantasies, and wishes from the self toward another, where it becomes sensed as an embedded quality of that other. This process is always invasive mental action, whether beneficial (exploratory, communicative) or destructive (omnipotent, expulsive, evacuative, defensive, coercive, attacking, violent, blurring or fusing boundaries). Its broad aim encompasses both information transfer and the reconfiguring of meaning.

The mechanism of projective identification operative in unconscious envy largely blurs value and salience distinctions between good and bad. Projective identification operative in ego-object relations blurs and conflates boundaries within intrapsychic aspects of the self and between self and objects. One's sense of reality—the distinction between what is internal and what exists independent of one's perceptions and evaluations—may be distorted by excessive projective identification.

Projective identification, in part, typically is exploratory and searching. This cognitional aspect of it may have a range of specific modifications that make its operation healthy or pathological. For example, in paranoid personalities or states of delusional paranoia, projective identification functions in an excessive and hypertrophied fashion. The paranoid individual feels compelled to scan an already mistrusted environment in a hypervigilant manner so that this detective work confirms previously held suspicions, usually of the ill will and malicious intent of others. The emphasis on this type of projective identification involves fear, anxiety, hostility, and anticipated persecution. Of note, a significant clinical feature of the paranoid patient is his guardedness and withholding. By contrast, envious projective identification searches for expected ideals but then destroys them because of the intolerability felt since they are unattainable.

Projective identification as defense (aggressive control) takes the form of unconscious phantasy: structured mental content whose function is to contain anxiety and instantiate conflict and defense in the form of internalized object relations. When used to effect an object-directed offensive attack, it is the crucial mechanism underlying envy and other paranoid-schizoid processes.

Projective identification as communication (unconscious sharing rather than rejecting) is a more nonaggressive interpersonal exchange affecting both the individual who projects and interpersonal figure toward whom it is directed. Projective identification is part of the broader cognitional mode *projective internalization*: the ego's core faculty for actively exploring, knowing, and understanding both the inanimate and animate worlds.

The ultimate aim of all mental defense mechanisms is self-defense and reduction of overwhelming anxiety. These homeostatic attempts try to maintain ego integrity and foster self-protective containment. The deep-seated anxiety states often elicited by separateness, envy, inferiority, fear, and persecution evoke projective identification processes. The nonconscious ego's defensive strategies for using projective identification include attempts to evacuate disturbing experiential content, to attack, efforts to control and dominate, fusion with the object, depositing vulnerable aspects of the self into the object for protection, and makeshift attempts to improve a less-than-optimal significantly regarded object. Unlike *projective internalization*, projective identification has a much greater share of passive and reflexively reactive responsivity, particularly to fear and anxiety. Attempts range from normal and healthy to excessive and pathological. The self and object become excessively spoiled and damaged in pathological outcomes. The route taken by pathological envy in the end leads to self-destruction.

In projective identification (Klein 1946, 1952a, 1957; Bion 1959, 1962a, 1963; Racker 1968; Grotstein 1981; Sandler 1987), disturbing, conflictual aspects of the self mobilize, split off, and become disowned. They are projected away from the nuclear center of the ego. Unconscious phantasy perceives and recognizes these unwanted parts as relocated in the selected object. This process, in fact, resides on the level of an intrapsychic interpretive creation. This represents the ego's enacted wish for omnipotent control of a seemingly irresolvable conflict. In this way, both the experience of the self and experience of the object become forcefully altered to suit the wishes of the projector.

## What Is Projected in the Complex Process of Projective Identification?

In projective identification, the following partial aspects of the self, often conjointly, are projected: parts of the ego, parts of the superego, id impulses in the form of hateful attacks or idealizing enrichments, part- and whole-object relations, and internal objects/mental schemata both good and bad. The aforementioned implies that formed unconscious phantasies, particularly component parts of these, constitute the principle currency and contents of the projections in projective identification.

In envy (Klein 1946, 1952a, 1955, 1957; Bion 1962a), this projective mechanism has a distinctly offensive target, the ideal object. Aggressive object relations result. The ego attacks a good, if not ideal, object precisely because of its goodness. These invasive, action states take shape as affectively charged unconscious phantasy structures in process of reconfiguring. They come to serve, in part, as templates that strongly influence and skew further mental operations in the envier. These pathways are part of nonconscious information processing.

A major, though not entire, part of projective identification is extinguishing mental distinctions and psychological boundaries. This occurs between psychic structures and in object relations, especially between ego and object. A mixture of dedifferentiation, fusion, and confusion, all of which blur distinctions, results. In this sense, projective identification, when used defensively or offensively, can instigate passive regressions, truncate processing, and downregulate cognition on all levels. This feature underlies the boomerang effect on the ego that the ego's attempted destructive spoiling of the object produces. *Narcissistic states increase while object-love diminishes to a degree commensurate with the amount of offensive projective identification used.* In other words, the envier becomes increasingly self-centered and decreasingly concerned about others.

In envy, spoiling by projective identification is twofold: (1) robbing the ideal object of its entire creativeness (deidealization) and (2) putting badness into it (vitiation). These dual destructive aims disfigure what was once made ideal. The results of this include an object that is blemished, crippled, impaired, or, in effect, nullified and deleted. It is worthwhile to emphasize that the last phase of projective identification results in the return to the ego of both the projection and its results. *The object spoiled becomes the ego spoiled.*

Projective identification, notably, is the transposition of aspects of the self into other aspects of the self, specifically into the ego's intrapsychic creation of its objects. It is primarily an intrasystemic, intrapsychic projective relocalization. In other words, it is *a powerful unconscious phantasy in the mind of its originator.* Moreover, because the nonconscious mental activity of projective identification is based on primitive primary process mechanisms, it has immense and compelling psychological power. Its spoiling effects, however, may be materially reflected, for example, in a patient's actual behavior and demeanor.

## Projective Identification:
## Interpersonal Effects

Besides its basis in intrapsychic information processing, projective identification plays a large part in interpersonal communication. When subliminal indicators of it impact an outside observer, they may be forceful enough to induce a mutual participation that includes a shared experience of attitudes, feelings, ideas, and even behaviors.

The psychokinetic effects on the object, in this case, the interpersonal other, underlie the way the unconscious receptors of the object accept and process the subject's projections. This unconscious communication remains an experientially nonconsciously lived phenomenon rather than explicitly recognized, especially in its initial stages. The recent discovery of actual "mirror neurons" in the central nervous system as described in chapter 2 lends neuroscientific understanding to this.

When the interpersonally communicated aspect of projective identification is consciously unrecognized in an interpersonal encounter, both parties are drawn into a collusive rapport. Empirically, the object of these unconsciously instigated attitudes and behaviors may seem confused and disturbed. For example, the subject using unconscious projective identification may behave in an extreme manner, excessively loud or extremely passive. This reflects underlying splitting processes characteristic of the paranoid-schizoid position. The degree of forcefulness that the projector uses to coercively influence the object is commensurate with how much the object/other person feels disturbed, intruded upon, bullied, or controlled. The ultimate aim of the projector is to coercively cause a change in thinking and behavior in the object—in the real interpersonal encounter.

The aggressive, forceful, and intrusive nature of such interpersonally used projective identification aims toward control and manipulation of the unwilling object by the subject. Both subject and object are urged or pressured to mutually respond in a mindlessly automatic way. Moreover, the strength of the coercive intent to control is reflected in the unrelenting tenacity that the projector exerts and that the object uncomfortably feels in the process.

Projective identification is also the basis for normal information transfers, especially when there is no manipulative, violent, or destructive intent. Noncoercive projective identification is more balanced. It seeks communicational containment to evoke a transformation of meaning. In contrast to its defensive operation, the normative communicational function of projective identification is experienced, for example, in the mother's "reverie" (nonverbal affectionate understanding) concerning her infant. In effect, this denotes maternal receptivity to assessing infantile states of body and mind with the aim of normalizing any perceived distress. It acts as the silent communicational conduit whose resonating synchrony mutually informs and benefits both participants in development-promoting ways.

Analogously, when the perceptual skills of an empathetic therapist are adequately attuned to the verbal and nonverbal communications of a patient, the therapist is better able to perceive nuances in the patient and in himself that, upon reflection, reveal hitherto unconscious processes. The entire conceptualization of countertransference in psychodynamic psychotherapies rests on these ideas. Hence, the projections of the baby toward the mother and the patient toward the therapist have strong communicational value. Their aim is to seek a resolution-producing confirmation, an understanding of dissonant affective and cognitive experience, in order for helping to occur. Distress, therefore, is remodulated, and subsequently shared in a less disturbing way.

## Projective Internalization and Introjective Internalization

Projective identification is an informational-processing mechanism having roots in, and an important part of what I have termed, *projective internalization*. Projective identification is a nonconscious subsystem of a broader cognitional function—*projective internalization, the principal mechanism of knowing, especially encoding complex relationships of data both animate and inanimate.*

Projective identification is the nonconscious process whereby the ego detects and recognizes ("projective") salient aspects in another ("the part-object") and then partially transforms itself ("identification") according to this recognition. Projective identification, in this sense, exerts an exploratory function.

Projective identification is a mechanism that uses paranoid-schizoid processes. *Projective internalization* is a mechanism that principally uses depressive-position processes although it is active earlier in the paranoid-schizoid position of infancy where its fidelity is less precise but rapidly developing.

Through the broader and more complex processes of *projective internalization, the ego, after exploring and detecting a kindred target, undergoes basic and complex learning by recognizing aspects of itself in the external environment of people and things as it internalizes them in the form of knowledge. Strong conscious elements of information processing are active here.*

Part of this orientation functions in a prop-like fashion to trigger the growth and development of innate, but undeveloped, traits and capacities.

This ability to orient attention and know the environment is a presymbolic experiential apprehension. It is the core of nonconsciously based knowing on all levels both affective and intellectual, and is rooted in the dynamic unconscious. It remains operative at all chronological periods. It both underlies and contributes to maturing conceptual capacities as they come online with growth, maturation, and further development over time.

To the extent that the depressive position has been successfully negotiated, a more realistic grasp of the environment occurs. With the gradual appreciation of objective features of the environment, empathy for the object develops. While *projective internalization* always remains the matrix of cognition in general, it is remodulated at selected periods of affectively charged interactions with objects and is complemented by its counterpart mode—*introjective internalization*.

*Introjective internalization*, while largely a nonconscious cognitive operation, is activated by consciously directed intention. It is a focused empathetic apprehension that enhances receptivity to the total experience of the other in a deliberate effort to more completely understand the gestalt of that other's current experiential state.

In the therapeutic encounter, for example, *introjective internalization* may be viewed metaphorically as the therapist's active engagement in surfing and periodically being submerged within the tidal wave of the patient's communicative and defensive projective identifications. Such transitory participation (empathy and intuition) over time may be reflected upon, be further developed more intentionally, and emerge as conscious conceptualizations. These become the therapist's insights into the patient's world. The mode of *introjective internalization* uses all these components to intentionally grasp, in the most intimate way, the cognitive-affective experience of another.

## Envy as Destructive Self-Dismantling: Sadistic Superego and Envy's Defenses

A last consideration in this chapter's discussion of envy's circuitry is the way envy becomes sequestered in the mind, the plethora of defenses envy instigates, and envy's lasting effects on mental functioning.

*Spoiling of object, and, in turn, spoiling of ego is the end product of envy's circuitry.* This results from perceived transgressions of fairness and equity. Phylogenetically conserved, neuromoral neurocircuitry provides the infrastructure for envy's perceptual and conceptual modus operandi. Retroflected hostility and self-destructiveness occur in parallel fashion with every projected attack on the object. Splitting mechanisms invade cognitive, emotional, and adaptive processes. The impulses in envy offensively rob and spoil. This results in widespread fragmentation and breaking connections that integrate the mind. *Links of meaning between thoughts, between thought and emotion, and between mind and body, for example, are loosened or severed by the robbing and spoiling attacks of envy.* Confusional states abound as one's sense of meaning diminishes as a result of these disconnections. This contributes to a confusing inner chaotic dispersal of previously orienting ideas and attitudes. In adult life, mental clarity, reflection, and insight begin to collapse. Reality sense degrades. Glimmers of existential despair and loneliness flood one's mood.

*Major defensive sequelae follow.* Envy produces direct offensive attacks in the ego by destructive projective identification mechanisms. The anxieties aroused threaten ego integrity and thus occasion the formation of self-protection, defense mechanisms. The mental and behavioral expression of these depends on the individual's level of maturation and development. Excessive and omnipotent idealization of the self (excessive narcissism and arrogant pride) and pathological manic grandiosity may emerge in a precarious attempt to hide a perceived sense of deep and unbearable inferiority and its subsequent emotional distress. Often, manic states of hyperidealization result in a negative idealization of objects. This gives object relations a menacing, grandiose air that is unstable and threateningly explosive. Examples are seen in individuals associated with dictatorial political movements promoting genocide and cults that sanction suicide.

When states of internally sensed agitation from a chronically sadistic superego/conscience become too intolerable, the defense of externalization may occur. The term "offense" may be more accurate to describe such forceful expulsion often entailing aggression. Although tenuous and unstable, externalization of conflictual attitudes and their enacted behaviors may temporarily dilute the unbearable pressure these exert in an individual. Externalized eruptions of sadistic behaviors, violence, and criminal activity are one path that people prone to these negative expressions of aggression may take. Antisocial personalities and persons with histories of criminality are characters that tend to have paranoid and schizoid traits. They are often brooding and isolative. Externalized behaviors, often paroxysmal and self-defeating, reflect unconscious phantasies composed of sadism and violence. Such prototypical envious unconscious phantasies may actually be enacted. These are feeble attempts to manage such harshly felt anxieties. They include mixtures of offense and feeble self-defense.

*Confusion* in the ability to adequately differentiate between good and bad may occur as well as a blurring within cognitive processes such as impaired discrimination, understanding, and learning. Excessive envy directly breaks links supporting meaningful discrimination. This results in confusion—the inability to distinguish realistic goodness from actual badness. In phantasy, envy behaves irrationally by attacking what it deems exceptionally good. This reflects a distortion in the capacity to appraise and differentiate goodness/safety from badness/danger, especially in the developmental course of achieving a normal reality sense.

Exaggerated, unrealistic feelings of injustice and unalterable shifts in perceptions of fairness emerge. Confusion regarding the equitable and fair distribution of assets in the face of contrary individual and social considerations abounds. The confounding influence of the sadistic superego's moral tone on how the ego experiences reality comes through clearly. Resistance to change, especially seen in the inability to receive and give, then becomes more entrenched and a difficult position from which to break out. An attempted flight away from the envied object becomes another defensive method of denying and avoiding participation in the conflicts and anxieties prompted by envy.

As idealization is gradually replaced by feelings of disgust, further devaluation of the envied object continues and may express itself as an increased awareness of more perceived faults, weaknesses, and defects. Spiteful, biting, and malicious criticism colors perceptions. Devaluation becomes malignant spoiling. These attacks on the object are paralleled by an eventually denigrated estimation of and disgust for the self.

In psychoanalytic terms, the *superego* is made excessively harsh, cruel, and demeaning as envy intensifies. The superego absorbs a great deal of envy's omnipotently ideal and debasing ("death instinct") energies. The superego serves as a major attractor and absorber, a repository, of experiential precipitates. These factors incrementally harden the superego and stultify experience and behavior. Emotional flexibility is lessened and normative qualities of playfulness, for example, are abruptly truncated.

When envy reaches malignant proportions, an almost delusional conviction in the belief that the self is bad, disgusting, and even contaminated may occur. The superego has a valve-like function that regulates the opening and closing flow of instinctual energies—love and hate—in the ego. This mostly nonconscious decision-making function exerts a profound effect on the personality. It may result in a rigidly fixed attitude that one is so bad that neither love nor being loved is possible. The belief that one's very being is fundamentally flawed, spoiled, and unlovable thus arises.

The defenses against unconscious envy, therefore, attempt to halt the progression of envy by making the originally envied object that was first seen as ideal (brilliant and attractive) but now spoiled (dull and disgusting) into a grotesque shadow. Such mechanisms are found in obsessional conditions as well. The individual with an obsessive-compulsive disorder feels intrinsically spoiled (contaminated, dirty, and out of balance). This manifests by the use of the evacuative function of projective identification—splitting off unwanted aspects of the self, projecting them outward, and identifying with them as they seem to exist apart from the self. The manifest expression of this can be seen in the obsessional individual's habitually noticing, even seeking out, variously dirty, spoiled, irregular, asymmetrical, and contaminated aspects of the environment in this anxiety-provoking manner.

*The belief that one does not deserve love results in the envier's rejecting not only any love given, but also rejecting the giver, and the very function of giving, itself.* In the envier, the function of giving manifests as the inability to be helpful. This implants itself as a deeply ingrained obstacle to receive love and, therefore, experience the enjoyment and satisfaction of feeling lovable, permitting oneself to be loved, and, in turn, of becoming loving. This state of impaired "loveworthiness" reflects the action of the sadistic superego as it sets in motion processes of masochism in the ego. The superego exerts barrages of devaluation on the ego resulting in the ego's suffering, felt as a need to be punished. The ramifications of this are enormous in considerations of self-worth and clinical depressions apparently resistant to treatment.

In one of her last contributions to the metapsychology of developmental processes in earliest infancy, Melanie Klein (1958) referred to the real presence and privileged status that the hidden psychodynamic phantasy configurations of unconscious envy take ("extremely dangerous objects," "terrifying figures," and "frightening figures"). This contrasts with the formation and less split-off (more consciously available) status of the healthy *superego*. In other contexts, she relates this to a type of mental splitting associated with fragmentation (1963a, 277) and with outbreaks of psychosis (1958, 243). She says:

> These extremely dangerous objects give rise, in early infancy, to conflict and anxiety within the ego; but under the stress of acute anxiety they, and other terrifying figures, are split off in a manner different from that by which the super-ego is formed, and are relegated to the deeper layers of the unconscious. The difference in these two ways of splitting—and this may throw light on the many as yet obscure ways in which splitting processes take place—is that in the splitting-off of frightening figures defusion seems to be in the ascendant; whereas super-ego formation is carried out with a predominance of fusion of

the two instincts. . . . The extremely bad figures are not accepted by the ego in this way and are constantly rejected by it. (1958, 241)

The construct of psychological "splitting" is fundamental to an understanding of envy dynamics. In psychodynamic theories, splitting denotes nonconsciously driven divisions in the ego or split attitudes regarding the object. Kleinian psychoanalysis correlates its operation with projective identification mechanisms—both of which can be antagonistic to cognitive and emotional integration. If splitting processes are not too extreme, they are considered healthy and adaptive. When splitting is extreme, for example, excessive idealization occurs and envious pathways open. When splitting is psychopathological, psychotic states are engendered.

*Envy theory* places splitting in the innate program of how nonconscious information processing, together with emotional states, operates. Primitive sensations, perceptions, attitudes, and cognitive apprehensions naturally occur as dualistic units—typically polarized dichotomies. This is the sine qua non of nonconscious, primitive primary processes and directly influences the conscious secondary processes of logic, reason, and rationality. Splitting processes are raw, harsh, and disparate rather than elastic, as is the mechanism of dissociation. The operation of unconscious envy, therefore, is always marked by splitting: ideal versus malefically devalued appraisals. Although envy is made up of positive and negative impulses, such impulses never exist in simultaneity. Unconscious envy is preambivalent. When unilateral feelings of excessive idealization are stimulated, they quickly fade into a deidealized array of spoiling forces. Dynamic splitting rather than simultaneity characterizes envy.

Envy, unlike love, is a strong mixture of both primitive love (inherent libidinal instincts or life instincts) and destructive forces (innate destructiveness or death instinct). More precisely, *the love component within envy takes the form of excessive idealization and the destructive component takes the form of spoiling.* Envy as such is not primarily ambivalent, which would strongly suggest an indecisive cycling of feelings of love and hate; envy erects polarized states.

In speaking of this "ego-destructive super-ego," Bion (1962a, 97) says:

It is a super-ego that has hardly any of the characteristics of the super-ego as understood in psychoanalysis: it is "super" ego. It is an envious assertion of moral superiority without any morals. In short it is the resultant of an envious stripping or denudation of all good and is itself destined to continue the process of stripping . . . till . . . hardly more than an empty superiority-inferiority that in turn degenerates to nullity.

On an interpersonal level, the sadistic superego—envy's dictatorial leader—manifests itself as the expression of harping criticism, scathing critique, and predilection to perceive the ideas of others in debasing ways—for example, perceiving them as apodictic, imperious, and dictatorial. To the extent that this attitude is a projection, it reflects these same qualities in the personal nonconscious experience of the perceiver. The harsher and more brutal the criticism, the harsher and more sadistic is the superego of the critic. The person riddled with envy needs to be first, have priority in all things, and claim a superior position. Empirically, one sees spontaneity and normal playfulness seriously withered.

Along with negatively affecting self-image, all interpersonal relationships, intimate partnerships, emotional attachments, bonding, and sharing love over time become disorganized, fragmented, and disabled by the sadistic superego. The inability to experience pleasure in receiving on all levels—emotional and cognitive—creates feelings of isolation, being lost, virtual perdition, anhedonia, resentment, hurt, bitterness, and misery. This envy-generated experiential "black hole" is an intimation of the experience of "aphanisis"—the extinction of pleasure—as described earlier concerning envious anxiety and its threats of annihilation.

Other defense mechanisms include the escalation of extreme possessiveness (stinginess, greed, and nonhelpfulness, for example), attempts to stir up envy in others, and efforts to mute one's own envy by reversing the situation and causing a pseudodistraction. A last consideration is the defense mechanism of trying to pervasively mute all envious feelings by attempting to become indifferent. This amounts to an indifference to both extremes of envy's polarized splits: the ideal and its opposite, the spoiled. This self-induced blindness to ideal qualities not possessed, therefore, is simultaneously a denial of self-impotency. This defensive posture is a regression to a state of narcissistic withdrawal and numbness either to an excessively idealized positive or to a malevolent object. It reflects a profound split in the ego, which becomes shrouded in an impenetrable veil of muted consciousness. This tenuous defense involves the ego's splitting aspects of itself and the ego's attempt to dissociate conflict from conscious awareness. This freezing of affective and cognitive life results in the continued condition of stalemate, passivity, and impasse. The lasting debilitating effect of these envy-elicited defense mechanisms on the personality cannot be underestimated.

A commonly encountered clinical expression of defense involves the projection of split-off envy into another person or persons. This is displayed in the form of the patient's perception of attitudes of others. Although envy is the driving force, manic defenses are also elicited. For example, a patient may feel unappreciated by his colleagues or superiors and use manic-like defenses that result in disparaging contempt for those unappreciative (and by implication more intellectually limited) others. These are associated with the patient's consciously perceived feelings of anger deriving from self-doubt and inadequacy. Obvious defenses include omnipotent control, denial, contempt, and sarcastic glee. When these more apparent defensive strata are clarified in therapy, an underlying core of projected envy from the patient into his perception of others can be revealed.

The patient's own sense of littleness and feeling of privation is intolerable. Destructive and spoiling attacks at the perceived instigation of these feelings are made in the form of such manic distractions. Envy in its relentless attempt to hide itself will typically marshal the distractions of manic defenses to eclipse its own pivotal location. The therapist's task, then, requires careful elucidation of all dimensions of the clinical presentation. This includes a sensitive selection of crucial matters, relevant to the patient's present moment of anxiety and urgency, to be introduced at decisive points in the treatment. The complex integration of affective-cognitive empathy, tolerance, preconscious intuition, and consciously developed insight—introjective internalization—is essential to understanding and strategic interventions. While all elements in a clinical presentation may be mentally "true," their root elements in envy are important to recognize for change to occur.

When several of these unconscious defense mechanisms occur in concert, as they usually do, envy's destructive omnipotence can be seen as the epitome of unyielding recalcitrance. The envy-traumatized personality becomes "wrecked" and knocked out of action. Entrenched narcissistic states (Klein 1957; Rosenfeld 1965; Kohut and Wolf 1978; Kernberg 1986) and self-absorption make the envier virtually impenetrable to outside influences. Therapeutic interventions, accordingly, are blocked. They reach an impasse. The concept of "psychic retreats" (Steiner 1993) also describes such states.

"Treatment resistance" is the phrase used in modern psychotherapies to describe this descent to the very bedrock of unyielding and adamant deterioration. The effects of envy on the entire fabric of the mind heavily contribute to this collapse in psychological vitality, overall functioning, and meaningful adaptation in everyday life.

## Summary

This chapter attempts to delineate a microscopic analysis of the pathways, routes, and attractor states that envy traverses once its nuclear genesis has activated. The concept of *envy's developmental triad* is introduced to delineate this progression—how envy unfolds.

*Developmental triad phase one* consists of the activation of *nuclear envy's* three roots: the primordial ache of innate privation, primal and preemptive anticipatory privation, and actual and phantasied experiential deprivation. *Developmental triad phase two* mobilizes idealization in an attempt to reilluminate the ego's experiential void. Such excessive and omnipotent idealization is far too rich for the ego to assimilate and so this overwhelmingly inflated infatuation becomes intolerable. This precarious defense rapidly collapses by deidealization to again expose the ego to its emptiness. This abnegation, a paradoxical denial of the self's ability to experience anything good on any level, is a devastating awareness that induces shock and numbing. To break this state of suspended animation, *developmental triad phase three* consists of the ego's explosive attempts to spoil the previously idealized object. By so doing, aspects of the ego and its inner world of which the ideal object is part become spoiled. Shock and autodestruction are set in motion.

This self-imposed reinforcement of the primordial narcissistic injury—wound of experiential privation—is so intense that further pervasive numbing ensues. The cataclysmic violence of envious emotions temporarily knocks the ego out of commission. All introjective processes come to a halt and *adaptive collapse* threatens the immobilized ego. At this juncture, two routes can be taken. A healthier modulation of this disrupted equilibrium may occur, or a pathological course mobilizing strong defenses may follow.

In this chapter, the psychodynamic pathways and defenses that excessive envy traverses are outlined. In chapter 9, the details of envy's healthy maturation will be addressed. Envy's multiple defenses with special attention to projective identification are described. Aside from its normal communicative and exploratory functions, projective identification is the premier mental mechanism that the ego in a narcissistic state of enviousness uses to spoil the goodness and creativeness sensed present in the other and absent in itself. Intolerable unhappiness at this explodes into both object destruction and self-destruction. The novel conceptualization of *projective internalization* elaborated in chapter 2 is reviewed. *Introjective internalization*, its counterpart, is introduced.

*Envy theory* contends that envy is an irrational, paradoxical dynamic that, if left unchecked, results in autoerosion. Although having qualities of both types of eruption, envy best characterizes an ego implosion rather than an object-directed explosion.

The inner world is the field on which the chaos and disintegration caused by envy spread. The defenses prompted by envy enlist the action of the sadistic superego, which spoils the once-envied object and, in the process, spoils the very ego of the envier. Obsessional disorders, fueled by the energies of the repetition compulsion (chapter 4), also reflect such mechanisms. The principal psychodynamic operation is projective identification in which the projector splits off conflictual and intolerable aspects of the self, relocates them outside the self, and in a frenzied fashion tenaciously tries to control them as they are perceived to exist in this state of vicarious identification. Envy, especially by the sadistic superego, brakes and fragments links of meaning and value on all levels. This aggressive action disorganizes all attachments, especially ego to good object and person to person.

# CHAPTER EIGHT

# Envy's Conscious Derivatives: Signs, Symptoms, and Surface Indicators of Envy's Inner Dialogue

### The Clinical Phenomenology of Envy: Envy Unmasked

Unconscious envy is a state of mind. Surface signs, symptoms, and markers organize and express themselves from this latent mental background.

*Nuclear envy* exists in the dynamic unconscious as unconscious phantasies. These repressed mental contents indirectly reach experience that is more conscious by releasing buoyant derivatives appearing in a variety of substitute forms. In everyday life, the expressions of envy and its defenses appear together and make each other indistinguishable. This "return of the repressed"—effects of envy—expresses itself in the waking state and in behavior in ways that mask its original nonconscious source. These envy screens are the ever-present, seemingly archaic revivals in everyday life that make the study of unconscious envy necessarily an indirect one.

Envy in the most general sense cannot be understood as a sign or symptom. It is not and cannot be understood as a unitary or discrete phenomenon. In current conceptions of psychiatric diagnoses, envy cannot be positioned neatly on Axis I as a mental disorder or exclusively on Axis II as a personality disorder. It has the properties of a stochastic phenomenon, a probability or distribution pattern that may be characterized but not predicted precisely.

For example, *hoarding behaviors* represent the expression of unconscious, *nuclear envy* and greed across the life spectrum. Ordinarily, transient forms of hoarding, ordering, and ritualistic behaviors are typical in early childhood development. When these become excessive and sustained to the point of significantly impairing biopsychosocial functioning, they are classified as major psychiatric disorders, the principal one being obsessive-compulsive disorder (OCD).

*Hoarding*, in general, is a heterogeneous occurrence with overlapping descriptive dimensions and phenomenological specifiers. Noncompulsive hoarding, which shows markedly different brain activity than compulsive types (Saxena et al. 2004), is observed in schizophrenia, dementia, and Prader-Willi syndrome. This noncompulsive hoarding has a strong genetic and biological loading. Unlike compulsive hoarding, obsessional fears of losing valuable or significant items do not drive noncompulsive hoarding; rather, it is related to delusions, cognitive impairments, or stereotypic rituals that are the result of coarse brain disease. In other words, it appears more biologically rather than psychologically driven.

Compulsive hoarding, as such, having strong psychological motivators denotes irresistible urges to save items, fears of losing materials believed meaningful, avoidance of discarding, indecisiveness, perfectionism, procrastination, disorganization of possessions, and circumstantial, overinclusive thinking and language. The envy and greed behind such conscious disturbances are accompanied by unconscious phantasies generating inordinate anxiety that instigates repetitive actions to reduce these recurring obsessional tensions. The *nuclear envy* prompting such hoarding is inordinately severe, entrenched, and seemingly intractable.

Additionally, symptoms with clear-cut features of acquisition and repetition are not restricted only to this category (OCD) of psychopathology. These also may be a significant feature of brain injury, dementia, schizophrenia, mood disorder, obsessive-compulsive personality disorder, eating disorders, and autism, along with other symptoms specific to these disorders (Frost and Steketee 1998). The repetitive, intermittent cycling of bipolar disorders, for example, reflects the way manic defense mechanisms are used to manage the excessive envy and subsequent depressive anxieties at their core. When the connection between unconscious envy and observable signs and symptoms is fully recognized, diagnosis and treatment is enhanced since this deeper understanding provides data for more effective interventions.

Although unconscious envy is quintessentially a subjective phenomenon, many *effects of envy—its surface indicators—*in the context of interpersonal relationships can be observed and described. Some directly felt conscious indicators include: striving for a greater advantage or reward than another; trying to avoid getting what is perceived to be less than another person receives; preventing others from doing better, especially by unfair, cheating means; and the inability to tolerate the success of others.

Unlike unconscious envy, conscious forms of envy or "everyday envy" are apparent in the emotions stirred by social and class differences, especially the possession of wealth. Class privilege of the "pampered elite" is often the target of conscious resentment fueled by a sense of perceived unfairness. All varieties of envy, however, are rooted in unconscious envy.

Envy may emerge as a series of subtle and not-so-subtle feeling states. Assessing whether significant envy is present entails evaluating realistic aspects of perceived occurrences of justice and injustice. Although the equitable distribution of personal assets and material acquisitions is often naturally skewed, people possess the capacity, if unconscious envy is not malignant, to discern these differences in realistic and tolerant ways.

When envy manifests in conscious awareness, it may express itself in distressing attitudes such as inordinate resentment or excessive hatefulness in the absence of any recognizable cause. Often, its instigations may be clear—unhappiness at another's good fortune. Perceived fortune in the object mirrors underlying perceived misfortune in the subject. This usually takes the form of resentful feelings of unfairness that cannot be rectified, feelings of inequality, and feelings of injustice, all of which are excessive and not reality-based. Conversely, envy may manifest as happiness at the misfortune of others particularly when it is overlaid with manic defense mechanisms. As an observable sign, envy may be reflected in inordinately withdrawn behavior, reclusiveness, prolonged staring, emotional detachment, or acutely impaired functioning in the absence of physical illness, external trauma, or emotional insult.

As envy escalates, the envier encounters a panoply of diffuse attitudes, thoughts, feelings, and even bodily conditions that are dysphoric and distressing. This experiential level of envy reflects its complications, more evident than *nuclear envy*, itself. Although envy is profoundly intrapsychic, its expression unfolds in social contexts. Interpersonal and social contexts typically act as props and cues setting off already formed innate envious programs. In infancy, envy centers itself between infant and mother. From about age three years, envy also tends to express itself in peer-related contexts. Hoarding, inability to share, and need to be first strongly suggest underlying envy. Stealing resulting from beliefs about the unfair distribution of desirable goods is based on envy.

In adolescence, the dysregulation of eating patterns found in anorexia and bulimia suggests an underlying core of impairing envy. Food that "tastes too good" implies excessive idealization, greed, and problems of self-regulation.

These are accompaniments of underlying envy. Wearing the same style of clothing, in effect a uniform dress code, is a defensive attempt at muting differences so that envy is not instigated. In adults, clothing on some level may represent both a defense against envy-based conflict in the wearer as well as a signal acting to incite envy in observers. In adult life, envious conditions may be reported by the patient or significant others in very indirect ways as nonspecific troublesome issues or part of a variety of conflicts, disturbing behaviors, and interpersonal/family/social problems.

Envy is at the root of boundary issues in adult relationships. This expresses itself clearly between intimate partners but may also manifest in any emotionally close relationship. Some men complain of discomfort when their female partner appears "too needy." This usually implies excess dependency behaviors and attendant conflicts. Typically, each person has a share in unresolved dependency conflicts although one person may seem relatively independent in contrast to a dependent other. Complicated amalgams of deep-seated problems need to be uncovered to make sense out of these relationship dilemmas.

*Envy alone may not be the sole cause of conflict and dysfunction.* Since the focus of this book is on envy and its manifestations, aspects of envy as leading and important contributing factors at the heart of significant conflicts are highlighted. The layering of character and personality over time with its complexity needs due consideration both theoretically and in clinical practice. Psychosocial tasks and real interpersonal engagements contribute to healthy and conflictual individual personality buildup in changing ways over time. Within these advances in development, pockets of sequestered envy may remain hidden. *Envy theory* stresses rational assessments and the need to have *sufficient and reasonable clinical evidence*, especially over time, to support the realistic identification of envy dynamics in any context.

## Envy in Everyday Life

While many threads make up the complex fabric of a clinical presentation, *envy theory* suggests that all clinical presentations have multiple features including elements of envy. Narcissistic personality disorders are accompanied by conscious feelings of envy; obsessive-compulsive disorders are characterized by hoarding, severe anxiety, irrational mental and behavioral repetitions that aim to "get things just right," and often by subtle feelings that something is incomplete. Good clinical work demands a comprehensive and balanced perspective in evaluations and making diagnoses. In everyday life, moreover, envy is present yet often undetected.

The following are some of the consciously felt emotional climates that suggest states of envy: resentment, begrudging, bitterness, bitter ill will, enmity, rancor, feeling hurt and assaulted, malevolence, the intent to be spiteful and destructive, gloating, the need to be first or have priority, hostility, pervasive unhappiness, ill temper, brooding, grievance, vengeance, spiteful criticism, carping, miserable complaining, gnawing, feeling a festering preoccupation with injustice and entitlement, resentment at unfair nonrectifiable distributions of wealth, seething tension, a frustrating sense of powerlessness, feeling frozen, feeling inhibited, miserliness, stinginess, hoarding, being uncharitable, being unduly suspicious or guarded, appearing excessively withholding, inability to be helpful, unwillingness to help, feeling trapped or unfairly victimized or having an unjustly merited deficiency, feeling abandoned, isolated, starved, impoverished, or poor, and also feeling the emotion of disgust.

Prejudices and strong biases of all sorts are often based on envy. Those who habitually "put others down" or are routinely critical are motivated by envy's impulse to mar, spoil, blemish, and devalue. *Spoiling the pleasure of others, especially around issues of pleasurable group activities, notably meals and special occasions, is pathognomonic of unconscious envy.* The aforementioned indicators, when detected, can be used as markers that may direct attention toward uncovering hidden envy dynamics.

*A major characterological indicator of underlying envy is the expression of unhelpfulness.* This apparently simple phenomenon expressed in interpersonal behaviors is a cardinal clinical sign instigated by envy. Unhelpfulness correlates with inhibitions in empathy. Those who withhold help, in effect, act to maintain a status quo and prevent potential improvement in another. Such a discouraging attitude thwarts positive achievements. On an unconscious level, the enhancement of another's proficiency acts as a threat to the envier's wish to maintain a façade of superiority. It reflects a defense against fears of the risk of highlighting personal shortcomings by attempting to retain a veneer of competence by contrast.

Another indicator suggesting envy at play is the absence of humor. Normal humor connotes a low level of anxiety, relaxedness, and prosocial sharing of mutually benefiting entertainment. Successful outcomes marked by happy and cheerful attitudes characterize humor. Normal humor correlates with smiling and may be traced to the first smiles noted in early infancy. Envy neutralizes humor. In common parlance, for example, the expression "eat your heart out" implies "I know you feel envy at not having the pleasure you crave; your frustration is gnawing you inside." This reflects envy's autodestructive mode.

Unhelpfulness in the envier is also associated with the impairing distress caused by the perception of unequal distributions of assets, often to the point of their proportions being viewed as unjust, unfair, and almost impossible to rectify. It is another dimension of envy's contribution to fostering inhibitions and preventing change. In such cases, the envier thwarts any attempt at creative problem solving, helping others improve, and fostering mutual learning from experience.

Attitudes and behaviors that reflect helpfulness, by contrast, indicate prosocial behaviors. They "level the playing field" and deemphasize asymmetrical proportions. Equal opportunities and mutual support are antithetical to envy's structure, perceptions, and aims. Helping behaviors are often associated with feelings of wellness, hope, optimism, and enthusiasm.

*Envy theory* highlights that the helpfulness-unhelpfulness spectrum demonstrates the pragmatic intersection of metapsychology and observable measures of mental processes. In other words, in real-life situations, the tangible expression of helpfulness—a set of behaviors—denotes that the superego is integrated in healthy ways rather than in a state where splitting and polarizations are dominant. Splitting here denotes wide divisions in attitudes toward "all-or-none" and "black-and-white" values. Integrated superego states characterize personalities that demonstrate a compassionate and empathetic concern for both self and other. Fear abates and is replaced with feelings of awe and respect. The ego ideal—aspirations—in such people maintains prosocial values that foster enthusiasm, humor, and optimistic outlooks toward personal and interpersonal achievements.

In her last contribution on the psychoanalytic interpretation of literary material, "Some Reflections on the 'The Oresteia'" (1963a), Melanie Klein focused on the concept of hubris, an attitude of insolence and pride. She stated that hubris is generally believed to be particularly detrimental to one's character because it is based on emotions felt to be dangerous to both others and the self. She linked this configuration with greed and envy.

In states of mind dominated by envy, the inability to recognize, or even experience, any semblance of joy is apparent. A conspicuous absence of primary depression, sorrow, bereavement, and guilt is obvious although depressive features—dysphoria—may be present. Those with excessive envy seem always unhappy, especially at other's good fortune and assets; yet they may not necessarily be depressed. They are demoralized and overtaken by a sense of meaninglessness. In addition, envy also lies beneath the attitude of indignation. Those who are haughty and carry an air of superiority, as found in some privileged, wealthy, or seemingly cultured people, are motivated by envious attitudes that are deeply rooted. Supercilious people, however, may be found in all walks of life.

When envy first stirs, it may express itself as a conscious feeling of positive overestimation or infatuation with the other or aspects of the other. This overpowering feeling of excitement is a state of excessive idealization—unreasoned, friable, and often short-lived. This may grow into a feeling of adoration, which can be a nascent form of envy. If inordinately excessive, this overvaluation may become an unrealistically exalting aggrandizement. Behaviorally, initial attempts at closer and closer contact are made since feelings of dependency and a growing need for contact with the idealized person become increasingly prominent.

When the potential for excessive envy is minimal or absent, this process may develop into forms of romantic love. Within realistic bounds, love is a normal emotional phenomenon that has its own characteristic set of features and developmental progression. *Healthy admiration and normal idealization are virtually synonymous.* The healthy ego and superego work in concert to experience both self and object in a normatively positive manner. These factors contribute to normal love relations.

If, however, this burgeoning attraction develops by an envious route, mechanisms different from those proper to the development of romantic love emerge. When the degree of desired closeness or personal attainment of the idealized properties is repeatedly blocked, what had been felt as simple longing and yearning transforms and, in the end, culminates in disabling envy.

As satisfaction is repeatedly thwarted in these cases, feelings of disbelief, shock, numbing, and impairment progressively emerge. Unmet dependency needs, frustrated neediness, residues of idealization, and inordinate possessiveness may fuel manic grandiosity and the ego's engorged omnipotence. Jealousy as a defense against envy may surface. These developments contribute to a sense of primitive rage and hostility. Excessive negative feelings traumatize and retard free-flowing mental functioning. The adaptive management of anxieties and conflicts ordinarily attending real-life problems and challenges suffers. The envier rapidly isolates and withdraws from the field of contact that, in itself, stimulates further envy. If, by chance, the envier is forced into proximity again, envy, rageful, threatening, or violent behaviors may emerge.

Chronic, excessive envy usually heralds the development of, and later instantiation of, psychopathology. As pathological envy consolidates, it expresses itself in a variety of ways. The detrimental effects of envy heavily impact the psyche. Activities of daily living and performance are negatively affected. Inhibitions on all levels of functioning, especially learning, can be significant manifestations of excessive envy and contribute to further emotional distress. Once inhibitions of this sort begin, they accelerate rapidly.

## A Note on Miserliness

Parallel to the force of envy's blockage of communicative receptivity (for example, attentive listening and empathetic concern), it exerts an equally strong block against giving and sharing anything. Emotional and material sharing is constrained to the degree that these are perceived to be valuable.

A state of *pervasive withholding* is set in motion. Being frozen in the ability to give or receive is at the core of the experience of unconscious envy. Mental and motoric inhibitions express themselves in a variety of ways. Often, the unwillingness to both offer help and attempt to be helpful in a variety of contexts, as mentioned before, suggests underlying envy and discourages positive advancement. In such states of unhelpfulness, help is withheld not only on an interpersonal level behaviorally but also an intrapsychic level of free-flowing thinking and creative problem solving.

The underpinnings of *miserliness and being stingy* lie in envy. This attitude of *envious possessiveness* is really a rigidly protective, strained containment, in effect, a *lifeless mummification, of the self by the self.* This costiveness arises from an impoverished sense of self. It is the envier's desperate attempt to preserve the few, devitalized bits of self still felt barely to exist. All of one's inner resources, wealth, and richness are perceived as scanty or virtually nonexistent. Thus, all are desperately held since so little is felt to be present.

This sort of habitual or forced stagnation reflects the underlying, inflexible envy dynamic that thwarts change on every mental level, in effect, producing a *degradation of adaptive learning from experience.* A simple recognizable expression of the pervasive spoiling aim in envy is seen when a person unexpectedly causes a meal or dinner with others not to occur or to become charged by bitter, negative dialogue. This withholds enjoyment from all.

Empirically, an individual in the throes of envy appears tense, "wound up," and "tight." This overall contraction of the body accompanies constricted thinking, feeling, and emotional expressivity. It is, in effect, a psychomotor state of frozen, suspended animation. Envy often manifests itself as a blunted, constricted, flat, wooden, and stunned appearance. The entire *biomental self* recoils under the impact of its own self-generated envy. Interpersonal withholding eventually turns into social isolation.

*Withholding, therefore, of valuables, especially creative goodness, love, nurturance, and understanding, is bidirectional: (1) withholding from another, and (2) withholding aspects of goodness from the very receptive/experiential capacity of the envier. The latter causes the envier to become impotent and unable to experience any possible enjoyment of what may be available. This withholding is a blend of unconscious and conscious components: automatic frozenness and intentional deprivation to self and others. Envy spoils enjoyment.*

For example, the phenomena of stealing, hoarding, or excessive collecting, especially seen in children, may reflect a deeper underlying envy dynamic. In these situations, a sense of inadequacy, lack, or deficit is defended against by the feverish pursuit of acquisition. Rigidity, fearfulness, secrecy, and anxiously compulsive activity replace healthy, spontaneous play when envy is dominant.

In all persons, obsessive-compulsive displays such as hoarding behaviors also reflect envy. From a metapsychological perspective, a high concentration of envy in a sadistic superego is presumed. Degrees of frugality, parsimony, and being stingy or miserly in adults may also reflect degrees of underlying envy. Envy, when unmodulated, always poisons pleasure on all fronts. This phenomenon and its psychodynamic origins in the actions of the sadistic superego on the masochistic ego were alluded to in chapter 7.

## A Note on Xenophobia—the Alien, Stranger, Outsider, Enemy, and "Other"

Xenophobia is the intense, irrational fear as well as hatred of others who belong to another group outside one's own. Others are perceived as foreign, strange, outsider, or alien. This form of paranoid-like repulsion and hostility is based on envy. This also implies a need to feel priority in the value of one's own position.

Underlying xenophobic attitudes is the recognition of differences that one considers qualitatively distinct, irreconcilable, and personally threatening. These attitudes arise from situations that range from contact with others in one's own community who hold slightly different values and beliefs to speculations about unknown others outside one's locality—for example, in foreign countries.

Perceived differences may be minor or apparently major. Inordinate attention to minor differences or hints of differences suggests stronger, well-defended enclaves of unconscious envy. Such seemingly obscure, peripheral similarities may have strong unconscious, idiosyncratic significance and so elicit unconsciously powerful discrepancies that activate envy. The "other" is then regarded as alien and strange—an outsider to be avoided. Subtle fears, strong biases, anger, and intricate forms of hatred may be based on perceived differences in race, religion, sexual orientation, political affiliation, geography, and so forth. When xenophobic attitudes are looked at carefully, their basis in envy may be uncovered.

Often, such attitudes have two reinforcing elements: (1) envy of an idealized yet amorphous unknown, and (2) fear and hatred of this unknown entity because of its threatening potential for harm. Fear of this unknown quantity may have both unwarranted and realistic elements. It always includes a presumption of personal inferiority in the envier and behaviors that appear withholding, not generous. Withholding and greed typically go together.

A veil of anonymity obstructs a more realistic recognition of the ominous "other" in both envy and persecutory anxiety. Successful working through of the depressive position brings about the ability to distinguish between paranoid persecutory danger and actual danger realistically understood.

Irrational fear of enemies is always referable to the ego's primordial split from its own id accompanied by feelings of amorphously understood, menacing presences. Anonymity-induced aggression is based on this. Fear, moreover, is the passively felt dread of a less recognizable enemy. Hate is an actively felt dread of a clearly perceived enemy. Xenophobic attitudes correlate with an array of social anxieties and other interpersonally avoidant behaviors.

## Envy, Greed, and Jealousy

Unconscious envy is often at the base of many complex amalgams of conflict. It also underlies distressing emotional impasses that defy easy description. These usually exist with developmentally advanced overlays that may express themselves in ways that are more conscious. This particularly applies to manifestations of greed and jealousy.

Greed and jealousy, however, are relatively less malignant than envy since they are based on impulses considerably more positive and, to some degree, substantially modulated by love. They are closer to conscious awareness, recognized more easily, and more open to personal, introspective analysis. Greed and jealousy are common themes in psychotherapeutic contexts. When greed and jealousy become pathological, however, deeper analysis reveals that their intransigence to change suggests *a core of hidden envy*. Distinguishing envy from greed and jealousy is important.

The central thesis of this book is the core role that envy plays in human psychology. On all operative levels, envy strives to maintain invisibility, to operate primarily within nonconscious mental activity. In this section, some central propositions fundamental to an understanding of envy will be reviewed. These will be contrasted to envy's more conspicuous and accessible manifestations or derivatives, the principal ones being greed and jealousy.

## Envy

Envy is a highly complex, psychodynamic constellation with both individual (monadic) and relational (dyadic) dimensions. On the subjective, molecular level, envy is a singular phenomenon that may occur spontaneously, awakening from its primordial, constitutional base without exogenous provocation. This sudden emergence is figuratively akin to an eye opening out of a sleeping state. Envy does not have to arise exclusively as a secondary response (root three of the nuclear genesis of envy), one provoked by frustration, deprivation, withholding, and a sense of injustice, although this is usually a significant part of envy's multiple triggers.

Envy always presumes an experiencing ego; its changing cognitive and affective perspectives are its aspects. Envy as a relational phenomenon has three fundamental aspects: (1) the intrapsychic dynamic between ego and its id (*id relations*), (2) the dynamic between ego and its intrapsychic object (*object relations*), and (3) the dynamic that arises on an interpersonal, molar level when the subject, in fact, empirically notices the presence of another person in the external environment (*interpersonal relationships*). Fully developed envy typically consists of the interplay of all its relational aspects as they arise in concert and interact with one another in highly complex ways.

The dyadic or relational aspect of envy reflects situations in which the envier perceives the envied one to be superior, possess a highly desirable personal trait or faculty, or possess an attractive and desirable experience—all of which are inferior or absent in the envier. Envy focuses only on partial perspectives or aspects of whole situations. Intolerable unhappiness at the other's perceived assets correlates with this recognition.

Crucial to understanding the profound nature of envy is recognizing that, *at the core of its elemental, experiential form, nuclear envy is the agonizing sense of lacking a quality or power that one believes one has never sufficiently possessed.* This is the experience of *true privation*, the painful ache and silent suffering stemming from feeling a primordial gap, absence, and hole in the very fabric of one's being. The envier feels an inner sense of devitalization or deadness, in effect, of being a living corpse.

*Envy is the feeling of the absence of something highly desirable yet not possessed, and which, in fact, never can be possessed even if a feeble expectation may be present. It is important to restate, however, that the kernel of truth that ignites envy is the actual possession of the desired feature—in ateliotic (nondeveloped) form—in the envier. This constitutional platform is the ego's background awareness of the vestigial remains of its id.*

The nonconscious id, in mental fact, makes up the overwhelming substance and majority of the self. For the myopic (semiconscious or rationalized) ego, its id is believed to be only vestigial, a nonfunctional remnant of the past—for example, of infancy or merely physiology. The energies of the id are, however, a nuclear part of the ego's wellsprings felt as its sense of omnipotence. The id fuels envy's shrouding power to paradoxically annihilate the shadow of the id's omnipotence on the ego and make the ego feel it instead as an experiential sense of voidness or being dead. The experience of envy is felt on a gradient ranging from an insidiously aching dysphoria to a sharp, biting, and destructive impulse to spoil.

From an interpersonal perspective, envy is instigated when one compares the results/value/merit/outcome (for example, payoff, compensation, reward, recognition, and so forth) of his own efforts with those of another. Since envy uses its own envy-based standard of comparison to evaluate outcomes, an individual with an excessive quota of dispositional envy will feel resentment when the value of his outcome is perceived by him to be less than that of another, despite the complexity and actual merits of the differing efforts of the two.

Such imbalances in reward are felt by the envier to be unjustified. If they are also perceived to be nonrectifiable, resentment and hostility emerge. The envier overwhelmingly wishes to rob and deprive the other of perceived assets and destroy and spoil them so no enjoyment can be had. Although such situations are often characterized by the term "jealousy," they are more accurately incisive descriptions of interpersonal envy.

*Envy seeks to spoil and nullify what provokes it.* In contrast to the acquisitive and appropriative nature of greed and jealousy, envy ultimately aims toward negation through destructively projective means (projective identification). The very existence of perceived goodness and value threatens the envier.

## Greed

Greed is based on underlying envy but its motives and how it operates differ significantly. Greed is a more consciously felt impulse. It is an empirical phenomenon that is directly observable since it is accompanied by measurable behaviors. Greed typically is experienced in insidious ways. It soon acts like a fever that becomes an all-consuming preoccupation driving real-time actions attempting to satisfy greedy impulses. Greed is the irrational impulse to rob.

For instance, the clearest example of the destructive role of greed in everyday life is the contemporary deterioration of financial markets. Although greed typically involves one person (the greedy one) and the acquisition (primarily introjective processes) of inanimate goods, groups and institutions also share greedy impulses.

The objects of greed include actual material items such as food, money, or assets, or nonmaterial items—for example, knowledge or superior rank. Empirically, greed involving food can have idiosyncratic meaning. By contrast, most other forms of greed involve conscious, premeditated excessive acquisitions of material having socially regarded objective value. Acquisition typically tends to border on unlawful action. Greed and exploitation have strong correlations. Greedy acquisitiveness often is hidden beneath a façade of seemingly lawful entitlements or rationalizations emphasizing arguably justified deservingness.

Greed denotes the mental state wherein one ruthlessly desires and aggressively attempts to take in more than one actually requires, or more than the giver is willing to supply. Destructiveness, although a significant factor in greed, is an incidental by-product, not a primary goal as found in envy. The destructive quality of greed, however, may be intense; often, a hateful, rapacious demeanor accompanies it.

Greed is based on an underlying feeling, often subliminal but frequently conscious, of always being "hungry," principally emotionally, and thus needing additional supplies to secure satisfaction. The emphasis is on hungriness rather than unhappiness. *The phantasies of being unsatiated that surround greed originate from the unconscious notion that what already has been taken in is somehow damaged and not sufficiently whole or complete enough to provide adequate satisfaction.*

The origins of this unconscious phantasy are the envy-based projective attacks on the ideal object. Once attacked and damaged, they are introjected and become an unassimilated and threatening part of the inner world. Greed is a precarious depressive-position operation used to protect the ego from the internally sensed persecution of these damaged introjects. Once greed begins, it starts a vicious circle that continues to perpetuate itself. Addictions of all kinds, including those with illicit substances, food, or inordinate ambition, for example, have greed as a major component. Introjective processes predominate.

At root, greed may correlate with complex unconscious phantasies whose fundamental goal is to hold on to life, itself. Since envy involves spoiling its objects and greed involves destructive acquisition of nonspoiled objects, the ego attempts to defend against the anxieties of both in many ways, one of which is the mobilization of excessive idealization. Since idealization is fueled by excessive amounts of life instinct, a precarious yet fervent attempt to maintain this grasp on life arises. In the broadest psychological sense, fears of losing life and fears of not having enough life and all it implies somehow typically drive greedy impulses and greedy behaviors. Excessive idealization makes objects of greed appear more valuable than they actually may be.

Whereas envy seeks to depersonalize, greed suggests an impersonal, materials-based activity. Difficulty maintaining consistently close interpersonal contact accompanies this. The individual in the throes of greed is nongregarious, at times, secretive. Greed is a clinically evident phenomenon. The greedy person is cognizant of his greed. Greed is often a defense against envy. Greed and indiscriminate identifications with objects are positively correlated.

Greed results in two related phenomena: (1) trends toward the feverish hoarding of inanimate objects, and (2) instability in the constancy of maintaining the same interpersonal relationships over time. Greed may take the form of hoarding behaviors. It is a clear-cut feature of obsessional disorders in which irrational collecting and excessive, repetitive ruminations are prominent. This excessive need also reflects defensive activity against the perception of spoiling and being spoiled, and also of damaging and being damaged. These have a base in greed and envy dynamics. In envy, emphasis is on spoiling; in greed, emphasis is on robbing.

In contrast to greed, normal ambition is the adaptive striving for improvement of self and significant others. When not excessive, healthy rivalry and competition, both of which are not destructive but prosocial, accompany this.

## Jealousy

Jealousy is distinct from greed and envy. Jealousy is a more social phenomena that has exteriorized, discernable behavioral accompaniments and is highly personal. It involves a triadic or three-person situation wherein the jealous one feels deprived of the positive attention of the loved person who once bestowed love but now is believed to give it to a third person judged a rival or competitor.

Jealousy is the feeling of conscious *deprivation*, of being deprived of something desirable that once was clearly believed possessed and enjoyed with sufficient satisfaction. Jealousy is the conscious feeling of being excluded and losing something. Fear, uncertainty, and ambivalence accompany this, especially since the jealous person feels dismissed from participation in a once enjoyed social context.

Jealousy feverishly seeks to maintain its dependent social bonds. Attempting to hold on to what is ambivalently loved and at risk of being lost constitutes jealousy-based possessiveness. Loss or the threat of loss in jealousy may be felt as sorrow, grief, sadness, bereavement, mourning, and clinical depression. If these feelings are not faced directly and worked through, then a nonconscious retreat to paranoid-schizoid feelings of persecution characteristic of envy may result. Alternatively, manic defenses may be stirred as an attempt to deny and mask depressive feelings. Jealousy, itself, has features of manic excitement, rage, control, and domination. Jealousy often serves as a more ego-syntonic defense against ego-dystonic envy.

Jealousy, however, always has a core of strong envy. This can be seen clearly in the jealous person's attitude toward the rival. The rival is hated. This hate is envy-based in that the competitor is seen as superior in contrast to the inferior, excluded envier. The envier feels a lack of a vital personal resource—a sense of impotence. In addition, jealousy is based on an envious wish to spoil the relationship between the other two lovers who also are seen as a combined unit.

Jealousy is powerfully driven by love "gone wrong." Although the jealous person aims to destroy or eliminate the rival, this is only secondary to his primary libidinal wish to regain the ambivalently loved person. Jealousy fears to lose what it has, whereas envy feels pain at seeing another have something desirable. A jealous person is threatened by the loss of a good; an envious person is threatened by the very existence of a good.

In addition, an important part of jealousy is its intimate connection with the Oedipus complex. The oedipal dynamic is a developmentally more advanced configuration of anxieties, defenses, and object relations than that inherent to envy, which is more primitive and elemental. Jealousy, always grounded in envy, is a more complex and discernible feature of conflicted object relations. It has more obvious expression in the realm of concrete, observable, interpersonal relationships.

Whereas envy is an intensely private, intrapsychic experience with relatively little "acting out," jealousy manifests itself as intensely passionate. It expresses itself on interpersonal levels where motoric and behavioral action and reaction, especially protests, are prominent and glaring. Envy is cold, seemingly dispassionate, and humorless. Jealousy usually expresses itself in a frenetic, passionate, hyperactive, and frenzied interpersonal drama that is more behavioral than quietly felt. As mentioned, clinically significant depressive and manic-like features accompany jealousy, not envy. In jealousy, emphasis is on exclusive possession of the best.

## Frustration Dynamics of Envy, Greed, and Jealousy

Envy, greed, and jealousy usually operate together in varying combinations after infancy. When one predominates, its own characteristic sense of frustration accompanies it. *Envy contains a feeling of elemental frustration and profound neediness. It is sensed as an aching privation*, attributable to the perceived absence of a highly desirable trait or tenuous possession never fully owned. Envy and withholding are almost synonymous.

*Frustration related to greed is the perpetual feeling of partial but disturbingly incomplete satisfaction.* It is the feverish pursuit of attempting to acquire, but never achieving, a satisfactory procurement of what is felt to be enough. The greedy person can never feel satiated.

*Jealousy is the feeling of depressive frustration.* This frustration, often accompanied by protest, nonacceptance, and fighting, is clearly reactive to the perceived real or threatened loss of what one once possessed but is now deprived of. It can also be a result of feeling the loss of what can realistically be had or could have been had but is not had. Jealousy is feeling excluded from adequately loving the loved object. The jealous person feels a strong sense of responsibility for this loss, for example, a damaged relationship, because of the belief of being the source of the damage.

*Jealousy awkwardly seeks to repair and restore this damage, unlike in the envy dynamic, which only seeks to spoil.* This amounts to a paradox of autodeprivation. The jealous one suffers because he has deprived himself of what he feels he wants (by his damaging) and is powerless to regain possession. There is a relatively indirect quality to the phenomenon of jealousy-based damaging (usually directed only to the rival) in contrast to the direct spoiling attacks incited by envy. Envy is rooted in the paranoid-schizoid position; greed and jealousy issue from the depressive position. The qualitatively different psychodynamics of these complex configurations shape these experiences in qualitatively different ways.

The expression of violent possessiveness suggests the threefold, blended operation of envy, greed, and jealousy. Violent possessiveness may be viewed as a composite of three major factors. They are (1) envious destructiveness of (spoiling as forceful violence to) something once prized, along with (2) defensively holding on to (greedy possessiveness of) what one senses he has damaged in the very process of grasping it, yet will lose to another (jealousy) because of (3) the perception of the other as more powerful and adequate—that is, ideal (envy).

## The Mask of Treatment-Resistant Depression

The clinical phenomenon of *treatment-resistant depression* denotes those severely clinically depressed persons who have long histories of emotional dysphoria, a feeling of being stuck, hopelessness, helplessness, dejected humorlessness, severely impaired job and interpersonal relations, various degrees of anhedonia, and worthlessness, and who are unresponsive to psychiatric and psychological treatment interventions.

A major contention of this book has been that envy rather than primary depression may be at the root of such intractable situations. Apparent depressions that are refractory to psychotherapies and combinations of psychotherapy and psychopharmacology may be found to have an underlying base of insufficiently integrated envy. This takes shape as a dysphoria that incorrectly becomes labeled as clinical depression.

In *envy theory*, what appears as treatment-resistant primary depression has its roots in unmatured, excessive envy. Its antecedents can be found in the earliest developmental units found in infancy, the paranoid-schizoid and depressive positions. Stultified developmental conflicts persist in the primary process as unconscious primitive mental activity, impaired information processing. They become fused into the secondary processes of rational cognition in the form of ever-present unconscious phantasies. Since they persist into later life, they influence experiential awareness, cognition, misapprehension, idiosyncratic construals, and behavioral choices. Thus, these underlying, unresolved nonconscious information processing conflicts manifest themselves as chronic, intractable dysphoric states.

To reiterate this in metapsychological, psychodynamic terms: When the ideal object (primary object: primal part-object breast and primary whole object mother) of infancy, in part, is experienced in excessively envious ways, it is defensively attacked by attempts to spoil it. It is then felt to be damaged and fragmented by the ego's own hand. *Early forms of unmatured guilt (persecutory guilt) about destructive envy directed toward the mother begin to consolidate and fester as personality development takes shape.* These highly tenuous feelings of premature guilt exert a persistent negative effect. Developmentally more dominant persecutory feelings of potential retaliation from the attacked and spoiled primary object reinforce the more primitive unresolved persecutory guilt feelings.

Since this object is in the ego's inner world, it becomes a feared, potential attacker to the ego. Whole clusters of diffuse anger, aggression, envy, and premature guilt become amorphously organized and contribute to an undercurrent of dysphoria, a feeling of being plagued by indistinct internal tormentors. What initially had been only a premature sense of guilt rapidly changes into *hybrid states of persecution.*

In the paranoid-schizoid position, excessive envious spoiling of the object produces this crude form of guilt. *It is qualitatively distinct from the empathetic and remorseful guilt experienced when and if the normal depressive position becomes dominant.* Envy breeds demoralization and a sense of meaninglessness. The templates, therefore, of later psychiatric disturbances often can be found to have their primitive origins in very early development. Recognizing the possibility of premature guilt at the base of apparently resistant mental disorders provides an asset to diagnosis and devising novel treatment strategies that may be effective.

States of such premature guilt, manifesting as "depression," treatment resistance, the negative therapeutic reaction, and various forms of parasuicidal behaviors such as cutting and drug addictions, may be more common than had previously been recognized. The important part that unconscious envy plays in complicated forms of obsessive-compulsive disorders may also have been underestimated.

## Summary

The *nuclear envy* concept has been developed using a phenomenological frame of reference to provide a clinical window into the inner world of unconscious phantasy. *Envy theory* contends that envy feigns its presence and refuses to expose itself in a frontal manner by insisting on manifesting in ruses and other indirect ways. Hence, this chapter addresses envy's multiple disguises. These reflect envy's inner, subjective dialogue.

Envy, at any given experiential moment, reflects a state of mind rather than discrete sign, symptom, or diagnosis. The psychodynamic structures and circuitry of envy connote more than merely characterological dispositions. One's constitutional envy quota and its experiential management over a lifetime significantly influence personality and character. The complexity and uniqueness of each individual reflects the heterogeneity of these contributing factors.

How an individual, from infancy through adulthood, experiences and reacts to perceived disappointments and unmet expectations reflects how envy is felt and handled. Envy's quality, strength, duration, and potential to impair adaptive functioning influence this response.

Attitudes, behaviors, and comportment that suggest envy include the following: unhappiness at the good fortune and assets of others, chronic resentment that an unfair situation will not be rectified or ameliorated in the future, feeling unfairly treated, unhelpfulness, miserliness, stinginess, excessive withholding, frequently experiencing disgust, a pseudodepression secondary to unfulfilled expectations and ambitions, xenophobia, excessively biased sentiments, and always seeming to notice what is absent, incomplete, or not just right. In indirect ways, greed and jealousy imply underlying envy. Whereas envy aims to spoil, greed aims to rob.

The mask of seemingly recalcitrant depression and other treatment-resistant mental disorders at any chronological period may cover an underlying base of the premature consolidation of guilt that results from unintegrated destructive impulses particularly characteristic of unintegrated, split-off envy.

# PART II

# THE HEALTHY
# MATURATION OF ENVY

# CHAPTER NINE

# The Healthy Maturation of Envy: Admiration, Emulation, Gratitude, Empathy, and Helpfulness

## Envy and Change

*Envy theory* is closely aligned with Melanie Klein's seminal propositions both about envy as well as change. Both perspectives abhor the erroneous idea of attempting to explain in a sufficient way envy based merely on its primary and innate foundations. It is wildly irrational to declare that one is envious solely because one has been born that way. Emphasizing this crucial point is important for theoretical clarity and, especially, in clinical applications where the aim is therapeutic change.

Personal change comes about from an intentional wish to change. Chronological age, developmental status, external circumstances, and much more contribute to this goal. It is complex and often fraught with ambiguities (Sebanz and Prinz 2009). The extent of one's capacity to change depends upon decisions that arise from unconscious and conscious sources. Considerations about personal change and its outcomes activate complex emotional networks. These include values, past conditioning, perceived locus of control, and sense of self-agency.

People typically find a "comfort zone" in which to maintain a status quo course of living. This reflects degrees of complacency and automatic behaviors—many of which appear safe, relatively pleasurable, and certainly not challenging. Inflexible patterns of thinking, feeling, behaving, and responding are established early in life and take on a rigidity making them, in fact, into antichange forces that preclude new learning and new modes of being.

Reasons prompting change are complex, often having hidden roots emerging clearly only over time. Life crises, precipitous and characterized by loss, however, can become markers opening opportunities for self-reflection and subsequent life revision.

Is substantive psychological change within the purview, let alone volition and praxis, of men and women? To address such a broad question, issues of the self as agent, intentionality, agency, and willed action among others need consideration. Change in this sense intersects both motivation and neuroscience. Both components have explicit and more nebulous, perhaps unknowable, features. Not only the wish to change but a sustained motivation over time that typically undergoes highs and lows of optimism and futility is foundational to any substantial efforts toward change.

Conscious determination and directed efforts, however, may not be the entire picture. Recent neuroscience studies are attempting to carry forward older studies (Libet 2004) to examine the neural correlates of what appears to be voluntary action. For example, researchers (Haggard 2005; Freeman 2000; Pockett, Banks, and Gallagher 2006) using transcranial magnetic stimulation and fMRI techniques seem to suggest that initial phases that precede action are unavailable to conscious awareness.

In other words, nonconscious process that herald what only later begins to express itself as reported conscious thinking (intentionally motivated volition) and manifest behavior (executed volition) can be objectively detected. Though still in their infancy, these studies purport to document an array of unconscious antecedents to what much later in time become conscious intention and subsequent action. Decision-making may be *unconsciously* prepared ahead of time although reversibility of such directives may still be an option.

*Envy theory* holds that psychological change is possible. A wealth of neuroscience data, for example, has demonstrated the plasticity of the brain and its capacity to learn and substantively reorganize (Cozolino 2002, 2006). A great deal of these research findings have been applied clinically to psychotherapeutic interventions.

Any personal change is difficult. Changes in thinking, feeling, attitudes, and behaviors come slowly, if at all. Most people harbor overvalued ideas about themselves, their values, and cultural traditions. These convictions firmly plant people in stable, perhaps rigid, unchanging positions. Significant personal change requires extraordinary efforts over time. Such self-development and refinement is demanding but possible. A great deal of self-reflection and tempering of narcissistic states of mind promote internal accomplishments. The activation of the epistemophilic impulse enhances odds of success.

Change must first focus on internal accomplishments; external accomplishments follow. The seeds of envy's maturation reside in developing substantive ego integration. This self-integration requires greater self-awareness and a focus on self-development.

The biological correlate is greater neural net profile integration in neural circuitry and greater organization and responsive reorganization among the brain's association areas. Greater integrative strength acts to link polar opposites and change functional structure—envy's information-processing circuitry. Such an emotional atmosphere prompts healthier identifications based on affiliation, admiration, respect, and emulation. These are preludes to developing gratitude in relations with people. Integration and gratitude reflect an enhancement of what *envy theory* considers the *epistemophilia* of the self, the search for and discovery of meaning.

*Envy theory* is predicated on dynamic interactions between the two normal developmental positions, paranoid-schizoid and depressive. The decisive psychological achievements of a successfully traversed paranoid-schizoid position include ego integration, less splitting, patience, and affective admiration. Building on these, the achievements of the depressive position advance ego integrity and include going beyond egocentric constraints to include realistic apprehensions of other persons.

Some of these advances include the developed capacity for configural apprehension of a whole object/person, ego-object differentiation and boundaries, empathy, awareness of inner destructive capabilities, acknowledgement of harm done to the ambivalently loved good object, sorrow and reparation, and enriched feelings of gratitude for loving impulses within the self and those received from others. In the broadest sense, loving attitudes manifest themselves in behaviors that are helpful and giving. All integration, moreover, is biomental integration. Psychological advancement and greater neural integration proceed hand-in-hand. This underscores the brain's neuroplasticity and ability to change.

The developmental origins of envy delineated in previous chapters are hallmarked by formidable recognition of sharp *distinctions in quality and kind*. The envier organizes the perspectives of experience in dichotomously split ways: ideal versus inadequate, perfect versus imperfect, superior versus inferior, rich versus poor, and so forth.

For changes in envy to occur, its crux—*the qualitative dichotomy*—experienced as categorically polar, opposite, antagonistic, asymmetrical, and irrevocably unalterable has to undergo an essential shift. The accomplishment of this feat, however, presents as an unassailable paradox. Being able to hold the paradox conceptually and emotionally without denying or dismissing the restlessness it instigates is a prelude to insights, especially in later life, leading to *the healthy maturation of envy*.

A shift in orientation such as this transforms rigidly fixed qualitative apprehensions to softer, less inflexible ones. This then releases the additional capacity for the appreciation of more subtle *quantitative and dimensional distinctions, distinctions in degree*. Quantitative distinctions in degree, not in kind, moreover, permit, and are based on, the ability to see similarities and to create and understand analogies. This mental set is more fluid, elastic, and adaptive. It recognizes a common core amid differences rather than seeing qualitatively different essences. Similarities in any structure and function residing on a continuum are more easily apprehended. Cognitively apprehending distributions with uneven proportions becomes sensed as more syntonic and acceptable.

These changes in inclusive epistemological continuities parallel an apprehension of self, object, *relationships*, and environment that is more reality-based and fluidly abstract rather than concrete and unchanging. Perception of the world—self and others—becomes less polarized, harsh, and widely split. Phenomenal awareness operates more synthetically. Perceptual recognition of unopposed binary opposites becomes deemphasized on nonconscious levels of cognitive processing. A substantive refinement of the capacity for the eduction of relationship links—namely, the ability to see the meaningful relations that make up the continuum between and among experiences—is thereby set in progressive motion. Reality sense is strengthened. Volition, moreover, as the bridge between desire and action is augmented.

Envy contains both *unmatured elements* (often coalesced as conflict, anxiety, a predisposition toward rigid binary splitting, and mental stasis) and the *"nondeveloped" seeds* that, when developed, *may produce envy's own transformative fruition*. For these reasons, the way envy may change is twofold: naturalistically and by psychotherapy. In other words, *the healthy maturation of envy* partially may come about naturally as typical development proceeds and learning from experience refines understanding. Self-development strategies also are aides to recognizing envy. This, however, is usually only an incomplete advance. A great deal of envy remains unmatured and unintegrated. This remaining unmodulated domain of unopposed envy acts to produce conflict and developmental lags. Therapeutic interventions best address these enclaves of unconscious envy.

As envy changes, attitudes and behaviors change. *The healthy maturation of envy* is indicated most clearly by the demonstration of a *genuine readiness to offer help: to be helpful and maintain an encouraging attitude in everyday situations.* These prosocial attitudes and behaviors, centered on the wish to help and the enactment of helpfulness, transcend mere altruism. Evolutionary biology and psychology have advanced such propositions as kin selection, inclusive fitness, and reciprocal altruism. Scientific evidence in these areas suggests an intrinsic capacity for *the healthy maturation of envy* (i.e., the individual "gene" recognizing itself in the "other") to enhance successful adaptation, which includes enhanced volition and a sense of self-efficacy in real-world performance.

As further advances in maturity are achieved, an individual's locus of control becomes more sufficiently internalized. This entails efforts to develop self-dependent leadership skills based on genuinely felt empathy rather than external mandates, reward expectations, or politically motivated ideologies. Sharing and rational helping reflect significant measures of personal confidence, a sense of safety over having adequately perceived assets (mental and material), and satisfaction derived from the sense of potency that accompanies giving. In this way, unconscious issues of power, powerlessness, and need modulate and soften their stridency. The omnipotence-impotence experiential spectrum indigenous to envy thereby becomes attenuated.

Intensive psychodynamic treatments, for example, deal with conflict and unconscious phantasy. Insights into the implicit unconscious, at times, uncover startling revelations too unbearable to easily accept. This intolerability is based on its underlying matrix, which, at root, is primal envy of the feeding breast, the very source of life. This has a dual reference: envy of the prototypical, primary object—the mother—and envy of the ego's own primordial progenitor—the id. *This necessitates a confrontation between love for and envy toward both one's actual mother and also with one's deepest relationship to experiential creativeness on a primordial and personal level.* The undeniably sensitive nature of these intimate insights makes their realization much more than mere intellectual problem-solving tasks.

The achievement of insight over time reconfigures previously fixed patterns of experience on all levels. Insight enables problem-solving abilities to perceive new functions within relationships and thus broaden and enrich the scope of all problem-solving capabilities. This working through of experiential data deepens insight and understandability and opens the possibility for longer-lasting psychological change.

This sort of perceptive learning is particularly efficient since it is framed to achieve a target response—insight. Insight is relevant in fundamental ways: emotionally (reduced anxiety), cognitively (increased meaningfulness), and behaviorally (higher quality of life from the enhanced sense of self-agency to act on both self and the real world). Additionally, when ego integration is firmly experienced, the capacity for attention is enhanced; subsequently, drifts toward boredom—rejecting present experience—are minimized.

## Paranoid-Schizoid-Position Achievements: Ego Integration, Patience, and Admiration

Achieving the capacity for integration is crucial for envy's healthy transformation. *Ego integration* in the organization and reorganization of self-experience implies developing dynamic, interactive communication among all aspects of the psychic system. This greater self-coherence is the potential to acquire a decisive ability—the mobilization of active mental trends toward self-unification. This qualitative attenuation of splitting processes, in turn, stabilizes the developing personality. Increasing cognitive constancy, more efficient information processing, greater access to memory, adaptive learning from experience, and greater mood steadiness result. These are the rudiments for the elaboration of *patience* over the lifespan.

The major task within the paranoid-schizoid position is integration so that more complex levels of biomental reorganization may occur in response to inner (introspective consideration) and outer (learning in an interesting and motivating environment) stimuli. While this first occurs in earliest infancy, it can be reworked retrospectively throughout life.

In psychodynamic terms, the principal trajectory toward this aim is the introjection of the breast experienced as a whole, good, feeding, nurturing, loving, containing, understanding, and creative object. The *ego's capacity to identify with this internalized good object*—in essence, the model of a mutually gratifying and constructive relation—becomes the nuclear core around which all stabilized integration occurs and progressively consolidates. This defining moment—an intimate coherence of self and object—launches the love relation to mother as a complete object. This stabilizes, enhances, and upgrades forward developmental progress across the lifespan.

In some sense, the ego's experiential emphasis in paranoid-schizoid configurations is on what is negative. Healthy advances within this emotional and cognitive framework trend toward a unification of polar opposites. To the extent that sufficient integration is successful, the achievements of the resulting depressive position all emphasize what is positive. For example, negative bias is superseded by bias that is more positive. More positive rather than negative emotional information, therefore, can be detected and extracted from experience.

Primitive love as excessive idealization transmutes itself into a more balanced loving relationship. This is how *envy theory* regards the vicissitudes of love's reparative and complex psychodynamic impact on the ego. *Normal idealization* enhances the ego's healthy perception of and positive regard, or *admiration*, for the object in infancy and subsequently all other objects and persons throughout life.

The raw fear that accompanies unmodulated envy becomes transformed, in part, to form the emotion of surprise. *Surprise* as a healthy sublimation of aspects of fear is a vivid emotional response that reflects an increased vigilance to unexpected events. Surprise correlates with emotional and cognitive receptivity—*a sense of wonder*—to new experiences as novel learning opportunities. Besides normal developmental progress in infancy, *the future capacity for insight*, often accompanied by astonishment and amazement, is directly related to the continual advances in incremental ego integration that occur over time.

Envy denotes insufficient ego integration. A major cause of the perpetuation of this state of disjointedness, anxiety, and dysphoria comes from narcissistic resistances to change. Change here denotes movement toward more adequate integration in the paranoid-schizoid position. This facilitates successful transitioning to higher levels of mental refinement in the depressive position. These early changes reconfigure the personality, are remembered on nonconscious corporeal, emotional, and intellectual levels, and affect future experience. Change and integration become repeating cycles throughout life. They reinforce one another and promote continual mental development.

*Unabated states of envy reflect obdurate states of narcissistic resistance. A major consequence of this is resistance to achieving insight since insight is the cognitive and emotional antithesis of envy.*

The overarching cause of *postponing* a fuller experience of depressive-position reparation at any developmental level can be traced to a "hang-up" or tenacity related to the narcissistic, envious clinging that is characteristic of unresolved paranoid-schizoid-position conflicts. The omnipotence fueled by the id is the impetus for the ego's clinging dependence on this primitive source of power. It stalls the free flow of paranoid-schizoid dynamics toward the goal of integration. The role of unopposed omnipotent impulses in psychic functioning retards the maturation of mental development. *The inability to manage premature persecutory guilt reinforces unhealthy adhesiveness in the paranoid-schizoid position.*

Coming to terms with paranoid-schizoid dynamics is arduous. Adequately confronting and managing destructive impulses and phantasies, however, launches integration. The beginning of this process entails recognition, naming, acknowledgement, ownership, and responsibility for unpleasant, negative, yet real innate destructive tendencies. This immensely complex process of matured identification is the basis for furthering *healthy integration of all aspects of destructive impulses in the ego. Its roots arise in the paranoid-schizoid position and its flowering occurs in the depressive position.* It is a lifelong challenge that oscillates continuously across life's chronological thresholds and opens new opportunities for further advancement.

## Normalized Projective Identification and Ego Integration

Since projective identification is a necessary part of mental functioning, its normalized use is beneficial as a means for psychological exploration and nonconscious communication. In technical terms, the normalization of projective identification denotes excessive features becoming reduced so that when activated appropriately a stabilizing, containment around affect and information-processing results. Pathological projective identification then becomes normalized projective identification. An increase in introjective and receptive capacities occurs simultaneously. *Normal ego integration always connotes a proper balance of projective and introjective mental mechanisms. Splitting processes decline. Emphasis shifts from paradigms of control to those of self-regulation and self-integrity.*

A clearly observable postinfancy measure of this is reflected in numerous real-life situations, especially attitudinal issues involving forceful control and intrusive behaviors that are overly manipulative. When the need to control, for example, goes beyond normal self-management, caregiving to dependent children or elders, and job-related responsibilities, it indicates the felt mental pressure that arises from excessive projective identification. This exhibits itself as staunch beliefs in one's own set of values and the compelling need to impose them on unwilling others. When these are excessive, abnormal and violent nonconscious splitting trends arise. They show up as perceived irreconcilable interpersonal and social differences, especially felt in an atmosphere of hostility. Child abuse, spouse abuse, combat, and war are concrete examples.

*Normalized projective identification denotes a relinquishment of omnipotent control on experiential and interpersonal levels.* This normalization reflects that strong reparative trends in the self (integration) and toward the other (helping) have superseded control issues. Excessive egocentricity abates and narcissistic self-centeredness becomes modulated. A realistic grasp of the other in the overall context of relatedness becomes more perceptually available. Rigid, idiosyncratic personalized emotional meaning becomes less instrumental in the apprehension of social stimuli—relations with other people.

This is the basis for a realistic *appreciation* of experiencing one's inner world as well as outer reality with balanced discrimination, pause, and mental equanimity. This process is a component of admiration and describable in a variety of ways: ego-object differentiation, self-regulation, the modulation of affective and cognitive reactivity, self-soothing, and a stable reality sense. A balanced sense of operational interdependence intrapsychically and interpersonally proceeds from this.

Hence, *the omnipotence-impotence default perspectives framed by envy become disabled.* Greater cooperation both interpersonally and socially subsequently ensues. Perceptions of differences remain, yet are recognized in a normative manner as agreeable givens rather than adversarial clashes.

Ego integration of destructive impulses is essential for the mitigation of their virulence. This diminishes the omnipotently negative impact they impose on thinking, feeling, and behaving. A radical acceptance of and balanced integration of one's own destructive, spoiling, and envious impulses, to some extent, must occur for change to proceed.

This view of personal reconciliation resonates positively with Melanie Klein's (1935, 1940) concept of the profound reparative trends that characterize the *continual*, normal mastery of the depressive position as an advance after integration in the paranoid-schizoid position. This deepening mastery is a decisive developmental accomplishment that continues throughout life. The depressive-position configuration of creative and restorative impulses adds to integration in the ego and consolidation of libidinal object synthesis (normative ambivalence)—apprehending both good and bad features in both simultaneity and balance. Greater cognitive constancy and emotional stability are interminable adjuncts to normal human psychic development.

## Why is the Successful Resolution of the Paranoid-Schizoid Position—Ego Integration—So Difficult?

Ego integration is difficult for many reasons. Adamantine resistances to integration are due chiefly to the *exquisite pain elicited by any attempt to integrate destructively opposing forces.* When significant advances are about to occur, the ego experiences a barrage of unbearable pain, which, in effect, attempts to slow and paralyze unification and forward progress. *Envy theory* sees "resolution" not as completion, but as the attainment of *ongoing states of manageable equilibrium.*

Three leading sources of this resistance are the following. First, ego integration results in a *partial deflation of omnipotence.* This is a partial giving up of unconscious phantasies of narcissistic omnipotence, narcissistic self-sufficiency independent of need for the object, and omnipotent control/domination of the object. These phantasy dynamics are based in deeply unconscious processes. Their adhesiveness typically approaches intractability to both access and change. The combination of forcefulness, obstinacy, and power inherent in omnipotence vehemently resists change. When we recall that omnipotence is another name for the *unconscious as a system*, this virtually impervious resistance is understandable. It has an autocratic and dictatorial hold on the ego since it is the ego's only direct link—by relocation—with the id's immeasurable primordial potency, fecundity, and creativeness. Omnipotence does not want to die. Moreover, the ego clings to it "for dear life."

Second, there is a *threat to the loss of excessive idealization—primitive love.* This particularly relates to the deflation of omnipotent narcissism, which threatens a loss of the expectation of limitless perfection. This includes the ego's having to give up its hope for unrestricted gratification.

*Envy theory* regards *suspense* as a crucial state of mind that, when developed, acts to enhance receptivity and intelligent responsiveness. This, in turn, encourages active anticipation and excitement, creative preludes to the future. Suspense may act as a significant mood regulator that engenders hopeful expectancy and a measure of emotional pause. *The healthy maturation of envy* fosters such patient states of mind. Unmodulated envy counters the adequate development of the capacity for sustainable feelings of suspense. This is an attempt to prevent the downregulation of the omnipotent wish for greater degrees of satisfaction on all levels. An adequate capacity for paused restraint becomes established by progressive integration in the paranoid-schizoid position. Subsequently, this self-modulation may further galvanize itself in the depressive position.

Third, as described previously, *the ego, to integrate in substantial ways, must recognize and take ownership of its internal destructive impulses—the primordial reality of the death instinct within.* This acknowledgement of ownership is a prelude to these destructive impulses being attenuated and integrated in the fabric of the ego. This is instrumental in assuaging premature guilt and thus affording proper recognition and acceptance of love and goodness. Confronting one's demons, as such, often comes as an alarming, dangerous, deeply anxiety-provoking, and appalling realization. It is a painful shock eliciting an almost reflexive retreat. When an acceptance of one's destructive potential is successful, however, the ego, aided by healthy libidinal energies within, is able to contain, soften, and mitigate the harshness of its own felt destructiveness. Superego relaxation is a large part of this integrative process.

Omnipotence, however, always continues somehow to act as a major resistance to ego integration and developmental refinement. The most underrated ballast, moreover, that perpetuates omnipotence is the dread and subliminal belief that reductions in its blinding brilliance—conscious attempts to face psychic reality—might expose one to one's own hidden core of latent insanity. This sense of being crazy, mad, or psychotic is a direct reflection of the destructive impulses that play such a large part in the inner world in both normal and psychopathological conditions. These destructive impulses, often taking nightmarish proportions, have subjugation of both the object and the self as their objective. For these reasons, complete and permanent ego integration can never be entirely achieved.

## Excessive Splitting and Idealization Diminish

To the degree that a healthy recognition of the multiple dimensions, good and bad, especially bad, of psychic life occurs, excessive idealization and inordinately wide splitting diminish. Only then can omnipotence and narcissistic states of the ego begin to abate. Extremes of emotion and other excessive polarizations of mental states soften.

As splitting processes normalize, they produce more coherently clear divisions and fluid distinctions in information processing. Archaic aims and primitive unconscious phantasies reconfigure. Although inclinations toward splitting and idealization always remain, greater integrative mental forces reconcile them more cohesively. The mind's part-object templates remain as unconscious influences but are much less dominant and are superseded by the ego's synthetic functions. In other words, objects now emerge as whole objects that are more realistically correlated with real persons in the interpersonal environment. This reflects the advances characteristic of the depressive position.

Cognition is more able to abstract experiential multiplicities and experience them as synthetic commonalities rather than alien repugnancies. Greater patience, along with the tolerance of ambiguity, uncertainty, and confusion, help consolidate the ego both affectively and cognitively. *The compelling pursuit for perfection in thinking, feeling, and behaving loses its harsh driving power.* These extreme states of mind, previously felt as intolerable, now rest in greater equipoise and balance. The experience of self becomes more singular, less plural. All the aforementioned reflect how the dynamics of envy—for example, excessively splitting to bits, excessive idealization, spoiling, and nebulous division between good and bad—are mitigated and assuaged.

What would have been the unrestricted emergence of full-blown envy, instead, expresses itself as a burgeoning capacity to perceive the other in a manner that preserves recognition and respectful acceptance of differences both good and bad. Reflexive splitting in cognition and affect abates; nuanced and transitional valuations become part of information processing's interpretive strategy. Equality is no longer a matter of comparisons that require virtual identity or a superior-inferior bias.

From an interpersonal and social perspective, *normalized splitting diminishes "win-lose" frames of reference underlying ruthless competition and rivalry. Fairness is felt as comfort in the recognition and acceptance of varying degrees of sameness and difference. Perceived discrepancies, in fact, are now experienced as welcomed novelty and surprise, both of which stimulate further healthy interest, pause, patience, suspense, anticipation, and productive exploration.*

Both the subjective experience of mental objects and actual experience of people in the real environment can now be perceived in moderately ideal ways. This reflects normal, not excessively expectant, interest. Extreme over-valuations become less frequent.

Empirically, volition and performance in real life improve. A greater sense of self-efficacy supersedes doubt and uncertainty. Inhibitions in taking action, for example, are not stifled by sacrificing the better for the sake of the best. Reasonable goals, and their performance, rather than unrealistic ideals are set and enacted.

These enormous shifts in attitude can occur naturalistically during normal development, especially if one's innate capacity for what I have termed *instinctive resourcefulness* under favorable circumstances (see chapter 4) is constitutionally strong. Self-development strategies along with teachers, coaches, mentors, and guides from a variety of disciples can enhance this. Ego integration, diminished splitting, and the normalization of idealization—*the healthy maturation of envy*—are specifically targeted and enhanced, however, in psychotherapeutic contexts.

## The *Epistemophilia* within the Self

*Envy theory* defines *epistemophilia* as the impulse and search for truth that manifests as the experiential sense of meaningfulness in cognitive and affective information processing. The innate epistemophilic impulse underlies emotionally and motivationally charged cognitive anticipation, expectation, and attention. It perceptively targets everything that might promote successful survival for that particular individual. The infantile prototype is the infant-mother relational link. Meaning is a function of the interpretation of connectedness derived largely from the social context. Linkages on all levels (emotional and cognitive) in the self, moreover, are felt as meaning laden and having significance.

Meaning and understandability versus indifference and confusion are on a par in value with the reward of love and penalty of envy. The primary reference point for the inherent search for meaning in *envy theory* rests in the infant's regard for the mother's body and mind in toto. The construct of the *epistemophilia* within the self has been referred to elsewhere as *adaptive intelligence* (Ninivaggi 2005, 2009).

*The innate predilection to seek out novelty is the primary search for good objects, the first of whom is mother, to insure both survival and a secure base in enduring creativeness.* This brings about a reduction in anxiety and confusion, and an increase in the pleasure of experiencing cognitive and emotional expansions. These are instinctively endowed nonconscious processes. They partially manifest in the preconscious and conscious attitudes of infants and mothers. All later intellectual and emotional exploration is grounded in this infantile base. Such impulses seek a novelty that conjointly engenders pleasure and reduces anxiety. This hedonic trait underlies the tonic responsivity in attention and the direction of focus.

All understanding—emotional and conceptual—emerges from these infantile sources that promote survival. The development of thinking and acquisition of knowledge are commensurate with developmental advances resulting from *the healthy maturation of envy.*

*As the paranoid-schizoid position is mitigated by expansions of love, developing integration, and reduced splitting, attitudes of pause, respect, admiration, and emulation crystallize.* These tools are necessary for mastering, or at least sufficiently managing, the developmental tasks of the depressive position and Oedipus complex. Hence, reparation may prevail and provide opportunities for further personality refinement, enrichment, and gradually expanding self-directive integration. Unmodulated envy in unresolved paranoid-schizoid processes thwarts the epistemophilic impulse. Envy knocks it out of commission and acts to congest its unobstructed flow. In effect, malignant envy acts to skin off the containing envelope that organizes meaning.

When sufficient advances in ego integration occur, however, degrees of intuition, insight, and *understandability* become progressively consolidated. They increasingly reflect an enhancement of the *epistemophilia* within the self. For example, the therapist's empathy, compassion, tolerance, and developing insight are crucial factors that facilitate the emergence of understandability. These help organize and link the individual's seemingly incongruent communications into meaningful realizations. Empathetic receptivity in a state of mental equipoise offers the patient a chance to participate in the transformative function of the therapeutic situation. This participation and identification gradually consolidate to become an internalized faculty for such empathy over time.

Theoretically, when life instinctual forces in the form of love (creatively affiliative trends) are strong, they facilitate the recognition of envious processes—psychological expressions of the death instinct. As this creative dialectic between the life-and-death instincts occurs, greater degrees of meaning and understandability emerge. This *epistemophilia* helps galvanize further ego advancement and integration, thus giving birth to creativity in all sectors of the personality. Thus, *the healthy maturation of envy* parallels the developmental achievement called the depressive position.

## The Depressive Position: Inception of Empathy

As Melanie Klein (1945, 1957) described, the depressive position is the psychodynamic state of mind repeatedly traversed and refined as the primary paranoid-schizoid position is developmentally resolved and restructured in intervals in both infancy and later life. This unfolding process results in emotional and cognitive complexity and an enrichment of the personality that also continues to consolidate. The healthy refinement of the depressive position correlates with the humanization of the id, harnessing the raw power of the psyche's dark side (nonconscious information processing and unconscious phantasy) toward greater personal integration and social creativeness.

This *process* can be formulated according to Bion's (1970) illustration: PS◆ ➜D. The paranoid-schizoid position (PS) oscillates with the depressive position (D) in dynamic ways throughout life.

In this context, *envy theory* advances the idea that the first developmental position—the paranoid-schizoid position—may be understood, in fact, to denote *the narcissistic position of envy*. The operation of excessive projective identification reflects an ego state in which boundaries are continuously made diffuse. Hanna Segal (1983) referred to the paranoid-schizoid position as the "narcissistic position." *Envy theory* adds and emphasizes a hitherto missing yet essential component—the envy dimension.

The hegemony of envious destructiveness to both self- and object-awareness prompts intense paranoid-schizoid anxieties. Intermittent mental states, largely dominated by splitting processes and periodic disintegration of the ego's normal attempts at containment, abound. Envy is deeply rooted in this state of mind. As fear, hate, envy, and persecutory feelings are mitigated by more loving feelings and cognitive differentiation and integration, however, the ego achieves more enduring states of *poised respect, quiet anticipation, and awe* regarding the now more securely felt goodness of the primary object needed for survival. Less fusion with the object and significantly diminished control-dominant omnipotence lead to feelings of separateness between ego and its object now seen as whole. These developmental advances signal the inception of the depressive position.

The essence of the *depressive position*, in contrast to the paranoid-schizoid position, is the ego's burgeoning recognition of its own differentiated destructiveness, a felt sense of having actually damaged a whole object that is ambivalently loved, and the urge toward resolution and repair of this. Experience becomes sensitized toward positive bias in detection and information processing.

Depressive guilt, sorrow, remorse, and mourning spark and reinforce these reparative impulses and feelings. Less splitting and polarity, a greater capacity for tolerating states of ambivalence, ambiguity, and doubt, and a newfound capacity for appreciating diverse and conflictual aspects of the whole object shore up patience and the emergence of basic trust in self and other.

Love and hate as attitudes and feelings now may simultaneously coexist toward the same one lovable person, for the first time perceived in more unified, configural ways. The capacity for tolerating ambiguity increases. Mental poise and a capacity to linger with these states, rather than reverting to automatic splitting as a response to frustration, are thus set in motion. This constitutes a life-long attitude, not a transient consideration. Profound empathetic caring inevitably ensues.

*Depressive-position restraint* is achieved as splitting processes are superseded by the ego's progressive integration. With this faculty, the ego is more able to function as an observer. A greater capacity for states of quiet anticipation tempers the craving for need satisfaction. Previously felt pressured needs for instantaneous gratification are softened. This results in states of lessened tension, frustration, impulsivity, and explosiveness. Depressive restraint reflects increased self-regulatory anticipation even in the face of ever-present ambiguities. Needs that inevitably arise are not reflexively responded to with immediate action. Impulse control further develops as inner security increases.

Clinically, one often sees a patient (adolescent or adult) on the verge of experiencing the intensity of depressive-position guilt unable to bear its intensity. Integration is thus blocked, and reconfigurations into the more psychodynamically refined depressive position cannot occur. This block, in part an effort to avoid experiencing the unsettling distress of ambiguity, ambivalence, dependency, self-reproaches, mourning, and loss, is erected as a defensive maneuver. It usually contains strong paranoid and persecutory elements. Hence, entrenchment in the paranoid-schizoid position with its omnipotence, splitting, and aversion to facing inner and outer reality endures.

When gradually increasing ownership over destructive impulses, concern for the welfare of the object, and reparative and creative urges escalate, however, they begin to transform the quality of object relations. Caring and concern also imbue one's intrapsychic self-relations. The experience of a more compassionate sense of self-worth and self-regard becomes ego-syntonic. The depressive position heralds an ego less split by envy. Together with more intact and whole-object cognition, the ego becomes more integrated, synthetic, and capable of feeling an expanding share of creativeness already latently present—*the id as resource of creativity*.

❖

*The depressive position is a transition from dyadic relations to triadic relationships.* It is also a shift from the earlier dominance of unconscious phantasy to a greater role for reality testing and a developing reality sense. Underlying this is the ability to comprehend objects as whole entities rather than as the part-objects experienced in the more primitive paranoid-schizoid position. This gives the ego an ever-greater capacity for mental looping, depth, and texture. This connotes both an emotional and cognitive capacity for progressively greater receptivity to and inclusion of perceived differences. It enhances the ability to synthesize polarities and integrate parts into more synthetic units as wholes. It also recalibrates the rhythmicity of the self: blind repetitions reconfigure and become healthier episodic cycles.

Cognitive expansions characterized by an increased capacity for abstraction, symbolization, concept formation, and the capability to infer links of meaning in relationships are further advanced. A more discriminative sense of reality develops. Integration and creativity in the ego, itself, as well as a more realistic appreciation of objects become mutually reinforcing dynamics. The fidelity of self-experience on all phenomenological levels becomes truer.

The ego's sparing the object its destructive intentions occurs simultaneously with the ego's sparing itself the damage that envious attacks inevitably cause. *Reparation* heals splits in ego and object. It functions experientially as creative restoration and new vitality. It pervades all dimensions of the complexity of self-experience and relations with others. Narcissistic self-destruction, autoerosion, and self-hatred are diminished as self-integration propagates.

Parenthetically, a major clinical parameter clearly reflecting the healthy negotiation of depressive-position dynamics is seen in individuals sensitive to the negative effects on others of disappointment. This denotes people who realize that disappointing others often provokes their frustration, anguish, and upset. In other words, those who have successfully resolved—to some significant extent—their own depressive-position conflicts and developmental tasks will act responsibly. They take accountability for their promises and especially their follow through in action.

While the PS-D (paranoid-schizoid oscillating with the depressive) dynamic is the prime developmental dynamic that characterizes earliest infancy, its lifelong occurrence refines and enriches the personality by using the vehicle of real interpersonal relationships experienced over time. The evolution and transformations in each configuration and between them reflects how the mind develops and people experience personhood. Degrees of mental health ultimately consolidate by the reworking of depressive-position psychodynamics throughout life once sufficient paranoid-schizoid integration has been achieved.

It is worthwhile emphasizing the vital importance not only of accepting but also of *lingering* with depressive-position feelings and ideation. It is unquestionably a complex and painful experience. The theoretical underpinnings of this crucial admonition rest on the premise that full ego development—cognitive and emotional maturation—occurs over extended periods of time. Remaining in this depressive state of profound sorrow, moreover, without impatiently or frenetically attempting to escape its exquisite distress, is crucial to its resolution. Time frames vary, but months rather than years is typical.

In everyday life, defensive reassurances from self-talk and from "sympathetic" others inevitably come to the fore to temporarily soothe distress, give evidence of love, and escape pain. Yet enduring this pain is necessary to work through—in sufficient ways—the depressive position. These roadblocks, which are forms of denial of the perception of psychic reality, need to be carefully detected, especially in all treatment situations. Parenthetically, good psychotherapeutic treatment is, in itself, not reassuring but appropriately empathetic and realistically encouraging—resolving conflict enough so that going forward in positive ways is facilitated. This correlates with a validation of realistic yet distressing states of mind that seek understanding, some resolution of anxiety, and transformation.

The depressive position, a chronological marker, exerts continuous influence as a maturational and developmental mediator. Sufficient ego strength—the consolidation of optimal cognitive capacity and balanced emotional fluidity—requires the kind of working through only provided by real time. The stress-vulnerability-coping model of health and biomental dysregulation has relevance in this framework. These considerations about proper integration of aspects of the self underscore *envy theory*'s intimate correlation of ego and time. While elemental developmental achievements may be launched in chronological infancy, only with the evolution of the ego—the experiencer in the person—over a lifetime can substantive self-development be achieved.

All too often, *the intensity of the depressive position at any age is so brutal that it elicits an almost reflexive reaction to deny its poignancy by fleeing. This may involve a regression to paranoid-schizoid defense mechanisms or to manic defenses against depressive anxiety*. The latter may take the form of *premature, mock reparation* and varieties of manic states. This false reparation by using caricaturized masquerades results in the manic drill of denial, control, contempt, and bogus triumph in a precarious effort to subdue the poignancy of feelings elicited in the depressive state. States of abnormal humor, irritable silliness, and mocking attitudes characterize the manic condition. The harsh, cutting, ironic derisions characterizing scorn strongly suggest the underlying glee of contemptuous manic attitudes.

*The manic constellation alluded to is a cardinal defensive response reflecting an inability to work through the depressive position*. Mania begins with an initial hyperidealization that turns into a hateful devaluation of the object. Manic defenses reflect attempts at manic devaluation of the object to reduce unbearable anxieties. This is rooted in an inability to accept recognition of the object as independent. Omnipotent denial, forceful control, contempt, and eventual triumph are defenses that cycle with depression in their precarious attempt to deal with the complexities of the unconscious phantasies underlying such attitudes.

It is imperative to recognize this common stumbling block during any psychotherapeutic intervention. One must always aim for balanced appreciation of all positive features, as well as relevant, even though disturbing, negative features. This fosters an inner sense of encouragement, which may act as impetus to further conscious reflection.

The continual process of refining depressive-position psychodynamics is the central hallmark of successful psychological development. It is difficult, however, to remain in this affective center of gravity before sufficient mastery is achieved. Defensive retreats are frequent and may go in opposite directions: either to the paranoid-schizoid position, or to attempts to massively deny needy dependency on the object by erecting manic defenses. Combinations of complex defenses are usual.

Mania reflects the omnipotent denial of dependence, helplessness, separation, and the oscillating feelings of both love and hate toward one, complete object. Manic hyperactivity in thought, engorged emotion, and impulsively driven behaviors indicate relentless attempts at distraction from realistically facing depressive anxiety and guilt.

Current trends toward an overemphasis on biological explanations and pharmacological therapies of depression, for example, can arguably be seen as containing strong manic elements. Exclusive reliance on psychopharmacology to treat mental disorders suggests a manic flight from exploring deep-seated conflicts. A balanced approach judiciously using all available resources (psychotherapies, psychoeducation, behavior therapies, and psychopharmacology) is more rational, and may be more effective.

It is incorrect to undervalue psychotherapies. Psychological interventions help explain the observed gap between research-setting statistics regarding drug efficacy and "real world" effectiveness or lack thereof using drugs alone. Psychiatric disorders, especially major disorders, express themselves with much more complexity than Mendelian inheritance and gene-only effects.

Tolerability, an important consideration in all drug treatments, certainly may be enhanced through psychotherapy and may give all aspects of treatment a better chance for successful outcomes. An important question to include in any rational therapeutic plan is, "In what experiential areas of the personality does anxiety lie?" rather than only asking, "In what areas of the brain are specific neurotransmitters dysfunctional?"

## The Role of the Id in the Depressive Position

The motor that drives the depressive position has its creative roots in the dynamic unconscious. In each developmental position—paranoid-schizoid and depressive—the id and unconscious processes manifest themselves in qualitatively different ways.

*Envy theory* postulates the virtually impersonal forces in the "id" propelling themselves in the ego so that they may become more external, more experienced, more personal and personalized. This underlies the overwhelming influence that the id plays in the primitive paranoid-schizoid position, and how its crude dominance is lessened in the developmentally advanced depressive position.

The depressive position brings with it a developing capacity to experience, in ever more exquisite ways, the broad range of how the corporeal self can be felt cognitively and emotionally. In other words, the depressive position offers the ego more direct access into conscious awareness of the sensitivities of the flesh. Body and mind are less split and felt as less alien to one another. Body image is experienced as an asset since it is felt as an integral part of the self.

*Transcendence of primitiveness as part of the refinement of the depressive position*, moreover, connotes deeper intrapsychic intimacy. In a figurative sense, *ego and id in this highly advanced state are realized to be—and therefore become—experienced as less split, less far apart, and less alien*. The whole personality becomes more integrated and unified. The primitive, elemental, and raw qualities of experience transform into more flowing continuities. This intrapsychic reparation is a healing unification or "at-one-ment" on a profound experiential level.

The integration achieved in the depressive position is not all or none. It resides on a wide spectrum. The aforementioned descriptions suggest transformations from primitive to more refined. Remaining stable in and having one's center of psychological gravity in the depressive position, in fact, is not absolutely secure. Reversions back to primitive paranoid-schizoid functioning occur. This reminds us that dynamic change and fluidity typically supersede inactivity.

What are some of the intrapsychic dynamics underlying depressive-position advances?

*The healthy maturation of envy* requires success in the depressive position and stimulation of creative reparative urges. *The breast mother as an unconscious phantasy that mirrors the interpersonal relationship with the mother of infancy, the prototypical model of all interpersonal relationships, henceforth is spared unbridled harm and spoiling.* Normal ambivalence, the capacity to simultaneously feel both love and hate toward the same object, becomes established. Normative and inescapable states of emotional and cognitive ambiguity thus become more easily tolerated. They are withstood without decompensations in psychic functioning.

In addition to the primary object of envy and of love—the *breast mother*—other new complete objects/persons are able to be cathected (apprehended and internalized) in a healthier relational way. In a sense, these new objects are secondary objects with which the subject may engage in more complex triangular and oedipal relations.

The primary object—*breast mother*—always remains the singular object of nurturance and reference point for all object relations. Nurturance includes feeding, love, and understanding. Secondary objects are always multiple objects (for example, father, siblings, grandparents, peers, teachers, and so forth) that are involved with the trends, tasks, and conflicts brought about by the capabilities realized as development proceeds. Such conflicts include, for example, genital impulses coming to the fore in adolescence (romantic interests) in the context of reworked self- and sexual identity and increased peer relations. The secondary objects experienced in the depressive position are grasped as whole objects—largely real people perceptions—in contrast to the part-object figural perceptual apprehensions of the earlier paranoid-schizoid position. After infancy and childhood, these secondary objects become the principal players in a person's life. They are secondary only in relation to the primary object of earliest infancy; in other words, so-called secondary objects are one's significant real-life companions.

Whole-object relations underlie the concrete interpersonal relationships between people and in social contexts. They benefit from the guiding template of the securely established "internal good object" at the core of the self, even though this varies in degree and is never complete. In the interpersonal relations after infancy, envy is much less potent since secondary objects are, in fact, not the primary object with whom primary, direct envy was originally transacted. The diffusion and dispersal of targeted envy in new and real interpersonal diversification cannot be underrated.

Depressive integration, therefore, denotes the ego's integration of previously split-off destructive impulses that were the matrix from which paranoid, envious, and hateful affects, object relations, and intrapsychic dynamics operated. As a result of such integration, anxieties of a more primitive nature are lessened.

The creative rather than destructive inclinations of id impulses in the ego come to the forefront. Reparative integration sets the stage for liberating the inner creative urges that underlie a more loving and well-balanced sense of self and capacity for mutually beneficial object relations. This is reflected in a realistic appreciation of the actual people in the real environment. It facilitates the capacity for greater interpersonal and social cooperation, healthy emotional exchange, and effective adaptation in a variety of activities of daily living.

In other words, one's emotional center of gravity becomes more loving, empathetic, and cooperative. Mental states of giving and receiving love become less conditional; feelings of generosity are more freely felt. This is reflected in the enactment of behaviors influenced by the actual reality of the interpersonal milieu. Sharing, fairness, helpfulness, and equity characterize such performance. Healthy depressive integration begins in infancy but is a lifelong process.

## Superego Softening/Integration: Self and Object Admiration

The normalization of envy emerges in a developing emotional configuration characterized by incipient pause, awe, admiration, and respect. When the long process of identifying, recognizing, and *appreciating* the value of all aspects of one's own experiential being begins, an intimate sense of self-admiration—healthy narcissism—arises. This is felt as an increase in healthy self-esteem.

Superego functioning denotes specialized mental processes in the ego for evaluation of the goodness-badness and rightness-wrongness of thoughts, feelings, and actions. This polar spectrum is wide with many nuances in between. Often referred to as the capacity for "conscience," it functions to judge and establish criteria for self-assessments. Conscience reflects *models of values and moral aspirations*. These range from self-confirmation to self-criticism and include their nuances. A primitive superego is characterized by wide splits between perceptions of extremely ideal judgments and extremely negative ones. With *the healthy maturation of envy*, as splitting lessens, the superego functions in more integrated and less strident ways. Less splitting, in effect, is a relaxation and softening of superego activity since envy has been significantly modulated.

Self-love becomes realistic when the superego becomes more relaxed by lessening some of its store of unmodulated envy and thus diminishing its tendency for excessive self-criticism. This makes possible a firmer belief and trust in the goodness of the self. This journey toward the integration of extremes and perceived polar opposites is launched in infancy and continuously evolves throughout life.

An example, in everyday situations, of an integrated superego is the phenomenon of "thank you." It implies the normalization of envy and an undercurrent of experiential gratitude for receiving something regarded as helpful. The helpee, both in turn and in simultaneity, can identify with and admire the commendable and meritorious features, traits, and faculties possessed by another, the helper. Genuine gratitude expressed as "thank you" to the other (the "object" of intrapsychic experience correlated with its reference to external figures in the environment) is felt in a more wholehearted way, with conviction.

In addition, an often overlooked and underestimated reciprocal phenomenon is the expression "you're welcome." In this case, the helpee's statement of "thank you" acknowledges the helper in the active role of helping. "You're welcome" connotes the helper's normalization of envy because the gratitude expressed by the phrase "thank you" is being received with pleasure and cordiality. It reflects the helper's agreeable and hospitable reception of the helpee's gratitude. When sincerely exchanged, both phrases imply that envy is minimal and that gratitude abounds. *When real admiration prevails, no heart suffers from another's perceived good fortune.* These processes seed themselves in infancy, only to flower over a lifetime.

Envy in its primitive state instantaneously creates a polarized split experienced as a personal sense of inferiority in the face of outside superiority. By contrast, soundly integrated, matured envy—in essence, admiration—enables one to recognize *degrees of interpersonal equity.* Since the self is felt as having intrinsic value and worth, it is also able to apprehend others as valuable and worthwhile. Normalized projective identification underlies this. In other words, projection lessens while introjection, assimilation, and integration increase.

*Recognizing others as different in kind yet equal in value, for example, connotes cognition capable of distinguishing among an unequal variety of differing qualities. Individuals are appreciated for the value of their differing characteristics, including both strengths and weaknesses.* The need for omnipotent control gradually becomes abdicated.

As superego softening proceeds, needing to view people in blanket and forced fashion as "absolutely" equal is no longer an imperative. As the superego becomes more integrated (intrasystemically within itself and intersystemically within the self-system of id, ego, and superego), its decision-making capacity becomes less prone to splitting between instinctively erected radical opposites. Balance and secondary processes of reason temper choice. *Human equality, accordingly, is perceived and understood as signifying the innate value and intrinsic worth of each differing and "unequal" person, including the "unequal" self of the perceiver.* All people, seen as unique by inborn and acquired differences, may now be recognized as equally worthwhile in principle.

However, since basic envy is never completely absent at any age, some feelings of inferiority and inadequacy naturally remain. Moreover, perceived interpersonal differences, while still noticed, are now grasped more realistically making them felt as more acceptable and less as stressors. These diverse personal givens then appear as *interesting variations* and the inevitable diversity that human nature typically exhibits.

An important consequence of superego softening is a reduction of mental rigidity and inhibition. As envy diminishes both quantitatively and qualitatively, ego functioning becomes more elastic, flexible, and spontaneous. This is reflected phenomenologically in a greater sense of emotional serenity, less fearfulness, greater intellectual creativity, balanced humor, and more appropriate behavioral playfulness. These are expressed in differing ways characteristic of chronological and developmental status.

## Aesthetics

A concrete example of how superego influences manifest themselves on individuals and the social group is seen in the cultural productions represented by art forms. The superego functions to set standards that include values, morals, and aspirations. The construct "aesthetics" embodies these considerations, especially when it reworks them in various harmonies, balances, exaggerations, and distortions. Art and culture within civilizations imply *values and aspirations.* Human cultures produce imaginative meaningful symbols implying shared social traditions, ethical mores, and aesthetic ideals. These shared social ideals, often imaginatively constructed and portrayed, are offered for communal contemplation.

*The healthy maturation of envy,* for example, is reflected in well-done works of art. *The roots of subjectively experienced aesthetic sensitivity, moreover, are laid down when the ego acknowledges both its goodness—beauty and benevolence—and inescapable but manageable destructiveness—ugliness and cruelty. In dialectical and reparative fashion, these underlie creativity* and reflect the integration of the superego both within itself, and as a more syntonic ally to the ego in the overall functioning of the self as a whole, especially self with other people.

The creation of a work of art, in whatever métier its form takes, is motivated more by the urge to recreate an unmatured, tenuous, and damaged ideal than to produce an ideal ex nihilo.

In *envy theory,* all expressed creativity is the externalization of the dynamics of raw and maturing unconscious phantasy. Art reflects the tension—the reworking of previously disjointed connections—between the ugliness of something felt damaged and the beauty of its restoration. The artist wishes to exhibit—to share this personalized materialization so that others may contemplate and partly identify with it. Imagination tempered by reality actualizes itself in "what-if" scenarios whether visual, auditory, or in artistic writing.

Art is an impulse prompting the restoration of a deeply perceived damaged ideal. The acknowledgment of this impulse requires a repeated working through of the contradictions and pains that ambivalence, uncertainty, and doubt along with the hidden anticipation of "something more, something wonderful" brings.

Art evokes rhythmical oscillations between feelings of dissonance and harmony. Art stimulates this tension of continued interest, unlimited explorations, and trying to figure out what is going on. How a work of art is constructed reflects both the underlying conflicts that stimulated it and the reparative attempts at its resolution. Aesthetic flaws in all great works of art attest to this. The *epistemophilia* within the self drives this.

All works of great art—like waves crashing on the beach that you can never still—have a sublime quality; they inspire awe—a feeling that the art does not need you since it is far greater. Each indefinable work somehow communicates a seemingly completed event—no more needs to be portrayed—at that moment.

Paradoxically, each piece of art is no longer subject to change; in itself, it is dead. This, however, is not true for the viewer. Each time a work of art—however unchanging—is contemplated, a new set of perceptions and conceptual reconfigurations is triggered so that the individual apprehends something new.

Art, in this sense, is primarily evocative rather than a static communication of data. For example, specific colors and how they are portrayed in dynamic movements often elicit attitudes and emotional states that defy simple articulation. Artistic processes stimulate the creative impulse within the *epistemophilia* of the self. Conditions are created that may bring about a renewed activation of the life instinct. This *élan vital* experience of "seeing" in a fresh way arouses feelings stimulating a renewal. This results in new opportunities for novel cognitive and emotional experience that has a reintegrating effect on the fabric of personality.

## Gratitude: Appreciation of and Thankful Regard for Coexisting Goodness and Badness

Gratitude is an outcome of advanced integration, especially in the depressive position. Polarized splits in information processing reconfigure into perceptual and conceptual apprehensions of contiguous contrasts. This results in a tolerable ambivalence able to see multiple perspectives simultaneously; it strengthens the capacity for empathy.

Gratitude is an achievement reflecting the dynamic integration of the self as it undergoes progressive developmental differentiation and intentional evolution. It is an operational shift. Narcissistic attitudes recede, egocentricity declines, and the needs of others are more clearly recognized. Boundaries between self and others become more distinct, yet not polarized.

The ego has access to more synthetic and complete views of the object as similar to itself even though sensed as different and more independent. The self, in turn, realizes the value of relationships that are *interdependent*. This obviates excessive dependency conflicts and intolerable frustration. Such attitudes characterize the broad range of normal depressive-position achievements.

On a theoretical level, *emerging gratitude takes a path away from narcissism*, a feature of paranoid-schizoid states, both early and later versions. Narcissism connotes a state of the ego wherein the majority of attentional cathexes gravitate in self-directed ego information circuitry. Subjective experience is principally intrapsychically oriented. The primitive ego fuses with an internal image of an idealized part-object. This profoundly intrapsychic affective cognition arises in an atmosphere of incomplete intersubjectivity—part-object paranoid-schizoid relations. Narcissism and omnipotence go hand-in-hand. Developmental immaturity (chronologically normal or produced by conflict or by constitutional atypicality) is the basis for an incapacity for ego-object differentiation. Excessive dependency needs remain in ascendancy. Excessive narcissism correlates with minimal capacity for empathy and sharing.

The *inception of gratitude* arises when sufficient ego-object differentiation—whole and complete object recognition—begins to arise. Phenomenologically, this occurs along with a clearer appreciation of and developing admiration of the attempts of another to be loving *even if that love is neither perceived nor felt to be perfect*. In such situations, the ego recognizes the less-than-optimal aspects associated with such less-than-perfect love. What is experienced, for instance, may be some "dirtiness" or unpleasant smell, some delay, faltering, or hesitation in whatever is involved in dispensing love. This is also the case when less-than-complete satisfaction is felt from love given.

Identification with this mixed recognition ensues if acceptance of this less than optimally apprehended love occurs. This entails a realization of the other's possession of, capacity for, and willingness to offer and share love, even if it is less than perfect and has shortcomings. Gratitude implies a more *realistic and respectful acknowledgment of and acceptance of what are perceived to be differences, especially weaknesses, shortcomings, faults, hesitations, uncertainties, and disadvantages in both oneself and others. Self-reconciliation and self-integration go hand-in-hand.*

A fuller sense of gratitude culminates in the ability to receive what is felt to be fundamentally good, desirable, and available in others and the extended social and cultural environments—even if not perfect. This can occur only when basic self-love becomes firmly established with sufficient conviction. Accordingly, one can become thankful that the other has such admirable and valuable qualities that, in turn, may be shared by this kind of emotional tasting. *This enriched feeling of gratitude becomes the pivot around which envy loses a significant portion of its malignant obstinacy.* The roots of gratitude are laid down in infancy and develop over time.

Gratitude, in effect, reinforces the salutary feelings of having received something experienced as initially good and satisfying. Satisfaction coupled with gratitude, in essence, becomes a prolonged experience. The personal sense of feeling good is optimized, perpetuated, protracted, and sustained as the combined process of actively experiencing and expressing gratitude occurs.

Gratitude, moreover, is the normative recognition of having received an adequate share of something perceived as pleasurable enough to be satisfying—*at least for now. This reflects normalized omnipotence. The infantile-based wish for an inexhaustible supply of gratification that will last forever is thus tempered. This satisfaction is always coupled with an expectation of, or hope for, the experience of a probable future pleasure. This hope is aroused from receiving something really felt as good. For these reasons, greedy impulses diminish since their roots in envy have become attenuated.*

Not only a feeling of indebtedness but also a normal and adventurous quality of suspense and wonderment arise even in the face of uncertainty. This wish "to return goodness for goodness received" is a large part of the maturing experience of gratitude. In this sense, *gratitude is the counterpart of greed. Envy may be seen to be greed's less developed form, which, if modulated, may mature into admiration and, subsequently, gratitude.*

The capacity to feel loved in an authentic way comes from two sources: self-acceptance and honestly felt satisfaction. The first is the progressive and balanced *recognition, acceptance, reconciliation, and integration* by the ego *of both good and bad aspects in the entire personality.* This necessarily entails a softening of superego severity, experientially felt as *self-forgiveness.* This softening is the relaxation of unmodulated destructiveness. It is made possible by greater degrees of integration stimulated and consolidated by the ego's use of life-instinct energies. This flows from an ego felt more unified and less split.

*Reparation* (Klein 1940, 1945) connotes a strong activation of the complex processes of love. *Such positive libidinal regard not only reflects sparing the object one's destructive and hostile assaults, but also sparing the self—in essence, self-forgiveness.* There is less self-hatred. This results in a deep sense of un-spoiled self-compassion and positive self-regard. The second source of being able to feel loved comes from the capacity *to receive, accept, and honestly feel satisfied from the love given by another.* As normal self-love is securely estab-lished, feeling loved becomes radically enhanced.

A more realistic and optimistic expectation of success, in general, and of fairness, in particular, accompanies these hopeful anticipations. The roots of the belief that equitable justice can and does exist emerge from this. The personality, in effect, feels more balanced and, accordingly, is perceived by others as less harsh, mean, cruel, withholding, and punitive.

Gratitude is also reflected in one's sensitivity to situations of disappoint-ment. The mature personality realizes that taking responsibility for one's promises and their follow through behaviorally is essential in mature inter-personal relationships. A more humane, compassionate, benevolent, caring, and helpful attitude may then typify interpersonal relationships. In some sense, there is a direct correlation and shared aims among such apparently different concepts as justice, righteousness, righteous conduct, and charitable sharing. In these, levels of envy, dishonesty, and fraudulence are low and sufficiently modulated by empathy, compassion, and benevolence. Of course, these mature attitudes need time to develop and can be observed after the period of childhood and adolescence.

## Helpfulness: A Major Behavioral Expression of *The Healthy Maturation of Envy*

*The healthy maturation of envy* is the outcome of psychological work on the self—self-development. Its initial focus is on internal accomplishments that, in turn, may translate themselves into external real-life performance and success.

*Envy theory* as an individual psychology emphasizes the subjective experiences accompanying envy as well as those attitudes, actions, and sets of behaviors reflecting its healthy maturation. The latter constitutes envy's social and more consciously developed dimensions including moral consciousness. From an empirical perspective, helpfulness is a leading behavioral expression of envy's healthy maturation. Volition and the capacity for implementing directed effort correlate heavily with this. In other words, personal will, "willpower," and getting things accomplished are strengthened.

*Helpfulness is associated with self-efficacy*—a sense of potency that accompanies giving. The inclination and readiness to help arises from a personal sense of security and self-confidence. *The healthy maturation of envy*, in fact, reflects that a person's unconscious sense of inordinate narcissism and omnipotence has been normalized. This sublimation implies that unconscious inadequacy and powerlessness have been tempered and become felt as a sense of self-efficacy.

Such adequate integration in one's diverse ego functions assuages both inordinate anxiety and fear, which often act as barriers toward helpfulness. Perceptions of harshness, cruelty, and negative criticism, in turn, about self and others become deemphasized. Along with rational self-dependence, feelings of interdependence and empathy become integrated in daily life and exhibit themselves between people. In other words, *how one performs interpersonally and socially demonstrates—in real time—the healthy maturation of envy*.

Helpfulness, as an attitude (aspirational dimension) and a set of behaviors (operational and instrumental dimension), draws from both one's sense of benevolence and one's normalized attitudes toward what is just, equitable, and fair. It reflects a sense of hopefulness and encouragement, both self- and object-directed.

Helpful behaviors—benevolent dispositions enacted between people—can be described as a kind of sharing having win-win outcomes. These may occur as a natural expression of one's inner attitude, or they may become highly developed through conscious reflection and practice—helping skills. When developed in this way, the intention toward helpfulness embeds itself over time in nonconscious, automatic, even procedural memory. *Envy theory* views this as the development of an intelligent character trait. Such mature helpfulness distinguishes itself by *timely and intelligent responsiveness*.

Although both kindness and justice are synchronized in mindful helpfulness, there is perhaps a heavier load of *kindness* imparting to it the benevolent outreach characteristic of all that is helpful. Humankind's major worldviews traditionally have held kindness, loving kindliness, charity, compassion, mercy, benevolence, and intelligent forgiveness as fundamental virtues toward which to strive. These *connotations of "love"* are characterized by nonviolent, intelligent mutuality. *Sentimentality, cheap pathos, blind faith, and indiscriminate attraction* are not included in such an understanding.

Different cultures, for example, refer to this experience in characteristic ways: *agape* (Hellenic), *caritas* (Christian), *metta* (Hindu), and *chesed* (Hebrew). Attitudes of helpfulness typically lead to helpful actions and good works. Both are essential in the development and expression of *the healthy maturation of envy*.

*Envy theory* as psychological theory adds analysis of unconscious dimensions to these laudable strivings and fleshes out some crucial subtleties. *Helpful behaviors (actions) and all attitudes (dispositions, impulses, preconscious intention, aspirations, and mental set) of helpfulness are particularly epitomized when displayed and enacted toward "strangers," those perceived as outside one's immediate group or culture.* Far from being an indiscriminate outreach, rational helping, whether asked for or merely offered as a helpful gesture, thoughtfully discerns goals appropriate and conducive to improvement.

Helpfulness that is sagacious and egalitarian has essential ingredients: avoiding unilateral control, forceful imposition, and actively eliciting wished-for cooperation. Groups that merely direct helpfulness toward their "fellow men and women"—inside members of an elite or privileged community, regarded as the only people worthy of help—have not achieved *the healthy maturation of envy.* These groups, by contrast, suffer from narcissistic, self-centered values, which are, in fact, envy-driven and foster schismatic polarizations and autistic-like insularity. In turn, envious spoiling in outside observers is provoked and may lead to persecution and violence.

*Envy theory* does not regard the cultural emphasis on cultivating "loving kindness" merely as reflecting sentimental platitudes or moral mandates externally imposed. As a psychological theory, it locates and describes envious processes and their management as part of humankind's genetic, mental/intrapsychic template—dispositions, predispositions, and shaping through environmental learning.

In contrast to some humanistic or faith-based systems that may mandate "loving thy neighbor" and "the obligatory nature of righteous charity," *envy theory* sees helpfulness originating intrapsychically through conscious and intentional self-development. In other words, morals and ethics are imposed principally from within. Outside influences, however, surely offer interesting standards that may reinforce or constrain these inner inclinations. Orchestrating and implementing help requires mutuality, negotiation, and rational strategies between people for it to be carried out successfully. Helpfulness, especially its real-time enactment, transcends being "monetized." Its value may include but goes far beyond what can be neatly calculated in dollars and cents.

From a neuroscience perspective, for example, envy and moral behavior (codes, values, and customs that guide social conduct) appear to correlate with distinct and measurable brain pathways (Mendez 2009). The neurobiology of moral behavior and its neuropsychiatric implications (for example, sociopathy) are grouped into two main categories: (1) no-harm as evidenced by discomfort felt on directly harming others, and (2) on fairness as evidenced by the need to punish those who violate rules of right and wrong. fMRI studies, therefore, are now able to map and measure aspects of the psychology of envy. These suggest phylogenetic origins significant enough to be conserved in the central nervous system.

*Envy theory* takes great pains to uncover the deeper psychological roots motivating empathy, compassion, and helping, especially how these may extend pragmatically in a social manner. Originating intrapsychically and expressed interpersonally, this individually based experience may secondarily promote prosocial behaviors. Helping orientations in individuals, in fact, contribute to stabilizing small groups, large groups, societies, and civilizations. Styles of professional helping—for example, in mental health, law, and religion as modulators of social systems—incorporate traits of helpfulness albeit in characteristically different ways.

Recent studies on the mechanisms and neurobiology of stress and overcoming adversity add to *envy theory*'s emphasis on the positive health value of helpfulness (Rutter 2007; Charney 2004). For example, fear responsiveness, reward and enhanced motivation, and adaptive social behaviors are character traits documented to be associated with resilience. Effective behaviors that, despite fear and learned helplessness, contain optimistic expectations, empathy, and cooperative teamwork correlate with successfully managed stress, individual and group resilience, and positive health outcomes.

## Unblocking the Capacity for Experiencing *Lived Goodness*

Feelings of paused admiration and appreciation, furthermore, free the ego's capacity to receive and identify with the newly perceived goodness now sensed as actually available in the environment. This marks a major developmental and dynamic shift from massive, reflexive projective processes (paranoid-schizoid dynamics) toward the increasingly advantageous, realistic processes of introjection (depressive-position dynamics).

Projection becomes more normalized—less destructive, attacking, egocentric, and narcissistically motivated. More reality-based introjective acceptance now works together with more normalized, less excessive projective mechanisms. A freer flowing emotional conduit is qualitatively established both intrasystemically (self-system: id, ego, and superego), in object relations, and in the interpersonal environment.

*The capacity for introjective processes such as listening, examining, and attempting to take in information—without spoiling it—through more focused efforts at comprehension is strengthened.* This further paves the way for opening one's emotional capacity to receive and experience love more easily and with fewer inhibitions—genuine gratitude. Empathy, compassion, and the capacity to forgive come to the fore. This sense of compassion and benevolence denotes both clemency to one's own self as well as kindness to others.

This newfound receptivity unquestionably extends to all aspects of the personality, especially cognitive functions. Learning fluency on all levels is increasingly unblocked since reflexive spoiling/soiling of incoming information has lessened. Previously experienced states of confusion, inattentiveness, or boredom diminish. These benefits increase proportionally as *the healthy maturation of envy* expands over time. Adaptive learning from experience is significantly increased.

Besides a renewed sense of receptivity, a broader range of insights occurs. This may express itself in a variety of ways, especially after childhood. For example, creative and reparative urges may take the form of aesthetic creations. Hanna Segal (1952) has elegantly described such processes in the developmental achievements previously discussed concerning the depressive position.

The greater capacity to identify, receive, accept, introject, and internalize goodness in all its diverse forms imparts a newfound sense of deep satisfaction—that is, a feeling of being nurtured, and experiencing more frequent states of truly satisfying nurturance. Nurturance includes being fed, feeling loved, and being understood. This also engenders profound feelings arising from the beneficially disarming impact of the more deeply gratifying enjoyment that *lived goodness* inevitably imparts. The self can now feel good—not excessively inferior and bad. This ego feeling, therefore, results in the lessening of negative self-feelings and self-estimations and an increase in healthy self-esteem.

Since perceptions of what was seen as bad and unacceptable are considerably lessened, self-rejection and self-hatred diminish and are partially mitigated. One now begins to feel more lovable. This state of feeling "*loveworthy*" entails a secure feeling that being loved by another is possible, and, in fact, genuinely deserved. "Deserved" in this sense strongly implies "earned." This positive self-regard fosters a series of progressive insights with integrative intrasystemic ramifications. A sense of self-constancy and greater sense of trust in both self and others reinforce one another. This is the foundation for the sense of caring. *Lived goodness* at any age enables one to feel happy when happiness in others is perceived. In addition, the realistic expectation of goodness from others rather than unrealistic anticipations of persecution becomes an internalized attitude.

# The Complexity of Mature Object-Love
# and Interpersonal Love Behavior

The maturational aspects of envy are energized by, modulated by, and work together with the constructive, esteem-promoting forces of love. Love expresses itself as the ability to spare the object intentional harm and more deeply care for its welfare. It is a benevolent attitude marked by ever-increasing empathy and a deepening range of kindness in attitude and tangible action.

Meaningful caring, in the sense proposed here, is not only a theoretical construct but also expresses itself in significantly changed emotional and behavioral dispositions. Impulses, attitudes, and actions that aim toward improving the quality of the life of the object as it exists intrapsychically, intersubjectively, and interpersonally in real time become a more regular part of daily living.

*Object-love is the subjective experience of what may be enacted as love behaviors with real people in the real world.* The joint interaction of one's mental attitude and capacities and the performance they impel attests to the biomental reality of human nature.

The complex experience of love, in this sense, is founded on a strong libidinal cathexis (imputed significance and meaningfulness) of the object. The object can now be experienced as a whole entity differentiated from the ego but experienced as an empathetically apprehended and intersubjectively shared reality. This is an affiliative investment. Its normative ambivalent dimension enduringly rests more on its positive, empathetic, and compassionate pole.

*Love is not understood here, however, in a simplistic way as an "antidote" to a "poisonous" substance—envy.* Envy, in fact, cannot be considered an "enemy." An individual's constitutional complement of primary love is a dispositional given. Love, together with destructiveness, determines one's constitutional proclivity to envy. Love, itself, is a constituent of envy, not simply a cure for it. Psychological work on the self in a pragmatic rather than lofty or romanticized manner enhances love's modulation of personal destructiveness.

*The healthy maturation of envy* is a complex development achieved over time. Through conscious efforts, gradually increasing introspection, self-reflection, and practice, elements derived from primary love may be mobilized and deepened. These developments, together with a wide variety of other reparative factors, coalesce toward achieving attitudes characterized by fairness, sharing, and the impulse to help. In other words, *the healthy maturation of envy* is experienced as an inwardly motivated sense of what may also be termed "righteousness," an attitude of loving kindness expressed in the performance of all forms of helping behaviors. Love becomes the center of gravity for *the healthy maturation of envy*, when it undergoes its complex developmental translation into behavior.

Forced attempts to inculcate "good behavior," whether in thought, attitude, or deed, are not significantly efficacious techniques useful in the modulation of envy. An envy-free psychology is not possible. A psychology that recognizes envy and *the healthy maturation of envy* is a comprehensive psychology. One cannot persuade oneself to be nonenvious just as one cannot significantly teach it to another. Effective and mutative psychotherapy is not achieved through didactic lessons or through homework assignments.

Ultimately mature self-love may be shared on differing personal and interpersonal levels with another (the intrapsychic "object" and the interpersonal concrete other) in mutually enriching ways. Mature self-love, made possible by *the healthy maturation of envy*, makes the experience of nurturance and mature object-love possible in real time. An attitude of benevolence and sense of happiness at the good fortune of others come to the fore as character traits. Nurturance as a mental attitude and an interpersonal behavior then becomes the dynamic process whereby the self is enabled to properly care for itself, and also extend and share this caring in the service of others.

*Spontaneity in the willingness to share and be helpful is an expression of deep-seated empathy and compassion. The capacity to receive nurturance from another is predicated on the ability to be nurturing, especially to oneself. It is normal narcissism, normal self-admiration, normal self-regard, and shared empathetic caring. These personal achievements characterize mature object-love.*

## Interpersonal Relationships and Social Psychology

The culmination of these healthy advances in refining the mind and personal development results in further progress in interpersonal relationships. These are the one-to-one interactions between people. Their extensions to groups—individuals in and making up groups and group-to-group attitudes and behaviors—are grounded in individual construals and actions. When a more positive self-image is established, one is enabled to regard and admire, in increasingly more loving and kindly ways, one's own self. This benevolent attitude begins to extend itself and generalize into attitudes and behaviors in the interpersonal world of social relations.

Admiration of and gratitude to others for freshly perceived positive qualities further evolves into the capacity to feel transitory, participatory, and
emotionally laden identifications—empathy for others. One's scope of concern expands, and a more extensive sense of caring as well as the *implementa-*
*tion of generosity, especially in concrete actions and behaviors,* may progressively
evolve. Mutually beneficial reciprocity and cooperation follow. This generosity may extend beyond the nuclear family. A perception of people initially
seen as strangers reconfigures itself to one that regards others as akin to one's
own self and as potential collaborators. As collaborators working together,
shared goals can become mutually enriching.

*Whereas admiration connotes a more passive sense of appreciation, the sensitiv-*
*ity characteristic of empathy expands this and opens the way for emulation, an ac-*
*tive striving to become like or even better compared to another.* One sees another's
admirable and desirable traits as inspirational models, able to be identified
with, and as personally customizable conscious emulations. This results,
moreover, in a recurring impulse to reciprocate received goodness. Often, *a*
*natural and genuine willingness to help* suggests this change. *Envy theory regards*
*this as the ultimate reflection of normalized envy.*

*The healthy maturation of envy* changes the psychodynamics of mental
mechanisms that sustain one's sense of personal identity, the self. The foundational role of projective identification now operates with a qualitatively
greater emphasis on its introjective, communicative dimension, on empathetic understanding.

One becomes more receptive to oneself, more self-reflective and realistically introspective. The corollary is greater receptivity in the form of
empathetic understanding regarding others. The healthy communicative
functioning of projective identification operates in this manner and is an
important basis for reciprocity, *interdependent cooperation,* and successful interpersonal relationships.

❖

An often asked question is "How does one respond to another when you
sense you are the recipient of envy?"

*The healthy maturation of envy* affords one the ability to quickly sense when
envy in others is mobilized and being projected. Typically, one discerns that
a special occasion or any event of significance is being spoiled. If you are the
target, feeling stunned results. After this period of numbness, a sharp feeling of
disappointment, hurt, and bewilderment follows. Soon an impulse to respond
in kind—with anger and violence—arises. Outside the therapeutic situation, in
everyday life, the best strategy to use is to pause and try to consciously recognize

and identify the way envy is operating in the other and having some effect on you, the recipient.

In general, *leaving the field for a time or longer is the only way to best manage such situations.* Trying to reason with the other only increases envy and risks further confusing envious attacks. Putting distance between the envier and the person feeling the spoiling attack tends to settle heated emotions. The recipient of such an attack can only ponder, perhaps consult with disinterested others, about what happened to make sense of such a baffling event. If another future contact with the envier arises, whether or not to discuss the envy dilemma, let alone continue the contact, rests on personal judgment. Only in a contained psychotherapy setting can envy be managed in more direct and therapeutic ways. This needs ample time. Effective handling of envy, of course, hinges on the skill, patience, and empathy of the therapist.

❖

Social psychology has its emphasis on behavioral action, especially interpersonal and intergroup attraction and repulsion. This psychology of groups develops out of an individual's past history of learning within groups, the primary group being the family. From this base, experiences in extended groups (peers, society, and the larger cultural context) further develop the personality and add to a sense of group membership, belonging to a community.

Social norms arise out of and are perpetuated by groups. These norms are made of expectations regarding what are viewed as typical role behaviors and, in addition, ideal, valued behaviors. The aim of these norms is maintaining and dynamically restructuring the group's survival. This occurs through adherence to social norms and their implied social constraints.

A natural, inverse correlation between individual (self) and group (civilization) aims results from differing priorities. In and between both, tensions arise. Conflicts caused by the struggle between conformity/compliance and deviation/oppositionality produce individual malaise and socially instigated discontent. Such experiential dissonance requires homeostatic regulatory guidelines by legal construction and democratic participation. To be accepted and effective, it must come from both directions. Hence, change is stirred on individual and social levels.

*Envy theory* contributes to a better understanding of the intersection between individual and social psychology, viewed not as competing paradigms, but mutually enlightening companions. The apparent challenges posed are opportunities that may set the stage for the potential salutary interventions implied in *envy theory*.

## Transcending the Constrictiveness of Envy: Self-Leadership and Mental Health

*The healthy maturation of envy* fosters mental health. A series of transformations occurs: states of passivity, helplessness, avolition, inferiority, withholding, resentment, and unrealistically feeling hurt, assaulted, and victimized transform to become attitudes of active self-competence, self-effectance, potency, self-esteem, and equitable sharing. Trust in one's capacity to change is a decisive factor enabling this advance. As successful ego integration brings about more self-cohesiveness, higher degrees of self-organization and single-mindedness are achieved.

*Personal competence, a developed capacity to bring about desired results in effective ways, launches a sense of leadership over the self. This quality of personal agency reinforces more consciously active self-reflection and goal-directedness whose locus of control is self-dependent rather than sought from the outside.* Feeling happiness and a measure of contentment, especially when seeing the happiness and good fortune of others, increases. By contrast, envy, if left unchecked, tends to destabilize the personality by weakening the integrative impulses that maintain ego containment and stable self-identity.

As envy gradually transfigures over time, a more consistent and unified sense of self is established. The whole personality responds with a gradually deepening capacity for the enjoyment of all aspects of living, as repeated experiences of being loved and, in turn, becoming more loving are activated and consolidated. Along with an overall upgrading in the functioning of the entire personality, a sense of self-leadership in the management of life is more confidently felt and successfully implemented. Integrity and strength of character reflect these developmental advances. A wise adage suggests that the love one receives reflects somehow the quality of love one bestows.

A sufficient recognition of the ubiquity of the envy dynamic is necessary for personal freedom. *Self-leadership* is the capacity to feel—with conviction—a sense of self-determination. Creativity in motivation becomes more psychologically available. A robust capacity for experiencing a clearer range of preferential choices rather than having to respond in habitual ways to rigid and narrow demands in thinking and feeling emerges as creativity increasingly informs personal choice. *Volition* in real-world performance is enhanced.

*The entire conception of envy presented here, moreover, rather than being inimical to a healthy model of mental functioning, underscores and reinforces a positive, constructive, life-promoting, and enhanced "quality of life" conception of human potential and its advancement. Acknowledging the influence of envy in the human condition is a realistic value appraisal that includes both the positive and negative psychological inclinations undeniably present in human nature.*

## Insight as a Prelude to Enlightenment: Wisdom in Everyday Living

Understanding the role of envy in human affairs is essential to any psychological, social, and behavioral perspective. As well, it can influence the development of an array of various interventions sustainably therapeutic. Therapeutic connotes degrees of resolution of conflict, repair of and relief from emotional trauma, restoration of a working mental equilibrium, enhancement of current strengths and potentials, and fostering the development of new mental resources, leading to more adaptive feeling, thinking, and behavioral skills in everyday living.

In psychoanalytic terms, ego integration and reparation are the principal aims that bring about advances (particularly facilitated by psychotherapies) in the quality of life. Achievements include strengthening a weakened ego, lifting repression by extending more conscious knowledge of the self as a whole, lessening the conscious and unconscious sense of suffering, and direct confrontation with and mitigation of internal destructiveness.

Achieving these therapeutic outcomes results in a better quality of life in specific and broader ways. Positive change—mental and behavioral—enhances quality of life. Besides learning and developing more refined information-processing skills, another level of psychological cognition—insight—is specific to the acquisition of knowledge derived from psychodynamically informed psychotherapies.

Developmental strengths across the lifespan accrue from genetic endowments, constitutional traits, and learned abilities. Insight produces dual expansions of covert mental abilities: skill know-how (adaptive capacity) and skill intelligence (the quality of cognitive infrastructure efficiency). These newly activated mental abilities express themselves behaviorally as performance skill competencies. Hence, insight produces functional outcomes not only in generating and uncovering covert mental abilities and observable successful behaviors but also in enhancing the overall quality of life. *Adaptive intelligence* is enhanced (Ninivaggi 2005, 2010).

*Experiential insight* is the intellectual and emotional understanding of the meaning and significance of previously unrecognized aspects of one's life. It is marked by highly charged cognitive and emotional convictions resulting from enduring reconfigurations of experiential outlook. Intermittent moments of insight ordinarily follow a sequential process—surprise, shock, amazement, mental pain, ambivalence, working through over time, and consolidation.

I use the term "insight" in a specific way, to denote a "moment of meaning" from which proceeds degrees of overall personal change. This may occur somehow at any developmental level certainly in very different ways. The term "insight" ordinarily connotes mental change in the postinfancy period, when language, introspection, and self-reflection are clearly more available and can be used as conscious psychological tools. Insight is an advanced achievement of substantial success in working through and mastering, at least, some aspects of the depressive position. Insight, typically an adult experience, indicates a deeper understanding of a variety of real-life issues. It reflects maturity, adaptive learning from experience, and degrees of wisdom. Insight connotes making contact with one's personal truth. Real insight is hallmarked by feelings that are "breathtaking" and stunning. Insight causes pause in the arresting grip of hitherto unrealized meaning.

Insight is not merely intellectual understanding; nor is insight solely the cognitive acquisition of new information. It is *a deep emotional reconfiguration of the understandability of the self in multiple contexts: self with self, self with others, and self in the environment.* As such, previous states of distressing ambiguity become demystified, new problem-solving strategies are realized, and quantum shifts toward a higher quality of life are set in motion.

The psychological concept of insight, moreover, should not be confused with the broader, perhaps more philosophical, concept of "enlightenment." An explicit distinction helps clarify the nature of the psychological changes resulting from the maturation of envy as discussed in this book.

Enlightenment represents a broad-based, sustained qualitative achievement characterized by enduring insight on a long-term basis, what I would call psychological *insight constancy.* This is a cultivated state of mind that can be equated with the notion of emotional and intellectual maturity developed over a lifetime of effective learning from experience. It connotes wisdom. It is not a final product, but rather a state of continuing achievements. This naturally includes the cognitive enrichment imparted by education and life experience in addition to the emotional and social learning that accrues from interactions with others. Emphasis rests on achievements of *sustainable* psychological learning. This insight is an understanding with deepening conviction occurring intermittently over time.

Enlightenment as a conception represents more a theoretical psychological achievement toward which one may aspire. It includes, accordingly, the broad range of personal, interpersonal, and social successes both cognitive and emotional that result from a life both satisfying and well lived. It is not merely restricted to momentary insights achieved through introspection, self-analysis, and mental exercise.

*Enlightenment, in many ways, is fluidity of consciousness. Experience becomes free floating to a greater degree—that is, emotionally diverse and cognitively less constrained. This denotes that attention is not inextricably attached to any specific object or groups of objects—for example, material resources, ideologies, and so forth. Healthy, intelligent desire makes objects of desire easily dissociable.* Enlightenment is a continually occurring state of becoming more deeply enlightened.

Insight, in contrast to enlightenment, describes a moment of the experience of meaning, characterized as a new understanding and marked by significant psychological awareness and partial mental restructuring. It is a direct look at the meaning of an experience. This direct look, in effect, is experienced as a novel discovery. Enlightenment, by contrast, denotes a higher level of accumulated and integrated insights and qualitative advances in adaptive psychological maturity sustainable on a daily basis.

Enlightenment, in the broadest psychological sense, is a characterological attitude marked by feelings of authenticity and meaningfulness that accompany activities of daily living and one's overarching reflection on their value. Insight may be viewed as the moment-to-moment tactic used in the overall strategy of sustaining enlightenment as an enduring psychological-mindedness. This attitude represents the continual achievement of wisdom in everyday living.

Achieving insight, though difficult, may be an intermittent triumph in comprehension that results from self-discipline and solid work aimed at optimizing one's personal best. States of enlightenment, in contrast, reflect enduring qualitative advances in mental integration, organization, and overall functional performance. These sustainable successes, like states of insight, occur in degrees, but, overall, may be much less common. In fact, one could consider them as values or guidelines used to approximate rather than "absolutely" consummate.

Insights accumulated over time, for example, in psychotherapeutic situations pointedly facilitate *the healthy maturation of envy*. Working toward achieving insight may be a more realistic expectation than the goal of achieving enlightenment. *The healthy maturation of envy* enhances the capacity for and probability of achieving increased insight over time. Such cognitive, emotional, and intuitive insight is an underlying precedent to an individual's overall adaptability to any situation, especially changing contexts.

Insight into personal motivation also becomes enhanced by *the healthy maturation of envy*. Motivation is a highly complex set of directing operations triggered by internally generated tissue/biological needs plus cognitive-emotional desires and externally recognized environmental incentives. Motivations arise from both what is innate and what is learned. Deepening degrees of wisdom as a sustained characterological attitude may emerge when insights are integrated with solid reality-based adaptations in everyday living over time. Efforts expended toward goals produce higher quality outcomes since one's performance platform, the infrastructure of mental processes, becomes recalibrated from the primitive dynamics of envy to admiration, emulation, and empathetic reciprocity.

## The Role of *Envy Theory* in Practice: *Envy Management Skills*

Psychoeducation is an educational strategy with therapeutic value that directly informs the patient/client about a variety of issues relevant to mental health and quality of life. In psychiatry, it may include information about mental disorders, their signs and symptoms, and the extensive interventions (psychosocial, psychopharmacological, self-help, dietary, hygiene, legal, and so forth) used to prevent, treat, and manage them. The goal of psychoeducation is to provide people with a practical approach to understanding and coping with illness, especially its prevention and consequences.

*Envy management skills* are a construct derived from *envy theory*. They comprise a form of psychoeducation. Psychoeducation, though often considered an important part of interventions within psychiatry, is not psychotherapy. It is a form of learning using conscious cognitive processes to convey and teach the logic and reasons for diagnoses and treatments. The unconscious dynamics of envy are not directly addressed. The acquisition of *envy management skills*, however, can be used alone or complement formal psychotherapies, even though these different approaches are distinct in aim and technique.

*Envy management skills* are psychological strategies and behavioral guidelines that can be taught as principles and models to facilitate adaptive coping skills, especially in social contexts. Two fundamental principles are (1) illustrating that change as such is real, inevitable, possible, and desirable; this helps restructure negative (malevolent or grim) expectations that have become chronic mind sets; and (2) exploring a set of alternative choices—cooperation, reciprocation, and sharing—in various contexts where disruptive envy is apt to emerge.

Respect and citizenship perspectives underlie these alternative choices. Respect is both an attitude and behavior that includes recognizing boundaries between persons, paused reflection in the face of interpersonal differences, and empathetic listening. Citizenship connotes behaviors that reflect an individual's respectful and helpful participation in smaller (family, peer, classroom) and larger (neighborhood, community, society) group situations. These principles emphasize that sustainable successes always require a "win-win" motivation and shared, favorable outcome. The value of equitable justice between people and within groups is addressed in this way.

*Envy management skills* helps people reorient motivation from subliminal pessimism and stagnation based on resentment, negativity, and destructive behaviors (attack, cheating, stealing, and dishonesty) toward more enthusiastic, flexible, option-focused thinking, and the anticipation of mutually enriching outcomes. *Envy management skills*, for example, may be especially useful for children and adolescents. A more sustainable development of these pragmatic skills is achieved by those techniques that emphasize the linguistic identification, clarification, and recognition of envy in everyday life.

Most clinical presentations have hidden aspects of envy. The demonstrated application of *envy theory* in a skills-based psychotherapeutic setting, for example, has a greater chance of being effective if *envy theory* is an explicit consideration in diagnosis, evaluation, and treatment planning. Since *nuclear envy* is unconscious, only its derivatives can be addressed. This counterpart side typically consists of situations characterized by frustration and deprivation, envy-specific amplifiers. These cognitive approaches use the secondary processes of logic and reasoning to achieve intellectual familiarity rather than the enduring conviction of emotional insight that develops in psychodynamic treatments over time. Any mode of therapy, however, that mitigates envy's sharp edge is worthwhile.

The face of modern civilization and the practice of psychotherapy over a wide range of populations, especially with children and youth, make including *envy management skills* a compelling consideration. *Envy management skills* is psychoeducation, not psychotherapy; therefore its goals and effects differ. Child guidance techniques with explicit psychoeducational aims (for example, defining and recognizing feelings, identifying triggers for specific feelings, and teaching coping skills) can also benefit from using the insights gleaned from psychodynamically informed envy management strategies.

Psychoeducation has a protective effect. As a *primary prevention*, it may decrease the incidence of envy-related problems. *Secondary prevention* using cognitive techniques incorporating principles of *envy management skills* may help lower the rate of malignant envy by early detection. The *tertiary level of illness prevention* directly treats established cases and so decreases the complications that may arise from latent envy. It behooves the astute clinician to recognize that, even in cases of apparent school difficulties or borderline intellectual functioning, the presence of important aspects of unconscious envy may be among the primary reasons for a child's difficulties (Ninivaggi 2005, 2009).

## Treatment Resistance Reconsidered

Psychological treatment resistance is not uncommon. Resistance toward change and recovery in a patient may be defined as the refusal to accept a new idea, take on a new attitude, and develop a new way of behaving. This opposition has both conscious and unconscious components. It impedes progress in a therapeutic relationship. Distressing attitudes, irresolvable conflicts, maladaptive personality patterns, and many mental disorders appear resistant to change.

Theoretically, it reflects the unconscious process of obdurate splitting. This prevents recognition of the unconscious determinants behind distressing and problematic conscious ideas, feelings, and behaviors. Resistance reflects the state of information maintained unconsciously—in repression. It serves a defensive function since the ego resists easily acquiring unconscious information that it fears may provoke feelings of danger, especially anxiety about the unmanageable unknown. It also reflects the nonconscious id's wish to maintain and repeat maladaptive processes (the "repetition compulsion") and, in effect, through the superego, to sustain the need for punishment and suffering, the self-spoiling action of unconscious envy.

Even with the advent of advanced psychopharmacological interventions, many children, adolescents, and adults remain impaired both psychologically and behaviorally. Recent studies paint a less than enthusiastic picture about the entire conception of mental illness and its treatment with psychopharmacological agents (Belmaker 2008; Horwitz and Wakefield 2007; Rush 2007).

Approaches that have a decidedly strong behavioral or cognitive orientation, alone, may also not have sufficient impact to produce effective change. The psychiatric treatment of depression, for example, includes the phrase "treatment-resistant depression" (TRD). Patients enter into a behavioral state of psychomotor retardation that includes anhedonia, an inability to feel pleasure and satisfaction and the loss of ordinary volition. TRD is recognized as an unmet medical need despite available therapies.

Psychopharmacological treatment resistance ordinarily connotes a failure to achieve at least a 30 percent reduction in symptomatology after two adequate courses of treatment, using medication and sometimes including psychotherapy, have been tried. An extreme form of nonresponsiveness is termed "treatment refractoriness." It is an almost complete failure to achieve any degree of improvement after three or more adequate trials of combined psychopharmacological interventions along with conjoint psychotherapies.

In fact, it is estimated that, although about two-thirds of treated depressed patients, for example, manifest an initial remission, after twelve months the relapse rate approaches 40 percent (Rush, Trivedi, Wisniewski, et al. 2006). Residual symptoms such as fatigue, concentration problems, sleep distur- bances, suididality, appetite and weight problems, guilt and worthlessness, depressed mood, anhedonia, anxiety, pain, vasomotor irregularities, sexual dysfunction, and excessive daytime sleepiness remain (Stahl 2008). Ad- ditionally, when hoarding is the prominent feature of obsessive-compulsive disorders, deeply entrenched envy may be a root factor and result in serious treatment resistance.

Nonetheless, newer and novel biological treatments are being offered for such challenging clinical situations. Advanced interventions, some requiring surgery, are neuroscience-based and include deep brain stimulation, neuro- genesis stimulators, and glutamate receptor antagonists. Research in expand- ing psychiatric treatment effectiveness is ongoing (Sanacora 2008).

Good treatment is comprehensive treatment effecting substantial and enduring change so that impairments in functioning and mental suffering are lessened. *Envy theory* suggests that all psychological therapies would benefit greatly from *including* a psychodynamic dimension. Recognition of unconscious processes, some exploration of these, and a joint interpretive articulation of relevant subliminal attitudes and personal meanings are es- sential components to effective treatments whose aim is facilitating sustain- able improvement, especially the achievement of an enduring good quality of life.

*Many treatment-resistant situations reach an impasse because their unyielding nidus may rest on insufficiently recognized and, therefore, unmanaged envy.* The "negative therapeutic reaction" is one such example. I submit that many cases of apparent "depression" are not depression proper but rather envy- based dysphorias. Intractable obsessional states may also have important roots in envy. They are fueled by projective identification and the feverish need to tenaciously control what has been mentally placed outside the self into some object that then takes on a compelling attractiveness, even if it generates frustration and intense anxiety.

In addition, any psychological disorder marked by self-endangerment, self- defeating choices and behaviors, self-undermining, and recalcitrance may have a strong dispositional envy load. Effective psychotherapies, therefore, need to recognize the existence and debilitating impingement of envy on mental functioning and interpersonal relationships. Therapies that recognize envy are optimized when they occur in the psychological intimacy of a professional, interpersonal relationship sensitive to the subtle as well as manifest expressions of unconscious *nuclear envy*. A therapeutic context such as this has the potential to mitigate envy's negative impact on mental functioning and behavior, and enhance successful adaptation in real life situations. Quality of life on all levels thus has a greater chance to improve.

A final note on the therapy of envy reminds us that the modulation of excessive omnipotence not only applies to the patient but also the therapist. It would be incorrect for a therapist to believe that he or she could directly change a patient's psychology. Such an attitude suggests degrees of omnipotence incompatible with reality.

*Proper therapeutic efforts, however, aim to create conditions that offer opportunities facilitating the patient's own, inwardly motivated impulses toward change.* Both spontaneous and intentionally instigated changes in the experience of envy primarily reside within the patient. A therapeutic position characterized by mental and emotional equanimity, observation, and judicious and reflective comments based on reasonable clinical evidence is optimal. This attitude may act to clarify the extent to which *the healthy maturation of envy* may be unfolding.

## Summary

In addition to advancing the proposition of *nuclear envy* as a ballast central in human psychological development, a qualified yet encouraging analysis of envy's potential healthy maturation is offered. For these reasons, this may be the most important, if not pragmatic, chapter in this book. A discriminative consideration and prudent use of *envy theory* is advanced. This review points to a range of potential achievements that may occur. In fact, these aims are approximations since *the healthy maturation of envy* is a lingering, lifetime enterprise. Theory rather than detailed technique is addressed.

Vulnerability to envy's pitfalls is an unpleasant psychological fact; yet significant change toward envy's healthy maturation remains a real possibility. Significant personal change is always challenging. People's natural inclination is maintaining a personal status quo, where living remains unconsidered and self-directed volition is sparse. Change requires significant attitudinal shifts from passivity to becoming active and assuming a self-determined locus of control.

Reasons prompting change are complex. Unexpected life crises, notably losses, for example, are not uncommon; these occurrences especially provide substantial opportunities for change. Change and self-exploration go to-gether. All these attend pursuits toward *the healthy maturation of envy*.

Core psychic shifts that foster *the healthy maturation of envy* are outlined. These principal changes pivot around the increasing integration of the ego. Integration increases as envy diminishes. Normalized projective identifi-cation, essential for ego integration, denotes the defusion of omnipotent control on all experiential and interpersonal levels. When projective iden-tification relaxes, less idiosyncratic material colors experience. Receptivity to new learning is enhanced. Excessive egocentricity abates and narcissistic self-centeredness becomes modulated so that a realistic grasp of others in the overall context of relatedness may occur. This becomes the basis for a more realistic distinction between and *appreciation* of inner world and outer reality. Balanced discrimination, pause, and mental equanimity character-ize this. Negative bias in information processing is superseded by a greater sensitivity to the positive, mutually beneficial aspects of interpersonal contexts.

As excessive splitting and idealization diminish, the ego gradually comes to grips with a more direct realization of the variety of destructive impulses indigenous to its mental life. *Nuclear love* in all its permutations comes to the fore and defuses *nuclear envy* of its spoiling bias. As momentary insights emerging from this accrue, more enduring psychological-mindedness devel-ops into *insight constancy*. This functions as wisdom in everyday living.

Using Melanie Klein's model of the paranoid-schizoid and the depressive positions, attention is called to the salient psychodynamic features that the ego traverses in relation to the object. This construct illustrates the psycho-logical drama of how self organizes structurally and functionally; in other words, how attitudes of love, hate, and envy toward others in infancy and adulthood shape personality.

The sound and fury of the internal death instinct's leitmotif is put in bold relief. This expresses itself as envy's inner dialogue, which plays itself out in the developmental inception of and later expressions of the *narcissistic position of envy*. This construct illustrates the ego's aggressive assaults on its objects, resulting in persecutory guilt and the arresting shock that a full real-ization of this destructive spoiling brings.

As continuing ego integration—patience and security—occurs, the re-parative urges in depressive-position dynamics—empathy and compassion—are released. Intentionality and volition are enabled toward actionable aims. Sublimations mix with sorrow and concern. This brings about both self and object repairs and restorations. As superego organization begins to detoxify its envy load through the greater integration made possible by increased libidinal forces in the ego, the ego itself becomes increasingly freer. It is less constrained by the dictates of envy and persecution from the sadistic super-ego. This flexibility launches a renewed appreciation of both itself and its objects. Anxiety and fear diminish.

*The healthy maturation of envy*, for example, is reflected in *aesthetic creations*— paintings, sculpture, music, dance, and poetry. It is here in aesthetics that the interplay of *nuclear envy* and *nuclear love* display their potentials for creativeness. The artist opens himself to receive inspiration from unconscious processes, transform them, and offer them as works of art to others.

The roots of aesthetic sensitivity, moreover, are laid down when the ego acknowledges both its goodness—beauty and benevolence—and inescapable but manageable destructiveness—ugliness and cruelty. In dialectical and re-parative fashion, these underlie creativity. Hanna Segal (1991) has elegantly discussed creativity in aesthetics in relation to the depressive position. *Envy theory* further illustrates this idea.

Such artistic productions are not primarily entertaining or merely decora-tive. They provoke in the viewer a need for psychological work on uncon-scious levels. Art is similar to dreaming in that a major aim of both is to work toward resolution of conflict and reduce confusion. Art, however, is unlike the dream in that the dream occurs in sleep where dreamwork is done by the unconscious ego.

Art, by contrast, requires enormous conscious intention reflected in the need for actual materials and their technical and logistical handling. All great works of art are produced by the artist's struggle to work, rework, create, recreate, and incarnate in the palpable world an ideal with missing parts that has its origins on unconscious levels. Such art has a sublime quality—like waves crashing on the beach that you can never still; they inspire awe—a feeling that the art does not need *you* since it is so far greater. Art reaches the beyond. It embraces in sentient awareness its nonconscious vitality. This is the subtle appeal of great art.

Cognitive functions expand and refine themselves as envy's lock on in-formation processing is released. Attention restructures its selectivity so it may now apprehend experience as increasingly more meaningful. The *epis-temophilia* within the self fosters a greater appreciation of similarities rather than highlighting differences. Differences both good and bad are appreciated; they are viewed as unified spectrums of normative variations. This cognitive and affective emphasis on unity then becomes more spontaneously experi-enced. This interpretive reframing is not a single or one-time event. Rather, this gradual experiential refinement extends its influence over a lifetime. Increased integration connotes the ability to experience the self as abidingly singular rather than a changing series of psychological pluralities. Mental stability thus consolidates.

Motivational urges arising from the epistemophilic impulse can foster significant change. Personal crises typically also offer opportunities that can stimulate change. These dual concepts are emphasized since personal change is exceedingly difficult and often requires extraordinary "shocks" both inner and outer.

Gratitude, which signals *the healthy maturation of envy*, becomes felt as the manageable tolerance of, profound appreciation of, and thankful regard for the simultaneous existence of goodness and badness in both self and object. What is offered is felt as both satisfying and enjoyable. This reconciliation eventually makes ambivalence no longer a stronghold of indecisiveness; its normalization enriches the capacity for a nuanced empathy. The withholding of love that envy had defensively instigated now releases its strictures. A greater capacity for what I call *lived goodness* comes to the forefront of the personality as freer flowing receptivity and expressivity; in other words, attentiveness to all that others offer is matched by generous reciprocation. Intrasubjective integration galvanizes itself; and intersubjectively shared communicational conduits are opened.

*Lived goodness* empowers feelings of happiness at the good fortune of others. Expectations about others, for example, become more positive rather than unrealistic, persecutory, malevolent, and grim. Transcending the constrictions that envy had imposed simultaneously fosters self-compassion and increasingly greater degrees of mental health. This, in effect, engenders the impetus, capacity, and greater willingness to engage more actively in mature "object-love relations." Greater reciprocity and more cooperation on real life interpersonal and social levels ensue. Helpful attitudes and pragmatic behaviors become more commonplace. *Envy theory* emphasizes that helpfulness—especially to those perceived as "strangers" outside one's group identity—is the empirical reflection of *the healthy maturation of envy*.

*Envy theory* helps bridge individual and social psychology. When the dynamics of love, hate, and envy are understood in their intrapsychic and object-related psychodynamic perspectives, their expressions in behavior, especially interpersonal attraction and repulsion, take on clearer meaning. Knowledge of these principles is an empowering instrument for positive change. Applications to social situations are numerous. Using envy-informed strategies in groups of any size can act to sublimate primitive impulses, enhance prosocial perspectives, and forge actionable policies.

Self-leadership and a greater range of creativity in motivation reinforce one another. Benevolent interpersonal, social, and occupational activities as well as pleasures in general are felt in more rewarding and reinforcing ways. Directed effort and intentional volition toward chosen goals take on an amplified trajectory for success. Personal will and "willpower" are enhanced. This has pragmatic value with real-life consequences.

Child and adolescent psychotherapies that include and thoughtfully use the diagnostic and treatment aspects of *envy theory* can be developed. Out of these, a range of *envy management skills* may provide a helping resource yielding more effective outcomes. Considerations of and studies based on *envy theory* may demonstrate the value of this therapeutic perspective in leading to lasting benefits, especially in situations where "treatment resistance" had been a stumbling block to change. In other words, *envy theory* asserts that *the healthy maturation of envy* constitutes "disease modifying treatment," not merely palliation.

# PART III

# ENVY IN HISTORY AND LITERATURE

# CHAPTER TEN

# Recognizing Envy:
# Historical and Clinical Contexts

## Overview: Seeing the Unmasked
## Face of Envy: A Challenge

Unconscious envy rarely appears discretely or transparently. When excessive, it stirs as a subtle undercurrent, a silent presence almost undetectable. Cloaked in obscurity, envy nonetheless works to undermine the integrity of people's sense of self, view of others, and, by extension, creative and productive interpersonal dialogue. Inevitably, this results in inhibitions, resentment, and confusing communication. These not only impair the smooth functioning of the envier's own mental equanimity but also play into and may alter the course of events in social and historical contexts.

Envy in history and narratives from biblical literature, illustrated below, produces twists in the direction history and culture take. In fact, many customs and beliefs gleaned from anthropological research may have their origins in the social impact resulting from envy's penetrating dynamics. While envy blinds insight, it also complicates and gives texture to human social dramas. Envy inevitably emerges in every contact between people and among groups.

Central themes in this book can be illustrated by culling selected examples from literature, mythology, philosophy, and the history of religion to illustrate unconscious dynamics, the dialectical interaction of id as passion and ego as reason, and the power of envy in shaping history. These examples, far from being exhaustive, portray the dramatic, inhibiting, and disruptive operations of envy.

John Milton, in his famous *Paradise Lost*, Book V, v.658–663 (1667 [1975, 131]), says:

> Satan, so call him now, his former name
> Is heard no more in heav'n; he of the first,
> If not the first Archangels great in power,
> In favor and pre-eminence, yet fraught
> With envy against the Son of God.

William Langland paints an early illustration of envy in the Middle English allegorical narrative poem *Piers Plowman* (w.ca. 1360–1399). Two men, one with malignant envy and the other with obvious greed, meet an elf who promises to bestow one of them with a wish only if the first candidate wisher agrees that the other be granted twice as much of the wish as the first. The greedy man decides to permit the envious one to make the first wish. The envious man wishes for blindness in one of his eyes so that the other, whom we assume he envies, becomes completely blind. This tale cleverly exemplifies the self-destructive and spoiling thrust of envy.

Another example of envy's themes is found in Friedrich Nietzsche's first book, *Die Geburt der Tradodie aus dem Geiste der Musik* (*The Birth of Tragedy from the Spirit of Music*) (1872 [1999]). Here he argues that Greek tragedy arose from the fusion of "Apollonian" and "Dionysian" elements, the former representing measure, restraint, and harmony, and the latter unbridled passion. He added his belief that Socratic rationalism brought about the death of Greek tragedy (passion). These ideas emphasize the power of the structures of the mind represented by what psychoanalytic psychology calls id (passion) and ego (reason). A central theme in Nietzsche's worldview is recognition of the id's passion expressed in literature being rationalized out of existence by the impact of excessive restraint and measured thoughtfulness—actions of the ego.

Last, *envy theory* suggests that envy, as such, is not "absolutely" destructive. The measure of destructiveness in envy, for example, is suggested in the frequent association between envy and the color green. The exact origins of this link are obscure. They are part of common folklore reflected in phrases such as "green with envy," "green with nausea," envy as a "green-eyed monster," and "the grass is always greener on the other side." The positive connotations of the color green, by contrast, are clearly connected to the greenery of nature, which implies growth and creativity, as well as green having been chosen as the standard color of all United States currency notes, implying the potential for wealth and prosperity.

## Envy and Mythology: The Dragon

Mythology, an imaginative invention reflecting psychological themes, often expresses universal preoccupations, especially conflicts, whose origins remain hidden in their fanciful presentations. These beliefs are formidably demonstrated in a variety of quasi-mysterious cultural traditions often characterized by commanding symbols.

Myths may take the form of a variety of oral or written narratives, ritualized behaviors, and concrete objects having symbolic, typically religious or perhaps supernatural, significance. Although myths employ a wide variety of motifs and recurring designs, they often express a limited number of relationships. Existing in every society, myths appear as basic constituents of culture. Hence, the examination of myths yields insight into psychology, society, and civilization.

Anthropologically and mythologically, envy has been represented in a variety of ways as a "green-eyed monster." In ancient times, cultures having no discernible geographical or communicational access to one another have produced similar mythological constructs taking the form of the dragon. The mind—in all cultures—conjures similar collective symbols. It dips into the unconscious and pulls together elements of universally shared meaning with commonly held significance. In both Eastern and Western mythologies, the figure of the dragon is found. Interestingly, these similarly powerful portrayals have distinctly contrasting meaning.

The dragon universally has been portrayed as serpent-like, having prominent, sharp, penetrating eyes, and linked with a kind of imperial power, evil in Western mythology and majestic in the East. The dragon's nature is not emotionally responsive and feeling—not mammalian—but reptilian, implying survival, fear, eating, and mating. Dragons are linked antithetically with creativity and destruction. The strength and power of the dragon's imperious forcefulness strongly connote the workings of envy.

In Eastern cultures—for example, China—it is associated in positive ways with fecundity, unrivaled wisdom, spontaneous changes in form, and invisibility. The superiority and splendor of Chinese emperors were explicitly identified as emanating from their dragon-nature in an almost literal sense. The dragon was for a long time the symbol of the Chinese nation. In traditional Chinese medicine, the gallbladders of snakes (in the East, a form of dragon) are still used as powerful medicines. In Buddhism, the term *mahanaga* (great dragon) is often used as a synonym for Buddha. In Hindu-Buddhist traditions, *nagas* (snakes) were believed to be powerful guardians of esoteric wisdom imparted only to a select superior few—for example, the luminary, Nagarjuna, second/third-century AD physician, philosopher, priest, and founder of Mahayana Buddhism.

In contrast, Western cultures see the dragon more diabolically. For example, the legendary Saint George (circa AD 300), patron saint of England, is classically portrayed as prevailing over and subduing a dragon that, in legend, was mythologized as attacking young, innocent, and pregnant damsels. One of the earliest cultures (circa 4000 BC), the Sumerian-Babylonian, relates an early creation tale of the god, Marduk, in conflict with the menacing dragon, Tiamat. Marduk prevailed and the dragon became his agent. An interesting side note is that some renditions of this tale describe Tiamat as the serpentine heavenly Mother who was displaced by the newer deity, Marduk, her son.

*Envy theory* suggests that the image and connotations the dragon evokes are universally shared symbols reflecting the operation of both the creative and destructively spoiling aspects of *nuclear envy*: namely, the mysterious dialectic at the core of primary conflict—the power of creativeness/love and that of destructiveness/envy and hate.

## Zoroastrianism, An Ancient Root of World Religions

The Zoroastrian religion of ancient Persia (modern-day Iran) has striking parallels to modern-day Judaism, Christianity, and Islam (Boyce 1979, 1990; Zaehner 1961; Boyce 2001; Godrej 2002). It is a root religion whose origins date from 1500 to 1200 BC in the Azerbaijan province near northwest Iran. It was the state religion of ancient Persia during the Sasanian period (AD 227–651) until its decline after AD 633 when the Muslims entered Persia, which then converted to Islam. When Zoroastrianism was at its Babylonian height at about 600 BC, a rigid dualism between good and evil appears to have consolidated.

The foundational Zoroastrian scripture, *Avesta*, is a compilation of historical, medical, legal, and liturgical texts (*Gathas*) composed over a one-thousand-year period. It was transmitted verbally from generation to generation until AD 400, when the Sasanid rulers had parts of it written in an archaic language called "Avestan," which is related to Sanskrit. This remains the only surviving example of these ancient, historical scriptures.

Zarathusthra (Greek name, Zoroaster) (circa 1500–1200 BC) is named as the founder of the Zoroastrian religion. He emerged out of a mass migration of Aryan peoples from Eastern Europe and central Asia southward into Persia. The modern name "Iran" means land of the Aryans, which translates as "noble ones." Others from this migration descended into India and mixed with the indigenous Dravidian or Dasa peoples to eventually produce the Hindu culture and medical system termed "Ayurveda." Alternative anthropological studies strongly suggest significantly more indigenous origins of Hindu culture (Ninivaggi 2001, 2008).

Some scholars believe Zoroastrianism was the first organized belief system to introduce the novel idea of monotheism in Western civilization (Duchesne-Guillemin 1988, 2006). This centrally positioned monotheistic proposition had an unequal, subordinate, and dialectical dualism as its leading subcategory, which typically eclipses its underlying monism. It has been called a nonabsolute monotheism. This was a departure from the previous Indo-Persian polytheism, and may be understood as the first formalization of nonbiblical monotheism.

One version of Zoroastrianism describes the divine creator by such names as "Zurvan," "Ahura Mazda," "Ormazd," and "Asha" (Truth). Zurvanism is theorized to be as close to monotheism as possible since Zurvan is held to be beyond good and evil. In one traditional chronology, Ahura Mazda produced twin sons named "Spenta Mainyu" (Beneficent Spirit or Mind) and "Angra Mainyu" (Destructive Spirit or Mind). The underlying dualism in the universe involved the perpetual battle for power between Ahura Mazda ("Wise Lord," creator of light and goodness working through Spenta Mainyu) and Angra Mainyu (the Destructive Spirit). Whether this set of dual principles were originally viewed as cosmic/ontological or ethical/psychological or both remains unclear.

The Destructive Spirit's essential nature was expressed in his principal epithet—"Druj," translated as "the Lie." This evil force was also known as "Ahriman" in the Pavlavi dialect of ancient Persian. It connotes absolute materialism devoid of spiritual, ethical, and moral qualities. The Lie expressed itself as greed, indignation, resentment, wrath, lust, and envy. Often, only three terms described its action: greed, anger, and envy. The five greatest ethical mandates countering the Lie were (1) truth, (2) generosity, (3) virtues that countered the Lie's greed, envy, anger, and shamefulness, (4) diligence, and (5) charitable advocacy (helping).

The overall structure of Zoroastrian society also contained other suggestive references to envy. It consisted of priests, warriors, and cattle breeders. The significance of the cow was ranked highly. It held supreme material, psychological, and spiritual value. Zoroaster is said to have banned the inordinate sacrifice of cows that previously played a large part in ancient Persian rites. Whereas the Hindus in India venerated the cow and refrained from eating its meat, Zoroastrians venerated the cow by only using it for food in a conspicuously respectful manner. One cannot but imagine how the mother-like quality of the cow with its large udders and copious output of milk may have held important psychological significance besides real survival value for both these ancient peoples. The prominence of these bovine features with attention to breast, feeding, survival, dependence, and ritualized respectfulness suggests an unmistakable reference to the human maternal-infant dyad and breast-feeding.

This brief look at, perhaps, one of the oldest of the Western world's religious traditions suggests their underlying awareness of the prominent role of envy in human affairs. Variants of monism and dualism are also obvious and prominent in the proposition of one deity and the dialectical struggle between good and evil. As mentioned earlier in regard to envy and related states of mind, *envy theory* regards the development of the capacity "to lie" and mask psychological truth as a direct result of the lie's etiological inciter—envy. This strongly reflects the fundamental and historical part these considerations (envy, monism, dualism, good, evil, and the lie) have played in human culture. This may be attributable to their being, somehow, axiomatic constructs intrinsic to human experience—that is, innate in how human intellectual and emotional information processing selects and constructs its reality, especially in externalized formalizations.

## The Vedas, Scriptural Texts of Ancient India

The Vedas are a large group of texts, originating in ancient India presumably about 1200 BC. Their orally based history dates them much earlier. They were comprehensive and included treatises on mathematics, astronomy, medicine, philosophy, and spirituality, to name just a few. Not only were they theoretical treatises, but they comprised a blueprint for living a life of quality, health, and morality. The influence of the ancient Vedas has shaped and continues to influence Hindu culture to the present day (Ninivaggi 2008).

The Vedas proposed four basic life goals. These *purusharthra* or prime values were *dharma, artha, kama,* and *Moksha. Dharma* is translated in several ways: destiny, purpose, duty, obligation, cosmic lawfulness, justice, and righteousness. This goal broadly referred to course of life, career, vocation, and ethical conduct. This was the prime obligation that made living a human life meaningful both individually and interpersonally.

*Artha* or possessions referred to the material resources needed to live with a reasonable degree of comfort. It also strongly connoted the actions or grasp of the five senses in perceiving the outer world. *Kama* was the experience of pleasure deriving from the capacity of desire and relating to the natural propensity of attraction to objects that satisfy needs, reduce tension, and yield wholesome enjoyment.

*Moksha* or liberation was the central goal under which the other three were subsumed. Proper attention to *dharma*, *artha*, and *kama* were principal strategies used to attain *Moksha*, the ultimate goal of physical, mental, and spiritual refinement. These guidelines suggest an explicit need for conscious regulation of desire and acquisitiveness—underlying features of envy. The Charaka (*Charaka Samhita*, Chapter VII, Sutrasthana composed about two thousand to three thousand years ago) and Vagbhata (*Ashthanga Sangraha*, Chapter V, circa AD 450) textbooks of Ayurveda, traditional Indian medicine, clearly single out envy as a destructive impulse needing attention and restraint.

*Moksha* refers to the gradual process of becoming freed from inordinate desire through the exercise of proper discrimination of a hierarchy of values that regards self-actualization and expanded (unified integration of) consciousness as the purpose of life. *Moksha*, in the Vedic sense, means to regain consciousness of the already extant primordial unity of individual spirit and its universal platform of extended existence. The theme of the one and the many, one being the individual focus of the gestalt of the unified many, underlies the *Moksha* idea (Ninivaggi 2001, 2008). In other words, the differentiation and multiplicities experienced in ordinary life are merely different aspects of the unity common to everything.

The conception of *dharma* as righteousness is consistent with the earliest traditions and records of humankind's efforts to achieve a meaningful quality of life amid the undeniable existence of human frailties and destructive impulses (personal communication with Manjari Dwivedi, M.D., Ph.D., dean of the School of Ayurvedic Medicine, Banaras Hindu University, India, 2005). Clearly, an awareness of envy and its regulation, especially its healthy maturation, was an implicit but intrinsic part of this ancient Vedic worldview.

## Envy in Biblical Literature

"It was the devil's envy that brought death into the world."

Wisdom 2:24

This summary statement is understood as a paradigmatic interpretation referring to the early parts of Genesis where the "Serpent" was regarded as evil personified and synonymous with figures variously called Satan, Devil, and the Adversary. The idea of death here denotes spiritual death followed by physical death. This notion sets the tone for the whole theme—both spiritual and psychological—of biblical literature. The idea of evil itself and temptation toward evildoing personified in the character of Satan can be found elsewhere in the Old Testament—for instance, in Satan's dialogue with God (Job 1:1–13). It illustrates the dualism set up between good and evil, life and death, and the challenges that temptation poses—that is, psychological forces (conflict) leading man to err in a self-destructive fashion.

In Judaic literature, for example, God asked Moses (Exodus 30:11–13) to count the Israelites—but only indirectly so no plague would break out among them. This was done with each one being represented by half a shekel. When doubled, the result gave the final census. Rashi (c. AD 1105), a renowned Talmudic scholar, interprets this to mean that one's possessions or wealth should never be counted publically for fear of incurring the "evil eye" (*ayin hora*) in those for whom envy would be stirred. In this tradition to present times, often when someone's good fortune is mentioned, it is followed by the expression "*kinnahora*," which denotes negating the *ayin hora*. The awareness of and defenses against envy are found in many cultures.

An interesting finding in surveying the Bibles of different faiths (for example, Hebrew, Roman Catholic, and Protestant) is the frequent confusion or exchange of the words "envy" and "jealousy" in the passages cited. The Hebrew and Protestant versions generally employ the term "envy" whereas the Roman Catholic translations usually use the word "jealousy" where envy would elsewhere have been adopted.

## The Sin of Adam

Now the serpent was cunning beyond any beast of the field. . . . He said to the woman, "Did, perhaps, God say: 'You shall not eat of any tree of the garden?'" The woman said to the serpent, "Of the fruit of any tree of the garden we may eat. Of the fruit of the tree which is in the center of the garden God has said: 'You shall neither eat of it or touch it, lest you die.'"

The serpent said to the woman, "You will not surely die; for God knows that on the day you eat of it your eyes will be opened and you will be like God, knowing good and bad."

. . . And the woman perceived that the tree was good for eating and that it was a delight to the eyes, and that the tree was desirable as a means to wisdom.

Genesis 3:1–6

The opening biblical drama portrayed in Genesis unfolds the story of the plight of the newly created human beings at the beginning of time. It demonstrates a variety of fundamental psychological themes. They include innocence (unconsciousness), dependency, curiosity, desire, temptation (assertive wish to expand consciousness), and willfulness (wish to become less dependent) in the face of mandates from an acknowledged superior authority, God. These are, *in statu nascendi*, the building blocks of envy.

A discrepancy between two contrasting states of being is recognized: first, one "more perfect" and filled with the supreme and ultimate knowledge of good and evil (God) and, second, one that is innocent, dependent, and almost helplessly inferior (man and woman). Subordinate man, nonetheless, has a mixed state of curiosity, puzzlement, and drive toward the desirability of acquiring more knowledge or power. The human path chosen is to disobey, spoil, or, in effect, destroy the divine command not to eat the forbidden fruit. There is a willful, though partly unconscious, thrust to violate this prohibitive command. What follows is a cascade of self-destructive and interpersonally destructive events.

The envy dynamic is suggested on two levels. On one level, we are given the implicit comparison of God (goodness) with the Serpent (evil). It can be inferred that the Serpent's pride—that is, his excessive narcissistically omnipotent wish to be, and to be viewed, equal in superiority to God—is his motivating impulse. This narcissistic self-aggrandizement is one pole of envy's superior-inferior frame of reference. The Serpent's characterization as "cunning" connotes qualities of attractiveness, false charm, skill, ingeniousness, and ingenuity in achieving his end by deceit (envy as the lie).

On the level of Adam and Eve, their wish to attain more knowledge and become less dependent reflects the envy dynamic of feeling inferior and attempting to undo this somehow. Of note in the biblical descriptions is that *the commandment not to eat of the tree was the very first (primordial, primal, and primary) negative commandment of God to man* (Genesis 2:17). Commentators say that man's violation of this command made him subject to death whereas before that he was not.

In addition, in describing Eve's state of mind, she is said to have perceived that the tree was good (ideal?), a delight (excessively ideal?) to the eyes (implied envy), and desirable as a means to wisdom (inferior to superior position). Idealization and the role of eyes in perceiving/appraising are key features suggesting envy. Awareness of inferior-superior status and upward social comparisons are also characteristic of envy.

Envy, therefore, was the cause of mankind's first breaking of the first negative commandment, mankind's first experience of sin, and mankind's first exposure to being subject to death.

## Cain and Abel

Time passed and Cain brought some of the produce of the soil as an offering
for Yahweh, while Abel for his part brought the firstborn of his flock and some
of their fat as well. Yahweh looked with favour on Abel and his offering. But
he did not look with favour on Cain and his offering, and Cain was very angry
and downcast. Yahweh asked Cain, "Why are you angry and downcast? If you
are well-disposed, ought you not to lift up your head? But if you are ill disposed,
is not sin at the door like a crouching beast hungering for you, which you must
master?" Cain said to his brother Abel, "Let us go out"; and while they were in
the open country, Cain set on his brother Abel and killed him.

God said to Cain, "Where is Abel your brother?" And he said, "I do not
know. Am I my brother's keeper?"

Genesis 4:3–9

After Adam and Eve crossed the line between deference and insolence
and set the tone of the envy dynamic, the Bible tells of the first murder committed in history, the murder by one of their sons, Cain, of the other, Abel.
The prohibition against murder was later to be codified as a central part of
God's major Ten Commandments—sixth commandment: "Thou shall not
kill" (*envy theory* reads as "Thou shall not psychologically murder/destruc-
tively spoil the innocent"). This first act of murder is also the introduction
of the first biblical reference to physical death in the world.

Although the scene is among three beings—God, Cain, and Abel—and
jealousy is prominent, a case for the existence of fundamental envy between
Cain and Abel can be made. Cain may have felt his brother superior and
more perfect than he. A hint pointing to this is given in the biblical passage
with its emphasis on the gift to God from Abel. It is described as "the first-
lings of his flock and from the choicest" (Hebrew Bible, Chumash). Cain's
offering from the fruit of the ground is not highlighted as "choice" like that of
Abel's, and so suggests that it was ordinary and inferior in comparison. Cain's
reaction was "angry and downcast." The Hebrew Bible says God's response
"annoyed Cain exceedingly and his countenance fell." This connotes a begrudging, resentful, and narcissistic withdrawal, silent yet observable characteristics of envy. Cain's very name in Hebrew, *Kayin*, connotes "acquisition."
There may also be a phonological suggestion of the word *ayin*, which signifies
eyes and looking, further suggestions of envy.

Two further issues of significance are Cain's replies to God. "I do not
know" may be one of the first accounts of a lie from one who is inferior to one
regarded as superior. "Am I my brother's keeper?" strongly connotes Cain's
resentment in regard to taking responsibility for Abel's welfare, the essence

of which may be understood as the abnegation of helpfulness and the brotherly attitude of empathetic caring. Both the lie and glaring unhelpfulness are key concepts in *envy theory*.

Of note, related to the word "Cain" are the Hebrew sounding words and the denotation of words for envy: *keen* (noun) and *lekane* (infinitive).

## Moses and Joshua

There is a vast literature of Hebrew commentaries called *midrash*, penetrating psychological interpretations by rabbinical scholars of biblical events. One such story relates to a text called "Parashat Pinchas," which is, in part, the narrative of Moses's handing over leadership of the Israelites to Joshua through a divine mandate (Numbers 25–29). Although the biblical story reflects an obedient and relatively smooth transition, the midrashic interpretation explicitly scrutinizes the conflictual emotional state presumed in Moses's actions.

When Joshua emerges out of a private conference with God, Moses asks him to relate what God has said. Joshua is adamant not to disclose what he describes as a privileged communication. Moses is shattered because he feels a burning jealousy (Plaut 1981). He turns to God and says, "Rather a hundred deaths than a single pang of envy. Master of universes, until now I sought life. But now my soul is surrendered to You" (Bialik and Ravnitzky 1992, 103). After this, Moses ascends the mountain, lies down, and "is gathered into heaven," that is, dies.

## Judgment of Solomon

The biblical passage in 1 Kings 3:16–28 relates the story of two women, each claiming to King Solomon rightful motherhood of a baby. The women, living together, each had a baby. Inadvertently, one smothered her child during the night. She then exchanged her dead baby for the live one of the other "by putting him at her breast." When the other woman realized this had occurred, she protested and both petitioned the king for rights to the living child.

In his legendary wisdom, King Solomon stated that justice would be served if the live baby were split in two and each woman were given half. Solomon's wisdom counted on the real mother's rejection of this killing; it is said, "she burned with pity for her son." The true mother strongly objected; the other woman, consumed with bitter envy, said, "He shall belong to neither of us. Cut him up." Solomon, recognizing the compassionate love of the real mother, gave the baby to her. This illustration demonstrates both the depriving and ultimate spoiling aims of envy.

## Further Biblical Citations about Envy

Rachel saw that she had not borne children to Jacob, so Rachel became envious of her sister.

Genesis 30:1

The life of the body is a tranquil heart, but envy is a cancer in the bones.

Proverbs 14:30

But if ye have bitter envying and strife in your hearts, glory not, and lie not against the truth. . . . For where envying and strife is, there is confusion and every evil work.
. . . You crave things you don't have, you are envious and jealous of things you cannot have.

James 3:14, 16; 4:1–2

Love envieth not.

First Letter to the Corinthians 13:4

The Bible does posit prohibitions against "covetousness" as the tenth of the major Ten Commandments in two slightly different versions. In Exodus 20:14, Moses is prohibited from coveting his neighbor's home, wife, servants, animals, and "anything that belongs to your fellow." The sense of covet used here suggests inordinately desiring.

In Leviticus 19:17–18, Moses is instructed "You shall not hate your brother in your heart," and "You shall not take revenge and you shall not bear a grudge . . .; you shall love your fellow as yourself." Here the commandment highlights hate, revenge, and bearing a grudge, all of which connote resentment and an underlying sense of unfairness (indicators of envy). What is emphasized is the positive commandment to love to counter the negative implications of such hate and its accompaniments.

These illustrations from biblical literature reflect the early recognition of envy as it plays itself out with love and hate in meaningful interpersonal dramas. Its often-central significance both in individual and social psychologies is hard to deny.

In early Christian literature, envy and jealousy were recognized and regarded as negative, often sinful, attitudes. Perhaps the earliest reference recorded is the text *Confessions*, Book 1, Chapter 7, verse 11. This is a highly regarded religious treatise by Saint Augustine of Hippo (AD 354–AD 430). He said, "I have myself observed a baby to be jealous, though it could not speak; it was livid as it watched bitterly another infant at the breast."

## The Seven Deadly Sins in the History of Religion

The classification of sin or evildoing in several discrete categories is also found in religious traditions. The seven deadly or cardinal sins are usually enumerated as pride, envy, anger, gluttony, sloth, lust, and greed. If one takes pride to denote excessive narcissism, then envy can be seen as the overarching frame in which the superior-inferior interpersonal dynamic takes shape, with pride as an exaggerated superiority.

In an interesting paper on the seven deadly sins edited for physicians of the twenty-first century, Francis Walker (2002) gives several examples of envy in medical practice: "An internationally known investigator-clinician is recruited to join a nonacademic surgical practice in a large city. The administration of a nearby medical school forbids its faculty members to collaborate with her." And, "A medical doctor quotes a professor as refusing to order an MRI on a patient, not because it wasn't indicated, but because the professor was sick of radiologists making so much money."

Therefore, the workings of envy in the human condition can be seen in the literatures of philosophy, religion, science, and the history of cultures. Envy has been recognized throughout human civilization as a ubiquitous dynamic in interpersonal interactions, even in sophisticated professional settings.

# Afterword

Is envy the force that makes the psychological world turn? Persistent and thoughtful struggle with this question for more than thirty-five years has yielded this monograph on *envy theory*.

The evolution of *envy theory* began by wrestling with some basic propositions. Mind, indeed a complex reality, refers to how people experience themselves both consciously and nonconsciously. The precise mechanisms and operations responsible for thinking and feeling—cognitive processing as a whole—remain largely uncharted. Psychoanalysis, psychology, and neuroscience offer partial explanations.

Although attempts at integrating these perspectives have yielded important correlations, gaps remain. Understanding the subjectively felt side of being human—self-experience—is an especially prominent conundrum. In many ways, the concept of "self" in psychology rests on a level of abstraction similar to that of "qualia" in the field of academic philosophy. Both refer to the experience of an entity (personal reference term and the idea, for example, of redness as a color, respectively) acknowledged as true by consensual validation; yet their underlying nature—how and why each manifests so uniquely—remains uncertain.

To answer questions like this, *envy theory* is advanced. It is a phenomenological analysis of self-experience. Besides defining self as a biomental entity, self always implies "other" or, in psychoanalytic jargon, ego (perceiver, experiencer) and object (perceived, experienced). Feeling, thinking, motivation, even complex executive functions are accessible to introspective and observer-based empirical description. Yet *envy theory* implies a broader substructure. It suggests a nonconscious envy-based platform of sensation, perception, emotion, and cognition. Together, these drive the experience of both self-identity and how people behave.

Although theoreticians have proposed conjectures about the causes of psychopathology, no theory sufficiently addresses people's passivity in the face of making changes in attitude and behavior even in the face of unbearable distress. In therapeutic settings, this is called treatment resistance. Inferences from clinical work plausibly show that obstacles to change are rooted in long-standing habits and inflexible modes. These include patterns of thought, feelings, behaviors, and reactions not accessible to ordinary logic and straightforward suggestions.

For these reasons, *envy theory* focuses on introspective analysis and insight to illuminate inferred unconscious mental contents responsible for conscious distress and troublesome behaviors, especially those appearing intransient and unchanging. Unconscious envy as primary and causative may be the key to unlocking mysteries behind mental suffering, resistance to changing attitudes, and behaviors that appear paradoxically self-destructive. This consideration points to the pragmatic yield of envy and its healthy maturation.

Unconscious envy is a subliminal sense of aching privation, powerlessness, and resentment. Its irrational core is rooted in intolerance of anxieties arising from an irresistible urge to spoil what is sensed as too good and too giving. This inversion of values—wanting to destroy what actually supports life—characterizes the primary inception of envy. It is envy's paradox. This indigenous envy is proposed as the permanent template guiding self-experience.

*Envy theory* is developmental both in origins and as an information-processing frame of reference. Human psychology at birth is described as the *infant's dilemma*. Past generations of theorists have dismissed the fact of functional mind being present at birth. Notable exceptions include the Melanie Klein school of psychoanalysis. Modern research and evolving sophistication in measurements of perceptual, physiological, and behavioral responses in infancy demonstrate much greater complexity in recognition and information processing than previously understood possible.

The *infant's dilemma* in *envy theory's* developmental psychology denotes that, with primary love/elemental idealization, the infant experiences primary envy (excessive idealization and spoiling) toward mother. This envy is not a craving for the advantages possessed by mother, but an intolerable anxiety that prompts the infant, in unconscious phantasy, to wish to strip and spoil those unbearable sensations, perceptions, and emotional states that connote the very existence of such value, salience, enjoyment, and goodness not felt as self-possession.

The core dilemma is maintaining primitive love in its healthy form—normal idealization, not excessive idealization. Although *envy theory* focuses on the dark side of human nature to illuminate envy, it tries unflaggingly to emphasize as clearly as possible that love and all its positive attributes are the essential foundations of all object relations and interpersonal relations. Healthy infantile development and mental health in adult life have this essential love as their underpinnings. In fact, recognizing envy helps in recognizing how fundamental and significant love and all other positive emotions are in real-life situations.

Empirically, mental health in infancy denotes healthy infant temperament, sleeping, feeding, and affiliative responsiveness to nurturant care. *Excessive idealization, however, provokes envious anxiety and leads to envious spoiling of what had been felt as extremely but unbearably good, not bad.* Envy theory suggests that this may operate in extremely passive or irritably nonconforming infants. They do not thrive in typically expected ways even in the absence of clear-cut problems such as physical illness and aberrant caregiving.

Normal love in all its permutations both opposes and modulates this conflict. The cognitive yield of this prototypical cognitive relation to mother is the unquenchable epistemic search for meaning to resolve uncertainty and reduce confusion. *Envy theory* calls this impulse the innate *epistemophilia*—search for meaning—within the self. It is the quintessential search for one's own psychological truth.

The evolution of the idea of *nuclear envy* began with some basic presuppositions, chief of which are love, destructiveness, and the *epistemophilia* in the self as primary driving forces underlying experiential urges. *Envy theory* sees these as the mind's overarching compass stimulating motivation, emotion, thought, and behavior. Primary drive denotes an organizing principle made of multiple brain-mind circuitries hierarchically tiered. Granting as valid the traditionally proposed binary "love and hate" orientation of psychological processes, *envy theory* introduces another, earlier, more primitive model—"love/elemental idealization and envy." Whereas hate is obvious, envy is obscure and unconscious.

Whence cometh love, hate, envy, and the *epistemophilia* in the self?

*Envy theory* uses the nature-nurture dichotomy as follows. Environment and learning accruing from it are essential to mental development from birth onward. They nuance personality and character and make personal change possible. The hardware and many activating programs making up mind, however, have innate and constitutional elements. Unconscious envy, *largely though not entirely*, pervades both mental hardwiring and its contents—ideas, emotions, and unconscious phantasies. These programs inform the complementary role of genes and the environment.

An individual's selective cognitive and affective encoding—*projective internalization*—makes the apprehension of experience uniquely meaningful. Meaning denotes the identity accruing from the self's recognition of aspects of itself in the environment of persons and things. *Envy theory* stresses the innate and bidirectional loop of all cognition—perception, projection, introjection, interpretation, perception, *ad infinitum*. Idiosyncratically preferred experiences reinforce undeveloped innate predispositions. Such novel experiences are actively sought. Biomental expectation pathways unfold and consolidate.

Emphasis is given to early development because the past is always present in the immediate moment. *Envy theory*, moreover, goes to great lengths to reiterate the vital importance of learning and change throughout life. The crucial influence of environment and context are undeniably significant.

The idea of *the healthy maturation of envy* attests to the presumption that real change is attainable. The evolution of this idea owes an inestimable debt to the work of Melanie Klein, who provided not only a developmental psychology but also the seminal discovery of unconscious envy. *Envy theory* has proposed an intricate set of conjectures about the nuclear genesis of envy and microscopic analysis of its dedicated pathways as a backdrop to its evolution, maturation, and refinement.

*In contrast to a bleak and pessimistic psychological theory, envy theory, guardedly optimistic, suggests a realistically enthusiastic blueprint for successful change and a better quality of life.*

Using the construct of a partly self-reflective ego as the self-system's beacon illuminating (cognizing) the vastness of its nonconscious brain-mind impulses, the phenomenology of personal change is described. Ego integration or increased connectivity among diverse mental functions and modules sparks and reinforces personal change. Splitting processes or cognitively polarized thinking, feeling, and attitudes thus become attenuated. Excessive idealization, fundamental to *nuclear envy*, diminishes and can become felt as normal love—admiration, emulation, empathy, gratitude, and compassion. When envy is recognized and made manageable, primitive urges to rob, spoil, destroy, and hate become humanized. A natural inclination toward helpfulness in attitude and performance comes to the forefront of experience. Inordinate violence and power struggles with self and others are mitigated.

In these concluding remarks, yet unaddressed research implications and further expansions of *envy theory* remain. Clearer scholarly distinctions among the definitions of envy as a conscious and an unconscious phenomenon remain. Whether envy is simply an emotion, a set of emotions, or a complex blend of urges, affects, cognitions, and motivations requires research. Delineation of envy's intrapsychic, interpersonal, and social dimensions is important. Related to this is how envious hostility and aggression negatively influence these domains.

*Envy management skills* as a form of psychoeducation, for example, has been alluded to in cursory fashion. This may prove a valuable addition to regular school curricula. It affords primary (education), secondary (detection), and tertiary (treatment) levels of prevention from a public health perspective. This can be a significant contribution to child and adolescent mental health. Organizational consultation, moreover, may discover new strategies in identifying, remediating, and improving business, leadership, and efficiency models, with the aim of supporting effective teamwork, through the clarifications and enhancements implied in *envy theory*.

In addition, *envy theory* may have applications in neuroscience, sociopolitical theory, and clinical practice. Details of *envy theory* may be formulated in valid, testable ways, and these hypotheses, in turn, may be subjected to rigorous scientific methodology. Research models and basic science measurements may develop from *envy theory*'s novel perspectives.

*Envy theory* has suggested new ways of exploring irrationally destructive trends—greed, aggressive control, suicide, homicide, and war—that appear resistant to change. Explanatory constructs have been proposed; these offer guidelines not only for the future development of strategic interventions but also for tactical—how to—applications in political science and sociology.

The place of envy and its role in development, conflict, defense, reparation, and adaptation have been alluded to in *Envy Theory* in sections on aesthetics and the superego. An expanded philosophy of aesthetics can be constructed on the principles of *envy theory*. This may give renewed insights into artistic motivations and enrich their varied expressions across different media.

A fruitful extension of *envy theory* also would be in the field of academic philosophy. Aristotle's (OBC) constructs of *physis* ("Being" in general), *morphe* (actual manifestation of specific being), *hyle* (additional being in the process of coming into manifestation), and *steresis* (privation dimension of manifest being—for example, "a blind eye") were incorporated in explicit ways into Heidegger's elaboration of existentialism (Sheehan 1983). Correlations of these ideas with the clinical metapsychology of envy could have pragmatic yields. Philosophical psychopathology, as well, might be able to expand a discussion of value attribution and idealization as central to cognitive processing and motivation.

Another important area left out has been a fuller discussion of psychotherapeutic technique specific to envy. Diagnostic screening, making diagnoses, and illustrative case examples remain for future presentation. The idea that treatment-resistant depressions and other mental disorders like hoarding may have a core in pathological envy treatable by psychotherapies is an encouraging prospect and adds a share of therapeutic optimism to this difficult area. Modern innovative research techniques, moreover, are now demonstrating the real and measurable effectiveness of long-term psychodynamically oriented psychotherapies (Leichsenring and Rabung 2008; Glass 2008).

Last, *envy theory* has emphasized the crucial significance of environment—the real context in which infant, child, and adult lives. The vital quality of mothering and parenting by both mother and father has been suggested throughout this text. The infant's capacity to deal with envy and *the healthy maturation of envy* is influenced by the physical, emotional, and cognitive ministrations of mother and father. This also is true of caregivers and the caregiving environment. Proper food, warmth, clothing, and shelter are obvious necessities. Emotional availability and empathetic understanding are essential factors in attunements and entrainments capable of refining and transforming envious experience.

*Envy theory* has elucidated the significant roles of projective identification, introjective identification, issues of entrainment, empathy, and intersubjectivity, to mention just a few, as they pertain to communication, understanding, and transformative change between persons. My own personal work with Wilfred Bion in 1979 in London amply demonstrated the effectiveness of containment and substantive intrapsychic transformations. Many of Bion's models already have informed psychotherapeutic technique in concrete ways. His model of mother-infant *reverie* (Bion 1962b) may be a rich source from which to glean in formulating guidelines for parents. *Envy theory* may also be a resource in this endeavor.

Since there are virtually an infinite number of personality configurations, expressions, and styles, effective child guidance requires one-to-one assessments of child-parent relationships. Only in this way can appropriate, custom-tailored suggestions be devised. Formulating details of these important considerations has been beyond the scope of the present text, but is an exciting challenge for the future.

It would seem now, in the history of ideas, that love, envy, hate, gratitude, empathy, and helpfulness and how they shape and modify one another may be likely candidates responsible for driving the motor that perpetually turns the world of human experience.

# References

Abraham, K. 1919. A particular form of neurotic resistance against the psychoanalytic method. In *Selected papers on psychoanalysis*, trans. Douglas Bryan and Alix Strachey, 303–11. London: Hogarth Press, 1948.

———. 1921. Contributions to the theory of the anal character. In *Selected papers on psychoanalysis*, trans. Douglas Bryan and Alix Strachey, 370–92. London: Hogarth Press, 1948.

Adolphs, R. 2009. The social brain: Neural basis of social knowledge. *Annu Rev Psychol* 60: 693–716.

Allen, J. G., P. Fonagy, and A. W. Bateman. 2008. *Mentalizing in clinical practice*. Arlington, VA: American Psychiatric Publishing.

Anderson, M. C., K. N. Ochsner, B. Kuhl, J. Cooper, E. Robertson, S. W. Gabrielli, G. H. Glover, and J. D. E. Gabrielli. 2004. Neural systems underlying the suppression of unwanted memories. *Science* 303 (no. 5655): 232–35.

Audi, R. 1995. *The Cambridge Dictionary of Philosophy*. New York: Cambridge University Press.

Augustine of Hippo (AD 354–AD 430). 1998 edition. *Confessions*. London: Oxford University Press.

Aurell, C. G. 1989. Man's triune conscious mind. *Perceptual and Motor Skills* 68: 747–54.

Baddeley, A. 2003. Working memory: Looking back and looking forward. *Nat. Rev. Neurosci.* 4: 829–39.

Badgaiyan, R. D. 2006. Cortical activation by unrecognized stimuli. *Behavioral and Brain Functions* 2: 17.

Balint, M. 1937. Early developmental states of the ego: Primary object-love. *Imago* 23: 270–88.

———. 1965. *Primary love and psychoanalytic technique*. London: Tavistock.

———. 1992. *The basic fault: Therapeutic aspects of regression.* Evanston, IL: Northwestern University Press. First published 1968 by Tavistock Publications.

Bandura, A. 1999. Social cognitive theory of personality. In *Handbook of personality: Theory and research,* second edition, ed. L. A. Pervin and P. P. John, 154–96. New York: Guilford.

Bargh, J. A., and M. J. Ferguson. 2000. Beyond behaviorism: On the automaticity of higher mental processes. *Psychological Bulletin* 126: 925–45.

Bechara, A., H. Damasio, D. Tranel, and A. R. Damasio. 1997. Deciding advantageously before knowing the advantageous strategy. *Science* 28 (February 275): 1293–95.

Beck, A. T., A. Freeman, and D. D. Davis. 2003. *Cognitive therapy of personality disorders,* second edition. New York: Guilford.

Beck, A. T., A. J. Rush, and B. F. Shaw. 1979. *Cognitive therapy of depression.* New York: Guilford.

Belmaker, R. H. 2008. The future of depression psychopharmacology. *CNS Spectrum* 13: 8, 682–87.

Berlucchi, G., and S. Aglioti. 1997. The body in the brain: Neural bases of corporeal awareness. *Trends in Neurosciences* 20 (12): 560–64.

Bialik, H. N, and Y. H. Ravnitzky, ed. 1992. *Book of legends/Sefer Ha-Aggadah: Legends from the Talmud and Midrash.* Trans. W. Braude. New York: Schocken Books.

Bion, W. R. 1959. Attacks on linking. *Int. J. Psychoanal.* 40: 308–15.

———. 1962a. *Learning from experience.* London: Heinemann.

———. 1962b. A theory of thinking. *Int. J. Psychoanal.* 43: 306–10.

———. 1963. *Elements of psychoanalysis.* London: Heinemann.

———. 1970. *Attention and interpretation.* London: Tavistock.

Boris, H. N. 1994. *Envy.* Northvale, NJ: Jason Aronson.

Bowlby, J. 1969. *Attachment and loss.* Volume I: *Attachment.* New York: Basic.

Boyce, M. A. 1979. *Zoroastrians: Their religious beliefs and practices.* Chicago: University of Chicago Press.

———. 1990. *Textual sources for the study of Zoroastrianism.* Chicago: University of Chicago Press.

———. 2001. *Zoroastrians: Their religion and beliefs,* second edition. London: Routledge.

Brass, M., and C. Heyes. 2005. Imitation: Is cognitive neuroscience solving the corresponding problem? *Trends in Cognitive Science* 9 (10): 489–95.

Braten, S. 2004. Hominin infant decentration hypothesis: Mirror neurons system adapted to subserve mother-centered participation. *Behavioral and Brain Sciences* 27: 508–9.

Carey, S. 2001. Bridging the gap between cognition and developmental neuroscience: The example of number representation. In *Handbook of developmental cognitive neuroscience,* ed. C. A. Nelson and M. Luciana. Cambridge, MA: MIT Press.

Carter, C., and M. Krug. 2009. The functional neuroanatomy of dread: Functional Magnetic Imaging insights into generalized anxiety disorder and its treatment. *Am J Psychiatry* 166: 263–65.

Charlton, B. G. 2000. Evolution and the cognitive neuroscience of awareness, consciousness and language. In *Psychiatry and the human condition,* 147–88. Oxford, UK: Radcliff Medical Press.

Charaka. 1902–1925. *Charaka Samhita* (vols. 1–4). Trans. A. C. Kaviratna. Calcutta: Girish Chandra Chakravarti Deva Press.

Charney, D. S. 2004. Psychological mechanisms of resilience and vulnerability: Implications for successful adaptation to extreme stress. *Am J Psychiatry* 161 (2): 195–216.

Choi-Kain, L. W., and J. G. Gunderson. 2008. Mentalization: Ontogeny, assessment, and application in the treatment of borderline personality disorder. *Am J Psychiatry* 165: 1127–35.

*Chumash*, Stone Edition [Hebrew Bible]. 1994. Brooklyn, NY: Mesorah Publications.

Collins, W. A., E. E. Maccoby, L. Steinberg, E. M. Hetherington, and M. H. Bornstein. 2000. Contemporary research on parenting: The case for nature and nurture. *American Psychologist* 55: 218–32.

Cozolino, L. C. 2002. *The neuroscience of psychotherapy: Building and rebuilding the human brain.* New York: Norton.

———. 2006. *The neuroscience of human relationships: Attachment and the developing social brain.* New York: Norton.

Damasio, A. R. 1994. *Descartes' error: Emotion, reason, and the human brain.* New York: Putnam.

Damon, W., D. Kuhn, and R. S. Siegler, ed. 1998. *Handbook of child psychology: Volume 2. Cognition, perception & language,* fifth edition. New York: Wiley.

Darwin, C. 1998 (1872). *The expression of the emotions in man and animals.* Introduction, afterword, and commentaries by Paul Ekman. New York: Oxford University Press.

Dawkins, R. 2006. *The selfish gene.* New York: Oxford University Press.

DeFries, J. C., P. McGuffin, G. E. McClearn, and R. Plomin. 2000. *Behavioral genetics,* fourth edition. New York: Worth Publishers.

D'Espositio, M., and B. R. Postle. 2002. The neural basis of working memory: Storage, rehearsal, and control processes. In *Neuropsychology of memory,* ed. L. R. Squire and D. L. Schacter. New York: Guilford.

Dehaene, S., and L. Naccache. 2001. Towards a cognitive neuroscience of consciousness: Basic evidence and a workspace framework. *Cognition* 79: 1–37.

Duchesne-Guillemin, J. 1988. Zoroastrianism. In *Encyclopedia Americana* 29, 813–15. Danbury, CT: Grolier.

———. 2006. Zoroastrianism: Relation to other religions. In *Britannica* (Online edition), www.britannica.com/eb/article-9207. Retrieved May 31, 2006.

Eisler, M. J. 1921. Pleasure in sleep and the disturbed capacity for sleep. A contribution to the study of the oral phase of the development of the libido. *Int. J. Psychoanal.* 3: 30–42.

Ellis, R. D. 2006. Phenomenology-friendly neuroscience: The return to Merleau-Ponty as psychologist. *Human Studies* 29: 33–55.

Etchegoyen, R. H. 1999. *The fundamentals of psychoanalytic technique.* London: Karnac Books.

Etchegoyen, R. H., B. M. Lopez, and M. Rabih. 1987. On envy and how to interpret it. *The Journal of the Melanie Klein Society* 68: 49–61.

Etchegoyen, R. H., and C. R. Nemas. 2003. Salieri's dilemma: A counterpoint between envy and appreciation. *Int. J. Psychoanal.* 84: 45–58.

Falck-Ytter, T., G. Gredeback, and C. von Hofsten. 2006. Infants predict other people's action goals. *Nature Neuroscience* 9 (7): 878–79.

Ferenczi, S. 1911. On obscene words. In *Sex in psychoanalysis*, 11. New York: Brunner, 1950.

———. 1924. *Thalassa: A theory of genitality.* London: Karnac Books, 1989.

———. 1927. The problem of the termination of the analysis. In *Final contributions to the problems and methods of psychoanalysis*, 77–86. New York: Brunner/Mazel, 1955.

Fitzsimons, G. M., and J. A. Bargh. 2003. Thinking of you: Nonconscious pursuit of interpersonal goals associated with relationship partners. *Journal of Personality and Social Psychology* 84, no. 1: 148–64.

Fodor, J. A. 1983. *Modularity of mind.* Cambridge, MA: MIT Press.

Fonagy, P. 2008. Being envious of envy and gratitude. In *Envy and gratitude revisited*, ed. P. Roth and A. Lemma, 210. London: Karnac Books.

Frankel, S., and I. Sherick. 1977. Observations on the development of normal envy. *Psychoanalytic Study of the Child* 32: 257–81.

Freeman, W. J. 2000. *How brains make up their minds.* New York: Columbia University Press.

Freud, S. 1900. The interpretation of dreams. *S. E.*, 4–5.

———. 1905. Three essays on the theory of sexuality. *S. E.*, 7.

———. 1908. Character and anal erotism. *S. E.*, 9.

———. 1909. Analysis of a phobia in a five-year-old boy. *S. E.*, 10.

———. 1910. The antithetical meaning of primal words. *S. E.*, 11.

———. 1911. Formulations on the two principles of mental functioning. *S. E.*, 11.

———. 1914a. On narcissism: An introduction. *S. E.*, 14.

———. 1914b. Remembering, repeating, and working through. *S. E.*, 12.

———. 1915a. Instincts and their vicissitudes. *S. E.*, 14.

———. 1915b. The unconscious. *S. E.*, 14.

———. 1916–1917. Introductory lectures on psychoanalysis. *S. E.*, 15–16.

———. 1918 (1914). From the history of an infantile neurosis. *S. E.*, 17.

———. 1918. From the history of an infantile neurosis. *S. E.*, 17.

———. 1920. Beyond the pleasure principle. *S. E.*, 18.

———. 1921. Group psychology and the analysis of the ego. *S. E.*, 18.

———. 1922. Some neurotic mechanisms in jealousy, paranoia, and homosexuality. *S. E.*, 18.

———. 1923. The ego and the id. *S. E.*, 19.

———. 1924. The economic problem of masochism. *S. E.*, 19.

———. 1925. Some psychical consequences of the anatomical distinction between the sexes. *S. E.*, 19.

———. 1926. Inhibitions, symptoms, and anxiety. *S. E.*, 20.

———. 1927. The future of an illusion. *S. E.*, 21.

———. 1930a. Civilization and its discontents. *S. E.*, 21.

——. 1930b. Introduction to the special psychopathology number of *The Medical Review of Reviews*. S. E., 21.

——. 1933a (1932). New introductory lectures on psychoanalysis. S. E., 22.

——. 1933b (1932). Why war? S. E., 22.

——. 1937. Analysis terminable and interminable. S. E., 23.

——. 1940 (1938). An outline of psychoanalysis. S. E., 23.

Fromm-Reichmann, F. 1950. *Principles of intensive psychotherapy*. Chicago: University of Chicago Press.

Frost, R. O., and G. Steketee. 1998. Hoarding: Clinical aspects and treatment strategies. In *Obsessive compulsive disorder: Practical management*, third edition, ed. M. A. Jenike, L. Baer, W. E. Minichiello, 533–54. St. Louis: Mosby.

Fulchiero Gordon, M. 2005. Normal child development. In *Kaplan & Sadock's comprehensive textbook of psychiatry*, eighth edition, volume II, ed. B. J. Sadock and V. A. Sadock, 3018–35. Baltimore: Lippincott.

Gabbard, G. O. 2000. *Psychodynamic psychiatry in clinical practice*, third edition. Washington, DC: American Psychiatric Press.

Gallese, V. 2005a. Embodied simulation: From neurons to phenomenal experience. *Phenomenology and the Cognitive Sciences* 4: 23–48.

——. 2005b. The intentional attunement hypothesis, the mirror neuron system, and its role in interpersonal relations. In *Biometric neural learning for intelligent robots*. Heidelberg: Springer.

Gallese, V., L. Fadiga, L. Foggasi, and G. Rizzolatti. 1996. Action in the premotor cortex. *Brain* 119: 593–609.

Gazzaniga, M. S. 1998. *The mind's past*. Berkeley, CA: University of California Press.

Gelman, R. 1993. A rational-constructivist account of early learning about numbers and objects. In *Learning and motivation*, ed. D. Medin. New York: Academic Press.

——. 2001. Cognitive development. In *The MIT encyclopedia of the cognitive sciences*, ed. R. Wilson and F. Keil. Cambridge, MA: MIT Press.

Gibson, E. J. 1991. *An odyssey in learning and perception*. Cambridge, MA: MIT Press.

Glass, R. M. 2008. Psychodynamic psychotherapy and research evidence. *JAMA* 300 (13): 1587–89.

Godrej, P. J. 2002. *A Zoroastrian tapestry: Art, religion, and culture*. Middletown, NJ: Grantha.

Gold, P. E. 2002. Memory modulation: Regulating interactions between multiple memory systems. In *Neuropsychology of memory*, ed. L. R. Squire and D. L. Schacter, 450–62. New York: Guilford.

Gopnik, A., and A. Meltzoff. 1997. *Words, thoughts, and theories*. Cambridge, MA: MIT Press.

Goswami, U. 1998. *Cognition in children*. Hove, UK: Psychology Press.

Greenspan, S. I. 1989. The development of the ego: Insights from clinical work with infants and young children. In *The course of life. Infancy*, ed. S. I. Greenspan and G. H. Pollack, 85–164. Madison, CT: International Universities Press.

Groddeck, G. 1923. *The book of the it*. New York: IUP (reprinted 1976).

Grotstein, J. S. 1981. *Splitting and projective identification*. New York: Jason Aronson.

———. 1985. The evolving and shifting trends in psychoanalysis and psychotherapy. *J. Amer. Academy of Psychoanal.* 13: 423–52.

Haggard P. 2005. Conscious intention and motor cognition. *Trends Cogn. Sci.* 9: 290.

Haggard, P., and B. Libet. 2001. Conscious intention and brain activity. *Journal of Consciousness Studies* 8 (11 November): 47–63.

Hane, A. A., and N. A. Fox. 2007. A closer look at the transactional nature of early social development and the case for phenotypic plasticity. In *Brain development in learning environments: Embodied and perceptual advancements*, ed. F. Santioanni and C. Sabatino. New York: Cambridge University Press.

Hartocollis, P. 1992. *The personal myth in psychoanalytic theory*. Madison, CT: International Universities Press.

Hartmann, H. 1939/1958. *Ego psychology and the problem of adaptation*. New York: International Universities Press.

———. 1964. *Essays on ego psychology*. New York: International Universities Press.

Hofer, M. A., and R. M. Sullivan. 2001. Toward a neurobiology of attachment. In *Handbook of developmental neuroscience*, ed. C. A. Nelson and M. Luciana. Cambridge, MA: MIT Press.

Horney, K. 1936. The problem of the negative therapeutic reaction. *Psychoanal. Quart.* 5: 29–44.

Horwitz, A. V., and J. C. Wakefield. 2007. *The loss of sadness: How psychiatry transformed normal sorrow into depression disorder*. New York: Oxford Press.

Iacoboni, M., and J. C. Mazziotta. 2007. Mirror neuron system: Basic findings and clinical applications. *Annals of Neurology* 62 (3): 213–18.

Isaacs, S. 1935. A symposium on property and possessiveness. *British Journal of Medical Psychology* 15: 69–78.

———. 1948. The nature and function of phantasy. *Int. J. Psychoanal.* 29: 73–97.

———. 1949. *Childhood and after*. New York: International Universities Press.

Jacobson, E. 1964. *The self and the object world*. New York: International Universities Press.

Jaspers, K. 1963. *General psychopathology*. Chicago: University of Chicago Press.

*Jerusalem Bible*. 1966. Garden City, NY: Doubleday.

Joffe, W. 1969. A critical review of the status of the envy concept. *Int. J. of Psychoanal.* 50: 533–45.

Jones, E. 1927. Early development of female sexuality. In *Papers on psychoanalysis*, fifth edition, 438–40. London: Bailliere, Tindall & Cox, 1950.

———. 1953, 1981. *The life and work of Sigmund Freud*, volumes 1–3. New York: Basic.

Joseph, B. 1986. Envy in everyday life. *Psychoanalytic Psychotherapy* 2: 13–30.

———. 1989. *Psychic equilibrium and psychic change: Selected papers of Betty Joseph*, ed. M. Feldman and E. B. Spillius. London: Routledge.

Kendler, K. 2005. Toward a philosophical structure for psychiatry. *Am J Psychiatry* 162: 433–40.

Kernberg, O. 1975. *Borderline conditions and pathological narcissism*. New York: Jason Aronson.

——. 1986. Further contributions to the treatment of narcissistic personalities. In *Essential papers on narcissism*, ed. A. P. Morrison. New York: New York University Press, 245–92.

Kihlstrom, J. 1987. The cognitive unconscious. *Science* 237: 1445–52.

——. 1996. Perception without awareness of what is perceived, learning without awareness of what is learned. In *The science of consciousness: Psychological, neuro-psychological, and clinical reviews*, ed. M. Velmans, 23–29. London: Routledge.

Klein, M. 1923. The role of the school in the libidinal development of the child. In *Love, guilt, and reparation and other works*, 59–76. London: Hogarth Press, 1975.

——. 1925. A contribution to the psychogenesis of tics. In *Love, guilt, and reparation and other works*, 106–27. London: Hogarth Press, 1975.

——. 1928. Early stages of the Oedipus conflict. In *Love, guilt, and reparation and other works*, 186–98. London: Hogarth Press, 1975.

——. 1929. Infantile anxiety-situations reflected in a work of art and in the creative impulse. In *Love, guilt, and reparation and other works*, 210–18. London: Hogarth Press, 1975.

——. 1932. *The psychoanalysis of children*. London: Hogarth Press, 1975.

——. 1935. A contribution to the psychogenesis of manic-depressive states. In *Love, guilt, and reparation and other works*, 262–89. London: Hogarth Press, 1975.

——. 1936. Weaning. In *Love, guilt, and reparation and other works*, 290–305. London: Hogarth Press, 1975.

——. 1940. Mourning and its relation to manic-depressive states. In *Love, guilt, and reparation and other works*, 344–69. London: Hogarth Press, 1975.

——. 1945. The Oedipus complex in the light of early anxieties. In *Love, guilt, and reparation and other works*, 370–419. London: Hogarth Press, 1975.

——. 1946. Notes on some schizoid mechanisms. In *Envy and gratitude and other works*, 1–24. London: Hogarth Press, 1975.

——. 1948. On the theory of anxiety and guilt. In *Envy and gratitude and other works*, 25–47. London: Hogarth Press, 1975.

——. 1952a. Some theoretical conclusions regarding the emotional life of the infant. In *Envy and gratitude and other works*, 61–93. London: Hogarth Press, 1975.

——. 1952b. On observing the behaviour of young infants. In *Envy and gratitude and other works*, 94–121. London: Hogarth Press, 1975.

——. 1955. On identification. In *Envy and gratitude and other works*, 141–75. London: Hogarth Press, 1975.

——. 1957. Envy and gratitude. In *Envy and gratitude and other works*, 176–235. London: Hogarth Press, 1975.

——. 1958. On the development of mental functioning. In *Envy and gratitude and other works*, 236–46. London: Hogarth Press, 1975.

——. 1959. Our adult world and its roots in infancy. In *Envy and gratitude and other works*, 247–63. London: Hogarth Press, 1975.

———. 1960. A note on depression in the schizophrenic. In *Envy and gratitude and other works*, 264–67. London: Hogarth Press, 1975.

———. 1961. *Narrative of a child analysis*. London: Hogarth Press, 1975.

———. 1963a. Some reflections on "The Oresteia." In *Envy and gratitude and other works*, 275–99. London: Hogarth Press, 1975.

———. 1963b. On the sense of loneliness. In *Envy and gratitude and other works*, 300–13. London: Hogarth Press, 1975.

Knowlton, B. J. 2002. The role of the basal ganglia in learning and memory. In *Neuropsychology of memory*, ed. L. R. Squire and D. L. Schacter, 143–53. New York: Guilford.

Knudsen, E. I. 2007. Fundamental components of attention. *Annu. Rev. Neurosci.* 30: 57–78.

Koestler, A. 1967. *The ghost in the machine*. London: Penguin.

Kohut, H. 1977. *The restoration of the self*. New York: International Universities Press.

———. 1984. *How does analysis cure?* Ed. A. Goldberg. Chicago: University of Chicago Press.

Kohut, H., and E. S. Wolf. 1978. The disorders of the self and their treatment: An outline. *Int. J. Psychoanal.* 59: 413–25

Kubovy, M., D. J. Cohen, and J. Hollier. 1999. Feature integration that routinely occurs without focal attention. *Psychonomic Bulletin & Review* 6: 183–203.

Kugiumutzakis, G. 1999. Genesis and development of early human mimesis to facial and vocal models. In *Imitation in infancy*, ed. J. Nadel and G. Butterworth, 36–59. Cambridge: Cambridge University Press.

Kuhn, T. S. 1996. *The structure of scientific revolutions*. Chicago: University of Chicago Press.

Lamb, M. E., D. M. Teti, M. H. Bornstein, and A. Nash. 2002. Infancy. In *Child and adolescent psychiatry*, third edition, ed. M. Lewis, 293–323. New York: Lippincott.

LaPlanche, J., and J. B. Pontalis. 1973. *The language of psycho-analysis*. New York: Norton.

Laverde-Rubio, E. 2004. Envy: One or many. *Int. J. Psychoanal.* 85: 401–18.

LeDoux, J. 1998. *The emotional brain*. New York: Simon & Schuster.

Leichsenring, F., and S. Rabung. 2008. Effectiveness of long-term psychoanalytic psychotherapy. JAMA 2008; 300 (13): 1551–65.

Libet, B. 2004. *Mind time: The temporal factor in consciousness*. Cambridge, MA: Harvard University Press.

Loehlin, J. C., R. R. McCrae, P. T. Costa, and O. P. John. 1998. Heritabilities of common and measure-specific components of the big five personality factors. *Journal of Research in Personality* 32: 431–53.

Loewald, H. 1980. *Paper on psychoanalysis*. New Haven, CT: Yale University Press.

———. 1988. Symbolism. In *Sublimation*, 45–65. New Haven, CT: Yale University Press.

Lohmar, D. 2006. Mirror neurons and the phenomenology of intersubjectivity. *Phenomenology and the Cognitive Sciences* 5 (1): 5–16.

McNab F., A. Varrone, L. Farde, A. Jucaite, P. Bystritsky, H. Forssberg, and T. Klingberg. 2009. Changes in cortical dopamine D1 receptor binding associated with cognitive training. *Science* 323: 800–802.

Meichenbaum, D. 1977. *Cognitive-behavior modification: An integrative approach.* New York: Plenum.

Meltzoff, A. N. 1995. Understanding the intentions of others: Re-enactment of intended acts by 18-month-old children. *Dev Psychol.* 31: 838–50.

Meltzoff, A. N., and M. K. Moore. 1999. Persons and representations: Why infant imitation is important for theories of human development. In *Imitation in infancy,* ed. J. Nadel and G. Butterworth, 9–35. Cambridge: Cambridge University Press.

Mendez, M. 2009. The neurobiology of moral behavior: Review and neuropsychiatric implications. *CNS Spectrum* 14 (11): 608–20.

Merikle, P. M., and M. Danemann. 2000. Conscious vs. unconscious perception. In *The new cognitive neurosciences,* second edition, ed. M. S. Gazzaniga, 1295–1303. Cambridge, MA: MIT Press.

Miles, D. R., and G. Carey. 1997. Genetic and environmental architecture of human aggression. *Journal of Personality and Social Psychology* 72: 207–17.

Miller, E. K., and J. D. Cohen. 2001. An integrative theory of prefrontal cortex function. *Annu. Rev. Neurosci.* 24: 167–202.

Milton, J. 1975. *John Milton: Paradise lost,* second edition, ed. S. Elledge. New York: Norton.

Neisser, U. 1967. *Cognitive psychology.* New York: Appleton Century Crofts.

Neubauer, P. B. 1982. Rivalry, envy, and jealousy. *Psychoanalytic Study of the Child* 13: 414–24.

*Neuropsychopharmacology* 2008; volume 33, no. 2; whole issue.

Newton, N. 2001. Emergence and the uniqueness of consciousness. *Journal of Consciousness Studies* 8: 47–59.

Nietzsche, F. 1999 (1872). The birth of tragedy from the spirit of music. In *Nietzsche: The birth of tragedy and other writings,* ed. R. Guess, R. Speirs, K. Ameriks, and D. M. Clarke. Cambridge: Cambridge University Press.

Ninivaggi, F. 2001. *An elementary textbook of Ayurveda: Medicine with a six thousand year old tradition.* Madison, CT: International Universities/Psychosocial Press.

———. 2005. Borderline intellectual functioning and academic problem. In *Kaplan & Sadock's comprehensive textbook of psychiatry,* eighth edition, volume II, ed. B. J. Sadock and V. A. Sadock, 2272–76. Baltimore: Lippincott.

———. 2008. *Ayurveda: A comprehensive guide to traditional Indian medicine for the West.* Westport, CT: Greenwood/Praeger Press.

———. 2009. Borderline intellectual functioning and academic problem. In *Kaplan & Sadock's comprehensive textbook of psychiatry,* ninth ed, volume II, ed. B. J. Sadock, V. A. Sadock, and P. Ruiz, 2479–90. Philadelphia: Wolters Kluver/Lippincott.

———. 2010. The psychology of the aging spine. In *The comprehensive treatment of the aging spine: Minimally invasive and advanced techniques,* ed. J. J. Yue, R. D. Guyer, J. P. Johnson, L. T. Khoo, and S. H. Hochschuler. Philadelphia: Saunders.

Nunberg, H. 1932/1955. *Principles of psychoanalysis: Their application to the neuroses.* New York: International Universities Press.

Oakes, L. M. 1994. The development of infants' use of continuity cues in their perception of causality. *Developmental Psychology* 30: 869–79.

[OBC]. 1976. "On the being and conception of physis in Aristotle's Physics B, 1," trans. Thomas Sheehan. *Man and World* 9(3): 219–70.

Ohman, A. 1999. Distinguishing unconscious from conscious emotional responses: Methodological considerations and theoretical implications. In *Handbook of cognition and emotion*, ed. T. Dalgleish and M. Power, 321–52. Chichester, England: Wiley.

Ortigue, S., and F. Bianchi-Demicheli. 2008a. The chronoarchitecture of human desire: A high-density electrical mapping study. *NeuroImage* 43: 337–45.

———. 2008b. Why is your spouse so predictable? Connecting mirror neuron system and self-expansion model of love. *Medical Hypotheses* 71: 941–44.

Ortigue, S., F. Bianchi-Demicheli, A. F. Hamilton, and S. T. Grafton. 2007. The neural basis of love as a subliminal prime: An event-related fMRI study. *Journal of Cognitive Neuroscience* 19: 1218–30.

Panksepp, J. 1998. *Affective neuroscience.* New York: Oxford.

Parks, C. D., A. C. Rumble, and D. C. Posey. 2002. The effects of envy on reciprocation in a social dilemma. *Personality and Social Psychology* 28: 509–20.

Parrott, W. G. 2000. Jealousy and envy. In *Encyclopedia of Psychology*, volume 4, ed. A. E. Kazdin, 391–94. Washington, DC: American Psychological Association.

Parrott, W. G., and R. H. Smith. 1993. Distinguishing the experiences of envy and jealousy. *Journal of Personality and Social Psychology* 64: 906–20.

Pascalis, O., and A. Slater. 2001. The development of face processing in infancy and early childhood: Current perspectives. *Infant and Child Development* 10: 1–2.

Perez-Edgar, K. E., and N. A. Fox. 2005. A behavioral and electrophysiological study of children's selective attention under neutral and affective conditions. *Journal of Cognition and Development* 6: 1, 89–118.

Phillips, M. L., A. W. Young, C. Senior, M. Brammer, C. Andrew, A. J. Calder, E. T. Bullmore, D. I. Perrett, D. Rowland, S. C. Williams, J. A. Gray, and A. S. David. 1997. A specific neural substrate for perceiving facial expressions of disgust. *Nature* 389 (6650): 495–98.

Piaget, J. 1952. *The origins of intelligence in children.* New York: International Universities Press.

Piaget, J., and B. Inhelder. 1969. *The psychology of the child.* New York: Basic.

Pittenger, C., and R. S. Duman. 2008. Stress, depression, and neuroplasticity: A convergence of mechanisms. *Neuropsychopharmacology* 33(1): 88–109.

Plaut, G. 1981. *The Torah: A modern commentary.* New York: UAHC Press.

Plomin, R. 2004. *Nature and nurture: An introduction to human behavioral genetics.* Belmont, CA: Wadsworth Publishing Co.

Pockett. S., W. P. Banks, and S. Gallagher. 2006. *Does consciousness cause behavior?* Cambridge, MA: MIT Press.

Racker, H. 1968. *Transference and countertransference.* New York: International Universities Press.

Rapaport, D. A. 1967. *Collected papers of David Rapaport,* ed. M. M. Gill. New York: Basic.

Reik, T. 1944. *A psychologist looks at love.* New York: Farrar and Rinehart.

Riviere, J. 1932. Jealousy as a mechanism of defense. *Int. J. Psychoanal.* 13: 414–24.

———. 1952. The unconscious phantasy of an inner world reflected in examples from literature. *Int. J. of Psychoanal.* 33: 160–72.

Rizzolatti, G., and M. Arbib. 1998. Language within our grasp. *Trends in Neurosciences* 21: 188–94.

Rizzolatti, G., and L. Craighero. 2004. The mirror-neuron system. *Annual Review of Neuroscience* 27: 169–92.

Rizzolatti, G., L. Fadiga, V. Gallese, and L. Fogassi. 1996. Premotor cortex and the recognition of motor actions. *Cog. Brain Res.* 3: 131–41.

Rizzolatti, G., and V. Gallese. 2005. Mirror neurons. In *Encyclopedia of cognitive science,* ed. L. Nadel. New York: Wiley.

Roediger, H. L., E. Tulving, and F. I. Craik, eds. 1989. *Varieties of memory and consciousness: Essays in honour of Endel Tulving.* Hillsdale, NJ: Erlbaum.

Rosenfeld, H. 1952. Notes on the psychoanalysis of the superego conflict in an acute schizophrenic. *Int. J. of Psychoanal.* 33: 111–31.

———. 1959. Envy and gratitude. Book review in *Int. J. Psychoanal.* 40: 64–66.

———. 1971. A clinical approach to the psychoanalytic theory of the life and death instincts: An investigation into the aggressive aspects of narcissism. *Int. J. Psychoanal.* 52: 169–78.

Roth, P., and A. Lemma, eds. 2008. *Envy and gratitude revisited.* London: Karnac Books.

Rubinow, D. R. 2006. Treatment strategies after SSRI failure—good news and bad news. *New Eng J Med.* 354 (12): 1305–7.

Rush, A. J. 2007. STAR*D: What have we learned? *Am J Psychiatry* 164: 201–4.

Rush, A. J., M. H. Trivedi, S. R. Wisniewski, et al. 2006. Acute and longer-term outcomes in depressed outpatients requiring one or several treatment steps: A STAR*D report. *Am J Psychiatry* 163: 1905–17.

Rutter, M. 2007. Resilience, competence and coping. *Child Abuse Negl* 31 (3): 205–9.

Salovey, P., and A. J. Rothman. 1991. Envy and jealousy: Self and society. In *The psychology of jealousy and envy,* ed. P. Salovey, 271–86. New York: Guilford.

Sanacora, G. 2008. New understanding of mechanisms of action of bipolar medications. *J Clin Psychiatry* 69 (supp. 5): 22–27.

Sandler, J., ed. 1987. *Projection, identification, projective identification.* Madison, CT: International Universities Press.

Sandler, J., A. Holder, C. Dare, and A. U. Dreher. 1997. *Freud's models of the mind.* Madison, CT: International Universities Press.

Sandler, J., and B. Rosenblatt. 1962. The concept of the representational world. *Psychoanalytic Study of the Child* 17: 128–45.

Sandler, J., and A. M. Sandler. 1998. *Internal objects revisited*. Madison, CT: International Universities Press.

Saxena, S., A. Broady, K. Maidment, E. C. Smith, N. Zohrabi, E. Katz, S. K. Baker, and L. R. Baxter. 2004. Cerebral glucose metabolism in obsessive-compulsive hoarding. *Am J Psychiatry* 161: 1038–48.

Schacter, D. L. 1994. Priming and multiple memory systems: Perceptual mechanisms of implicit memory. In *Memory systems*, ed. D. L. Schacter and E. Tulving, 233–68. Cambridge, MA: MIT Press.

Schoeck, H. 1966. *Envy: A theory of social behavior*. New York: Harcourt Brace.

Schore, A. N. 2002. *Affect dysregulation and the damage to the self*. New York: Norton.

Schur, M. 1966. *The id and the regulatory principles of mental functioning*. New York: International Universities Press.

Sebanz, N., and W. Prinz, eds. 2009. *Disorders of volition*. Cambridge, MA: MIT Press.

Segal, H. 1952. A psycho-analytical approach to aesthetics. In *The work of Hanna Segal*, ed. R. Langs, 185–206. New York: Jason Aronson, 1981.

———. 1968. Notes on symbol formation. In *The work of Hanna Segal*, ed. R. Langs, 49–68. New York: Jason Aronson., 1981.

———. 1973. *Introduction to the work of Melanie Klein*, chap. 4. New York: Basic.

———. 1983. Some clinical implications of Melanie Klein's work. *Int. J. Psychoanal.* 64: 269–76.

———. 1993. On the clinical usefulness of the concept of the death instinct. *Int. J. Psychoanal.* 74: 55–61.

———. 1991. *Dream, phantasy, and art*. London: Routledge.

———. 2007. *Yesterday, today, and tomorrow*. London: Routledge.

Schmidt, L. A., and N. A. Fox. 2002. Molecular genetics of temperamental differences in children. In *Molecular genetics and human personality*, ed. J. Benjamin, R. P. Ebstein, and R. H. Belmaker. Washington, DC: American Psychiatric Press.

Shapiro, T., and D. Emde. 1989. Psychoanalytic perspectives on the first year of life: The establishment of the object in an affective field. In *The course of life. Infancy*, ed. S. I. Greenspan and G. H. Pollock, 271–92. Madison, CT: International Universities Press.

Sharp, C., P. Fonagy, and I. G. Goodyer, eds. 2008. *Social cognition and developmental psychopathology*. Oxford: Oxford University Press.

Sheehan, T. 1983. On the way to Ereignis: Heidegger's interpretation of physis. In *Continental philosophy in America*, ed. H. J. Silverman, et al., 131–64. Pittsburgh: Duquesne University Press.

Smith, R. H., ed. 2008. *Envy: Theory and research*. New York: Oxford.

Smith, R. H., and S. H. Kim. 2007. Comprehending envy. *Psychological Bulletin* 133 (1): 46–64.

Smith, R. H., W. G. Parrott, E. F. Diener, R. H. Hoyle, and S. H. Kim. 1999. Dispositional envy. *Personality & Social Psychology Bulletin* 25: 1007.

Smith, R. H., T. J. Turner, R. Garonzik, C. W. Leach, V. Urch-Druskat, and C. M. Weston. 1996. Envy and schadenfreude. *Personality & Social Psychology Bulletin* 22: 158.

Spielman, P. M. 1971. Envy and jealousy: An attempt at clarification. *Psychoanal. Quart.* 40: 59–82.

Spillius, E. B. 1992. Clinical experiences of projective identification. In *Clinical lectures on Klein and Bion*, ed. E. B. Spillius. London: Routledge, 59–73.

———. 1993. Varieties of envious experience. *Int. J. Psychoanal.* 74: 1199–1212.

Spitz, R. 1965. *The first year of life.* New York: International Universities Press.

Spruiell, V. 1979. Freud's concepts of idealization. *J. Amer. Psychoanal. Assn.* 27: 431–40.

Stahl, S. M. 2008. *Essential psychopharmacology*, third edition. New York: Cambridge University Press.

Stanley, D., E. Phelps, and M. Banaji. 2008. The neural basis of implicit attitudes. *Curr Dir Psychol Sci.* 17: 164–70.

Stapel, D. A., and H. Blanton. 2004. From seeing to being: Subliminal social comparisons affect implicit and explicit self-evaluations. *Journal of Personality and Social Psychology* 87: 468–81.

———, eds. 2007. *Social comparison theories.* New York: Psychology Press.

Steiner, J. 1993. *Psychic retreats: Pathological organizations in psychotic, neurotic, and borderline patients.* London: Routledge.

Stern, D. 1985. *The interpersonal world of the infant.* New York: Basic.

———. 1987. Affect in the context of the infant's lived experience: Some considerations. *Int. J. Psychoanal.* 69 (2): 233–39.

Swain, J. E. 2008. Baby stimuli and the parent brain: Functional neuroimaging of the neural substrates of parent-infant attachment. *Psychiatry* 5 (8): 28–36.

Takahashi H., M. Kato, D. Mobbs, T. Suhara, and Y. Okubo. 2009. When your gain is my pain and your pain is my gain: Neural correlates of envy and schadenfreude. *Science* 323: 937–39.

Torgersen, S., S. Lygren, P. A. Oien, I. Skre, S. Onstad, J. Edvardsen, K. Tambs, and E. Kriglen. 2000. A twin study of personality disorders. *Compr Psychiatry* 41: 416–25.

Trevarthen, C. 1993. The self born in intersubjectivity: An infant communicating. In *The perceived self*, ed. U. Neisser, 121–73. New York: Cambridge University Press.

Trevarthen, C., and K. Aitken. 2001. Infant intersubjectivity: Research, theory, and clinical applications. *J. Child Psychol. Psychiat.* 42 (1): 2–48.

Tulving, E., and D. L. Schacter. 1990. Priming and human memory systems. *Science* 247: 301–14.

Uddin, L., M. Iacoboni, C. Lange, and J. Keenan. 2007. The self and social cognition: The role of cortical midline structures and mirror neurons. *Trends in Cognitive Science* 11 (4): 153–57.

Vagbhata. 2006. *Asthanga Sangraha*, trans. R. Vidyanath. Varanasi, India: Chaukhamba Surbharati Prakashan Press.

Varela, F., E. Thompson, and E. Rosch. 1991/1993. *The embodied mind*. Cambridge: MIT Press.

Velmans, M. 1991. Is human information processing conscious? *Behavioral and Brain Sciences* 14 (4): 651–69.

Walker, F. O. 2002. The seven deadly sins revised and edited for physicians of the 21st century. *Neurology* 58 (11): 1700–1703.

Wertz, F. J. 1987. Cognitive psychology and the understanding of perception. *Journal of Phenomenological Psychology* 18: 103–42.

Wynn, K. 1992. Addition and subtraction by human infants. *Nature* 358: 749–50.

Yantis, S., and J. Jonides. 1996. Attentional capture by abrupt onsets: New perceptual objects or visual masking? *Journal of Experimental Psychology: Human Perception and Performance* 22 (6): 1505–13.

Zaehner, R. C. 1961. *The dawn and twilight of Zoroastrianism*. New York: Putnam.

# Index

# About the Author

**Frank John Ninivaggi**, M.D., is an associate attending physician at Yale–New Haven Hospital, an assistant clinical professor of child psychiatry at Yale University School of Medicine, Yale Child Study Center, and a member of the Yale–New Haven Community Medical Group. He is the medical director of the Devereux Glenholme School in Washington, Connecticut. He is board certified in psychiatry and neurology, and in 2004 was certified as a fellow of the American Psychiatric Association. He received training at Johns Hopkins School of Medicine in Baltimore, Maryland. He currently holds university and hospital appointments at the Yale Child Study Center, Yale University School of Medicine, where he earlier received fellowship specialty training in child and adolescent psychiatry. He is in private practice in New Haven, Connecticut. Dr. Ninivaggi has also contributed chapters to the 2005 (eighth edition) and 2009 (ninth edition) *Kaplan & Sadock's Comprehensive Textbook of Psychiatry*.

Breinigsville, PA USA
11 August 2010
243265BV00001B/2/P